For
Tammy,

May you find some [...]
that empowers you to
your Shayn-[...]

Love
Dad

EMPOWERMENT

EMPOWERMENT
THE COMPETITIVE EDGE
IN SPORTS, BUSINESS & LIFE

GENE N. LANDRUM, PH.D.

Brendan Kelly Publishing Inc.
2122 Highview Drive
Burlington, Ontario
Canada L7R 3X4

ISBN 1-895997-24-0

CREDITS

Chapter 1: Excerpts from *JIM THORPE: WORLD'S GREATEST ATHLETE* by Robert W. Wheeler, copyright © 1979 by the University of Oklahoma Press.

Chapter 4: Excerpts from *WILMA* by Wilma Rudolph and Bud Greenspan, copyright © 1977 by Bud Greenspan. Used by permission of Dutton Signet, a division of Penguin Group (USA) Inc.

Chapter 5: Excerpts from *MY LIFE AND THE BEAUTIFUL GAME* by Pelé with Robert L. Fish, copyright © 1977 by Licensing Corporation of America. Used by permission of Doubleday, a division of Random House, Inc.

Chapter 6: Excerpts from *THE GREATEST: MY OWN STORY* by Muhammad Ali with Richard Durham, Copyright © by Muhammad Ali and used with permission.

Chapter 7: Excerpts from *MARTINA* by Martina Navratilova and George Vecsey, copyright © 1985 by Martina Enterprises, Inc. Used by permission of Alfred A. Knopf, a division of Random House, Inc.

Chapter 8: Excerpts reprinted from the book *BREAKING THE SURFACE*, copyright © 1995 Greg Louganis and Eric Marcus, with permission of its publisher, Sourcebooks, Inc. (800-432-7444).

Chapter 11: Excerpts from *JEFF GORDON: Racing Back to the Front–My Memoir* by Jeff Gordon with Steve Eubanks. Copyright © 2003 by Jeff Gordon, Inc. Reprinted with the permission of Atria Books, an imprint of Simon & Schuster Adult Publishing Group. All rights reserved.

Chapter 12: Excerpts from *IT'S NOT ABOUT THE BIKE* by Lance Armstrong, copyright © 2000 by Lance Armstrong. Used by permission of G. P. Putnam's Sons, a division of Penguin Group (USA) Inc.

Chapter 14: Graphs from pp. 98 and 99 and brief excerpts from pp. 100, 103–4 from *HUMAN ACCOMPLISHMENT* by Charles Murray. Copyright © 2003 by Charles Murray. Reprinted by permission of HarperCollins Publishers.

*To those who seek self-empowerment
and believe that
life is a do-it-yourself kit.
These are the people
who pursue their goals relentlessly
until they achieve their dreams
and, in the process,
illuminate the path ahead
for the rest of humanity.*

Contents

Acknowledgments

The idea for this publication evolved over several years. It began as interesting research into the psyches of the greatest athletes of the 20th century, morphed into a blend of biography and sports psychology and ultimately evolved into a self-help book on winning behaviors. In the process, I discovered that integrating the latest psychological research into the psychobiographies of the athletic superstars and casting these in a self-help format to empower the reader was an ambitious undertaking. It has only been with the help of a talented and dedicated team of colleagues that I have been able to complete this project and share with my readers the winning behaviors and emotional dispositions that empower individuals to attain their goals.

Of the many people who have contributed to this book, I am particularly indebted to Rockne Sybyrg. Rockne went out of his way to contribute a wealth of important research data and books without which this book would not have been as comprehensive. Tennis friend John Burton, father of Ward and Jeff Burton of the NASCAR circuit, offered valuable insights into the nature of succeeding in the grueling sport of stock car racing. Justin Scott, founder and president of Syzygy I/O, applied his considerable artistic talents to create the impressive cover of this book.

Empowerment would have been far less readable and reader-friendly without the generous help of the readers who perused the various drafts, offering encouragement, suggestions and important embellishments. Listed alphabetically by surname, they include, David Bailey, Russ Bayes, Tim Cestnick, Len Collins, Gary Cusson, Hilda Cusson, Bernard DeOre, Keith Deviney, Robert Gatley, Ted Hughes, Gerry Keay, Aaron Kelly, H. Michael Kelly Q.C., Shannon Kelly, Teresa Kelly, Don Schafer, Graham Shiels, Steve Smith, David Street, Nancy Street, Dr. Joe Vitale, Blair Warren and John Wood. Their insights and suggestions resulted in numerous revisions of the manuscript that enhanced the clarity and flow that you see in the final result. The depth and scope of their collective expertise and perspectives have made the book extremely readable while further strengthening the scholarship of its content.

Editing is a long and enduring process. Entrepreneurs like myself are hard-pressed to deal with the tedious work and patience it demands. Consequently, I am eternally grateful to Rosemary Tanner who came to the fore, tackling the Herculean task of preparing the final edit of the manuscript. Her professional expertise and meticulous scrutiny has purged the text of the inconsistencies, ambiguities and inadvertent oversights that inevitably emerge in a work of this magnitude. Teresa Kelly also dedicated many hours to checking the manuscript for readability, coherence and consistency. Such contributions are invaluable.

Brendan Kelly, the publisher of this work, transcended the normal definition of this role in his unrelenting research into the principles of empowerment as exemplified by the subjects in this book and for the rewrites and unending revisions that no other publisher would have undertaken. His untiring work has made the psycho-biographical aspects of this book flow into a self-help methodology for the reader aspiring to self-empowerment. Brendan bought into focus the importance of the underlying motivations, drives and psychology that enabled these superstars to achieve at eminent levels.

The collective efforts of this stellar cast of brilliant individuals have made *Empowerment* a powerful self-help resource for aspiring athletes, entrepreneurs and anyone wishing to tap into the virtually infinite potential that resides within. Their suggestions pertaining to issues of content, cosmetics and flow were invaluable in rendering the high-quality book you are about to read. I hope you enjoy the ride ahead and that it takes you into a new, more highly-empowered phase of your life.

Introduction

The difference between a successful man and a failure is not one's better abilities or ideas, but the courage one has to bet on his ideas, to take a calculated risk–and to act.

–Maxwell Maltz, *Cybernetics*

Why this book? For starters it is needed to show all competitors–whether in the game of sports, the game of business or the game of life–that success resides not in the body but in the mind and heart. Most people live their lives accepting less than the full attainment of their dreams. Goals formulated in youth gradually fade as obstacles appear. Striving to achieve is replaced by coping to survive. The optimism of youth slowly erodes into the pessimistic conviction that those youthful fantasies were unrealistic–a perspective that becomes a self-fulfilling prophesy. As the dreams fade, the void is filled vicariously through the achievements and triumphs of others–the celebrities and superstars. In the absence of detailed psycho-biographical information about these superstars, it is tacitly assumed that their success is a direct result of a superior mental or physical gift, a genetic endowment peculiar to them.

This book is dedicated to empowering you by revealing the fallacy of that belief and by sharing with you the mental and emotional dispositions that lead to success. In my previous book, *Entrepreneurial Genius: The Power of Passion*, I identified the behaviors common to the great entrepreneurs of the 20th century. As an entrepreneur myself and founder of the *Chuck E. Cheese* chain of restaurants, I studied the entrepreneurial mind and determined the behaviors that made these people great. I never expected these same principles to apply to the athletic superstars because it seemed obvious to me that athletic preeminence was primarily about physical prowess. What I discovered in my subsequent research hit me like a bolt out of the blue! My extensive study of the backgrounds and psychological makeup of the greatest athletic superstars of modern vintage revealed that physical attributes were of secondary importance, subordinate to mental and emotional dispositions as determinants of success in athletics. Furthermore, the winning behaviors of athletic superstars mirrored those of the preeminent entrepreneurs. Excited by these findings, I felt compelled to share this discovery in a book to show how each of us can apply these same behaviors in our own lives and become more than we could otherwise be.

Empowerment reveals the mental and emotional dispositions of those preeminent athletes who reached the highest echelons of achievement, dominating their sport and changing it forever. Though most great athletes appear psychologically normal, they are dramatically different from the rest of us in their behaviors. They walk onto the field of play with a relaxed state of being that belies the raging passion bubbling within.

Each chapter in this book describes a particular empowerment principle that is exemplified by a psycho-biography of the athletic superstar of the 20th century who most conspicuously models that principle. Together, these profiles constitute a collection of psycho-biographies rather than biographies, focusing less on what these superstars achieved than on why and how they succeeded. Featuring larger-than-life personalities such as Babe Ruth, Michael Jordan, Lance Armstrong and Tiger Woods, *Empowerment* investigates the motivations and behaviors that transformed these relatively normal people into charismatic icons in their lifetime. What imprints molded them to be superstars? Did childhood influences and role models contribute to their becoming special? Did they possess some unique physical attributes or was it something more? The analysis of their behavioral patterns investigates their propensity for risk-taking, source of competitiveness, passion, divergence, response to crises, holistic vision and a plethora of other factors. I delved deeply into what made them tick mentally, physically, emotionally and spiritually.

Why These Superstars?

True eminence in any endeavor is not just what you achieve, but how you achieve it in relation to your peers. Sammy Sosa, Mark McGuire and Barry Bonds were magnificent home-run hitters at the millennium. But when compared to Babe Ruth, their feats, although magnificent, were just *very good*. When the Babe began annihilating the home-run records, he moved into the stratosphere of batting performance. Had he not pitched for five years, the Sultan of Swat may have hit 1000 career home runs. In 1920 Ruth hit 54 homers. The runner-up hit 19. The next year Babe hit 50 homers. The runner-up hit 24. In 1929 Ruth hit more homers than 14 of the 16 entire teams in all of baseball! Writing in the *Baseball Research Journal*, Gabe Costa compared Ruth's achievements with those of modern-day stars and concluded, "No one was close to him [Ruth] as a hitter or as an all-around performer." His statistical analysis showed that modern-day superstars would have to hit about 200 home runs in a season to be as dominant as the Sultan of Swat. By the time Ruth hit his 700th homer, only two players had hit 300. These are the reasons I selected Ruth to represent baseball.

I applied similar analyses in the selection of the other athletic superstars profiled in this book. For example, Wayne Gretzky annihilated the scoring records in the National Hockey League by the time he was 24. His #99 jersey was retired not only by those teams for which he played, but also by every team in the NHL–a tribute of the highest order. Soccer superstar Pelé was beyond comparison. He retired with twice as many goals as his nearest competitor. Although Joe Louis won more heavyweight title defenses than any other boxer and could have been included along with Ali, I chose Muhammad Ali for his long-term dominance in the field of boxing. Jack Nicklaus was more than just "The Bear" in golf. He was preeminent. But if Tiger Woods maintains his current momentum, he will break almost every record in the history of this popular game. On the basketball court Wilt Chamberlain was The Big Dipper who holds a record–100 points in one game–that will probably never be broken, yet Michael Jordan's domination of the game made him a more natural selection. For the same reason, I chose to profile Martina Navratilova rather than Aussie Rod Laver or Pete Sampras as the representative in tennis. Inevitably, I may have left out your favorite player in a particular sport, but in the final analysis, we will find that similar principles emerge no matter who we study, as long as we select from the very top echelon of the sports hierarchy.

Selection Criteria for the Sports Represented

In selecting the sports to represent, it was important to choose those that have the largest spectatorship as well as those that are most widely played. Although NASCAR racing has a large following in the United States, a relatively small number of people actually participate (except perhaps on the highways). Golf, on the other hand, has a relatively large number of fans and boasts a growing number of active participants. Football is a very popular spectator sport in the United States, but to the rest of the world the term "football" means soccer. For this reason I have included Pelé, but hope that (American) football aficionados will delight in Jim Thorpe as the representative of the gridiron.

Many of the superstars profiled actually played sports that are not featured in this book. Martina Navratilova is an expert alpine skier, Jeff Gordon is an avid and exceptional water-skier, Michael Jordan is a scratch golfer. There was not enough space to include all the sports or even twenty of them. The most popular were selected. Though I was involved, for a number of years, in amateur racquetball at a highly competitive level, I have left out that fast and exciting sport because it is not as universal as those selected. For similar reasons, softball, wrestling, weightlifting, figure skating, gymnastics, downhill skiing, handball, polo, American football, dressage, table tennis, swimming, horse racing and volleyball are not represented.

What Are the Most Difficult Sports?

People often debate about what constitutes athleticism and this discussion inevitably leads to questions such as "What sports represent true athleticism?" and "What skill presents the greatest athletic challenge?" Is it hitting a baseball thrown at 95 mph? Or is it negotiating turns on a NASCAR track at over 200 mph? Could it be returning a tennis serve hit at 130 mph? Or maybe it is flying down a mountain on skis at 80 mph. None are easy. In a study reported in *USA Today* (March 7, 2003) involving 42,000 respondents, the skill that ranked #1 in difficulty was hitting a baseball pitched at 90 mph. Racing a car around an oval track at 200+ mph ranked #2. Pole-vaulting came in at #3 while returning a tennis serve launched at 130+ mph came in #5. Hitting a golf ball came in at #4 in this study, but Tiger Woods would not agree because for him it is almost instinctive. Understandably, those who perform these skills don't find them difficult at all. Why? Because they have been trained in that discipline. What we find easy, others find difficult, even world-class athletes. For example, Dale Earnhardt Jr., a man who lives life in the fast lane, told *USA Today*, "Never in a million years would I try skiing down a mountain at more than 80 mph," even though downhill racing on skis came in at #10 and behind NASCAR. Lance Armstrong's cycling up the mountain peaks in the Tour de France ranked #8, yet Lance told *USA Today*, "I could drive a race car, swing a golf club and run a marathon, no problem. The rest I doubt."

The Sports Superstar: Is it Physical or Mental?

Are superstars born with a genetic predisposition for success? Do they have a distinct physical advantage over their competitors? Wayne Gretzky broke every scoring record in the history of hockey by the time he was 24. He was so dominant that Canadian psychologists tested him to find the secret of his superior play. To their amazement, Gretzky tested surprisingly normal in terms of physical and neurological factors. The Great One dominated his sport like few others in history, but his success had far more to do with his holistic sense of the game and his passion and mental attitude.

Many sports mavens tried to find the mystery behind the superiority of Babe Ruth, Pelé, Michael Jordan and Tiger Woods. They tested them, evaluating their hand-eye coordination, jumping ability, muscle strength and twitch speed. They came up blank. Are these players special? Of course they are. But it had far more to do with their mental magic than any physical attributes. There are literally millions of people in any given sport with superior physical characteristics to those at the top. Consider size. Size doesn't matter except when everything else is equal. At 5'6" and 150 pounds, Jeff Gordon is hardly a robust physical specimen and almost not big enough to withstand the grueling task of handling a metal missile flying around a track in excess of 200 mph. Journalists characterized Babe Didrikson Zaharias as a Muscle Moll in the 1930s. But Babe, considered the best all-round female athlete in history, was small by today's standards at 5'7" and 125 pounds. Her success went beyond the physical. Driving a golf ball over 250 yards in 1940 with those antiquated clubs demanded timing, club-head speed and a will power beyond the norm. At 6'6" Michael Jordan was tall for playing the guard position in basketball, but many were taller. Michael's outstanding performance derived from his head and heart, rather than his size. Tests revealed that he had above average jumping ability but others had more. He was a zealot and that's what set him apart.

Superstars go that extra mile, driven by an invisible force that propels them into the rarified atmosphere of superstardom. The "have to" is what makes them "want to" more than anything else in the world. In the words of the 19th century poet, E. R. Bulwer-Lytton, "Genius does what it must, and talent does what it can." Passionate energy pervades their very being. It transcends money, family, friends and even the gold at the end of the contest. What the eminent possess is something beyond the physical. That is what we will explore in this book.

The Findings Transcend Sports

This book is not just about athletic prowess. It is about the game of life, chess, business, bridge and ping-pong. The same behaviors that lead to athletic superstardom also apply to business tycoons and politicians. What works in one area is universally adaptable to other areas. In the words of sports psychologist and author Timothy Gallwey in his book *The Inner Game of Golf* (p. 212):

Potentially, sports have a greater value to a culture than as a mere outlet for releasing tensions or providing heroes. They can become the laboratory in which research and experimentation about human motivation, performance and self-interference take place.

Indeed, what I have found in my research laboratory of athletic competition is both fascinating and empowering and I look forward to sharing these findings with you. However, it would be glib to suggest that developing these 13 mental and emotional dispositions is easy. Anyone who has struggled to lose a bad habit, change an eating pattern or stick to an exercise program knows that behavioral changes are very difficult. You may decide that the success you desire is not worth the effort or the risk. That is up to you. Achieving a goal comes at a price that is usually commensurate with the size of that goal. However, if you decide to pay that price, then learn the behavioral and emotional dispositions described in the *13 Principles of Empowerment* presented in this book. They will give you the competitive edge in attaining your dreams. Whether you are reading this book to enhance your athletic or business prowess, or whether you are merely seeking some information about the personalities of your favorite athletes, I hope you find something that will inspire you to find your game and push it beyond its previous limits.

Chapter 1

PRINCIPLE #1: VALUE YOUR DIFFERENCE

If a man does not keep pace with his companions, perhaps it is because he hears a different drummer. Let him step to the music which he hears, however measured or far away.

–Henry David Thoreau

Do You Fit In?

Have you ever felt that you didn't fit in? When you were in high school or college, did you feel excluded from the "in group"–that inner circle of people at the center of a social microcosm around whom everyone else was in orbit? Have you sometimes wondered why you weren't accorded by your colleagues a level of respect that you deserve? Have your opinions and perspectives often been at odds with those around you? If your answer to any of these questions is "yes," then you are in good company. Most of the world's eminent in all walks of life, were significantly different from others. They were different in their personalities, beliefs, behaviors and perspectives, and it was this difference that spawned their exceptionality. The superstars in the human cosmos who revolutionized science, technology, business and sports were virtually all renegades who differed dramatically from the norm, destroying accepted beliefs and creating new paradigms that changed forever the nature of their enterprise. Philosopher Friedrich Nietzsche acknowledging this truth asserted in *Thus Spake Zarathustra*, "Whoever wants to be the creator of good and evil must first be an annihilator and break values…but that is being creative."

In most cases, the potential of these superstars was not recognized until they reached exceptional levels of achievement; in many cases their opinions and aspirations were ridiculed, and in some cases they, themselves, were persecuted for their difference. En route to eminence, these renegades faced opposition, discrimination and denigration. Their ability to persevere was empowered by regarding their difference as an asset, rather than a liability. They trusted their instincts and marched to the tune of their own drummer. Valuing their difference from others enabled them to push through adversity and reach new heights never before imagined. In so doing, they blazed the trial for the generations to follow, leaving their footprints in the sands of time.

What Drives Us to Fit In?

From the time we are born, society gives us guidelines to follow, indicating which behaviors are acceptable and which are unacceptable. Ralph Waldo Emerson explained in his *Essays: First Series:*

> *Society everywhere is in conspiracy against the manhood [and womanhood] of every one of its members...The virtue in most request is conformity. Self-reliance is its aversion. [Society] loves not realities and creators, but names and customs.*

A system of rewards and punishments are established to encourage us to serve and support the existing social order. This structured indoctrination is a necessary part of building a social order that allows for a stable and sustainable civilization. Without this structure, anarchy would prevail. Indeed, it is the indoctrinated multitude who form the backbone of a society, maintaining the social structure and perpetuating its values. However, this pervasive indoctrination exacts a toll on the autonomy of the individual that becomes evident early in a child's life.

Childhood educator and psychologist Paul Torrance said, "Most kids begin life with a creative spark, but have it knocked out of them by the 4th grade." Schools, like most institutions, promote the status quo. Don't rock the boat. Sit and do what I say. Don't be different. If you aren't prepared to program your own journey, it will be programmed for you and that program is for journeys into orthodoxy and conventionality.

By the time they reach puberty, most children have become accustomed to surrendering their individuality to the collective will. We see this most transparently in the behavior of adolescents in their peer group. Insecure in their quest to assert their independence from the adult world, these youngsters follow slavishly the behaviors and fashion dictates of a harshly judgmental and ruthless peer group. It's a mini-society, not unlike that depicted in Goldring's *Lord of the Flies*, that punishes difference with ostracism, ridicule and sometimes violence. These pre-teens and teenagers learn quickly what brand names are acceptable in clothing and what behaviors are considered "cool." Individuals violate these norms at their own peril.

Submission to group norms follows these adolescents into adulthood, residing quietly beneath a veneer of confidence as they age. The workplace reinforces the importance of fitting in. Those who are not perceived as team players are regarded as mavericks and either purged from the staff or passed over for promotion. The contestants on Donald Trump's television production *The Apprentice* who are not regarded as team players are shown the door and told, "You're fired!" Similarly the individualists on *The Apprentice: Martha Stewart* are dismissed with the tagline, "You just don't fit in." Such are the punishments that encourage us to conform.

In addition to punishments for non-compliance, there are considerable rewards that society offers those who move with the current of accepted practice. Those who take this path of least resistance are less likely to become embroiled in a life of conflict with friends, associates and the establishment. Their lives are more predictable and less encumbered with struggle than the lives of those who march to their own tune. Monetary rewards, elevated status and social acceptability often accrue to those who perform well as part of the herd. Through these incentives, society gradually comes to own their soul the way that Mephistopheles bought the soul of Faust.

At What Price?

Hidden within these rewards is an insidious trap. With the gradual accumulation of relationships and material possessions comes an increased vulnerability that is felt as a deep-seated fear. It is a fear of losing the money and the material possessions that have become the surrogate for one's original goals and aspirations. It is a fear that is gradually transformed into a dull pervasive ennui that is linked to the potential loss of the love of a spouse, parent, child or friend–and ultimately, the loss of self-esteem. This is the conundrum that Bernard Levin, columnist of the *Times* of London, expressed (as quoted in Ferguson, p. 40):

> *Countries like ours are full of people who have all the material comforts they desire, yet lead lives of quiet (and at times noisy) desperation, understanding nothing but the fact that there is a hole inside them and that however much food and drink they pour into it, however many motorcars and television sets they stuff it with, however many well-balanced children and loyal friends they parade around the edges of it...it aches.*

The gradual surrender of one's individuality brings with it a benign acceptance of imposed limitations and an abandonment of the hopes and dreams of youth. The idealism and optimism seen in early life eventually give way to the pessimism and cynicism evident in the later years, taking with it the passion that makes life exciting. The jaded and the disillusioned are the people Henry David Thoreau observed 150 years ago when he said, "The mass of men lead lives of quiet desperation."[1] In trading their individuality for comfort, the masses have lost the very passion for life that is needed for high achievement and, more importantly, the joy that psychologists call *self-actualization.* Very few people escape this enculturation and even fewer march to the tune of their own drummer. Why do so few people escape the early indoctrination that dooms them to an unfulfilled life? The answer is seen in the behavior of other animal species.

The Pike Syndrome

The high priests in every field of human endeavor speak about doing things "by the book." Who wrote the book? In every endeavor, "the book" is in continuous revision, driven by breakthroughs made by those who actually play outside the book. The masses take the book as gospel. Slavish adherence to the book is referred to in business psychology as the *Pike Syndrome.* In an experiment with pike (a fresh-water fish), a glass barrier was placed between the fish and their food. When the fish tried to get to the food they hit the glass. After repeated failures, the fish stopped trying for the food. Surprisingly, when the barrier was removed they still refused to swim to the food. Early enculturation has led most of humanity to suffer from the Pike Syndrome –forever inhibited from the pursuit of their dreams by an invisible "glass" barrier of convention.

The Pike Syndrome molds us to believe we know what can and can't be done. Before 1954, it was generally believed that running the mile in less than 4 minutes was not humanly possible. However, Roger Bannister, who had frequently run a quarter of a mile in less than one minute while a student at Oxford, visualized combining four such runs in succession. The result was his famous 3-minute-59-second mile. Once people realized it was possible, running the mile in less than 4 minutes became commonplace. Bannister's triumph shows clearly that the greatest barriers we encounter in life are those that are self-imposed. Victims of the Pike Syndrome would rather starve than go where the glass barrier threatens failure. Such negative inner beliefs prove debilitating.

---

[1] a phrase borrowed by Levin in the quote on the previous page.

Abnormal Deeds Are Done by Abnormal People

Normal people achieve normally and abnormal people achieve abnormally. This is a fundamental truth: to be special, we must be different. Abnormal people are those who are abnormally driven, abnormally tenacious, abnormally competitive and abnormally passionate. If you aren't willing to go where the pack isn't, you are not likely to make your mark in the world and you will become part of the pack.

What differentiates the superstar from the also-rans is freedom of thought and action. Superstars are less constrained by inner limits to their success. Jim Thorpe and Babe Didrikson Zaharias, two of the greatest athletes who ever lived, never questioned their ability or put any limit on their achievements. Both were free spirits who wandered unfettered and unsupervised as children. Thorpe ran away from home at a very young age and spent months alone in the wilderness. Who could have imagined that this solitary rebel who resisted structure and instruction would reach the highest levels of success in Olympic track and field? Babe Zaharias also grew up unfettered, running away from her Texas home for the circus in California when still a teen and indulging her appetite for risk by jumping off moving freight trains. The Texan Tornado bowled 200 the first time she tried because she saw no limits. When banned from playing amateur golf, she shrugged and went on tour playing exhibitions.

Superstars transcend the norm both mentally and emotionally. All have a prescient sense of destiny without limits. They don't know they *can't*, so consequently they *do*. Such a mental fix outside reality allowed Babe Ruth to hit not only more home runs than anyone ever thought possible but to hit more than almost every other entire team in the American League.

The Renegade Attitude

The eminent in almost every field of human endeavor are those who march to the tune of their own drummer. These superachievers are renegades who live life on the edge, energized and empowered by their unrelenting struggle toward their goals. They are never predictable. When it is noon, traditionalists want to eat; the eminent may eat if it fits their fancy. Sunday night is a time for rest and relaxation for most, but for the superstar, Sunday night is just one more opportunity to hone skills. When opportunity strikes, the superstar will be there, willing to play the game no matter the time or day.

Mavericks live outside convention. They seldom follow slavishly the instructions of a coach, preferring to take the coach's instructions under advisement. Though they may masquerade as team players and may give credit to teammates, when it comes to crunch time they listen only to their own counsel. Though Michael Jordan's coaches thought he listened intently to them, he confessed shortly after his retirement that he seldom listened to a coach in his life. He told biographer Bob Green (p. 231):

> *I never follow along. I'm never paying attention to what they are telling the team. I don't think the coaches are aware I'm not listening. I'm looking at them, but my mind is totally somewhere else. I don't want to hear it.*

Off-the-wall Dennis Rodman of the champion Chicago Bulls is an iconoclast, actually pushing the envelope of eccentricity. A careful look at the demeanors of Rodman and Michael Jordan reveals that they march to the tunes of similar drummers. Neither listens to his coach. Neither drives within speed limits. Neither dresses conventionally. Both love to gamble. However, they differ from each other in their respect for other people. Rodman is radical and eccentric, appearing in drag and flouting the status quo. Jordan, in contrast, projects the flashy persona of Armani and Lamborghini. Rodman uses shock to get attention; Jordan uses winning and power to make his mark. Both are cocky, flamboyant and passionate about life.

The Inner Voice of the Individualist

In your quest to achieve excellence–athletic or otherwise–you will be advised, coached, denigrated and praised. Traditional beliefs will be used as a basis for the coaching and the advice will generally be given in good faith. However, the new breakthroughs will be made by those who move outside the accepted techniques and keep counsel with their instincts. These are the rugged individualists who become the superstars.

Individualists have a strong sense of self that psychologists call *self-efficacy*. (I will address this in more detail in Chapter 6.) Without such a strong inner belief system it is impossible to function effectively outside the mainstream. Operating outside convention, these visionaries tend to see what others do not, relying heavily on an inner voice that speaks without the prejudice of tradition. They seek opportunities and pursue life's possibilities while others are following the well-trodden path of conventional thought. The visionary is willing to live life unfettered, avoiding the quagmire of the status quo. Traditionalists see visionaries as defiant or even eccentric because they see the world through a different lens.

Unfortunately in today's lexicon, non-conformity is often associated with lawless rebellion and criminal behavior and hence portrayed in a negative light. Yet, it is the non-conformists who have spawned the ideas captured in great literature, brilliant science and powerful technologies. Most non-conformists are merely chasing their dreams and surfing the waves of triumph and defeat.

Self-empowerment begins with valuing your uniqueness–your difference from the masses. It's not about being eccentric, perverse or different for the sake of being different, but rather, listening to your inner passions, your dreams and the motivations that give you goose bumps. It's about risking failure, rebounding from defeat and persevering through your inner limits and external constraints.

Resistance to free thinking has been the norm since Socrates was poisoned for teaching the young to question traditional beliefs. Those who aspire to high achievement *must* value their difference–that is the hallmark of all high achievers. Though all the superstars profiled in this book valued their uniqueness, I have chosen one–Jim Thorpe–as the model of a rugged individualist and the embodiment of the difference that makes a difference. What follows is his brief psycho-biography that outlines the early imprints and the cultural influences that enabled him to develop his athletic skills to a level that set him above all other male athletes in the 20th century. However, before delving into one of the most fascinating stories in the annals of sport history, you may want to assess your own level of individuality by taking the test on the following pages.

INDIVIDUALISM SELF-ASSESSMENT–Are You an Individualist?

Choose a number 1–5, with 1 the lowest and 5 the highest, to indicate the degree to which you believe the statement describes you or how you feel. Record for each statement the number you have chosen. The scoring key is on the next page.

There are no "right" or "wrong" answers. In making your selection, answer the questions as candidly as possible without anticipating how you will be classified.

	Strongly Disagree				Strongly Agree
1. I prefer to do my own thing rather than participate in groups.	1	2	3	4	5
2. The well-being of my co-workers is important to me.	1	2	3	4	5
3. One should live one's life independently of others.	1	2	3	4	5
4. If a co-worker of mine received an award, I would feel proud.	1	2	3	4	5
5. I treasure my privacy.	1	2	3	4	5
6. If a close relative were in financial difficulty, I would help.	1	2	3	4	5
7. I try to be direct and forthright with others.	1	2	3	4	5
8. It's important to me that there be harmony among my friends.	1	2	3	4	5
9. I see myself as a unique individual with special qualities.	1	2	3	4	5
10. I like sharing confidences with my friends and neighbors.	1	2	3	4	5
11. What happens to me is generally a result of my own actions.	1	2	3	4	5
12. I follow rules only to the extent that they don't interfere with my achieving my goals.	1	2	3	4	5
13. I feel good when I cooperate with others.	1	2	3	4	5
14. When I succeed, it's usually because of my abilities.	1	2	3	4	5
15. My happiness depends very much on the happiness of those around me.	1	2	3	4	5
16. I enjoy being unique and different from others.	1	2	3	4	5
17. To me, pleasure is spending time with others.	1	2	3	4	5
18. I have trouble relating to people who have different beliefs from me.	1	2	3	4	5

		Strongly Disagree			Strongly Agree	
19. When working in a group, I find it difficult to compromise.		1	2	3	4	5
20. If you want to get a job done well, you shouldn't depend on others.		1	2	3	4	5
21. I find it stressful to have others in my group outperform me.		1	2	3	4	5
22. I am excited when I am part of a group that is energized and productive.		1	2	3	4	5
23. I believe in the adage, "Clothes make the man [or woman]."		1	2	3	4	5
24. I prefer to have my own bank account rather than a joint account with a spouse.		1	2	3	4	5
25. I like to put things together without reading the instructions.		1	2	3	4	5

Instructions

Total the numbers you chose for these items:
#1, 3, 5, 7, 9, 11, 12, 14, 16, 19, 20, 21, 24 and 25.
Then use the scoring key below to assess
your individualist tendencies.

Scoring Key

57–70: Strong individualist.
43–56: Tendency to individualism and cooperation.
29–42: A team player and a social animal.
Below 29: Tend to follow the crowd and established practices.

JIM THORPE

- Voted the "Best All-Round Athlete of the 20th Century" by the Associated Press.
- Won the decathlon and pentathlon at the 1912 Olympics in Stockholm, Sweden.
- Led professional football team Canton Bulldogs to Championships in 1916–1918.
- Played professional baseball with the New York Giants for 6 years.
- In 1919, became the first President of the National Football League.
- Voted to the National Track & Field Hall of Fame and NFL Hall of Fame.

Jim Thorpe: Rugged Individualist

On May 27, 1999, Resolution 198 of the House of Representatives of the United States designated James Francis Thorpe as "America's Athlete of the 20th Century." No other athlete in the history of this nation has been so honored. This tribute to Jim Thorpe was recognition of his legendary athletic prowess. He embodied many–if not all–of my *13 Principles of Empowerment*. But none did he more conspicuously model than Principle #1: *Value your difference*. Jim was an individualist of the first order: He did everything his way. And the Thorpe way was ethereal. Rules were unimportant distractions for this free spirit. He saw himself as a son of nature and returned there when life became too difficult.

© Bettmann/CORBIS

**Jim Thorpe
1888–1953**

In 1950, the Associated Press voted him the greatest male athlete of the first half of the 20th century. The table shows the tallied votes for the others in the top ten. What achievements brought Jim Thorpe to be unequivocally recognized as the world's (or at least, America's) greatest male athlete? As you scan the list of the top ten candidates, each name will bring to mind a particular sport in which that athlete made his mark–except for Thorpe. Some will associate Thorpe with his outstanding performance in track and field at the 1912 Olympics when he decimated the competition by the largest margin in history. Others will link him with his legendary open field running on the gridiron. This football prowess was later dramatized in the 1951 Hollywood film, *Jim Thorpe–All-American*, starring Burt Lancaster. There may be others who know him as the professional baseball player who hit

Greatest Athletes: First Half of the 20th Century	
Athlete	Total Vote
Jim Thorpe	875
Babe Ruth	539
Jack Dempsey	246
Ty Cobb	148
Bobby Jones	88
Joe Louis	73
Red Grange	57
Jesse Owens	54
Lou Gehrig	34
Bronko Nagurski	26

three home runs into three different states in the same game. (When playing in a stadium in Texarkana, a Texas town that borders on Arkansas and Oklahoma, Jim hit home runs over the right, center and left field fences, landing the balls respectively in Oklahoma, Texas and Arkansas.) But most of those who recognize the name Jim Thorpe will know him as the consummate athlete who dominated virtually every sport he played.

As a member of the Sac and Fox Indian tribe, Thorpe possessed the deep spiritualism for which the Native American culture is known. His ability to commune with nature and with his inner soul manifested as an inner strength of mythical proportions. Jim Thorpe was the consummate visionary. He saw himself succeeding in his mind long before he participated in an athletic event. In an eerie display of visualization technique, he was able to win the most complex and grueling track and field events without ever practicing on a track. In the voyage across the Atlantic to Stockholm, Sweden (the site of the 1912 Olympics), coach Mike Murphy questioned his selection of Thorpe for the Olympic team. While the other players were diligently running and working out on the deck of the ship, Murphy found Thorpe sitting alone on deck in a meditative mode. The reflective Indian told coach Murphy, "I am visualizing how far I will jump when we get to the games." At that time, long before the benefits of mental rehearsal were understood, such a comment seemed, at best, a rationalization for laziness and at worst a mystical super-stition. Murphy would soon discover that Thorpe's vision was deeper and more farther-reaching than his coaches and teammates.

History will remember Thorpe as the peerless and arguably the most adept multi-sport athlete in history. He could do it all. No matter what sport he tried, he excelled. Thorpe bowled 200+, played golf in the 70s and showed remarkable prowess in lacrosse, tennis, handball, rowing, hockey, billiards and figure skating. This athletic prowess did not derive from an advantage in size, since he was of comparable size to his competitors. However, Thorpe had a will to win that was forged from internal conflict. The only way to be accepted and find freedom was to compete, and compete he did. In a football game against the heavily favored Army team, Thorpe annihilated the opposition with running skills that prompted the *New York Times* to report:

In and out, zigzagging first to one side and then to the other, while a flying Cadet went hurtling through space, Thorpe wormed his way through the entire Army team. Every cadet in the game had his chance, and every one of them failed...It was a dodging game in which Thorpe matched himself against an entire team and proved the master.

Thorpe's Carlisle College team defeated Army 27 to 6. A player on the losing Army team commented years later, "Except for [Thorpe], Carlisle would have been an easy team to beat. On the football field, there was no one like him in the world." That player was future General and U.S. President, Dwight Eisenhower.

JIM THORPE'S TREK TO THE TOP

Early Imprints

Born on May 28, 1888, Jim Thorpe was raised as a member of the Sac and Fox Indian tribe on a reservation in Oklahoma before that region had gained statehood. His father, Hiram, was half Irish and half Indian and a trapper by trade. His Indian mother, Charlotte, had some French blood. Thorpe's Indian heritage–a need to be free or not be at all–was ingrained and inculcated in him. Jim's Indian name, *Wathohuck*, meant *Bright Path*, reflecting his mother's hopes for his bright future. Both parents were immersed in the white and Indian cultures and wanted their children to enjoy the advantages of education in the country's dominant culture. To this end, they sent their offspring to the Agency schools on the reservation, which were run by white teachers.

Jim Thorpe was a rebel in school from the very first day. He was not interested in submitting to the white man's ways or in losing the freedom inherent in the Indian culture. Nature was in his blood and conforming was not. Furthermore, many of the teachers were intolerant of the students whom they regarded as either lazy or slow to learn. As well, since the government ran these Agency schools, English was the language of instruction. In the words of one of Jim's classmates (Wheeler, p. 12):

I knew Jim was not very happy at school. I wasn't myself and neither were any of the other children...We could not speak or understand English when we were taken there at the age of six. It took us a long time to learn our lessons in kindergarten because most of the teachers had very little patience with Indian children. Some of the teachers were kind, while others were very mean. We got a licking many times when we could not spell a simple word. As a result, we could not learn very much because most of us were afraid of our teacher.

When Jim's twin brother Charlie died of pneumonia at the age of eight, Jim was devastated. They had been inseparable. Without his soul mate, Jim no longer wanted to attend the school. To escape his pain, he took off to the woods where no one could find him. The tragedy left an indelible mark on his fragile psyche. In his personal scrapbook, he wrote, "After Charlie died, I used to go out by myself with an old dog and hunt coon. Often I would make camp and stay out all night."

In 1896, just a few months after the death of his brother, Jim left school one day and walked home–a distance of 23 miles. Insistent that Jim was to have an education, his father hitched up the horses and drove him back to school. Unwilling to remain there, Jim at 8 years of age, ran home via an 18-mile shortcut, arriving there ahead of his father! It was this deep-seated spirit, motivated by his intense need for freedom, that propelled Jim forward and made him different from other boys.

After Charlie's death, Jim was responsible for many of the chores on the ranch, such as feeding the livestock and breaking wild horses. Jim particularly enjoyed the challenge of lassoing, saddling and riding these free-spirited animals–an activity that he later claimed had made him strong, active and alert. (He began breaking horses at age 10 and proudly announced that by age 15 there was not a single wild horse he couldn't tame.)

When Jim was 10 years of age, his father took him on his first hunting trip. Hiram was known in the community for his strength and endurance, and he set a grueling pace for his son. Years later, Jim waxed with pride over his father's physical prowess, commenting (Wheeler, p. 10):

[My father] could walk, ride, or run for days without ever showing the least sign of fatigue. Once, when we didn't have enough horses to carry all our kill, my father slung a buck deer over each shoulder and carried them twenty miles to our home.

Though Jim and his father had become closer after Charlie's death, Hiram ran out of patience with Jim's frequent escapes from the classroom and his appearance at home in the middle of the day. When Jim was 10, Hiram sent him to the Haskell Indian Junior College in Lawrence, Kansas–over 200 miles from home. However, shortly after arriving at the new school, the restless renegade developed a penchant for jumping onto freight trains to find his way home.

In the spring of 1900, Jim was 12 and beginning to adjust to the student life. He received word that his father was dying from a gunshot wound received in a hunting accident. Without consulting with school authorities, Jim ran to the town of Lawrence where he jumped a freight train that was homeward bound–or so he thought. Some time later, he discovered that the train was northbound instead of southbound. Responding in his usual fashion, he decided to rely on his own resources and walk home–a distance of 270 miles. When he arrived home on foot a week or so later, he was delighted to discover that Hiram had recovered.

Shortly after Hiram's recovery, fate took an ironic twist and Jim's mother Charlotte, always in robust health, fell victim to blood poisoning. In that pre-antibiotic era, there was no defense against such infections and Charlotte died within a week.

On one occasion, Hiram left Jim and his older brother George to tend to the livestock, but the boys decided to go fishing instead. On their return, they found the livestock in chaos and their father irate. Hiram's anger translated into what Jim later described as the first thrashing he had ever received from his normally gentle father. At the age of 12, Jim found himself without direction and without connection to the ranch. While he still loved and admired his father, Jim had reached an age when he would no longer accept parental punishment and he ran away to Texas. Though only 4' 11" tall and 102 pounds, the loner quickly adapted to life as a cowboy on the Texas ranches. In less than a year, Jim was able to earn enough money to buy a team of horses and return home. Warmly received by his father who had lamented his departure, Jim took on a major portion of the chores at the ranch while he simultaneously attended Garden Grove Public School.

During his early teen years, Jim had established a reputation as a superb athlete. News of this talented youth reached "Pop" Warner, a staff member at the Carlisle Indian School in remote Pennsylvania, who was recruiting students of exceptional athletic prowess. One thing led to another and by 1904, at the age of 16, Jim Thorpe was enrolled at Carlisle and about to establish himself as one of the greatest athletes who ever lived.

An Early Hint of Exceptionality

At Carlisle, Jim attempted to straddle the divergent cultures of the Indian and the White man. But fate intervened once again, taking him on another detour. Shortly after his arrival at Carlisle, his father who was both his hero and mentor died of septicemia (blood poisoning) that he contracted during a hunting accident. Jim was devastated and felt very much alone in the world. As before, he sought solace in escape and left Carlisle. During the next two years, he obtained employment at farms where he earned enough money to keep body and soul together. Finally in 1907, at the age of 19, the lure of competitive sport brought Jim back to Carlisle. Having reached a height of 5' 9 1/4" and a weight of 144 pounds, Jim was still considered too small to play on Pop Warner's varsity football team, so he played instead in the intramural football league at Carlisle.

How Jim Thorpe ultimately joined Pop Warner's track team is one of the great stories of athletic achievement and one that was dramatically represented in the movie *Jim Thorpe–All-American*. Jim was meandering around the campus when he stopped to watch the athletes competing for a place on the track team. They were trying unsuccessfully to clear a high-jump bar set at a height of 5' 9". Jim was wearing overalls and an old pair of gym shoes. He asked if he could try the bar. The frustrated athletes, anticipating the young upstart's humiliating defeat, exchanged all knowing glances as the bar was set to the school record height. The neophyte ran towards the bar and sprung upward with the grace of a gazelle, clearing it easily as the track team stood gaping in amazement. Thorpe, in typical nonchalance, began to walk away. But the coaches, overwhelmed by this display of athletic prowess, led him off to see Pop Warner. Jim Thorpe had been discovered, but no one yet had even the remotest inkling of the magnitude of the star that would emerge from this self-effacing free-spirited youth.

The Competitive Genie Escapes the Bottle

Pop Warner was quick to place Jim on the track team after this high-jump incident. However, in spite of his relatively small stature, Thorpe expressed his wish to play football on the varsity team. Warner resisted, fearing that his star track-and-field athlete might be injured. The aspiring player implored Warner, asserting, "They can't tackle Jim Thorpe!" These pleadings fell on deaf ears until the 1908 season when Pop Warner, finally acquiesced and played Jim against Conway Hall. Thorpe's performance was outstanding. He scored five touchdowns himself and threw a 30-yard pass for another–and that was in the first half! In the game against Villanova, Pop Warner kept Jim on the bench again, fearing injury to his track star, but the fans chanted, "We want Jim! We want Jim." Warner put Jim in the game and a star was born. Chief Johnson, who observed the game himself, reported years later (Wheeler, p. 67):

> *What followed was the single most dramatic play I have ever seen in sports. Jim took the very first hand-off and blasted into the line with the loudest crash I've ever heard. When he was able to continue into their backfield, I couldn't believe my eyes! He didn't use one block on his way to the goal line 70 yards away while all the time he kept hollering, "Out of my way! Get out of my way!"*

Throughout the remainder of the 1908 football season, Jim Thorpe continued to build his reputation as an outstanding football player. A fellow player on that team reported (Wheeler, p. 73):

Jim was a terrific runner, passer and kicker. He weighed around 190 and had tremendous leg drive. Often you'd see him knock out would-be tacklers simply by running right over the top of them. He didn't try to overpower you if he didn't have to, for Jim was a snaky ball carrier in a broken field. He gave you the leg and then took it away.

The track-and-field season of 1909 began a few months after the end of Jim's spectacular 1908 football season. His performance in track was even more stellar than his remarkable prowess in football. In a meet against Lafayette, he scored six gold medals and one bronze in the seven events he entered and Carlisle won 71 to 41. Thorpe achieved his gold medals in the 120-yard hurdles, the 220-yard low hurdles, the broad jump, the high jump, the shot put and the discus. His bronze was in the 100-yard dash. Some claimed that Jim defeated the entire Lafayette team single-handed.

A Brief Hiatus–Then a Return with a Vengeance

At the end of the 1909 academic year, as Jim prepared to travel to his summer job, he ran into some friends who were going to play baseball in North Carolina for $15 a week. Preferring to earn money from sport rather than from work on a ranch, Jim opted to join his friends. What started as a substitute summer job turned into a two-year stint in what might be called the "semi-pro" baseball leagues, although the stipend was less than the remuneration for a comparable summer job. During the next two years, the free-spirited Indian was a cowboy, hired hand and semi-pro baseball pitcher for Rocky Mount in the Eastern Carolina League. In this latter role, that would come back to haunt him years later, Jim batted .248 and won 19 games as a pitcher.

In 1911, Pop Warner enticed Jim back to Carlisle to play football. As an incentive, he invited him to try out for the 1912 U.S. Olympic track team. Jim trained for track and field while playing football for Carlisle. During this year, Jim's gridiron prowess won him the admiration of all football fans. Pop Warner described Jim as "an absolutely fearless competitor," having a better ability to see the essence of things than other athletes. When he set his mind on the end zone he was virtually unstoppable. Warner summed up Thorpe's talents saying (Wheeler, p. 82):

No other college player I ever saw had the natural aptitude for football possessed by Jim Thorpe. I never knew a football player who could penetrate a line as Thorpe could...As for speed, none ever carried a pigskin down the field with the dazzling speed of Thorpe. He could go skidding through first and second defense, knock off a tackler, stop short and turn past another, ward off still another, and escape the entire pack; or, finally cornered, could go farther with a tackler [hanging on] than any man I ever knew.

In 1911, Thorpe led Carlisle to a winning season with 10 wins and only one loss. Game after game, Thorpe was the outstanding player in both offense and defense. At the end of the year, he made First Team All-American. In 1912, he led Carlisle to 10 wins, two losses and one tie. Again he made First Team All-American.

It isn't possible to separate Thorpe's athletic prowess from his cultural heritage. Freedom to play and run was in his blood. That freedom to run with abandon was replicated on the football field where Thorpe unconsciously associated defensive players with those authorities who forced him to sit in a schoolroom at a desk. When he hit them, many didn't get up. That inner rage was released on opposing players despite the fact he was placid and non-aggressive by nature. He wasn't quite aware of the derivation of his intensity and neither were the opposing players. But they sensed this was a man on a mission and not about to lose his freedom. Thorpe wrote of his sense of competing, "I've always liked sport, and only played or ran races for the fun of it and never to earn money." The great ones seldom strive for money. If they do they are competing for the wrong reasons. However, when they execute well, the money comes in bundles.

By the end of 1912, Jim Thorpe was already widely acknowledged as the greatest football player ever and sports columnists gushed over his ability to do everything well. When little Carlisle faced the behemoth Army team in November of that year, Thorpe led them to a dramatic upset victory. On that day he kicked four field goals and ran the ball for 175 yards. A number of Army's defensive players ended up in hospital from trying to tackle the irrepressible Indian. In reporting the Carlisle victory, the *New York Times* waxed eloquent:

Standing out resplendent in a galaxy of Indian stars was Jim Thorpe, recently crowned the athletic marvel of the age. The big Indian Captain added more luster to his already brilliant record, and at times the game itself was almost forgotten while the spectators gazed on Thorpe, the individual, to wonder at his prowess...It was like trying to clutch a shadow. Thorpe went through the West Point line as if it was an open door; his defensive play was on a par with his attack and his every move was that of a past master.

The *New York Herald* effusively extolled Thorpe's abilities, ending a tribute with the statement, "So summing everything up, Jim Thorpe appears to have possessed about every quality necessary to make a player close to perfection."

"The Greatest Athlete in the World"

During and after the 1911 football season, Jim trained under Pop Warner for the 1912 Olympics in Stockholm, Sweden. He agreed to compete in the pentathlon and the decathlon–the ultimate tests of all-round athletic supremacy.

The Fifth Olympiad opened with all the pomp and ceremony befitting a world-class event. The stadium was crammed with 30,000 expectant fans who came to witness the gladiatorial struggles that would bring honor to some and disappointment to others. Teams from 28 countries paraded around the track, past the Royal Box where His Majesty, King Gustav V of Sweden, presided over the contests. A chorus of 4400 lifted their voices to the heavens, declaring that the universal test of athletic prowess was about to begin.

What happened during the days that followed ensconced Jim Thorpe in the history books as one of the greatest athletes of all time and simultaneously launched the legend of Jim Thorpe. The pentathlon (no longer included in the men's Olympic games) consisted of five track and field events: running broad jump, javelin throw, 200-m race, discus and 1500-m race. The Scandinavians, known for their endurance in the long races and their domination of the javelin throw, were favored to win, but Jim Thorpe was not one to be intimidated. He came first in all of the events except the javelin throw in which he came third, earning him the gold medal for the pentathlon by a margin that has never since been achieved.

JIM THORPE'S PENTATHLON		
Broad Jump	23' 2.7"	first
Javelin	153' 2.95"	third
200-m Race	22.9 s	first
Discus	116' 8.4"	first
1500-m Race	4 min 44.8s	first

The decathlon, still considered the ultimate test of athletic speed, power and grace,
is a grueling competition consisting of ten
events spread over three days. It would be an
understatement to say that Jim Thorpe annihilated the competition. He won the decathlon
gold medal with a score of 8412 (out of the
possible 10,000 points), exceeding his closest
rival by almost 700 points. This is equivalent
to winning a football game by a score of 45–0
or a baseball game 15–0. Journalists
described him as a modern-day Paul Bunyan.
However, the crowning glory bestowed upon

JIM THORPE'S DECATHLON		
Event	Thorpe's Result	Status
100-m Race	11.2 s	second
Broad Jump	22' 2.3"	second
Shot Put	42' 5.45"	first
High Jump	6' 1.6"	first
400-m Race	47.6s	second
110-m Hurdles	15.6s	first
Discus	121' 3.9"	second
Pole Vault	10' 7.45"	third
Javelin	149' 11.2"	third
1500-m Race	4 min 40.1 s	first

Jim Thorpe was the tribute paid by royalty. After King Gustav V presented
Jim with the gold medal for the pentathlon, the crowd of 30,000 broke into a
thunderous applause and tumultuous cheers that seemed to go on forever.
Later, when Jim came forward to receive the wreath and the gold medal for
the decathlon, the fans exploded. Overwhelmed with emotion, King Gustav V
extended his hand to Jim, shook it warmly and declared, "Sir, you are the
greatest athlete in the world." Exuding characteristic poise and humility, Jim
Thorpe responded, "Thank you, King." On his return from what has been
called the "Jim Thorpe Olympics" he was honored with a ticker tape parade
in New York City. Amidst the adoring cheers from a multitude of ecstatic
New Yorkers, Jim mused, "I heard people yelling my name–and I couldn't
realize how one fellow could have so many friends."

Paradise Lost through Politics

On January 28, 1913, about six months after New York had celebrated
Jim Thorpe's achievements, the *New York Times'* headline blazed "Olympic
Prizes Lost–Thorpe No Amateur." Apparently the American Athletic Union
(AAU), guardian of rulings regarding amateur status of athletes, had learned
of Jim Thorpe's earnings of $15 per week during 1910–11 when he played
semi-professional baseball. Though many amateurs had engaged in such
employment, most used pseudonyms to avoid being caught. Unaware that this
modest income would jeopardize his amateur status, Jim had not tried to hide
his identity. He wrote to the AAU:

I was not wise in the ways of the world and did not realize this was wrong, and that it would make me a professional in track sports...I am very sorry, Mr. Sullivan, to have it all spoiled in this way and I hope the Amateur Athletic Union and the people will not be too hard in judging me.

Unfortunately, the AAU took a hard stand–ruling that Thorpe had violated his amateur status–either as a misguided attempt to preserve the integrity of amateur status or with a more malevolent motive. The news media wrote about the injustice, but to no avail. The *Buffalo Enquirer* observed:

Jim Thorpe, amateur or no amateur, is the greatest athlete today in the world. They can take away his tin medals and his pieces of pottery and they can hold him up to the scorn of a few "pure athletes," but the honest world, the thinking world, the great majority of men and women will always consider him the athlete par excellence of the past fifty years in this country.

Avery Brundage, a man whom he had defeated in those 1912 games and who now served on the AAU, adamantly refused to consider returning Jim's medals. Though public opinion was on Jim's side, the AAU invoked their authority. Jim was not only required to return his Olympic medals and prizes, but his records were stripped from the record books. Jim Thorpe was humiliated by the ruling and the implicit charge of dishonest behavior. For a man known for his integrity and sincerity, the accusation and subsequent ruling were devastating. Years later, when asked about losing his medals, the unassuming Thorpe told the media, "The King of Sweden gave me these trophies. But they took them away from me and I won them fair and square." Jim never recovered emotionally from this travesty and this point marked the beginning of a downward spiral in his life.

After college, Jim played professional football for the Canton Bulldogs. He led that team to the world football championships in 1916, 1917 and 1918 and his presence was a major attendance draw. In 1919, he was elected as the first president of the American Professional Football Association (later the National Football League). From 1913 through 1919, he also played professional baseball for the New York Giants. In 1922, Jim organized the Oorang Indian football team that lasted two seasons. During the next seven years, he jumped from team to team, finally ending his career shortly after reaching his fortieth birthday.

Jim Thorpe was a mythical man who lived and played with spiritual intensity. Playing was freedom for him. Despite all the rhetoric about his outstanding physical prowess, it was his emotional and mental power that accounted for a major part of his success. In his world, if you could envision it you were better equipped to achieve it. When he was no longer able to envision a life in a white man's world, he crawled into a bottle to live out his days. Jim suffered financial hardship during the Depression, finding temporary employment as a laborer at 50 cents an hour, a bouncer, and as a Hollywood extra often playing an Indian chief. When the press learned that the great Jim Thorpe could not afford a ticket to the 1932 Olympics in Los Angeles, there was a public outcry. Charles Curtis, Vice-President of the United States and himself an Indian, invited Jim to sit with him as he officially opened the games. Though Thorpe was still highly revered and respected by the American public, this never translated into an economic benefit. When the film *Jim Thorpe–All-American* was released in 1951, Jim received nothing because he had previously sold his life story for a paltry sum.

Though used and abused, Jim Thorpe never held grudges. He had competed to satisfy an inner spiritual sense and a competitive need to excel. He married three times and sired eight children in a continual search for happiness and a resolution of an inner lack of meaning. Jim was trapped between his natural heritage and a world that revered Jim Thorpe the athlete, while discriminating against Jim Thorpe the Indian.

Legacy

In his later years, Jim began to reap some of the rewards and recognition that were his due. In 1950 the Associated Press named him the Greatest Football Player of the half-century and the Greatest Male Athlete of the half-century. This honor was followed in 1951 with his election to the National College Football Hall of Fame, and in 1953 with the naming of the Jim Thorpe Stadium in Shawnee, Oklahoma. Jim Thorpe had earned the adulation of the world through his athletic prowess, but more importantly had earned their respect through his strength of character. When he died suddenly on March 28, 1953 from a massive heart attack in his 65th year, the world lost a great human being. His widow, (and third wife) Patricia, who had married him in 1945, said of Jim (Wheeler, p. 226):

He was so easy going, so trusting. He was always concerned about people in distress. One of his friends needed $105 to pay his wife's hospital bill. Jim gave him the $100 he had and borrowed the extra $5. I discovered later that the friend didn't even have a wife. I guess you could say Jim had two-way pockets...You wouldn't think a man could be so perfect. He didn't have a mean bone in his body.

After Thorpe's passing, his daughter Charlotte wrote of him as a "strong individualist." His second wife Freeda told the media, "Jim wanted to do things his way all his life." Jim himself had written, "I was always of a restless disposition and was never content unless I was competing." In following his passion, Jim Thorpe had run afoul of various rules such as those that defined amateur status. Like the hero in a Shakespearean tragedy, his greatest strength–rugged individualism–became his greatest vulnerability and he paid an outrageously high price for minor transgressions. Near the end of his life he had reflected, "Rules are like steamrollers. There is nothing they won't do to flatten the man who stands in their way."

Throughout the six decades following the 1912 Olympics there were numerous efforts by various groups to petition the AAU to reinstate Jim Thorpe's amateur status and re-enter his records in the annals of Olympic history. Finally, on October 12, 1973, Jim Thorpe's amateur status was restored by the AAU. However, it was not until October 13, 1982 that the International Olympic Committee returned Thorpe's achievements to the record books and returned his gold medals to the family.

At the millennium, the Associated Press voted Jim Thorpe the Best Male Athlete of the 20th century. It is indeed appropriate that the epitaph on the Jim Thorpe's red granite memorial in Mauch Chunk, Pennsylvania reads:

"SIR, YOU ARE THE GREATEST ATHLETE IN THE WORLD"
KING GUSTAV, STOCKHOLM, SWEDEN
1912 OLYMPICS
1888 JIM THORPE 1953

Chapter 2

PRINCIPLE #2: TO WIN BIG, BE WILLING TO FAIL BIG

Failure is good. Everything I've learned about coaching, I've learned from making mistakes.
                                        –Rick Pitino, basketball coach

Risk-Taking Propensity

After exploring in the "rough outback" of an Arabian desert and finding nothing but dry holes for four years, a renegade wildcatter found himself teetering on the brink of financial ruin. It was 1953 and he had lost $20 million of the $21-million fortune he had amassed over four decades. Bankruptcy was imminent and his friends advised him to take his last million and run. Yet his instinct told him that there was a sea of oil beneath those desert sands. At the age of 60, when most would cut their losses and run, he put all of his cash at risk. Suddenly, he hit the big one–a gusher that tapped into the Middle East Neutral Zone oil reserves. Within four years, the intrepid wildcatter, later known to the world as Jean Paul Getty, founded Getty Oil and became the richest man in the world.

Few people have the temerity to handle risk. Rather than suffer the embarrassment of failure or pay the price of losing, they avoid challenges or abandon a quest when failure seems likely. Psychologists have found that most people opt for a sure thing with a lower payoff rather than a riskier option with a significant payoff, *even when the returns favor the higher-risk option.* In a famous study, people were invited to choose between receiving a payment of $80 or taking an 85% gamble on winning $100. Which option would you choose? Most people chose the sure gain of $80 to avoid the 15% possibility of winning nothing. Yet probability theory tells us that on average, the riskier option would yield $85.

When Bill Gates, the richest man in the world, was queried about the secret of his success, he reflected, "We've bet the company many times." Why would someone build so successful a company as Microsoft and then risk it all? Bill Gates understands that avoiding risk eventually leads to a mediocrity that ultimately ends in collapse. Most people protect their assets instead of betting them. However, this is not true of the superstars in business or sports. Those not willing to bet it all can't have it all. Do some of them lose it all? Of course they do. But that is the price of reaching the top–having the courage to bet big and risk big.

Permission to fail is really permission to excel, but few people learn this early enough to make a difference in their lives or careers. Those who take pride in having made few mistakes usually work for someone who has made many and expects to make more. The skier who never falls down has not challenged himself or herself enough to master the techniques of navigating double black-diamond runs. In all endeavors, failure is the price paid for learning how to succeed. Ironically, most people abandon the quest even when they are on the right road to the right goal with the right spirit. They merely fail to persevere in the face of adversity. Thomas Edison, an icon who parlayed a life of failures into blockbusting successes, once observed, "Many of life's failures are people who did not realize how close they were to success when they gave up."

Risk and Reward: An Immutable Law of Business and Sports

Risk and reward are inextricably intertwined in life and sports. It is impossible to mitigate risk by saying, "I think I'll just play it safe this one time," because the lowering of any risk simultaneously lowers the size of the potential reward. That is the nature of the game of life. Buy bonds and you limit your downside, but you are also limiting your upside. Furthermore, high-risk bonds pay a higher yield than low-risk bonds. The risk-reward relationship does not tell us that high risk is better than low risk. It merely tells us that high risk offers greater potential rewards *and losses* than low risk.

Superstars understand the need to live on the edge and to risk going down in flames on their climb to eminence. Risk, whether physical, psychological or financial, is a major part of the price every athlete pays to be at the top. For a NASCAR driver the risk of injury is significant; for the golfer, the risks are more likely financial or psychological. Not everyone is willing to pursue a career to which many aspire and in which few succeed. Those with a low tolerance for risk shouldn't enter the fray.

Avoiding risk-taking in sport and in life has its justifications. The heaviest prices are paid by those who take big risks; sometimes the price is one's health or one's life. In other cases the price is financial ruin or the loss of a relationship. In spite of the benefits of risk aversion, one thing is sure: there is a sub-stantial penalty attached to

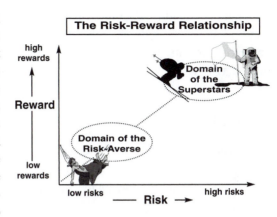

the avoidance of risk. A person who is consumed by a fear of injury will never learn to ski, snowboard, dive or fly. Fear of failure may prevent a person from learning golf or tennis, and fear of economic loss may prevent a person from investing. Life is a risk, as anyone who drives on a freeway in America is well aware. The key to a successful life is not the *avoidance* of risk, but its *management*. The most persuasive reason to engage risk at some level is the classic risk-reward relationship shown in the graph. The graph indicates that reward is greatest when there is a high risk. Conversely, low risk yields small rewards. However, when the risk is high, the large potential rewards are mitigated by the reduced chances of winning them and the likelihood of substantial losses.

Risk-Taking and Winning in Sports

A study at San Jose State University in 2002 reported that those who took the most chances were conditioning themselves to take greater and greater risks. Over time, what these people regarded as risky changed dramatically. What was previously regarded as high risk was soon regarded as somewhat routine and what was previously regarded as dangerous was perceived as merely "risky." The study concluded, "The more we race [vehicles] or experience adventure, the more likely we are to take big risks. The more we race the less likely we are to consider the activity risky."

This finding is self-evident to anyone who has played sports at any level. For a child riding a bike for the first time, the experience is about risk. After a little practice, the child begins to enjoy riding the bike and, perceiving less risk, starts looking for more worlds to conquer. Soon the parents see their child riding with no hands. The same is true for many sports. In alpine skiing, for example, people at first tread cautiously, but after a time they can be found bombing down the hills with abandon. What was at first intimidating is later perceived as fun. Clearly, a significant part of risk is in the eye of the beholder. What is risky for the normal person is typically a walk-in-the-park for those with more experience.

The Big T Personality

Research psychologist Frank Farley wrote extensively on the psychology of thrill seeking: what he labeled Big T (testosterone) personalities. These types are most likely to live on the edge. According to Farley (*USA Today*, Jan 10, 2001):

> *Type T's value variety, novelty, and change. They like challenge, have high energy levels and tend to be self-confident, to feel that fate is in their own hands. They respond to fear by taking action.*

Farley classified Big T's as people who are prone to take more chances and therefore tend to be the most likely to fail. But their failures are what contribute to their successes. Bravado is the stuff of Big T's. Most drive fast cars, get a rush from betting on #13, are competitive to a fault, tend to be creative and are sexually voracious. They drive fast, think fast, walk fast, work fast and even eat fast. The bigger the challenge, the bigger the thrill and that includes romantic conquests. Most are impatient to a fault. Such individuals are intense, passionate and brimming with vitality. Their risk-taking propensity dwarfs that of mere mortals. Jim Thorpe told opposing linemen where he would run the football and challenged them to tackle him. For him it raised the competitive stakes, while others saw it as an exercise of ego. Jeff Gordon was always willing to risk a crash to win. The same mentality drove Pelé, who believed that the only way to play soccer was to attack, not play defensively. It was the same mindset that led Martina Navratilova to charge the net rather than play a more cautious baseline game. Big T's are always willing to lose in order to win.

Failing in Order to Win

The quest for security–the flip side of fear of failure–is the surest path to mediocrity. People who never make mistakes never achieve anything worthwhile. Mistakes and failures are a by-product of action. In basketball, winning is more about losing than anything else. NBA coach Lenny Wilkins won more than any other coach. Who lost the most? Yep! It was Lenny Wilkins. John Stockton annihilated the record books for assists and steals in the NBA. Yes, it was Stockton who holds the record for the most turnovers in the NBA. Most people don't have the self-esteem to handle such failures. Michael Jordan did. He told the media (*People Weekly*, October 9, 1995):

Look, I've missed more than 9000 shots in my career. I've lost 300 games; 26 times I've taken the game-winning shot and missed. I've failed over and over again in my life. And that is why I succeed.

Jordan once lost a million dollars on a game of golf and $250,000 on a putt.

Failing in order to win was never more evident than in the success of the immortal baseball pitcher Cy Young. Each year the best pitcher in baseball is honored with a Cy Young trophy. Why? Because Cy Young pitched more winning games than any other pitcher in baseball history. In fact, he won almost 100 more than the runner-up. What isn't well known is the fact that Young also holds a more dubious record. Young lost more games than any other pitcher. Tiger Woods reinforced this perspective when he told *Good Morning America* after his PGA loss in 2002, "Inherently, you are a loser in golf. You are going to lose many more tourneys than you can possibly win." The moral of this story is that if you win a lot you will probably also lose a lot. So get used to losing if you want to win.

The most admired golfer before the days of Tiger Woods and Jack Nicklaus was the intrepid Arnold Palmer. Palmer didn't swing like Snead, never had the power of Nicklaus or the skill of Gary Player. But what Palmer had was the willingness to go for the impossible. When behind, Arnie always went for the big, high-risk shot. That was something weekend warriors were afraid to try themselves and they loved him for it. When his gambles succeeded, they were spectacular. When they failed, the result was disaster. Arnold's willingness to risk all made him a media darling and for years he was the top endorser in all of sports. Galleries continued to idolize and follow him relentlessly long after Jack Nicklaus had taken over as the king of the links. Palmer came to golf armed with a modicum of raw talent but the heart of a lion. That is what made him special. His approach validated T. S. Eliot's observation, "Only those who will risk going too far can possibly find out how far they can go." Arnold brought golf to the fore.

In his book *Spirit of Enterprise*, author and journalist George Gilder offered insight into winning and losing in the competitive game of business, explaining:

The investor who never acts until statistics prove his choice, the athlete or politician who never fails to move until too late, the businessman who waits until the market is proven–are all doomed to mediocrity by their trust in a spurious rationality and their feelings of faith.

Of all the qualities that differentiate the high-achievers from the underachievers, none is more prominent than the propensity for risk-taking. If you are reluctant to take risks, you will forever hide your light under a bushel, never translating your hopes and dreams into realities. The trek to the top is characterized by risks, failures and redoubled efforts involving additional risks. A vitally important winning behavior is a willingness to take calculated risks, to learn from failures and to pursue your goals relentlessly.

In the previous chapter, I included a table showing the top ten athletes of the 20th century chosen by the Associated Press. Jim Thorpe was voted the greatest by an overwhelming majority. This chapter profiles the icon who was second only to Thorpe in that vote. George Herman "Babe" Ruth was named the greatest baseball player because he achieved a stature that rendered him a legend in his own time. Was it innate talent that set him so far above his contemporaries? Dr. Lisberger, professor of neuroscience at the University of California in San Francisco told the media "baseball is probably 90% mental." In an extensive study of hand-eye coordination, he concluded, "Hitting a baseball is one of the most complex tasks you can imagine." Why? Hitters have only 200 milliseconds (2/10ths of a second) to decide whether to swing the bat or not. (In the Introduction, I cited a *USA Today* study in 2003 that rated "hitting a fastball" as the most difficult of "the ten hardest things to do in sports.") After Ruth's 1921 season, during which he annihilated the record books, Columbia University psychologists analyzed his sensory and cognitive reaction time. They found that his hand-eye coordination times were better than average, but not that much better to have made him the Sultan of Swat. His supremacy resided in a combination of qualities, but none was more dominant than his high risk-taking, big T persona. How did Babe rise to the top of the world of celebrity and become an American legend that defined an era in his country's history? This is a real-life Horatio Alger story in which the protagonist is displayed in an array of colors, showing all the contrasting shades and shadows of greatness.

Before delving into this story, I encourage you to complete the following assessment. There are no "right" or "wrong" answers. To measure your risk tolerance accurately, answer the questions as thoughtfully as you can.

RISK-TAKING SELF-ASSESSMENT–Are You a Risk-Taker or a Care-taker?

For each of the following statements choose "True" or "False" to indicate whether you believe the statement to be true or false.

There are no "right" or "wrong" answers. In making your selection, answer the questions as candidly as possible without anticipating how you will be classified.

1.	I'd rather be master of my destiny than depend on others.	True	False
2.	I would rather stay put than move up in the organization.	True	False
3.	My friends think of me as a high roller in gambling.	True	False
4.	I am an initiater rather than a follower at work.	True	False
5.	I would never quit my job until I had another job confirmed.	True	False
6.	I prefer investments with fixed returns over investments with big potential, but unknown or unproven returns.	True	False
7.	I often take chances on new concepts if they will advance my career.	True	False
8.	Working on incentives with larger potential is not my style.	True	False
9.	I would love to have the opportunity to go white-water rafting.	True	False
10.	I'd be reluctant to change jobs now to make big money.	True	False
11.	I usually eat at new restaurants rather than those that I have enjoyed in the past.	True	False
12	I am content with life as it is and don't need new things to excite me.	True	False
13.	I would enjoy the chance to take flying or skydiving lessons.	True	False
14.	I have been told that I have a creative bent.	True	False
15.	I don't go to casinos to bet because the odds are against me.	True	False
16.	I would like to travel to different parts of the world to see how other people live, even if there is some danger involved.	True	False
17	I never play the "float game" (writing a check in hopes to cover it before it hits the bank in a few days.)	True	False
18.	A less secure career choice with greater long-term opportunity is appealing.	True	False
19.	I follow the rules, even if they don't seem quite right to me.	True	False
20.	I would not enjoy walking through a foreign city without a map.	True	False

Instructions	Scoring Key
Give yourself one point for each "True" answer on items: 1, 3, 4, 7, 9, 11, 13,14, 16, 18 and one point for each "False" answer on the other items. Then use the scoring key to determine your risk propensity.	**16–20:** High risk-taker. **10–15:** Moderate risk-taker. **5–9:** Risk averse; prefers structured environs. **1–4:** Security conscious and almost always plays within the rules.

BABE RUTH

- In 1999, voted the "#1 Athlete of all time" by the Associated Press.

- Best pitcher in American League from 1914 to 1918 with ERA of 2.28.

- His slugging percentage in 1920 was .847–a record that stood for 80 years.

- Hit 60 home runs in 1927 and 714 in his career. His lifetime batting average was .342.

- Winner of the 1915, 1916 and 1918 World Series with the Boston Red Sox and six World Series with the Yankees.

Babe Ruth: Consummate Risk-Taker

**Babe Ruth
1895–1948**

In America, the decade from 1920 to 1929 was called "the roaring twenties." The First World War had come to an end, the troops were returning and America was ready to party. It was the era of *The Great Gatsby*, grandiose living and the celebration of life. Unbridled optimism pushed the stock market ever higher and women's hemlines rose in accordance. Celebrating a new freedom, women threw off the long formal gowns of tradition and danced the Charleston in the boyish flapper fashion designs of Coco Chanel. Although prohibition had been instituted in 1920 to outlaw consumption of alcohol, American people flouted the rules and partied hard. They were ready to inaugurate a new, high-risk-taking, rule-flouting champion who would symbolize excess in the extreme.

It was out of this exciting new era in American history that one of the greatest icons of Americana emerged. He was larger than life during his days on Earth and even larger in the legend he left behind. Most Americans knew him as "The Babe" or simply "Babe." The large Italian-American population of New York affectionately referred to him as "Bambino" (Italian for "child" or "baby"). He was also given titles of royalty including "Home Run King" and "Sultan of Swat." His surname "Ruth" morphed into the adjective, "Ruthian" to describe greatness of the highest order. His "Ruthian" home runs not only sailed out of the ballpark, but they seemed to go into orbit. When Walter Johnson, the famous Washington pitcher with the all-time record for shutouts, was asked to compare the length of Babe's homers with those of Jimmie Foxx and Hank Greenburg, he replied, "All I can say is that the balls Ruth hit out of the park got smaller quicker than anybody else's."

In Babe's day, long hitting was not valued the way it is in the modern game, because a cautious approach to the game, called "inside baseball," prevailed. Home runs were rare and therefore regarded as high-risk, low-yield hits. The popular strategy among most coaches was to try for a single to get a man on first base. If the runner could steal second base, the next batter could hit a (sacrifice) ball into the outfield, enabling the man on second base to move to third. Finally, a sacrifice by the third batter would enable the runner on third to score. In short, inside baseball was a low-risk strategy that denied fans the drama of the big hit. It was Babe Ruth, a high-risk taker and renegade, who ushered in a new era in baseball by swinging for the fences in his "take-no-prisoners" approach to hitting. In his own words, "I hit big or I miss big. I like to live as big as I can." Describing his all-or-nothing swing and its dramatic impact on the spectators, sportswriter Grantland Rice wrote, "To watch Ruth go down, swinging from the heels, often sprawling from the sheer violence of his cut, was almost as exciting as seeing him blast one out of the park."

Babe changed baseball because he was prepared to fail big in order to win big. By swinging for the fences, he won the twin titles "Home Run King" and "Strike-out King." In his own words, "Once committed…once my swing starts,…I can't change it or pull up. It's all or nothing at all." That Babe understood the fan-appeal of his all-or-nothing-at-all approach was evident when he told a sports columnist, "I could have hit .600 if I had settled for hitting singles, but the fans were paying to see me hit home runs."

When Babe Ruth came into baseball, he was ready–ready to out-pitch, out-hit and out-party all of his contemporaries. The roaring 20s set the stage for Babe's explosion on the American scene as the standard-bearer for high-risk, high-stakes living. Babe Ruth and the American public enjoyed a symbiotic relationship–he fed their fantasies and they responded by transforming him into a legend. Teammate Harry Hooper said many years later:

> *I saw it happen, from beginning to end…this nineteen-year-old kid, crude, poorly educated, only lightly brushed by the social veneer we call civilization, gradually transformed into the idol of American youth and the symbol of baseball the world over–a man loved by more people and with an intensity of feeling that perhaps has never been equaled before or since. I saw a man transformed from a human being into something pretty close to a god.*

In 2003, *Sports Illustrated* polled its readers for their nomination of today's greatest *living* player. Strangely, Babe received eight votes even though Babe, the mortal, had been dead for a half-century and had not played a game in almost 70 years. The Babe's legend lives on.

BABE RUTH'S TREK TO THE TOP

Early Imprints

George Herman Ruth, born February 6, 1895, was raised on the Baltimore waterfront. He was exposed early to the seamy side of life, residing above a saloon with his parents. By the time he was seven, he was proving too much to handle, so on June 13, 1902, his parents "enrolled" him in St. Mary's Industrial School for Boys–a Catholic reform school. Today this wayward boy would be classified as ADHD (Attention Deficit Hyperactive Disorder). One of Babe's teachers and mentors, Brother Gilbert, wrote of George's renegade spirit at St. Mary's, "His defiance of ritual got him in the doghouse. Ruth broke rules with childlike impunity." He spoke with tongue-in-cheek humor of Ruth's antics. He recalled on one occasion catching Ruth and teammates sitting in the clubhouse with a .22 caliber rifle, betting money on who could shoot out doorknobs. This was a harbinger of things to come.

A compassionate mentor, Brother Mathias, directed George's mania into baseball. Mathias was a giant of a man who could hit a baseball out of sight. His 6' 6" height alone was intimidating. When George saw him hit fungoes out of sight with one hand, Mathias became his hero. He trained George to be flexible and play every position on the field. Forty years later, Ruth wrote in his memoirs, "At St. Mary's I met and learned to love the greatest man I've ever known–Brother Mathias. He bunted balls to me by the hour when I was eight…I tried to do things as he did them. He was the father I needed."

Later, Ruth reflected, "I look back on St. Mary's as one of the most constructive periods of my life. I'm as proud of it as any Harvard man is of his school." And so he should be. St. Mary's saved him from an unsavory life on the streets, or worse. The school allowed him to expend his enormous energies on sports and taught him some semblance of discipline. It taught him how to win and how to lose. When the movie about his life was released, Babe told Bob Consodine, "I was a bad kid. I hardly knew my parents and I was incorrigible."

Like most superstars, Ruth adamantly refused to conform to rules or regulations. From the day he started playing baseball he was unorthodox. The big kid did things that were verboten in baseball, then and now. Ruth loved to catch but left-handers rarely play the catcher position. He also played shortstop and third base, two positions not played by left-handers. While playing for St. Mary's, he would wow the audience by playing every position on the field–a different one each inning. By his late teens George could play all positions with equal skill. His most impressive talent was his pitching prowess that included a blazing fastball. At 6' 2" and 190 lbs, George was much bigger than the average 5' 9", 168 lbs of that era. His reputation as an outstanding pitcher grew until one day Jack Dunn, owner and manager of the Baltimore Orioles, heard of the young sensation and asked St. Mary's if he could take him under his wing. The rules at the reform school required that a student remain "enrolled" until he was twenty-one. On February 14, 1914, Brother Paul, who as superintendent of the school was George's legal guardian, released him to the custody of Jack Dunn. Although George was just 19 years old, the release enabled him to sign a contract with the Baltimore Orioles and begin earning an income as a professional baseball player.

Flight from St. Mary's to the Orioles

After George's release from St. Mary's, he headed off to spring training with the Orioles. For the first time in his life, George Herman Ruth had cash in his pocket. His first acquisition was a bicycle. This overgrown kid was hell on wheels riding his bike each day to the baseball park. Cycling with abandon through traffic, he raced across busy streets oblivious to the dangers around him. His daughter Dorothy later wrote, "He left St. Mary's like a caged animal set loose on the world." At 19 Ruth was now a professional ballplayer with a paycheck of $100 for the first month. Years later, reflecting on those trips to the ballpark, he explained, "I bought a bicycle, something that I had wanted and often prayed for through most of my young life. Most of the Orioles, of course, had cars, but none of them was as proud as I was, riding the first possession of my life through the streets of Baltimore."

When his income increased, George graduated to an Indian motorcycle. On taking ownership of this new marvel of technology, his only question was "How do I start it?" He ignored such subtleties as how to shift gears, throttle up and down, or negotiate high-speed turns. He jumped on the motorcycle and took off for St. Mary's to show it to his friends. During the drive across town, Ruth almost died twice. This man-child showed up at St. Mary's looking like a punch-drunk boxer after a bad beating. The fun-loving Ruth saw the glee in the eyes of the students as he spent the day riding them back and forth across the grounds. With the generosity that was to become one of his most endearing characteristics, he donated his prized possession to the school. Unmitigated passion for life and its rewards contributed to his charismatic persona. That same passion also contributed to a life of unparalleled partying and philandering.

George's image as a wild, untamed youth was already in the making when rumors circulated about this big kid who almost killed himself cycling to the ballpark. Ruth's reputation for childlike behavior was further enhanced when Sportswriter Roger Pippen of the *Baltimore News-Post* described how this wild kid ate a dozen hot dogs and washed them down with two quarts of ice cream before taking the mound against the National League champion Phillies. In a column written March 14, 1914, Pippen described with amazement how this "babe in the woods" had beaten the Phillies 4 to 3 after such a display of gastronomic activity. The nickname stuck, and George Herman was known ever after as "Babe."

Professional Baseball with the Boston Red Sox: 1914–1919

Mid-way through the 1914 season, Jack Dunn fell into financial difficulty. To cover his debts, he sold three players, including Babe, to the Boston Red Sox for a total of $25,000. After only a few months with the Orioles, Ruth became a member of the Boston Red Sox and a player in the American League. Babe's career and personal life were about to move into a higher gear.

Shortly after arriving in Boston, Babe entered Lander's Coffee Shop for his usual gargantuan breakfast of bacon and eggs. There he was captivated by a 16-year-old waitress named Helen Woodford. She was a beautiful young woman with a personality that might be described as sunnyside-up. Turning on the legendary Ruthian charm, he courted her favor during the countless breakfasts that followed. On October 17, 1914, within three months of their meeting, 17-year-old Helen Woodford became Mrs. Babe Ruth. Since Babe was only 19, he had to get his father's permission to marry. After the wedding Helen and Babe moved into the apartment above his father's saloon in Baltimore, where they spent the winter before moving back to Boston.

Big Leagues for the Big Kid

In 1915, Babe enjoyed his first full season in the Major Leagues. Throughout that year the Sox played defensive "inside baseball," hitting singles, stealing bases and hitting runners home. Pitching was paramount and "hitting" rather than "slugging" was the preferred method of scoring runs. By season's end, Babe Ruth had 29 hits in 92 at bats giving him a batting average of .315. Of those hits, only four were home runs. The other members of the Sox had a combined total of 9 home runs. In spite of the defensive style, Babe was a critical factor in the Boston Red Sox becoming the World Series Champions.

The 1916 baseball season was another successful season for the Sox who won the pennant and, for the second time in a row, the World Series. In that year, Babe established himself as the best left-handed pitcher in the American League. He pitched 9 shutouts, had 23 wins and led the league in earned run average, the true barometer of pitching excellence. However, this season wasn't much different from the previous year in the hitting department. Babe had a batting average of .300 and hit only three homers.

The next year Babe's pitching was even better. In 1917 he won 24 games including 6 shutouts and he pitched an amazing 35 complete games in 38 starts. He did this while batting an incredible .325–an average exceeded only by Hall of Fame legends Ty Cobb, George Sisler and Tris Speaker. The only home run he scored in that year was a spectacular smack that sailed into the centerfield bleachers at Fenway Park–the first ball ever to reach that destination. The home run, perhaps the most exciting event in baseball, had not yet come into its own. However, Babe Ruth, with his swing-for-the-fences approach, would soon change all that.

His high psychic energy caused Ruth to live each day as if there were no tomorrow. It made him a horrible mate, impossible to manage, and led to over-indulgence in virtually every vice known to man. Moderation was not part of the Ruthian lifestyle. Excess was his forte whether it was food, booze, women, cards, cigars or hitting a baseball. For him it was all or nothing. When he ate he was a gourmand. One or two women were never enough. There was always a cigar in his mouth and a beer bottle in his hand. Too much smoking, too much beer, too much food, too many women and too many fast cars would ultimately become part of his legacy.

During the 1916 and 1917 seasons, it was evident that Babe Ruth was becoming a prima donna. On June 23, 1917, when his disagreements with umpires escalated from verbal to physical abuse, he was suspended for 10 days. On another occasion, he stopped his car in the middle of a busy Boston intersection to chase after an opposing ballplayer who had insulted him on the field. The traffic jam he created was monumental—but lost on the impetuous Ruth. Consistent with Ruth's Big T personality was his fascination with speed. In his 1948 memoir he spoke of his love of fast cars (Gilbert, p. 109):

There wasn't any greater thrill in life for me than stepping on that baby's gas (new 12-cylinder Packard). During the 1921 season I nearly killed myself and four others. I hit a turn too fast and we turned over and rolled like a ball with bodies flying out in every direction. The car was completely wrecked. I just left it there and bought a new one the next day.

In another incident, Babe attempted to beat two trolley cars through an intersection and ended up squashed between them. The car was reduced to an unrecognizable heap of metal. Babe and an unidentified lady friend escaped without serious injury. Babe's overt philandering was also taking a toll on his marriage. It seemed that Babe Ruth was a free spirit who would not allow anyone or any institution to fetter his desires. But what made him incorrigible also contributed to making him the Sultan of Swat. It was no accident that Babe never considered following the coach's suggestion that he change his swing when there were two strikes against him. Other batters would choke up on the bat and try for a single. Not Babe! He liked to say, "Why choke up? Those who do, take a chance on hitting into a double play rather than take the shame of striking out. They're quitters." Pure abandon was his style. The magnitude of his magical persona grew among his teammates when he would beat them bowling left-handed, then double the bet and beat them bowling right-handed.

Babe's excessive lifestyle between the 1917 and 1918 seasons caused his weight to increase from 194 to 215 lbs. His salary also increased from $5000 to $7000 as his talents and crowd appeal became increasingly more evident. From the 1918 season on, dramatic home runs that dazzled the spectators began to be a major attraction. On May 6, 1918, Babe was moved out of the ninth position in the batting order (the standard position for pitchers) to the cleanup position. When the season ended, Babe had tied the league lead with 11 homers out of 317 at-bats. Sports writers referred to him as "the Home Run King," but they hadn't seen anything yet. In the 1919 and 1920 seasons, Ruth smashed 29 and 54 homers respectively, setting new major league records in both years. George Sisler, the runner-up in 1920, had only 19 home runs. As the decade came to an end, Babe Ruth's reputation as a slugger grew exponentially, eclipsing his pitching prowess. Realizing that his spectacular home runs had more fan appeal than excellent pitching, Babe demanded to be relieved of his pitching duties and placed in the outfield. His wish was eventually granted and Babe was able to concentrate on the glamour of the big hit that would become the jewel in the crown of the Home Run King.

To some extent, Babe's reputation as a slugger overshadowed his all-around prowess in baseball. He could play virtually every position. For three years he was arguably the best pitcher in the American League. From 1914 to 1919 he won 94 of 140 decisions with an ERA of 2.28. His record of $29^{2}/3$ consecutive scoreless innings in World Series play (spanning the 1916 and 1918 series) stood for 42 years and it was the record of which he was most proud. However, by July 1919, Babe's pitching career was behind him. When his reputation for hitting reached mythical proportions, Babe would often remind people, albeit with minimal success, of his exceptional pitching prowess.

During the off-season in 1919, the cash-strapped owners of the Red Sox sold this emerging star to the Yankees for an unprecedented $100,000. It was a remarkable coup for the New York Yankees and the embarrassed Sox owner, Harry Frazee, justified his decision by saying Ruth was wild and unmanageable. After this infamous trade, the Boston Red Sox fell from prominence in baseball and did not win a world series until October 27, 2004 when they defeated the St. Louis Cardinals in four straight–after an 86-year drought. Sportswriters referred to the long Red Sox hiatus without a World Series victory as "the curse of the Bambino."

Ruthville and the House that Ruth Built

When the Yankees paid Ruth $20,000 in 1920, it was the highest salary in baseball. The Babe promptly bought a brand new Cadillac for $5,000–one-quarter of his annual pay. Then, in a display of generosity for which he was famous, he gave the car to his mentor, Brother Mathias. Brother Gilbert of St. Mary's wrote of Ruth's love of the game and disdain for money. He wrote, "Money could never mean as much to him as hits." In describing Ruth's ethics he said, "He wouldn't cheat at solitaire" (Gilbert, 1999, p. 152).

In the first season following Ruth's trade from the Boston Red Sox, the Curse of the Bambino kicked in. By himself, Babe hit more home runs than the entire Boston team and continued to do that for the next 12 seasons. Ironically, his first home run that season occurred on May 1, 1920 against the Boston Red Sox. Babe smashed what has been called a truly amazing drive, far over the roof of the Polo Grounds, the Yankee's home field. Ruth was at the pinnacle of his awesome prowess. The home runs that he hit were truly Ruthian and the prospect of witnessing such colossal power had fans swarming into the Polo Grounds in record numbers. Two weeks after Babe's opening smash, 38,600 aficionados crammed into the Polo Grounds and

15,000 more had to be turned away from the ticket windows. Babe Ruth mania was in full swing and money was flooding into the Yankee coffers. When the stellar 1920 season came to a close, Babe had hit an unprecedented 54 home runs and achieved a .847 slugging percentage (total number of bases divided by at bats). Sports researcher George Russell Weaver said it was "the best single season any major league hitter has ever had." The next year (1921) Babe hit 59 home runs and his slugging percentage was .846. Until Barry Bonds achieved a .864 slugging percentage in 2001, no player other than Babe had exceeded .800.

Babe Ruth mania caused attendance at the Polo Grounds to skyrocket. The New York Giants, who had been sharing the Polo Grounds with the Yankees as their home field, were being outdrawn by the Yankees and served notice that the Yankees would have to locate elsewhere. The Yankee owners, flush with cash, purchased a site for a new home field. Construction began in 1922 and by the 1923 season the New York Yankees were playing in a new home, officially called Yankee Stadium and unofficially called "the House that Ruth Built." The section of the right field bleachers into which most of the Ruthian homers were hit was named "Ruthville."

In 1920, Babe Ruth dared to participate in a barnstorming tour of Cuba (playing exhibition games after the end of the regular season) in defiance of the commissioner's rule against it. For that tour, he received the unbelievable sum of $40,000. In typical Ruthian style, he bet it all on the horses and had to borrow the return fare from his wife Helen.

His continued defiance of rules during those first years with the Yankees grew in proportion to his fame. In fact, during the 1922 season, he was suspended a record five times for personal and professional misconduct including fighting with the umpires. Through it all, the Bambino continued exercising his gargantuan appetites for food, drink, gambling, cigars, ice cream and women. The Sultan of Swat was notorious for chasing down ham and eggs with a glass of whiskey. Few men could have played–let alone excelled–on such a diet. More often than not he would show up at the ballpark directly from some party. Women were his weakness and nobody's wife was off limits when Ruth was nearby. In spite of his fast living, Babe continued to dazzle the fans. In 1923, he won the Most Valuable Player award, batting .393 and hitting 41 homers in helping the Yankees to win their first ever World Series. In the following year he batted .378 and hit 46 home runs.

As Babe approached the pinnacle of his career, his fame became ubiquitous. In 1923 the Curtiss Candy Company released the Baby Ruth candy bar without endorsement fees or even consultation with Babe. The firm said the bar was named for Grover Cleveland's deceased daughter, who had died 17 years earlier. This allegation was ludicrous, but the jovial fun-loving Ruth just shrugged it off as an amusing marketing ploy. By a strange coincidence, the candy bar hit the market just after the Babe had virtually rewritten the record books, averaging over 50 home runs in each of three successive years.

A Fall from Grace

Eventually the fast living took a toll on the Babe. By the 1925 season Babe's weight had ballooned up to 256 lbs and he began to experience stomach problems. This caused him to miss most of the 1925 season and bat under .300 for the first time in his career. The Babe's voracious sexual appetite continued to dominate his activities off the field. His continuing infidelity was a source of constant domestic conflict that eventually led to the breakdown of his marriage. Helen packed up and moved back to Boston. As a Catholic, she was not permitted to divorce so she and Babe remained estranged. Ruth's excessive lifestyle, his declining performance and his prima donna antics, including conflicts with umpires and hostile fans, were triggering a public backlash against the former hero. In the public tradition of placing heroes on a pedestal and subsequently tearing them down, many fans began booing Babe Ruth. The Home Run King took the abuse in good spirit when in his Dr. Jeckle mood, but reacted explosively when his psyche was hijacked by Mr. Hyde–a classic display of bipolar behavior.

What saved the Babe from reaching villain status was a charming assortment of redeeming qualities that made his undisciplined exploits easy to forgive. Among these were his child-like honesty, his instinctive generosity and his unselfish dedication to children. One of the incidents that made him an icon and endeared him to the public is alleged to have occurred during the 1926 World Series. According to the legend, he was visiting 11-year-old terminally ill Johnny Sylvester in hospital and asked (Gallico, p. 37), "If I hit one out [of the park] will you get better? Ya know what I'm going to do this afternoon? I'm gonna hit a home run just for you. You watch. It's gonna be your home run." Babe was true to his word that afternoon, hitting the promised home run and lighting up the life of a young boy. Then in game four, the Babe hit three home runs, a mark that would stand for another 50 years. The home runs are fact, though the story may well be the kind of embellishment that grows with the reputation of a superhero. In any case,

Babe Ruth's dedication to children is irrefutable. Despite his larger-than-life persona he never lost his childlike sense of adventure. And it was the children whom he adored and who adored him. Other stars would sign a few autographs but not the Babe. He would stay an hour or two after every game signing autographs for admiring youngsters and would not leave the stadium until he had fulfilled their requests.

The Sixtieth Home Run

The 1925 season was the nadir of Babe's career with the Yankees–the time when his health and his personal discipline hit bottom. However, early in 1926, the Babe showed up at spring training a sleek 212 lbs, a result of several months of training in the gym. During that season, he hit 47 home runs and batted .372. Though the Yankees lost the World Series to St. Louis in 1926, it was clear that Babe Ruth was once again at the top of his game. In 1927, the Yankees, led by the Sultan of Swat, won the American League pennant and went on to defeat the Pittsburgh Pirates in four straight to win the World Series. On September 30, 1927, Babe hit his historic record-breaking 60th home run, exceeding the total of any other team in the league. To put this in a modern perspective, those 60 home runs constituted 14% of the home runs in the league. That would be equivalent today to Barry Bonds hitting 300 homers in a season. Ruth's 60-homer mark stood intact from 1927 until 1961 when Roger Maris hit 61 homers, albeit in a season that was eight games longer. Many fans vilified Maris for daring to break the Bambino's record, attesting to the lasting power of Babe Ruth's presence as an American icon.

The Yankees continued their winning ways in 1928 by capturing the pennant, and Babe finished the season with 54 home runs. In the World Series they met the St. Louis Cardinals who had defeated them in the World Series two years earlier. It was a chance for the Yanks to avenge their previous humiliation. The Sultan of Swat rose to the occasion, getting 10 hits in 16 times at bat for a batting average of .625, a World Series record. Three of his hits were home runs–all hit in the same game! The Yankees swept the Cardinals four games straight and retained their title as World Series Champions. The 1928 World Series win was the zenith of Babe's career, but it was not the end of his home run prowess.

On January 11, 1929, Babe's estranged first wife Helen died in a tragic fire. Three months after her death, Babe married Claire Hodgson, a beautiful 28-year-old who had played in The Ziegfeld Follies. Babe's raging libido was beginning to slow as the roaring 20s came to an end. The Market Crash of 1929 ended the decade of excess and followed it with a decade of deprivation for the common man, who needed entertainment more than ever to escape the hopelessness of a dismal reality.

In the three years that followed, the Yankees were unable to win the pennant and were therefore closed out of the World Series. Babe Ruth's performances were still exciting, but his best years were behind him. In the 1930, 1931 and 1932 seasons, Babe hit 49, 46 and 41 home runs respectively. A story that is often told as an important vignette in the Babe Ruth legend occurred at the end of the 1931 season. During this tough year of the Depression when jobs were scarce and people were starving, Ruth was earning $80,000 per year and the President of the United States, Herbert Hoover, was earning $75,000. One of the reporters asked the Babe how he could justify making more than the President. Ruth responded, "Why not? I had a better year than he did."

The Famous Called Shot

Ruth's flair for the dramatic reached a climax in the fifth game of the 1932 World Series against the Chicago Cubs in Wrigley field. The Babe, tired of the taunts and catcalls from the jeering fans, stepped to the plate with the score tied 4-4. The ball whizzed past him and the umpire called "Strike one!" In an act of pure defiance he raised his index finger to acknowledge the first strike. The Chicago fans went wild with insults and taunts. The next two pitches were called balls. There was a brief troubled silence. The pitcher Charlie Root sent another sizzler into the strike zone and the umpire called "Strike two!" Babe raised two fingers acknowledging the second strike. The Chicago dugout went wild, shouting jeers and insults at the Sultan of Swat, hoping to break his quiet composure. The Chicago fans lobbed lemons at Ruth who in good-natured style lobbed them back into the stands. Then Babe pointed towards the flagpole in center field as if to say, "That is where the next pitch is going to go." The fifth pitch, a changeup curve, was low and away. Babe reached for it with full extension and launched it into a fast-rising orbit that landed deep in the center field bleachers. It was described as the longest home run that had ever been hit in Wrigley Field. Sports journalists in the stands that immortal day went wild. Paul Gallico wrote, "[Ruth pointed to the center field bleachers] and that is exactly where the ball went!" The man who was never predictable had done the impossible. The President of the

United States, Franklin Roosevelt, who was in a box seat near ground level, threw his head back and laughed. The media gushed over this epoch-making achievement. Many have questioned whether Babe actually gestured to the center field bleachers, but sportswriter Gallico insisted, "I saw him do that."

The *New York World Telegram* headlined Ruth's called home run in their evening paper: RUTH CALLS SHOT AS HE PUTS HOMER #2 IN SIDE POCKET. Journalist Joe Williams reported (Miller, p. 145), "In the fifth with the Cubs riding him unmercifully from the bench, Ruth pointed to center and punched a screaming liner to a spot where no ball had ever been hit before." The Hearst papers wrote, "Ruth pointed out where he was going to hit the next one and hit it there." Westbrook Pegler wrote an extensive play-by-play account of the game and Ruth's call, saying (Creamer, p. 364):

Many a hitter may make two home runs, possibly three, in World Series play in years to come, but not the way Ruth hit these two. Nor will you ever seen an artist call his shot before hitting one of the longest drives ever made on the ground in a World Series game, laughing at and mocking the enemy, two strikes gone.

After the game, a reporter asked the Babe, "What if you hadn't connected?" With childlike simplicity Ruth responded, "I never thought of that."

Time: The Superhero's Greatest Foe

Babe was 38 as he entered the 1933 baseball season. The euphoria of the 1932 World Series Championship was now in the distant past. The Depression was at its lowest point and money was tight. Babe was offered a contract for $50,000–a $25,000 decrease from his 1932 salary of $75,000. Although he ultimately negotiated $52,000, it was becoming clear to the Babe that he was not able to bargain as hard as in his high-performing years. By the end of the 1933 season he had 34 home runs and a batting average of .301, but this dropped to 22 home runs and an average of .288 in the season that followed. Finally in 1935, the inevitable happened. The Yankees let it be known Babe Ruth was on the trading block. The other Boston team, the Braves, offered Babe a contract that intimated a possible future role for Babe as a manager, but the managerial role was illusory. The Braves wanted Ruth as a player, knowing that his presence could generate substantial revenue at the box office. Babe signed the contract with the intention of retiring at the end of that season. However, he was not about to leave the stage without adding a dramatic closing signature to a colossal career.

On May 25, 1935 Babe Ruth was 40 years old and entering the final act of his epic career. In the seventh inning of a game against the Pittsburgh Pirates, he came up against Guy Bush, the pitcher who had hit him in the arm with a fastball in the 1932 World Series. This time it was Babe who hit the ball. In the words of Guy Bush (Creamer, p. 397):

I never saw a ball hit so hard before or since. He was fat and old, but he still had that great swing. Even when he missed, you could hear the bat go swish. But I can't remember anything about the first home run he hit off me that day. I guess it was just another homer. But I can't forget that last one. It's probably still going.

Biographer Creamer reflected (p. 397):

It was unbelievably long, completely over the roof of the double-decked stands in right field and out of the park. Nobody had ever hit a ball over the roof in Forbes Field before. Gus Miller, the head usher, went to investigate and was told the ball landed on the roof of one house, bounced onto another and then into a lot, where a boy picked it up and ran off with it. Miller measured the distance from the first house back to home plate and said it was 600 feet. His measurement may have been imprecise, but it was still the longest home run ever hit in Pittsburgh.

That home run was Babe Ruth's 714th and the last in his major league career. It stood as the record for total career home runs for almost four decades until Hank Aaron set a new record of 755. When Babe hit his 700th homer, no other player had hit 300. Ruth's record of 72 multiple-homer games still stands. All these records set him apart from other greats such as Ty Cobb, Barry Bonds and Nolan Ryan. All were great but none were so far above their peers as the Bambino.

The Final Inning

Babe Ruth finally retired at 40 years of age at the end of the 1935 season. He was spent on the field of play and dejected because he had been unable to secure a job as the manager of a baseball club. Though he was acknowledged as the greatest player the game had ever seen, his reputation as a renegade had convinced team owners that he would not make a suitable manager. The ultimate insult to his ego came in 1936 when he requested complimentary tickets to the opening game. The person handling the ticket sales asked the Sultan of Swat to send a check for the tickets. His prestige as baseball's ultimate superhero had lost its leverage. This stinging insult occurred just four years after Jim Thorpe's humiliating attempt to secure tickets to the 1932 Olympics.

In 1939 at the age of 44, Babe Ruth suffered the first of two heart attacks that would threaten his life. In the months that followed, he curtailed his indulgent lifestyle and dropped 40 lbs. from his previous 270. Near the end of 1946, Babe experienced pain over his left eye that was eventually attributed to a tumorous growth that encircled the left carotid artery. Unaware that the radiation treatment he was receiving was to stop the growth of a cancerous tumor, he thought that the pain was due to a gum infection. Actually, he was suffering cancer of the larynx. Recognizing the imminence of Babe's death, the Commissioner of Baseball, A.B. Chandler, declared Sunday, April 27, 1947 as Babe Ruth Day. On that festive occasion, Babe gave a public address and it was apparent that he was in the final stages of cancer. However, by June of that year the cancer appeared to have gone into remission. On June 13, 1948, Babe attended the celebration of the 25th anniversary of Yankee Stadium. As the foremost celebrity on that occasion, he appeared before a huge crowd, supported by a bat that served as a cane to support his weight. He received numerous ovations fit for a superhero. Although never told he had cancer, Babe eventually understood the essence of his pain and announced, "I think the termites have got me."

The great Babe Ruth was given the last rites of the Catholic Church on July 21, 1948. On July 26, less than a week later, he attended the film premier of his life story titled *The Babe Ruth Story*, and apparently disturbed by its contents, left the theater before its conclusion. On August 16, 1948, Babe died, but the colossal legend he left behind lived on. Babe became one of the most important icons in American history.

Legacy

Babe Ruth was not merely a baseball superstar, but was so far ahead of his peers that he redefined the sport and raised the bar to an entirely new level. In 1920 he hit more home runs than 14 of the 15 teams in the league. Gabe Costa analyzed all eras and concluded (*Baseball Research Journal*, p. 102),

"No one was close to him as a hitter or all-around performer. It seemed he should play in a higher league." In a statistical analysis involving baseball data from Ruth's time through the 2002 season, Costa compared Babe's "Individual Home Run Ratio" with those of his contemporaries. Ruth ranked first in the years 1920, 1921, 1927 and 1928, as well as far above the superstars in subsequent eras. In "Isolated Power"–the sum of home runs, runs-batted-in and total bases divided by at-bats–Ruth scored way ahead of his nearest competitor and far ahead of modern-day superstars Mark McGuire and Barry Bonds. In 2005, Princeton University Press published *Baseball's All-Time Best Sluggers*. In that book, Michael J. Schell, Professor of Biostatistics at the University of North Carolina, presented the results of his statistical analysis of the hitting prowess of the greatest baseball players of all eras. Again, Babe Ruth was unequivocally rated #1 as baseball's best hitter and slugger.

For the generations who arrived too late to see the Sultan of Swat in action, we have only the vivid descriptions of past writers to help us recapture the drama of Babe at the plate. Sportswriter Paul Gallico of the *New York Daily News* wrote (Miller, p. 48):

> *It was impossible to watch him at bat without experiencing an emotion. I have seen hundreds of ballplayers at the plate, and none of them managed to convey the message of impending doom to a pitcher that Babe Ruth did with the cock of the head, the position of his legs and the little gentle waving of the bat, feathered in his two big paws.*

In an eloquent eulogy on Ruth's passing, teammate Waite Hoyt explained, "Babe was no ordinary man. He possessed a magnetism that was positively infectious. When he entered a clubhouse or the field it was as if he was the whole parade. All the lies about him were true."

In 1969 the Baseball Writers Association of America, in celebration of the Centennial Year of Baseball, voted Babe the Greatest Baseball Player of All Time. Three decades later, Sportswriter Bill Koenig wrote of Ruth's huge impact on the game, "If Babe Ruth were alive today, he'd be Mark McGwire, Ken Griffey Jr. and Sammy Sosa–rolled into one."

Sports editor Roger Pippen of the *Baltimore News-Post* wrote a memorial on Ruth in 1955, six years after his death. Pippen described Ruth as a man who transcended the game, a key figure in the nation's national pastime. "You stand immortal as a symbol of America–the greatest rags-to-riches story, the boy from a reform school who fired the imagination like no one before."

Chapter 3

PRINCIPLE #3: FOLLOW YOUR PASSION

My goal was to be the greatest athlete that ever lived.
                                                    –Babe Zaharias

The Origin of Passion–The Sex Drive

Sigmund Freud asserted, "Unsatisfied libido is responsible for producing all art and literature." Expanding on this idea, author of the classic self-help book *Think & Grow Rich*, Napoleon Hill wrote (p. 184–5):

Sex energy is the creative energy of all geniuses…The desire for sexual expression is by far the strongest and most impelling of all the human emotions, and for this very reason this desire, when harnessed *and* transmuted *into action, other than that of physical expression may raise one to great accomplishment.*

Most psychologists agree that high achievement results from the *sublimation* or transference of the sex drive into creative activity. Libidinal or sex energy is the fuel that drives us to pursue our dreams. Great works of literature, breakthroughs in scientific knowledge, giant skyscrapers, and spectacular athletic feats are all products of creative effort driven by passion. Conversely, males who have been castrated are seen to be less aggressive and diminished in their passion and their drive to produce. Similar effects are seen in females who have been sexually altered. Since all of us have sex energy, we all have passion, yet it sublimates into creative activity in only a small segment of the population. Why is it that some people have enough passion to aim for the stars while others amble aimlessly through life, aspiring to little and achieving less? A natural inference would be to attribute such differences to genetic factors. Though genetics account for some differences, they do not explain why some people are fiercely passionate early in life, others acquire productive passion later in life and the majority pass through life without transmuting much of their latent libidinal energy into creative activity.

Early Imprints– The Most Common Origin of Creative Passion

Anyone who has observed a school playground or a sandlot baseball game will recognize that levels of energy, psychic passion and commitment vary from child to child. Though the propensity for passion has an inherited component, the dramatic differences in passion among siblings and even between identical twins indicate that there is a strong environmental influence. Frequently an event or occasion serves as catalyst igniting a latent passion and setting it ablaze. My study of the biographies of world's highest achievers, including the greatest entrepreneurs and superathletes, reveals that most of them can trace their lifelong goals–goals that became a raison d'être or obsession–to a single incident that sparked a vision. We call this vision an *early imprint*. Babe Zaharias won a marbles tournament at age seven that made her obsessively driven to win any and all competitions. Early on, she formulated her personal goal to be "the greatest athlete that ever lived." Many journalists and sports aficionados would say that she achieved her goal.

Henry Ford's early imprint, when he was 12, was his first glimpse of a steam-driven self-propelled vehicle that moved without the aid of horses. Forty-seven years later he would say, "I remember that engine as though I had seen it only yesterday." This vision inspired Henry to build a dynasty that revolutionized the automobile, refined the process of mass production, and created a middle class in America.

Though "early imprints" often occur prior to or during puberty, they sometimes occur in early adulthood. Michael Dell, billionaire founder of Dell Computer Corporation, told in his autobiography how his dream to beat IBM in the PC market drove him to abandon his plans for medical school and become a school dropout at the end of his freshman year at the University of Texas (Dell, p. 10):

> My Dad started. "You've got to stop with this computer stuff and concentrate on school," he said. "Get your priorities straight. What do you want to do with your life?"
> "I want to compete with IBM!" I said.
> He wasn't amused.

In 1999, fifteen years after this conversation, Dell turned 35 years old and his corporation surpassed IBM in sales of personal computers.

The Genesis of Creative Passion in Late Bloomers

Are those who have never experienced an early imprint doomed to live out their lives in a limbo without creative passion or self-fulfillment? Happily the answer is a resounding no! Some high achievers were late bloomers whose creative passions came into full flower in middle age or later. Sometimes adversity was the catalyst that triggered the transmutation of sexual energy into creative passion and sometimes it was merely a state of readiness that connected with opportunity.

Charles Robert was a person who encountered adversity early in life and opportunity later. His mother died when he was only eight and the young lad was shipped off to Shrewsbury School in his native England. Though not a distinguished student, he had come from a family of physicians and was sent to study medicine at Edinburgh University. When it was determined that he was unfit for medicine, he was sent to Christ's College, Cambridge to become a clergyman. Upon graduating without honors at age 22, Charles discovered that he had no passion for any particular career or calling, especially theology. With no particular dream in mind, he set out on a five-year voyage on the H.M.S. Beagle, serving as a naturalist to study the geology of various islands scattered throughout the seven seas. While on this protracted voyage, his observation of the varied life forms on these strange and diverse ecosystems ignited his creative passion. Fascinated by the differences between animals on the islands and those on the contiguous mainland, he gradually formulated theories about how animal species change in form and function. Nine months after his 50th birthday, he gave birth to his classic *Origin of the Species by Means of Natural Selection, or the Preservation of Favoured Races in the Struggle for Life.* Charles Robert Darwin's theory of evolution changed forever the way humans perceive the world and themselves in the universe.

Harland was another person who was on his own at an early age. His father died when Harland was six, forcing his mother into menial work to provide for him and his two younger siblings. At age 12, Harland left home to work on a farm in Greenwood, Indiana. In the decades that followed, he held a variety of jobs including streetcar conductor, railroad fireman, steamboat ferry operator and insurance salesman. At age 40, he was the owner of a small service station in Corbin, Kentucky where many travel-weary customers stopped to fill their tanks. Offering the hospitality for which the South is famous, he began serving meals to his hungry customers using a small room in the living quarters of his service station. The popularity of this service prompted Harland to open a motel and restaurant across the road. With seating for 142 patrons, the restaurant was large enough to enable Harland to devote himself full time to cooking. As he perfected his recipes and his culinary skills, word of his restaurant spread far and wide. By the early 1950s, the prospects for Harland's enterprise were rosy. Then the construction of Interstate Highway I-75 was announced. This highway would bypass Corbin and Harland's restaurant, leaving him without the patrons that had been the mainstay of his business. Devastated, Harland auctioned off his assets and paid his debts. Suddenly, at the age of 65, he was reduced to living on Social Security. Picking up the pieces of his broken life, he drove to restaurants across the country offering to cook batches of chicken for the restaurant owners to sample. When the response was positive, he would offer to share his secret recipe if the restaurant would pay him a nickel for each piece of chicken sold. The idea was a blockbusting success, launching one of the first restaurant franchises in history. When Harland sold his business in 1964 for $2 million, he had 600 franchised outlets across the United States and Canada. Harland Sanders, who had been made a Kentucky Colonel by the Governor of Kentucky, became known to the world as Colonel Sanders, serving as spokesman for the Kentucky Fried Chicken dynasty. Harland Sanders, a man who harnessed his passion at age 65, became an icon for southern fried chicken and licked his fingers all the way to the bank.

Hierarchy of Passionate Performance: Pathway to Peace

Though creative passion is often ignited early in life, it can come at any time, but it needs a stimulus from within or without–in either case it begins with a dream. The diagram titled "A Hierarchy of Passion for a Dream," on the facing page, is derived from the work of psychologist Abraham Maslow. In essence, it shows the stages of passion through which you can move to reach the ultimate peace that Maslow called *self-actualization.*

About 90% of us have some wish or dream that we carry with us daily in our conscious or subconscious. Some of us dream of obtaining great wealth and enjoying all the luxuries that money can buy. Others dream of becoming media or sports celebrities and enjoying the status of someone who is perceived to travel in the circles of the rich and famous. Yet others dream of achieving prestigious awards like an Olympic medal or a Nobel Prize. However, for most people these dreams are not held with sufficient passion to bring them to fruition. At a subconscious level, these people believe they will

Hierarchy of Passion for a Dream

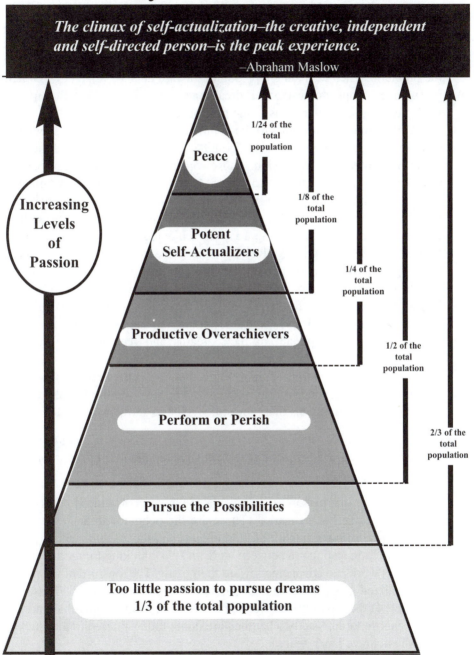

The climax of self-actualization–the creative, independent and self-directed person–is the peak experience.

–Abraham Maslow

Increasing Levels of Passion

Peace — 1/24 of the total population

Potent Self-Actualizers — 1/8 of the total population

Productive Overachievers — 1/4 of the total population

Perform or Perish — 1/2 of the total population

Pursue the Possibilities — 2/3 of the total population

Too little passion to pursue dreams
1/3 of the total population

never achieve their dreams and are therefore reluctant to commit much effort to their realization. Many people who dream of great wealth buy lottery tickets and then they wait and hope. Big dream–small investment! Hundreds who dream of becoming golf professionals become discouraged and abandon their dream when their game hits a plateau and lessons don't seem to solve the problem. When achieving a prestigious award appears to be beyond their grasp, many people downsize their dreams and settle for more easily achieved goals, leaving the loftier goals to the passionate.

Approximately two-thirds of the population makes at least one attempt to achieve their goals, however, only about half the population reaches the next stage in the hierarchy of passion. Those who reach this "perform or perish" stage constitute the more pro-active half of the population, placing themselves in a position where they risk or invest significant personal resources to achieve their dreams. These people possess enough passion to carry them past the "one-shot" approach to achieving their dreams to the point where they persist against adversity. The more passionate half of those reaching the "perform or perish" stage push forward to the level of the "productive over-achiever." These people exude sufficient passion to achieve interim goals en route to the achievement of their ultimate dreams. Productive over-achievers–the top 25% of the population–achieve significant self-fulfillment from the pursuit of their dreams and reap rewards with the achievement of each immediate goal.

In his book *Search for Meaning*, Viktor Frankl described his observations during the Holocaust and reported that those who survived the ordeal were the very ones who had dreams that they still wished to fulfill. Frankl observed:

Fear brings about that which one is afraid of...success like happiness cannot be pursued; it must ensue as the unintended side effect of one's personal dedication to a course greater than oneself.

Only about one person in eight of those who dream actually reaches the state of potent self-actualization. These are the people who achieve a high degree of joy from the pursuit of their dreams and the achievement of goals. They make little distinction between work and play, looking forward each day to going to work and advancing toward their goals. The top third of the potent self-actualized group have enough passion to become actualized. These are the people at the top of the passion hierarchy who, given all possible options, would choose to do exactly what they are doing today. These are the "lucky" few who achieve inner peace.

Passion is an intangible personality trait fuelled by a deep reserve of energy somewhere within the psyche. Though not directly observable, passion shows itself in a variety of behaviors that I call the *faces of passion*. These faces reveal the high intensity of the passion residing within superachievers, driving them onward toward their goals with unrelenting force.

The Fundamental Face of Passion: A Positive Attitude

The power of positive thinking has been widely promoted, and for good reason. Positive thoughts tend to result in positive outcomes. Henry Ford once observed, "Whether you say you can or you say you cannot, you will be right." The weak are victims of self-imposed negativity. Strangely, they seldom realize that the enemy lies within. It is no coincidence that losers keep losing and winners keep winning.

Your game begins and ends in your head. Clearly, everyone experiences ups and downs when competing at a high level, but some people–those with a positive attitude–have a much higher batting average. The reason is that positive mental models are as self-fulfilling as their negative counterparts.

High self-confidence, what psychologists call *self-efficacy*, is a prerequisite for success in any venture including business and athletics. Tycoon Donald Trump antagonized many with his egoistic machinations (and what some interpreted as an arrogant style) but this shameless flaunting of his successes brought him attention and respect as a deal-maker and entrepreneur. His willingness to praise the accomplishments of others reveals his respect for those with the passion to pursue their dreams. Daring to go where mere mortals only dream makes such people compelling personalities. The media understands this and seeks out those who provide controversial and provocative interviews.

Negative thoughts invoke negative actions–they cause their possessor to play tentatively or to opt for safe havens. As we found in the previous chapter, big wins do not come from safe havens; they come from scaling tough obstacles. The competitive arena is hostile to the timid and the faint of heart because a person who thinks negatively is incapable of thinking positively at the same time. On any given day you have approximately 16 hours of time at your disposal. Every minute spent thinking negatively lessens the available time for positive thoughts. Conversely, if you spent 16 hours thinking positively, there is virtually no time left for negative thoughts. While this observation may seem trite, it identifies a major attitudinal difference between mediocrity and superiority. It's up to you. You can fly Pessimist Air–the airline that carries life's victims to nowhere–or Optimist Air that jets its passengers to the destination of their choosing.

Tiger Woods exemplified the positive attitude in an interview (*Sports Illustrated*, July 14, 1997):

> *If I play my normal game, I should be able to win. I think my game is good enough that I can do that. I think the biggest thing is to have the mind-set and the belief that you can win every tournament going in. That's where a lot of guys have their faults…So it's nice to win a tournament with your mind because that's what wins majors.*

The Physical Face of Passion: Body Language

Passion is manifested in body language. Those who are possessed with an intense desire for victory display in their eyes an intensity that often strikes fear in the opponent. Our eyes reveal much about our inner needs. Michael Jordan often said he could look into the eyes of his defender and know whether he was in for a battle or if his opponent was intimidated. He told a journalist, "I see it in their eyes." NBA player Roy Hinson offered insight into the Jordan passionate persona from his seat on the bench. He told the press:

> *I was sitting on the bench and MJ [Michael Jordan] came dribbling past us at full speed. Then he shifted into another gear and went to the hoop. I'll never forget that fire in his eyes; that look of determination. It scared me to see that look. I've never seen it before. I've never seen it since.*

The Chemical Face of Passion: The Big T Personality

Psychologists have discovered that testosterone levels are higher in winning athletes than in losers. Elevated levels of testosterone have also been associated with added creativity, hyper-aggression, higher risk-taking propensity and more sex drive. (You may recall from Chapter 2 that Frank Farley, former President of the American Psychological Association, described the thrill-seekers with high testosterone as the Big T personality type.) *Sports Psychology* (1993), a textbook on athletic competition, asserts, "Heightened arousal enhances athletic performance." The book supports

Farley's hypothesis on arousal as a factor in winning. The high-arousal athlete tends to be blessed with high psychic energy manifested as passion. Ardor and zeal can overcome many limitations in skill, speed or athletic ability.

Examples of this principle abound in nature. Those who study animal behavior tell us that lions catch their prey in only about one chase in twenty. Polar bears also come up empty much more often than they succeed in securing a meal. Even though the predator has more physical skill, speed and power than the prey, the latter has a much greater motivation to win the contest. For the prey, losing the contest means losing its life. For the predator, losing the contest means losing a meal. Only when the predator has suffered extended deprivation does his ardor approach that of the prey. There is a kind of "Darwinian law" underlying the link between passion and success. In simplest terms, it reads: He who wants it most, wins.

Those with high sex energy are hyper about almost everything. They are driven more than normal people and are often viewed by friends and family as ticking time bombs. They exude perpetual energy, wearing out others with their constant action. Commenting on such behavior 2500 years ago, Socrates said, "Exertion makes weak people strong, sloth makes strong people weak." Without passion, it is difficult or impossible to reach the highest echelons of achievement. Passion is the fuel that accelerates the motivated person to the top of their field.

Enhancing Your Performance and Achieving Your Dreams

In your trek to the top, remember that passion will ultimately prevail. Without the passion to push you beyond internal and external constraints, you will not be able to reach the Holy Grail of self-actualization and internal peace. Formulate your goals clearly so that you carry them with you daily and pursue them relentlessly. Then focus only on the positive, blasting through those moments of self-doubt by redoubling your efforts. Celebrate your interim successes and use them to motivate your future actions. When naysayers attempt to discourage or intimidate you, imagine how they will respond to your success and use this vision as a call to arms.

A self-assessment instrument follows that will provide you with some insight into your level of passion and your propensity for enlightenment. Life is too short to pursue the dreams of others, so choose your own and pursue them to the limits of your being.

PASSION SELF-ASSESSMENT–How Passionate are You?

Choose a number 1–5, with 1 the lowest and 5 the highest, to indicate the degree to which you believe the statement describes how you feel about the issue. Record for each statement the number you have chosen. The scoring key follows.

In making your selection, be careful not to confuse passion with sex (male predilection) or romance (female). Passion in the sense used in this chapter refers to inner needs as manifested in exterior drives.

	Strongly Disagree				Strongly Agree
1. Physical beauty is important in mates, dates and my possessions.	1	2	3	4	5
2. Losing in a sport makes me even more resolved to win.	1	2	3	4	5
3. I have been described by friends as being ambitious or competitive to a fault.	1	2	3	4	5
4. The inner sense of power from winning is more important to me than some title.	1	2	3	4	5
5. I will go for the gold even if it causes the loss of a valued relationship.	1	2	3	4	5
6. When I find myself in a non-stimulating environment, I move on to a more exciting one.	1	2	3	4	5
7. I am often described by my friends as highly enthusiastic.	1	2	3	4	5
8. Prior to a competition, I worry about my performance.	1	2	3	4	5
9. I thrive on the excitement of a new venture, even when I don't know where it might lead.	1	2	3	4	5
10. Prior to an international trip I have trouble sleeping.	1	2	3	4	5
11. The chance to excel in any enterprise is more important to me than the money involved.	1	2	3	4	5
12. I follow rules only to the extent that they don't interfere with my achieving my goals.	1	2	3	4	5
13. Emotionally-charged stories involving personal loss and sad movies make me want to cry.	1	2	3	4	5
14. When sexually aroused, I lose inhibitions about where I consummate a relationship.	1	2	3	4	5

		Strongly Disagree			Strongly Agree	
15. I would give up most things to engage in a wine and cheese sunset vigil with a special partner.		1	2	3	4	5
16. Even when fatigued, I am willing to give up sleep for an exciting new adventure.		1	2	3	4	5
17. I enjoy flirting and displaying my sexuality.		1	2	3	4	5
18. Sexual metaphors are a means of communicating with close friends.		1	2	3	4	5
19. I am considered spiritual even by close friends who don't know my religious affiliations.		1	2	3	4	5
20. Sexual fantasies are an important part of my life.		1	2	3	4	5

Instructions

Total the numbers you chose for all 20 items.
Then use the scoring key below to assess
your level of passion.

Scoring Key

90–100:	Super passionate
80–89:	Passionate
65–79:	Normal level of passion
50–64:	Austere
Below 50:	Ascetic

BABE ZAHARIAS

- In 1999, voted the "Top Female Athlete of the 20th Century" by the Associated Press.

- Set four world records in the 1932 Olympics.

- All-American basketball player in 1931, 1932 and 1933; scored 106 points in one game.

- Won all but 12 of the 634 track events she entered.

- Won 82 professional golf tournaments including 17 consecutive wins in 1946–47.

- Founder and first President of the LPGA.

Babe Zaharias: Passion Incarnate

Superstars don't just show up, they come prepared for war. No athlete, male or female, personified this more than the 20th century's greatest female athlete, Babe Didrikson Zaharias. Babe wasn't deterred by closed doors. If they weren't open, she knocked them down. This passion flared when an All-American basketball player bragged that no man could throw him. Babe responded by grabbing him by the shoulder and tossing him to the floor! That kind of inner passion is not often found in a graceful female athlete, but the Babe was something special–she was passion incarnate.

**Babe Zaharias
1911–1956**

Mildred "Babe" Didrikson Zaharias was a model of the athletic superstar. She exemplified the winning behaviors vital to athletic success and exuded the fierce competitive spirit that defines what it means to be the best. At the relatively normal height of 5' 7" and weight of 125 lbs., Babe was a human dynamo who could outperform most male athletes in track and field. She could best them in tennis and out-drive all but a few of the longest hitters on the (men's) PGA Tour–hitting drives in excess of 250 yards with equipment that was antiquated by today's standards. So profound was her superiority over her competitors that she became an icon of athletic achievement and a legend during her lifetime.

Her life story inspired two movies. The first, a light upbeat fiction in which she made a cameo appearance, was the 1952 movie *Pat and Mike* (starring Katharine Hepburn and Spencer Tracy). The second, a 1975 production titled *Whatta-Gal: The Babe Didrikson Story*, was a more serious biography that examined her persona and some of the underlying relationships of her life in more depth.

It was the refined and socially acceptable sport of golf that Babe Didrikson Zaharias ultimately chose as her field of battle and it was on this battlefield that she established her stellar reputation. The story of how this roughly-hewn, unsophisticated renegade from east Texas rose to the pinnacle of the haughty country-club society of golf is one of the most fascinating in the annals of athletic achievement. Her dazzling performances inspired Grantland Rice, preeminent sports writer of the *Chicago Tribune*, to describe her as "the greatest woman athlete and perhaps the greatest all-around muscle machine of both sexes." Testimonials from celebrities, including not only those at the top of the golfing world but also such icons as President Eisenhower, reveal the esteem in which she was held. Bob Hope, an ardent golfer and a generous patron of the game, once observed, "There's only one thing wrong with Babe and myself. I hit the ball like a girl and she hits it like a man."

In the sections that follow, I profile "the Babe" and chronicle her rise to the pinnacle of athletic accomplishment. More importantly, I examine the personality traits that launched her into the rarified atmosphere of the greatest athletic superstars. In this you will find powerful ideas that will provide you with some insights into what makes a superstar and some ideas on how to enhance your own competitive performance.

BABE ZAHARIAS' TREK TO THE TOP

Early Imprints

Mildred Ella Didrikson was born on June 26, 1911 in Port Arthur, Texas, the sixth of seven children. During the short time that she was the youngest, she was called "Baby" and the name stuck even after the arrival of her younger brother. For the rest of her life, Mildred Ella was "the Babe" or merely "Babe." Her parents, Ole and Hannah, were immigrants from Norway, lured by employment in the oil-refining business of that harbor town. When Mildred was still a toddler, a hurricane destroyed the Didrikson home, prompting Ole to move his family to Beaumont, Texas where Mildred spent her formative years.

From the beginning, Mildred was mentored by her older male siblings whose rough-and-tumble treatment transformed her into the consummate tomboy. She reported in 1932 to the International News Service:

> *I am what I happen to be today because I had three brothers who were plenty rough and I lived in a neighborhood in Beaumont, Texas where the neighbor boys weren't any nicer to little girls than my brothers were to me.*

At seven years of age, she competed in marbles against older children and won. From that day in the second grade, she was driven to win. Thirty-five years later, she wrote in her memoirs "All my life I've had the urge to do things better than anybody else. From as far back as I can remember I played with boys rather than girls."

Biographer Cayleff wrote (p. 36), "Babe roamed the streets [of Beaumont] untethered. The street was her playground. The children's games she played were unbridled–at times dangerous." Her older sister Lillie, who idolized her, described how Babe coaxed her and some friends to climb aboard a moving freight train and then:

> *It started goin' faster 'n' faster 'n' faster…Babe hollered us to jump off but I froze, so she had to get back up on the car and push me off. We got skinned up, but we never got no worse hurt than that.*

Lillie noted that Babe was always the best at everything: baseball, roller-skating, marbles, jumping and throwing. Those early experiences of competing and winning left an indelible mark. They instilled in her an indefatigable self-confidence that never waned and a will to win of gargantuan proportions.

Shortly after her entry into Beaumont High School in 1925, it became clear that Babe was an emerging athletic star. At age 16 she was the basketball team's leading scorer. She was also a member of the school golf and tennis teams. Her reputation as a pugilist was also well founded. On one occasion, "Red" Reynolds, star halfback for the school football team, challenged Babe. "Hit me as hard as you can," he taunted. "You can't hurt me!" Years later, Reynolds confessed, "The next thing I knew, I was lying on the gym floor and they were pouring water on me to clear the bells and birdies out of my head. That gal really gave me a K.O."

The Industrial League

By the time Babe was in her senior year, her reputation as an outstanding athlete had spread across Texas. Melvin McCombs, coach of the Employers Casualty Insurance Company's basketball team, the Golden Cyclones, came from Dallas to Beaumont to watch Babe play. He was so impressed that he offered her a secretarial job with the understanding that she would play basketball for the Golden Cyclones in the semiprofessional industrial league. On February 14, 1930 and with the consent of her parents, Babe Didrikson accepted the offer and withdrew from Beaumont High School, on the condition that she could return in June to receive her diploma. She moved to

Dallas where she soon earned the name "Mighty Mildred" as the star of the Golden Cyclones, earning All-American honors in three consecutive years–1930, 1931 and 1932. She often scored more points than the entire opposing team.

The Babe also played on the company's baseball and track and field teams. It was during this period at the Employers Casualty Insurance Company that she trained to compete in the 1932 Olympic games. The unparalleled triumphs that Babe experienced in her late teen years and the adulation she received made her increasingly more arrogant. She delighted in projecting a cockiness that alienated friends but enhanced her sense of self. Jean Shiley, captain of the 1932 Olympic team, said, "I had to room with her in Denver because no one else would. She certainly did have a big mouth." McCombs, her coach and mentor and one of Babe's strongest supporters, often had to rein her in. He said, "Babe Didrikson was the easiest girl to coach and the hardest to handle of all the athletes I have had in the past 15 years."

Babe Enters Track and Field Competition

To qualify Babe for the 1932 Summer Olympics, McCombs entered her in the 1932 national AAU (American Athletic Union) track and field championships as a one-woman team against teams of up to 22 members. She entered eight of the ten events. In her inimitable style, she antagonized her 250 highly-trained competitors by asserting, "Ah'm gonna lick you [all] single-handed." As Babe's extreme aggressiveness began to surface, her internal goals and the drive that flowed from them became apparent. She recalled in her memoirs, "My goal was to be the greatest athlete that ever lived."

Babe's performance in this national championship was an unprecedented display of energy, power and raw athleticism. In a period of three hours, she rushed from one event to the next, winning six of the eight events in which she competed. Her undeniable supremacy stunned the competition and mesmerized the press. With minimal training and maximum commitment, she captured six gold medals and set four world records! As a one-woman team, she placed first with a score of 30 points–8 points ahead of the second-place Chicago Athletic Club. In the closing ceremonies, as the teams were called onto the field, Babe burst forth as the victorious "one-woman team" amidst the thunderous applause of an overwhelmed audience. Decades later, she described this as one of the greatest moments of her life.

Her triumph at the AAU championships was a harbinger of things to come in the 1932 Olympics. In those days there was no decathlon event for women. Each female competitor was allowed to participate in a maximum of three events. Babe chose the javelin throw, the 80-meter hurdles and the running high jump. Though her training had been minimal and her European competitors were much more highly rated, Babe alarmed the media and offended fellow competitors by predicting that she would win gold medals in all three events. When a reporter asked if she was going to try to win a gold medal in the 1932 Olympics, Babe responded, "I'm not goin' to try. I'm goin' t' do…I didn't come all this way to lose."

In her first event, the javelin throw, she won gold easily against the highly favored German competitors with a toss of 143 feet 4 inches, shattering the world record by more than 11 feet! In her second event, the 80-meter hurdles, employing a style described as "unrefined," she achieved a time of 11.7 seconds, establishing yet another Olympic and world record. In her third and final event, the running high jump, she scaled a height of 5' 5", tying her team-mate Jean Shiley for the gold medal. However, the judges ruled that Babe's head had cleared the bar before the rest of her body and they awarded her second place. In spite of this rather arbitrary ruling, Babe's outstanding achievement–two golds and a silver with two world records–made her the celebrity of the 1932 Olympic Games and the talk of the world athletic community.

As a result of her spectacular performance at the Olympics, Babe Didrikson became a household name throughout America. She was honored by a ticker tape parade in Dallas and featured in newspaper headlines. The *Dallas Journal* declared her "World's Greatest Woman Athlete" and the *Dallas Dispatch* called her the "Reigning Queen." The *New York Times* deemed her "America's Girl Star of the Olympics." Other newspaper headlines across the country referred to her alternately as "The Texas Tornado," "The Iron Woman" and "The Amazing Amazon."

Receiving a silver medal rather than a gold in the high jump, in which she had tied teammate Jean Shiley, was the first of a series of "political" rulings that would relentlessly impede Babe's ability to showcase her true potential. She would find the political hurdles ahead to be much more challenging than the 80-meter hurdles she had so skillfully surmounted.

Politics Rears its Ugly Head

Her outstanding success in the 1932 Olympics brought Babe the national recognition and adulation that she had always craved, but it also brought with it her depiction as a "muscle moll"–a mannish woman lacking the grace and elegance expected of a female superhero. When she appeared in an advertisement in the *Chicago Times* endorsing a Dodge automobile, the AAU assumed she had received remuneration for the endorsement. On December 14, 1932 they suspended her amateur status pending an investigation. This suspension disqualified her from playing for the Cyclones and from participating in any AAU events for a year. It also removed her as a candidate for the James E. Sullivan Memorial Medal, a prestigious award to be bestowed on the amateur deemed to be the best all-round athlete of 1932. (Babe's performance in the AAU national track and field competition and her performance in the 1932 Olympics would have made her a top contender for the award.) In spite of her claims (supported by Chrysler) that she received no money for the ad, the ruling was not revoked. *Coronet* magazine wrote (Cayleff, p. 100):

> *In retrospect, it seems clear that the AAU was determined to eliminate "muscle molls" from its ranks. No official ever put it that bluntly, of course, but the decision was called "for the best interest of the game."*

At the dawn of 1933, Babe found herself, at age 21, excluded from amateur standing and therefore without any venue for competing in tournaments. (Sports like golf had no professional organizations for women that could sponsor tournaments and offer a purse.) Many, including Babe herself, believed that the ruling was invoked to keep her from participating in women's amateur golf and tarnishing its long-standing image as a refined sport for ladies of culture and breeding. The female contingent of the country club set was immersed in a culture of lacy frills. Babe was racy and "no frills." In Babe's own words, "They didn't want me to beat the rich dames."

Babe Hits the Road

In the absence of outlets for her competitive spirit, Babe went on the road with a series of stunts, sideshows and demonstrations of athletic prowess. These included exhibition matches with and against top professionals in billiards, basketball and baseball. When money for these events dried up in the Depression years of 1933–34, Babe joined the all-male baseball team called the "House of David." As their star pitcher and the only member of the team without a beard, she was earning over $1000 per month when most of those lucky enough to have a job were earning less than $20 per week.

The Olympics ruling that denied her a gold medal and the AAU ruling that revoked her amateur status made it increasingly clear to Babe that her emerging image as a bawdy, unrefined muscle moll was becoming an impediment to her career. In the culture of the 1930s, this image could slowly undermine her status as a national hero, her reputation as a female athlete, and ultimately her ability to pursue a career in sports. In a desperate attempt at damage control, Babe began cultivating a more feminine persona. She began wearing cosmetics, sporting fashionable hats and styling her hair. She also abandoned the rigors of track and field in favor of sports like tennis, golf and bowling that were deemed more appropriate for women. Power and strength capitulated to finesse and, like few others in history, Babe made this transition.

A Career in Golf

To launch her golf career, Babe booked herself into exhibitions with high-profile male golf pros like Gene Sarazen and Sam Snead, thereby generating publicity and exploiting widespread interest in "the battle of the sexes." Bill Nary, a golf pro and frequent golfing partner, explained to biographer Susan Cayleff in a 1989 interview (Cayleff, p. 118), "The galleries were huge because they wanted to compare Babe's distances to the men stars of that era."

When asked how she developed her golfing skills to a professional level so quickly, Babe responded (Cayleff, p. 118):

Most things come natural to me and golf was the first that ever gave me much trouble...[but I] determined to learn to play and kept plugging away at the ball.

According to Babe, she scored over 100 in her first game of golf on account of poor putting. Then after three or four rounds, she broke 100. A few rounds later, she broke 90 and shortly after, she broke 80. However , although she liked to promote the idea that she was introduced to golf in 1932 and developed her proficiency easily and naturally, other sources tell a different story. A photo of Beaumont High's golf team in the 1929 yearbook *Pine Burr* shows Mildred Didrikson pictured along with six other women, suggesting that she was already somewhat proficient at golf at the age of 18. In fact, Beaumont High's physical education teacher, Beatrice Lytle, claimed to have coached Mildred in golf as early as 1927. The media understood that Babe was a shameless self-promoter, frequently taking license with the truth and employing creative hyperbole in attempts to capture public interest and further dramatize her accomplishments. However, the media was not about to diminish a great story and sometimes aided and abetted the promulgation of some inaccurate legends. In truth, Babe earned her golfing skills the old-fashioned way–through hard work.

Perhaps anticipating her return to amateur status at the conclusion of her suspension, Babe announced in July 1933 (Cayleff, p. 119), "I have enough money to last me three years and I intend to win the women's amateur golf championship before these three years–and my bankroll–are gone."

To achieve this prediction, Babe moved in with her sister Lillie in Santa Monica, California, where she poured every ounce of energy into honing her golf skills. Focusing her psychic energy with laser intensity, she executed a practice regimen that even today's most committed professionals would regard as formidable. According to her golf coach, Stan Kertes, she would arrive at the practice range at 9:00 a.m. every morning and hit balls until dark. For a period of 8 months, she hit an average of 1500 balls a day–often until her hands would bleed. Kertes reported that he had to plead with her to stop and rest. Lillie also reported standing beside her compulsive sister as darkness settled in, begging her, in vain, to quit hitting golf balls. Gene Sarazen once observed, "After we'd played 18 holes, she'd practice for hours more…I only know of one golfer who practiced more than Babe and that was Ben Hogan."

Babe Enters the Amateur Tour

In April 1935, two months before her 24th birthday and with reinstated amateur status, Babe entered the Texas State Women's Golf Championship at River Oaks Country Club in Houston. Her reputation as an unrefined, mannish upstart preceded her. Well-read and well-bred she was not. Among the female members of the Country Club ran an undercurrent of disapproval in her participation. Attempting to disparage Babe's lack of pedigree, Peggy Chandler, a three-time winner of the Texas State Championship and member of the Texas Women's Golf Association, remarked, "We really don't need any truck driver's daughter in our tournament." Babe resolved to make the cultured set pay for that remark.

In a touch of irony fit for a Hollywood script, it was this same Peggy Chandler whom Babe would meet on the last day of the tournament in a final head-to-head 36-hole match for the championship. Babe was clearly the underdog to the top-ranked Chandler. However, the final round would turn out to be one of the most dramatic matches the fans would ever see. After a fiercely-contested 33 holes, Chandler and Babe were even as they approached the 34th hole–a challenging par 5. Babe crashed a 250-yard drive straight down the fairway, only to discover to her horror that the ball had rolled into a ditch that cut across the fairway. On her next shot, Babe bladed a 3-iron, "air mailing" it over the green into a rut containing an inch of casual water. Meanwhile, Chandler was sitting pretty on the green in 3, with an almost certain birdie. In what would have been an implausible outcome even in fiction, Babe took a sand wedge and approached the ball where it lay, partially obscured by muddy water. Concentrating with all the intensity she could muster, Babe chipped the ball onto the green. It rolled as though guided by remote control toward the cup. Fans who had been watching from the edge of the green ran forward to witness the impossible and inadvertently collided with Babe, catapulting her into the muddy puddle. Regaining her composure, Babe heard the cheers of the gallery exploding in ecstatic disbelief. The ball had found the cup! Babe carded an eagle 3 to win the hole.

When the two adversaries subsequently tied the 35th hole, Chandler found that the 3-hole lead she had enjoyed at the end of the 26th hole had evaporated and she was now trailing by one. This meant she had to win the final hole to tie the match and force a playoff. However, it was not to be. Babe handily won the 36th hole, sending a delirious gallery into a thunderous acknowledgement of one of golf's most remarkable upsets. This was for Babe her first tournament victory in golf and an important moral victory in her quest for social acceptance.

On the Road Again

In spite of this triumph, Babe's quest for social acceptance still eluded her. Two weeks later, she was once again banned from amateur competition–this time by the United States Golf Association (USGA). Her earlier participation as a professional in baseball, basketball and billiards was used as a pretext to declare her a professional athlete and revoke her amateur status as a golfer. This ruling also excluded her from the 1935 national golf championship. In spite of objections from the Beaumont Country Club and other supporters from east Texas, the ruling was upheld by the USGA. Babe was banned from amateur golf for three years.

Forced once again to return to the ranks of professionalism to find a venue for her golfing skills, Babe signed a contract with P. Goldsmith Sons sporting goods company. The contract paid her $2500 per year to endorse and promote their products and to participate in exhibition golf with Gene Sarazen, the current top-ranked golfer on the men's pro circuit. He mentored Babe, providing continuous instruction that enabled her to hone her skills and eliminate weaknesses in her game. During these exhibitions, Babe developed a banter with Gene to entertain the gallery. On one occasion, after executing a poor shot, Gene offered a sympathetic "Too bad." Babe retorted, "Too bad!? What's too bad? Didn't you see me make that long drive a few minutes ago? Better than yours, wasn't it?"

With a combination of sharp wit and pithy humor, Babe exploited her down-home, folksy, east-Texas drawl to build a friendly rapport with her adoring fans in a self-mocking delivery (Cayleff, p. 122):

> *Heah, you all! You-all come closah mohaw,' cuz you-all've heerda Waltah Hagen and you-all heerda Bobbuh Jeeones, but today, folks, you-all ah lookin' at th' veruh best of 'em all–yoahs truleh, li'l ol' Babe Didrikson.*

Four decades before Lee Trevino delighted golf fans with his quips and good-natured homilies, Babe had mastered the art of delivering one-liners and self-deprecating comments. On one occasion, when a photographer was attempting to take her picture, she taunted, "Hey, you've got your thumb over the lens. Maybe I'm no beauty, but I'm not that homely!" On another occasion, she solicited gallery empathy with the disclaimer:

> *Folks, don't you go holdin' anything I say today against me. It's just to keep you-all enjoyin' yerselves. We like havin' you follow us around. Only time Gene and I object to a gallery is when it stays home.*

The exhibition tour with Gene Sarazen was a watershed period that provided Babe with the opportunity to sharpen her golf skills under his tutelage and, at the same time, develop a charismatic rapport with her fans. When it concluded, Babe packed her belongings and moved back to Los Angeles where she resumed golf lessons with her old mentor, Stan Kertes.

By January 1938, at the age of 26, Babe felt herself ready for real competition, even though her amateur status had not been reinstated. The Los

Angeles Open, an event on the professional men's tour, had been closed to women, but Babe Didrikson's popularity with the golfing public offered the promise of substantially increased revenue for the tournament. Consequently, the rules were waived and her entry was approved. Babe was placed in a threesome with a minister and a professional wrestler–a kind of "bless 'em and press 'em" duo. The "press 'em" part of the duo, known as the "Crying Greek from Cripple Creek," was a rugged looking, 235-pound world-class wrestler named George Zaharias. As one might suspect from George's sur-name, by which Babe is most widely known, love blossomed during the tour-nament. The threesome missed the cut, but the twosome tied the knot before the year was out. Babe Didrikson became Babe Zaharias on December 23, 1938.

George's experience with professional wrestling had taught him the importance of self-promotion, public exposure and celebrity status. He became not only her husband but her most aggressive promoter, booking her into tournaments, exhibitions and anything else that would give her the opportunity to showcase her talents. In April of 1939, George took Babe to Hawaii for a belated honeymoon and then on to Australia for a rigorous tour on the golfing exhibition circuit. Babe's golfing prowess wowed the Australians who were charmed by her banter and captivated by her skills. At the Yarra Country Club, she competed against the Australian PGA champion, Charley Conners. They played men's rules and they both hit from the back tees. In typical "Babe" style, she finished with flair and panache, following a long drive with a huge 4-iron shot to the pin of the final par 5 hole. Then she sank the putt for an eagle 3. Babe Zaharias carded a score of 72, just one higher than Conners' 71.

Babe had made remarkable progress in the battle of the sexes, but a much greater battle was looming on the horizon. The dark clouds of World War II were gathering in the fall of 1939 and the newlyweds decided it was time to return to Los Angeles.

A Three-Year Probation

By early 1940, George was earning enough money to keep them in a comfortable lifestyle and to enable Babe to abandon her income as a professional and apply to the USGA. The USGA promised to restore her amateur status if she underwent a 3-year waiting period during which she earned no income from golf. To hone her skills in the interim, she entered and won the Western Women's Open in Milwaukee, refusing to accept the prize money in accordance with the terms of her probationary period. She followed this victory with a win at the Texas Women's Open at Fort Worth, Texas. However, the golfing exhibitions failed to satisfy Babe's voracious appetite for competition, so she decided to devote herself to tennis. After a year of intense practice, she was beating some of the best female tennis pros. Near the end of 1941, Babe applied to enter the final tournament in the women's amateur tennis circuit, but was barred from participation on the basis that professional status in any sport was equivalent to professional status in tennis. Bitterly disappointed, Babe decided to give up tennis forever.

After the attack on Pearl Harbor on December 7, 1941, Babe resumed playing exhibition golf to raise money for the war effort. She participated in charity fundraisers with celebrities Bing Crosby and Bob Hope, entertaining enthusiastic fans with their antics and clever repartee on golf courses across America. She also played golf exhibitions with fellow Texans Byron Nelson, the top male golfer in the war years, and Ben Hogan who was at that time a rising star. Impatient to find a venue for her competitive spirit while waiting out her probationary period, Babe flirted for a time with professional bowling. She developed such skill that she was described by several journalists as one of the best female bowlers in Southern California.

Freedom to Compete

Finally, in early 1943, Babe's amateur status was reinstated. She now had a venue for unfettered competition in golf and an opportunity to show what she could do. Because few women's golf tournaments took place during the war and gas rationing restricted travel, Babe entered as many local tournaments as possible and won almost all of them. Among these was the Western Women's Open, which she won for the third time in 1945. Then in the fall of 1945, she won the Texas Women's Open for the second time. Recognizing the enormous achievement in these remarkable victories, the Associated Press named her Woman Athlete of the Year in 1945. This recognition merely whetted Babe's appetite for more conquests. In 1946, she announced to the press, "I want to establish the longest winning streak in the history of women's golf."

In August 1946, Babe won a tournament in Denver, another in Colorado Springs, then the All-American Championship at the Tam O'Shanter Country Club in Illinois. Her first national victory–a dream she had cherished from her earliest days in golf–came in the U.S. Women's Amateur national competition at the Southern Hills Country Club in Tulsa, Oklahoma. At the end of 1946, Babe had a string of five consecutive tournament wins and was once again named Woman Athlete of the Year.

Babe Zaharias' winning streak continued unbroken through to the end of August, 1947: 13 consecutive victories. Though elimination in the fourteenth tournament broke her winning streak, she won her next four tournaments, including the prestigious British Women's Amateur Golf Championship. (Babe subsequently commented that this tournament victory brought her more widespread fame than all the other tournament victories combined.) She was the first American woman to win this event, doing it in such style that she captured the hearts of the reputedly dour Scottish fans. When she drove a ball deep into the woods, she would exclaim in self-deprecating style, "Must be some scotch in there." Babe had achieved (save a minor blip after number thirteen) a string of 17 consecutive tournament victories in a single year. To accomplish such a feat in the sport of golf, a player must not only excel beyond her peers, but must possess skill that is at least one magnitude greater than all other competitors. It was a surprise to no one when the Associated Press named Babe Zaharias Woman of the Year in 1947, along with Helen Hayes, Helen Traubel and Ingrid Bergman.

Return to Professional Status

After this outstanding performance, Babe Zaharias became a commodity. Businesses sought her endorsement and lucrative offers flooded in. Though reluctant to relinquish her amateur standing, a series of proposals offering her a total of about half a million dollars finally convinced her to announce on August 14, 1947 that she would be turning professional at the end of the season. She subsequently signed a lifetime contract with Wilson Sporting Goods Company who would market Babe Zaharias golf equipment. Babe also added to her income by returning to athletic exhibitions, including pitching to Joe DiMaggio in Yankee stadium and participating in a golf driving contest with Ted Williams in Sarasota, Florida. In 1948, with earnings of only $3400, Babe was the leading money winner of all the professional women golfers. However, her endorsements and performances had yielded in excess of $100,000. It was clear that there was no way for a woman to make a living by merely dedicating herself to playing golf.

Birth of the LPGA

Within a short time, Babe's golf game began to deteriorate because there were few tournaments in which she was allowed to participate. She sought entry into the men's National Open, but the eligibility rules of the USGA had been recently revised to enforce the "men only" provision. It was apparent to Babe and George that a professional tournament tour for women was needed. Their early efforts in 1949 led to the birth of the Ladies' Professional Golf Association (LPGA). It was incorporated in New York State in 1950.

In 1950 Babe earned $14,800 by winning most of the tournaments on the LPGA circuit. The Associated Press once more honored her athletic achievements–this time, by voting her the Greatest Female Athlete of the first half of the 20th century. Babe was also the dominant player on the LPGA tour during 1951 with seven victories in the 12 tournaments she entered. When she began the 1952 season with several victories, it looked like she would once again dominate the pro circuit though the competition was becoming stronger as the LPGA expanded. Then in May of that year, Babe began to feel intense pain in her left side that turned out to be a strangulated hernia in her upper left thigh. An operation to correct the problem sidelined her for several months. Finally, in October 1952, Babe entered and won the Texas Women's Open. She finished the 1952 season with four victories out of twenty-four tournaments.

A Harbinger of Doom

Early in 1953, Babe was plagued with severe fatigue that sapped all her energy, leaving her weak and listless. Mustering all her strength in a superhuman effort, she entered the tournament that had been named the Babe Zaharias Open because she had won it so often. Impelled by the desire to win the tournament for her hometown crowd in Beaumont, Texas, she pushed through the pain and lassitude and won the tournament by a single stroke on the last hole of the competition. The delirious fans carried her off on their shoulders. It was to be her last victory for awhile.

In April of 1953, two months before her 42nd birthday, the source of Babe Zaharias' extreme fatigue was discovered. She was diagnosed with colon cancer. For anyone, such news would be devastating, but for an athlete of the first magnitude, the impact of such news is incomprehensible. Babe's body was her temple of worship. It was the machine that brought her fame, wealth and full actualization. To have it desert her at the pinnacle of her career was as cruel an irony as Beethoven's loss of hearing–substantially magnified by the threat of imminent demise. When a colostomy was performed on April 17, 1953 it was discovered that the cancer had spread to the lymph nodes. The prognosis (unknown to Babe) was that she had a year to live.

After the operation, Babe spent 43 days in hospital. During that time she plunged into a rigorous program of exercise to rebuild her muscles and condition herself for a return to professional golf. Defying all medical predictions, she entered the All American tournament three months after her surgery. Two days later, Babe entered the World Championships and shortly after, the Texas Women's Open. Although she didn't win, she displayed remarkable endurance and tenacity. At the end of 1953, she was awarded the Ben Hogan trophy for the Greatest Comeback of the Year.

Accelerating in the Home Stretch

Babe charged into the 1954 season with renewed vigor, winning the Serbin Women's Open on the final hole. She went on to win five tournaments in that year, including the All American Open in which she carded a 72-hole score of 294–one stroke higher than the course record. President and Mamie Eisenhower hosted her at the White House where she opened the Cancer Crusade in a ceremonial presentation. As a symbol of someone who had beaten cancer, Babe was an inspiration to millions of people throughout the world who were also battling this disease.

However, as the 1954 season grew to a close, Babe was beginning again to experience the extreme fatigue that had plagued her prior to her colostomy. In spite of ever-increasing lassitude and excruciating pain in her back, she pressed on into the 1955 season, winning the Tampa Open and the Peach Blossom Classic–a total of seven tournament victories after her cancer surgery. She was also reelected president of the LPGA. But near the end of July, 1955, her doctor announced that her cancer had returned. Babe, convinced once again that she would beat the cancer, began taking radiation treatments. To spare future cancer victims the ravages of this disease, Babe and George formed the non-profit Babe Didrikson Zaharias Cancer Fund, using her high profile to raise money.

After she left the hospital and returned home, her close friend and fellow golfer Betty Dodd came to live with Babe to administer drugs and nurse her. This was the most prolonged and agonizing fight of Babe's life and she did not yield easily to its unrelenting attack. Finally, on September 27, 1956, at the age of 45, Mildred "Babe" Didrikson finished the 18th hole in the game of life–more than two years beyond the original prognosis. She gave more to the world than she took from it and, in the process, may even have achieved her dream to become the greatest athlete who ever lived. In her eulogy, President Eisenhower observed:

> *Ladies and gentlemen, I should like to take one minute to pay a tribute to Mrs. Zaharias, Babe Didrikson. She was a woman who in her athletic career certainly won the admiration of every person in the United States, all sports people over the world. I think every one of us feels sad that finally she had to lose this last one of all her battles.*

Chapter 4

Psychological suffering, anxiety and collapse lead to new emotional, intellectual, and spiritual strengths.
                    –Ilya Prigogine, from *Order out of Chaos*

The Bottom Is a Springboard to the Top

The concept of transforming a breakdown into a breakthrough is most profoundly portrayed in the story of Notre Dame fullback Mario Motts Tonelli. At age six, Mario suffered third degree burns to 80% of his body and was not expected to live, let alone run. Doctors gave up hope that he would ever walk. However, his immigrant father nurtured him back to health and inspired him to become an outstanding athlete in football, basketball and track. Mario went on to star for the Notre Dame football team, almost single-handedly beating archrival University of Southern California in 1937. Prophetically, another young student was in the USC stands that day watching Tonelli annihilate his team. That student, who was Japanese, became an officer of the Japanese army during World War II.

During the war, Tonelli joined the U.S. military and was captured while fighting in the Philippines. As a prisoner of war, he became part of the infamous Bataan death march in which 10,000 men perished. During this grueling ordeal, a Japanese soldier noticed Tonelli's Notre Dame ring and took it from him. The officer-in-charge was that same Japanese student who had witnessed Tonelli's brilliant performance against USC. On recognizing the ring, he confiscated it from his subordinate. He then returned the ring to Tonelli with his compliments, explaining that he had seen him devastate USC on that day in 1937 and that he admired his spirit. Tonelli, who had been close to exhaustion and breakdown from the punishing march, took this as a symbol of hope and was inspired to keep going.

By the summer of 1945, the once powerful football player, ravaged by malaria and starvation, had wasted away to 100 lbs. A shadow of his former athletic stature, he was then moved to Nagoya prison camp. "I thought I would die," he told the press later. But in that prison, another serendipitous occurrence sent shivers up his spine. The guards issued him a prison outfit and the number inscribed on the back was 58–the number of his Notre Dame jersey. At that instant Tonelli felt a mystical surge of energy race through his emaciated body. "From that point on I knew I was going to make it," Tonelli told the media on the 50th anniversary of that nightmarish ordeal. First the ring, then the number 58! Some mysterious force was at work and he felt deep inside that fate had intervened and he was a chosen one. The world around him was perishing and offered little hope, but he sensed he would make it and he persisted relentlessly. For Tonelli, his belief that he would survive the worst possible atrocities gave him the tenacity to transform an imminent breakdown into a breakthrough.

One of the principles derived from Ilya Prigogine's Nobel Prize-winning work was that breakdown often leads to breakthrough. That is, what doesn't kill you, makes you stronger. In his landmark work on *dissipative structures*, he wrote "Many systems of breakdown are actually harbingers of breakthrough."

This is precisely what happens often in the lives of highly successful people. Tour de France winner Lance Armstrong, reflecting on the breakdown that launched his later successes, said, "The truth is that cancer is the best thing that ever happened to me. I don't know why I got the illness, but it did wonders for me and I wouldn't want to walk from it." When individuals like Armstrong and Tonelli reach the depths of despair, they often recover to be more than they were prior to the trauma. This suggests that unless you have been to the bottom, the top is not as easy a target. Why? Those who hit bottom go through a metamorphosis, not of the body, but of the mind and emotions. Their inner tapes are reprogrammed to believe in themselves and to deal with adversity far better than those without such experiences. Do some people hit bottom and self-destruct? Of course! But for the many who self-destruct, a few others experience an epiphany and reemerge stronger than before the breakdown.

It is no accident that Sigmund Freud made his breakthroughs in psychology while in a state of emotional collapse. In 1895, while in the throes of a psychotic state, he discovered the importance of dreams and the subconscious. Carl Jung admitted in his writings that he also was in a psychotic state when he developed his greatest contributions, such as personality types, the collective unconscious, archetypes, syzygy and synchronicities. Renowned scientist Stephen Hawking learned that he had Lou Gehrig's disease while a graduate student. He sought relief from this horrific discovery through alcohol, but after he hit bottom he emerged stronger than ever. Since then, he has developed theories of cosmology that have earned him the admiration of the scientific world and the Lucasian Chair of Physics, a post once held by Sir Isaac Newton. (Ironically, Sir Isaac Newton, one of the greatest mathematicians and scientists of all time, is also reported to have suffered a nervous breakdown.) Why did all three of these intellectual giants achieve greatness only after they suffered breakdowns? All had to transcend normality into abnormality to allow their creative geniuses to explore possibilities outside accepted theory. This is also true in sports. Until you stop doing what is expected on the court or course, it is very difficult to win over others who are better at the expected than you are.

Many business superstars also used adversity as a catalyst to reach the top. Fred Smith of Federal Express fame required crutches when he was a child and was never expected to walk. By age 14, he had cast away the crutches and earned a pilot's license. By 16, he was a successful entrepreneur and a star high-school football player. By his twenties he was flying jets in Vietnam. An even more dramatic story of recovery comes from famous female entrepreneur Linda Wachner. During the 1990s, Linda was the highest paid female executive in America. *Fortune* magazine in 1992 called her "America's most successful businesswoman." But she spent her childhood in a body cast. "The focus I have today," she told the media, "comes from when I was sick. When you want to walk again, you learn to focus on that with all your might and you don't stop until you do it." *Cosmopolitan* (June, 1990) quoted her as saying, "Oh, if I could walk, I know I would never get tired. I know I could do more. It's a psychological thing." These breakdowns were the catalysts for her later breakthroughs.

During the 1990s, a ubiquitous bumper sticker unabashedly asserted, "Shit happens." So what! It isn't what happens to us but rather how we deal with it that counts. In my research into the lives of the superstars in business and athletics, I was amazed at how many of them faced early challenges that transformed them into extraordinarily successful people. It was surprising to me how often hitting the bottom served as a springboard to reaching the top. I concluded that their early battles against adversity were major learning tools that paid handsome dividends throughout the rest of their lives. These people came away with far more resolve, a willingness to go where others fear, and an awesome tenacity seldom witnessed by those who have life too easy.

Most of our Limits Are Self-Imposed

Both empowerment and ineptitude are learned qualities. We learn to be excellent and we learn to be mediocre. Our heads and hearts are the limiting variables in life, limits that are self-imposed. We know too much about what we can and can't do. As long as we set those unconscious limits within ourselves, we can never attain goals that lie outside those limits.

We must stop questioning our ability to execute anything new: those questions only detract from performance. Trying and failing is not destructive, it is instructive. Failing merely alerts us to areas that require our attention, although most people don't see it that way. I have met multitudes who try downhill skiing and fail or try unsuccessfully to blast a golf ball out of a deep sand trap. Eventually they give up trying to learn. They have programmed themselves with what I have labeled "failure imprints" as opposed to "success imprints." The superstars, however, understand that failure is the path to success.

Over a century ago, British poet Rudyard Kipling described the elements of a strong character in his poem *If*:

> *If you can meet with triumph and disaster,*
> *And treat these two imposters just the same...*

Kipling was reminding the reader that success often masquerades as failure and failure sometimes appears to be success; it all depends on how we interpret events. Every time Thomas Edison failed in his attempt to create a light bulb, he celebrated the failure as the discovery of yet another method that would not work. We all know people who never try anything outside their comfort level for fear of failing and embarrassing themselves. The only true disability in life is negative mental predisposition. The mind is a database wherein previous failures are recorded to define future limits. Winners record failures as unsuccessful experiences on the way to success. Losers record failures as a series of *faits accomplis* and thus become victims of the Pike Syndrome described in Chapter 1.

What do these internal limitations have to do with hitting a baseball, golf ball or tennis ball? A lot! This inner knowledge is the law of life that regulates what we will try or what opportunities we will pursue. Contrary to the common perception, athletic success is an outward manifestation of our inner sense of knowing. Blasting a ball out of a fairway bunker onto the green 200 yards away is as much about believing it can be done as it is about talent for doing it. Hitting a tennis backhand down the line is seldom attempted by amateurs because of prior negative preprogramming; consequently they never try it and never improve. Successful execution is but an external manifestation of an inner belief system. Did Babe Ruth have such limits? No! Think Tiger ever tried a shot he didn't *think* he could make? Never!

Self-Confidence Emanates from Inner Programming

Those who don't know they *can't*, can. Those who don't know they *can*, can't. There are myriad examples of athletes who achieved unbelievable feats because they had no preconceived limits in their minds. Jim Thorpe was too uneducated, too steeped in Indian lore, and far too naïve to know that he should not be traveling to Europe to compete in the decathlon without ever having tried the event. That is unheard of in any sport. Most athletes would not even consider competing with world-class athletes who have been training for years. Thorpe had no preconceived limits to anything, which allowed him to achieve the impossible. He won the Decathlon in the 1912 Olympics, outscoring his nearest rival by an incredible 700 points. The key to Thorpe's success was far more mental than physical.

We observed in our discussion of the Pike Syndrome in Chapter 1 that the educational system is often guilty of programming limits into its students. Mass education evolved out of the Industrial Age and classrooms were designed as replicas of the factory production line. The admonitions "Don't get out of line," Don't try new things," "Sit in rows and don't speak until asked" were antithetical to individualistic thinking and exploratory behavior. Mass education produced an environment that was hostile to exploration, discovery and learning through mistakes. Facts and dogma were delivered in didactic fashion to be memorized and regurgitated without analysis or interpretation. In spite of recent attempts to promote discovery learning, the inertia of tradition has made educational reform glacially slow. It is no surprise that many of the world's great minds hated school. Einstein, Edison, Tesla, Fuller and Gates resisted the insidious limits imposed by forced conformity. Both Walt Disney and Dr. Seuss were summarily dismissed from art school for daring to draw outside the lines. Whose lines?

Isadora Duncan and Amelia Earhart detested school for the same reason as Einstein and Disney. Why? Because they were constantly told what they could and could not do. Are those teachers justified in their approach? Of course! They too are by-products of living and fitting into a preordained system where order is sacrosanct. Students should be allowed the freedom to err so they learn both how to deal with failure and how to overcome it. The most powerful educational environments are those that encourage exploration and celebrate failures as paths to discovery. Learning how to hook and slice a ball in golf (normally considered errors) helps us to learn how to hit one straight.

Great success in sports (or any other endeavor) requires a break from the norm. This can occur through a breakdown or a reprogramming of our inner sense of limits. A breakdown is outside our control and can be transformed into a breakthrough only if a person has the kinds of positive beliefs and behaviors described above. However, it is not necessary to suffer breakdown to achieve a breakthrough. By taking a proactive approach to reprogramming our inner limits, we can achieve blockbusting breakthroughs beyond our wildest dreams. Valuing our differences (Chapter 1), taking risks (Chapter 2), tapping into our passion (Chapter 3) and embracing failure as a path to success (Chapter 4) are four critical components in moving outside the box that traps most of us in mediocrity.

John Diamond said, "Optimizing potential is about balancing the cerebral hemispheres–eliminating the negative and promoting the positive." He had found that all success comes from an inner belief and positive envisioning. All failure is a function of negative thinking that generates stress. Worrying about what might happen makes it happen. Think about that water hazard between you and the green and how it induces the negative thoughts that result in a poor golf shot. Diamond asserted, "Your thoughts have the power to alter the physiological response of your muscles." He also found that many people who were ill wanted to be, while those who were well had an inner mantra that said, "I want to be well." In his seminal work, *Life Energy*, Diamond wrote (p. 227), "To change a negative into the positive, just say the appropriate affirmation with conviction and visualize it strongly and clearly and the negative becomes positive."

One of the most remarkable stories of triumph over adversity is embodied in the life of sprinter Wilma Rudolph. Her steely resilience in the face of overwhelming physical and emotional obstacles enabled her to rebound from the depths of despair to the pinnacle of triumph. Before embarking on that story, I invite you to assess your own level of resilience by taking the Resilience Self-Assessment on the opposite page.

RESILIENCE SELF-ASSESSMENT–Can You Bounce Back?

Choose a number 1–5, with 1 the lowest and 5 the highest, to indicate the degree to which you believe the statement describes you or how you feel. Record for each statement the number you have chosen. The scoring key is at the bottom of the page.

There are no "right" or "wrong" answers. In making your selection, answer the questions as candidly as possible without anticipating how you will be classified.

	Strongly Disagree				Strongly Agree
1. I become motivated when someone tells me I can't.	1	2	3	4	5
2. I am willing to sacrifice my time and money to achieve.	1	2	3	4	5
3. Even when I fail repeatedly at something, I never give up.	1	2	3	4	5
4. I tend to use failure to learn how not to fail.	1	2	3	4	5
5. When my plans fall apart, I tend to abandon them.	1	2	3	4	5
6. Breakdowns for me are merely opportunities to prove myself.	1	2	3	4	5
7. I look on failure as a learning process.	1	2	3	4	5
8. When things fall apart, I become discouraged and re-formulate my goals.	1	2	3	4	5
9. I seem to be more motivated when I lose than when I win.	1	2	3	4	5
10. I believe that success is rarely possible without hard work.	1	2	3	4	5
11. I find it difficult to stay on a diet or a training routine.	1	2	3	4	5
12. I don't believe that people can beat me on talent alone.	1	2	3	4	5
13. Whenever I achieve my goals I seem to set new goals.	1	2	3	4	5
14. After I set a new goal, I have trouble maintaining enthusiasm.	1	2	3	4	5
15. All the work involved in striving to attain goals isn't worth it.	1	2	3	4	5
16. A 40-year-old can never have the body of a 20-year-old no matter how hard they work out.	1	2	3	4	5

Instructions	Scoring Key
A. Total the numbers you chose for items: #1, 2, 3, 4, 6, 7, 9, 10, 12, and 13. B. Total the numbers you chose for items: #5, 8, 11, 14, 15 and 16. Subtract the total in B from the total in A.	**33–44:** Highly resilient under adverse conditions. **21–32:** More resilient than average during adversity. **15–20:** May or may not bounce back after setbacks. **10–15:** Tend to be defeated by adversity. **Below 10:** Need to use failure as a learning device.

WILMA RUDOLPH

- In 1960, voted the "Female Athlete of the Year" by the Associated Press.
- In 1960 Olympics in Rome, she became the first American female to win three gold medals in track and field.
- In 1962, won the Babe Didrickson Award as the Top Female Athlete in America.
- In 1983, inducted into the Olympic Hall of Fame.

Wilma Rudolph: Irrepressible Spirit

© Bettmann/CORBIS

**Wilma Rudolph
1940–1994**

Those who believe that superhero status is attainable only by those who are dealt a hand of genetic aces are destined to attribute their mediocrity to factors outside their control. No one more than Wilma Rudolph has shown the fallacy of such thinking. Her life stands as irrefutable proof that trouble, trauma and tribulation, visited on someone who refuses to be defeated, can be the most powerful inducements to high achievement. In fact, a reflection on the life of this incredible woman makes one speculate that adversity, particularly in the formative years, may be one of the strongest trump cards we can hold.

Wilma Rudolph spent her formative years in Tennessee during the 1940s and early 1950s. As the 20th in a poor black family of 22 children, she was accustomed to doing without material luxuries. But Wilma, unlike most of us, was denied the most important of all luxuries, good health. At the age of four, she contracted polio as the disease swept through America unchecked, ravaging thousands every year and leaving them paralyzed or dead. Wilma survived, but with a deformed, paralyzed left leg that was twisted grotesquely inward and all but guaranteed she would never walk again. In those days, people with such disabilities were labeled "cripples" and were believed by some to have been "cursed by the gods." Unfortunate children with such handicaps were mercilessly ridiculed by other children and quietly shunned by adults. In her autobiography *Wilma: The Story of Wilma Rudolph*, Wilma recalled those early years with some pain (Rudolph, pp. 15, 19):

> *I was six years old before I realized that there was something wrong with me...But I did have this crooked left leg, and my left foot was turned inward. It didn't hurt me physically, and the only times anybody noticed it was when I was out playing with the other kids, and some of them would start teasing me and calling me "cripple"...and they would try to make me cry by saying that I was adopted and a cripple, things like that. I used to cry, but no more.*

Wilma had to struggle through life against the silent discrimination by the healthy. However, societal discrimination against physical disabilities was only one strike against Wilma in her struggle to realize her aspirations. Like Babe Zaharias, she would also face sex discrimination, the second strike against her. As we observed in the previous chapter, many people believed that women would injure themselves or their ability to reproduce if they participated in high-intensity sports. Wilma described the prevailing ideas about women and sports in Tennessee during the '40s and '50s, echoing what Babe Zaharias had encountered two decades earlier in Texas (Rudolph, p. 43):

Down South, there was the old "ladies-don't-do-such-things" way of thinking. You couldn't be a lady and a good athlete at the same time. There was a lot of talk about "playing sports will give you muscles, and you'll look just like a man." They would say, "If you run around too much as a girl, you'll never be able to have children." The running was supposed to be too much strain for your body, and your body would never be the same again.

In 1989, Wilma explained to the *Chicago Tribune* (Jan. 8, 1989) the catalytic role that her struggle against discrimination had played in enabling her to triumph:

Believe me, the reward is not so great without the struggle. The triumph can't be had without the struggle. And I know what struggle is. I have spent a lifetime trying to share what it has meant to be a woman first in the world of sports so that other young women have a chance to reach their dreams.

Perhaps the toughest of all the discriminatory obstacles facing Wilma was racial. The South was segregated during the 1940s and early '50s, and black schools and communities had very limited financial resources to support amateur athletics. Wilma and her teammates traveled to track meets in a nine-passenger DeSoto station wagon and enjoyed few of the luxuries that were normally afforded traveling athletes. The track team packed their meals because blacks could not get served in restaurants. Racial discrimination was the third strike against Wilma Rudolph. However, even with three strikes against her, Wilma didn't strike out–she struck back.

Wilma's superhero status was born of a tenacious will that refused to bow to the fate that had dealt her what most people would regard as an atrocious hand–no ace, no face, no trump. But the hand dealt is not nearly as important as the one played and Wilma played hers with panache and style. Her courage and tenacity brought her to the pinnacle of athletic achievement and made her an inspiration to all of us who struggle against adversity. For Wilma, running was freedom, the freedom to escape abject poverty, to gain acceptance, to get a college education and later to fight discrimination. "You can accomplish anything," she wrote, "if you think you can." The woman destined to be a cripple never became one. And when competing for the gold, she remembered a time when she was unable to do anything. "I never forgot all those years when I was a little girl and not able to be involved in sports," she wrote. "When I ran I felt like a butterfly that was free."

The story of Wilma Rudolph is an inspiration to anyone who feels unable to surmount the obstacles that stand between them and their dreams. She refused to give in to polio, high school pregnancy or a sprained ankle on the eve of the Olympic 100-meter dash. She was an indomitable spirit who spent her life helping others overcome adversity. United States track coach Nell Jackson wrote, "Wilma's accomplishments opened up the real door for women in track because of her grace and beauty. People saw her as beauty in motion." Olympic champ and member of the U.S. Olympic Committee Anita DeFrantz told the media (Herzog, p. 241), "She is immortal. We'll know about Wilma Rudolph forever." As you read of Wilma Rudolph's challenges and triumphs, you will understand why she was elected to the Black Sports Hall of Fame and the U.S. Olympic Hall of Fame and won numerous awards and honors. You will also understand why she is included in this book as one of the 13 greatest athletes of the 20th century.

WILMA RUDOLPH'S TREK TO THE TOP

Early Imprints

On June 23, 1940, Wilma Rudolph entered the world prematurely as a puny, four and one-half pound baby. The 20th of 22 children in a poor black family in St. Bethlehem, Tennessee, Wilma was challenged even before she left the starting blocks of life. Her father Ed Rudolph provided for his family by working as a porter for the railroad. He had eleven children by a first marriage and another eleven through his marriage to his second wife, Blanche. Blanche worked as a domestic to help provide for the needs of this huge family.

When Wilma contracted polio at age four, the family doctor told Wilma she would never walk again. Her left leg was paralyzed and her left foot turned inward. Horrified by the prospect of life in a wheelchair, she refused to accept the doctor's prognosis. Years later she wrote, "The doctors told me I would never walk, but my mother told me I would, so I believed my mother." The polio had left Wilma's immune system in a weakened state and she subsequently fell victim to scarlet fever and double pneumonia. Wilma later recalled that she spent the first decade of her life being sick.

Since she had lost the use of her left leg, Wilma was fitted with a steel brace. When her mother told her that she would not be able to attend school like her siblings at age six, she just cried. In her own words (Rudolph, p. 18):

Being sick so much kept me alone a lot. Whenever the other kids went out somewhere, I was left behind...Being left behind had a terrible effect on me. I was so lonely, and I felt rejected...I cried a lot."

The unrelenting assault of various illnesses at such an early age ignited in Wilma an anger that gave her the courage to launch an all-out battle against her infirmity. She later described this fury that would serve as her springboard to good health (Rudolph, p. 19):

After the scarlet fever and the whooping cough, I remember I started to get mad about it all...I went through the stage of asking myself, "Wilma, what is this existence all about? Is it about being sick all the time? It can't be." So I started getting angry about things, fighting back in a new way, with a vengeance. I think I started acquiring a competitive spirit right then and there, a spirit that would make me successful in sports later on.

Wilma received a great deal of support from her siblings who would massage her left leg in attempts to restore feeling and stimulate the muscles. When Wilma reached six years of age, the massage treatments alone were no longer adequate and she began a series of twice-weekly therapy treatments in Nashville. Her mother would ride with her on the one-hour trip into the city where Wilma would undergo a four-hour ordeal involving traction, twisting and hot whirlpool treatments. On those interminable bus rides from her hometown in Clarksville, she would fantasize about what it would be like to be normal. As she explained to the *Chicago Tribune* (Jan. 8, 1989), "I would visualize myself in this gigantic white house on the hill and being married and having children." Those long trips to Nashville continued for four years.

At age seven, Wilma's confinement to her home finally came to an end. She was enrolled in the second grade at Cobb Elementary School–an all-black school that Wilma later described as having an inferior curriculum and inadequate resources. However, most of the teachers were caring individuals who encouraged Wilma and helped her develop the self-esteem and confidence that would serve her so well in the years to come. During her first years at Cobb, Wilma continued to be encumbered by a steel brace on her left leg. Whenever she was at home alone, she would slip off the brace and practice walking without it, pretending that she could walk normally. Such unrelenting persistence, combined with daily massages and her twice-weekly treatments in Nashville, eventually enabled Wilma to walk normally.

At age nine and a half, Wilma went out in public for the first time without her leg brace. It was one of the proudest moments of her life as she walked into church knowing that her peers who had ridiculed her deformity and called her "cripple" now had to accept that she was just as normal as they. But Wilma was no longer merely striving to be normal. Her desire for acceptance now extended beyond normal achievements to loftier goals. In her own words (Biracree, p. 52), "I was determined to go beyond them, to do something that none of them would ever do, so then they'd have to accept me." By the time Wilma reached the age of ten, her therapy in Nashville was no longer required and she wore the leg brace intermittently. By age 12, she shed the leg brace forever. She announced triumphantly, "I was free at last." A new chapter in the life of Wilma Rudolph was about to unfold.

Wilma's First Passion: Basketball

Grade seven was to be described later by Wilma as one of the "pivotal years of [her] life." Now attending the new Burt High School in Clarksville and unencumbered by the leg brace, Wilma resolved once and for all to never again be relegated to the sidelines. Her first venture into the active world was to try out for the Burt basketball team. However, the coach, Clinton Gray, was not impressed with Wilma's skills and she sat on the bench for three seasons, playing only in the dying minutes of games that were already decisively won or hopelessly lost. Finally in her sophomore year, Coach Gray seemed to notice her. She had grown to a height of almost six feet and her spindly stature gave the impression of a loosely connected concoction of arms and legs as she buzzed around the basketball court. This conjured up the image of a mosquito to Coach Gray who nicknamed her "Skeeter." The nickname stuck, and thereafter Wilma Rudolph was affectionately known as "Skeeter."

The raw speed born of a tenacious will was apparent every time Skeeter ran up and down the basketball court. In her sophomore year, Wilma became a starting member of the basketball team. She exploded onto the court, unleashing the pent-up energy that had been percolating for three years. Averaging over 30 points a game, Wilma was now a revered star of one of the best teams in the state. The next year, as a junior, she averaged 35 points a game with the team, often scoring over 100 points a game. Burt High went undefeated and won the Tennessee State Championship. Wilma's tenacity and fierce competitive spirit had catapulted her from a disabled recluse to a popular high-school athletic hero.

Discovering the Secret of Winning

By 15, Skeeter was playing basketball at a very high level but she had been performing at an even higher level in the Burt High School track and field events. Her success in track and field was such that she was invited to an interstate track meet in Tuskegee, Alabama. At this point in her life, Wilma had achieved nothing but success in track and field and she felt unbeatable. She observed (Rudolph, pp. 63–4):

When we got to the track, these girls from Georgia really looked like runners, but I paid them no mind because, well, I was a little cocky. I did think I could wipe them out because, after all, I had won every single race I had been in up to that point. So what happens? I got wiped out. It was the absolute worst experience of my life. I did not win a single race I ran in, nor did I qualify for anything. I was totally crushed...It was the first time I had ever tasted defeat in track, and it left me a total wreck...I can't remember ever being so totally crushed by anything.

In the weeks that followed, Skeeter stood on the precipice between abandoning her quest to excel in track or pushing past the painful defeat and pressing on to victory. In a flash of insight, she mused (Rudolph, p. 65):

But looking back on it all, I realized somewhere along the line that to think that way wasn't necessarily right, that it was kind of extreme. I learned a very big lesson for the rest of my life as well. The lesson was, winning is great, sure, but if you are really going to do something in life, the secret is learning how to lose.

Fortunately, she chose to use the defeat to learn how to win. In early 1956 when playing in the Tennessee State Championship in basketball, she caught the attention of Ed Temple, coach of the University of Tennessee track team in nearby Nashville. Temple recruited Wilma as a Tigerbelle (his track teams had been called "Tigerbelles"–tigers on the track, but Southern belles when not in competition.) Temple became Wilma's mentor, surrogate father, friend and coach. Preparing her for life in the fast lane, he trained her as anchor of the Tigerbelle track team. Life was rosy for Skeeter–just 16 years of age and already a high-school hero and prized recruit of the University of Tennessee.

The 1956 Olympics in Melbourne

During that summer, Wilma trained hard. Ed Temple taught her how to explode out of the starting blocks, optimize performance by releasing tension in the muscles, and pass the baton in a relay. By the end of the summer, the University of Tennessee track team was primed to compete in the AAU competition in Philadelphia. Skeeter was entered in the 75-m and the 100-m dash as well as the 440-m relay. She won all the preliminary heats and the finals–nine races in total. In the ceremonies that followed, Wilma was asked to stand for a photo beside Jackie Robinson, at that time a star player for the Brooklyn Dodgers. She was overwhelmed when Mr. Robinson turned to her and said, "I really like your style of running and I really think you have a lot of potential." That endorsement inspired Wilma and gave her a black role model to relate to. She later wrote (Rudolph, p. 79):

> *All the way back to Tennessee, I thought about Jackie Robinson and what he said, and for the first time in my life I had a black person I could look up to as a real hero. Jackie Robinson, after that day, was my first black hero.*

Following the AAU track meet, Coach Temple invited Skeeter to go with the College track team to Seattle, Washington to qualify for the 1956 Olympics in Melbourne, Australia. It was in those trials that Wilma came into her own. Her internal competitive spirit now burst forth in all its glory and she qualified for the 200-m race and the 400-m relay at the Olympics. At age 16, Wilma was the youngest member of the U.S. Olympic team. She lost in the 200-meter sprint, but her team won the bronze medal in the 400-m relay. Though the mixed victory/defeat was a bittersweet experience for Wilma, she was inspired by the performance of Betty Cuthbert who won gold medals in the 100-m, 200-m and 400-m for Australia. She recalled (Rudolph, p. 97):

Watching [Betty Cuthbert] win those three gold medals motivated me into making a commitment to do the very same thing someday. I was determined that four years from then, no matter where the Olympics were held, I was going to be there and I was going to win a gold medal or two for the United States.

When Wilma returned from Melbourne, she discovered that Burt High School had been closed for the day to hold a special assembly in her honor. Wilma Rudolph had arrived! She was now a celebrity in her own school and her hometown–and about to learn about the joys and sorrows of celebrity status.

Wilma enjoyed the adulation that rained down upon her when she returned to Burt High School. However, once the honeymoon phase of her new celebrity status had passed, she began to feel the inevitable backlash that follows a hero's homecoming. Wilma lamented (Rudolph, p. 104):

They either put you on a pedestal, or else they put you down. There was no in-between. It was the same with my own peer group at school; all the kids acted differently toward me after I came back from Melbourne. I was starting to feel that it was difficult to go out in the world and accomplish something, and then come back and be friends with everybody again.

Wilma was experiencing a fall from grace similar to that suffered by the Sultan of Swat shortly after his canonization by the public. Though Wilma continued in her struggle to reconcile her desire to be accepted with her desire to excel, she intuitively understood that the only real choice is the pursuit of the latter. Wilma was at the top of her game and her life was within her control. What could possibly go wrong?

Wilma's Second Passion: Robert

In the fall of 1957, Skeeter entered her senior year at Burt High School. Among her friends was Robert Eldridge, who had been a childhood sweet-heart since early elementary school. Robert was the football and basketball star at Burt High School and everyone looked upon them as the "golden cou-ple." The friendship matured into physical passion and Wilma soon realized that she was in love. Wilma wore his football jacket during the fall. By the time basketball season arrived, however, Wilma's pre-season medical exami-nation revealed that she was pregnant. The usual recriminations followed and the pregnancy almost ended her career before it began, as so often happened with other aspiring female athletes. However, once the dust had settled, Wilma's family agreed to pull together to help her. When Wilma graduated from Burt High School in May 1958, she was seven months pregnant. In July 1958, she gave birth to a beautiful daughter Yolanda. Knowing that Wilma had her heart set on participating in the 1960 Olympics, Wilma's mother and older sister Yvonne made arrangements to raise Yolanda until Wilma made it through the Olympics and college.

Destination Rome

In the fall of 1958 at the age of 18, Wilma entered Tennessee State University on a track scholarship. She continued to train with the track team, improving her speed and techniques. At the end of her sophomore year, she participated in the National AAU meet in Corpus Christi, Texas and then the Olympic trials at Texas Christian University. In the 200-m dash, she achieved a time of 22.9 seconds, the fastest 200 meters ever run by a woman. This new world record stood for almost eight years. As a result of her outstanding performance at the Olympic trials, Wilma qualified for the Olympics in the 100-m dash, the 200-m dash and the 400-m relay.

The City of Rome was an appropriate site for the Eighteenth Modern Olympic Games. In this ancient city, gladiators had fought to the death in the Coliseum. From the opening moment of the Olympic Games, the enthusiasm and excitement of the spectators crackled as though the stakes were no less than in ancient times. Indeed, the stakes for Wilma were of the highest magnitude. In her first 20 years of life, Wilma had undergone a grueling regimen of treatments followed by a rigorous program of training and conditioning to get to this one moment of truth–this ultimate test of speed to determine the fastest woman in the world. Wilma's entire lifelong struggle was coming to a climax–a climax of approximately 11 seconds–that would determine how the rest of her life would unfold.

When the moment of Wilma's first race–the 100-meter dash–arrived, she approached the tunnel that led to the track on the stadium floor. Suddenly the paralyzing fear and the "butterflies" sensation of flowing adrenaline began to wane. She said goodbye to Coach Temple and entered the tunnel alone. Wilma later described what she was feeling at that moment (Rudolph, p. 130):

> *When I got into the tunnel with the other runners, a strange calm came over me. I was nervous in a sense, yes; but I also got a chance to take a look at the runners I would be going up against, and I felt, deep inside, that I could beat any of them.*

More than 80,000 people crammed into the stadium. The Italians who knew of Wilma's prior achievements were chanting, "Vil-ma! Vil-ma!" The stadium was throbbing with the heartbeat of anticipation as Wilma and the other runners took their positions on the starting blocks. When the starter's pistol fired, the runners exploded out of the blocks. Though Skeeter was not the first out of the chute, she quickly closed the gap and by the 50-m mark had taken the lead. By the time she reached the finish line she was more than 3 meters ahead of the pack. Wilma Rudolph had won a gold medal and set a new world record of 11.0 seconds for the women's 100-meter dash. The fans went mad. By achieving her dream, Skeeter proved that even the most apparently outrageous fantasies are within the grasp of virtually anyone with enough tenacity and commitment to pursue a goal relentlessly.

Wilma's winning the gold medal in the 200-m dash with a time of 24.0 seconds, and then another gold in the 400-meter relay, was almost anticlimactic. Yet, in doing so, she became the first American woman ever to win three Olympic gold medals. Wilma Rudolph had used her early physical and emotional challenges that brought her to the brink of breakdown to motivate her to hobble, to walk, and finally to run until she could run so fast that no one could catch her. She was now on the top pedestal of the 1960 Olympics and at the top of the athletic world. Though this would, indeed, be the climax of her competitive athletic career, it was only the beginning of her contribution to generations of young people.

Life after Olympic Triumph

Newspaper journalists worldwide gushed over Wilma Rudolph's Olympic triumph. The Italians referred to her as "La Gazzella Nera" (The Black Gazelle) and the French called her "La Perle Noire" (The Black Pearl). Their praise was effusive. Wilma visited Pope John XXIII at the Vatican and then traveled to Britain before returning home.

On her return to the United States, Wilma Rudolph was showered with honors including several ticker-tape parades. When her hometown of Clarksville planned to hold a parade and banquet in her honor, she insisted that it be integrated rather than organized in the traditional segregated format. Her wishes were honored, and what followed was a hugely successful parade that Wilma described as "the first integrated event in the history of that town."

Official honors bestowed on Wilma included the Associated Press Female Athlete of the Year Award and the United Press Athlete of the Year Award in 1960, the James E. Sullivan Memorial Trophy as America's Top Amateur Athlete in 1961, and in 1962, the Babe Didrikson Award as the Top Female Athlete in America. (The Babe Didrikson Award was particularly appropriate since Babe, just one generation earlier, had also been one of the trailblazers for the acceptance of women in competitive athletics.) She was also invited to the White House by President John F. Kennedy. However, in spite of all the glory, fame and honors bestowed upon Wilma Rudolph, she received little monetary reward from her achievement. Today's huge fees for commercial endorsements and public appearances that accompany Olympic stardom were not widely available in 1960, particularly to black females. In her exposure to the rich and famous, Wilma experienced a taste of life at the affluent level and realized how difficult it is to be poor after you've lived rich. Speaking to *Ebony Magazine* she lamented:

> *You become world famous and you sit with kings and queens, and then your first job is just a job. You can't go back to living the way you did before because you've been taken out of one setting and shown the other. That becomes a struggle and makes you struggle.*

Wilma Rudolph announced her retirement from competitive athletics in 1963 and in that same year graduated with a major in elementary education from the University of Tennessee. On graduation, she accepted a job as a second-grade teacher at Cobb Elementary School, her own alma mater, and served as the girls' track coach. She also married Robert Eldridge, her high school sweetheart and the father of their daughter Yolanda. Together they had three more children. She and her family later moved to Evansville, Indiana, where she was director of a community center. A variety of different jobs that involved work with young people took her to various locations across the country. During that time, she divorced Robert and raised her children on her own. She married once more and that marriage also ended in divorce.

Legacy

Though not living the lifestyle of the rich and famous, Wilma still enjoyed celebrity status in the decades that followed. In 1967, Wilma worked with Vice-President Hubert Humphrey on Operation Champion, a project designed to bring professional coaching to potential athletic stars from urban ghettoes. In 1977, she wrote her autobiography *Wilma: The Story of Wilma Rudolph*, which was scripted by NBC as a television movie that served as an inspiration to physically challenged youths who were struggling with their disabilities.

In June 1993, President Bill Clinton honored Wilma Rudolph along with other athletes, including Muhammad Ali, at the first National Sports Awards. Wilma Rudolph and Muhammad Ali had met and become friendly verbal sparing partners during the 1960 Olympics, when Ali, then Cassius Clay, had won the gold in boxing. *USA Today* reported (November 14, 1994):

> *When Ali asked Rudolph to accompany him on a goodwill trip to Iran, Rudolph shot back, "How much money do you have these days?" When Ali said, "I don't have any money, Wilma," Rudolph answered, "Then I'm not going." They both laughed.*

Seventeen months after the National Sports Award ceremony, Wilma was dead. On November 12, 1994, Wilma Rudolph, who had defeated diseases that destroyed others, succumbed to brain cancer at age 54. Her contribution to athletics is indisputable, but even more than this is her enormous contribution to all of us who believe that we can surmount any obstacle if we have enough tenacity. Her story is living proof of how we can use breakdown or near breakdown as a springboard to breakthrough.

Wilma used the insurmountable obstacles she faced to motivate a breakthrough of heroic proportions. In transforming herself from a poor "cripple" raised in a black community in the segregated South to the fastest woman in the world, she not only blazed the trail for women and blacks in athletics, but she gave hope to the physically challenged. When Wilma Rudolph retired from athletic competition, she dedicated herself to helping young people believe in themselves. To this end, she established in 1981 the Wilma Rudolph Foundation. Prophetically anticipating her epitaph, she reflected:

> *I would be very sad if I was only remembered as Wilma Rudolph, the great sprinter. To me, my legacy is to the youth of America to let them know they can be anything they want to be.*

Chapter 5

Intuitively, at any instant, I knew the position of all the other players on the field, and saw just what each man was going to do next.
—Pelé (Edson Arantes Do Nascimento)

What Brain Research Tells Us about Our Instincts

Near the end of the 20th century, research into brain physiology revealed that different cerebral functions are housed in different locations in the brain. For example, logical deduction and language capability, both of which involve sequential processing, are situated in the left hemisphere. However, spatial perception, balance and face recognition, processes of a holistic nature, are situated in the right hemisphere. It is believed that much of our creativity derives from processes that occur in this hemisphere. Consequently, those who are described as "right-brain dominant" are seen to be intuitive, creative and holistic thinkers. "Left-brain dominant" people, on the other hand, are described as rational, deductive and sequential. The ideal for optimal athletic performance seems to be a harmonic balance between the two hemispheres. In his book *Life Energy* (p. 84), Physician John Diamond observed, "Life energy is high when brain hemispheres are balanced–psycho-biological harmony."

PEANUTS: © United Feature Syndicate, Inc.

Brain research provides a framework for understanding how the brain processes and internalizes athletic skills. In practicing a complex movement such as the golf swing, we experiment with different grips, positions and swing movements, analyzing each in terms of the results it yields. This is a conscious, left-brain process. Once we identify those elements of the swing that produce the desired results, we rehearse them over and over again in an attempt to record them permanently in "muscle memory." In this way, we internalize the swing as a kinesthetic feeling that we trust to recreate the desired swing on demand. This internalization transfers the swing from a consciously controlled left-brain function to a more intuitive or automatic right-brain function. This description, albeit an oversimplification of the actual processes involved, serves as a model for the interaction between conscious and unconscious actions in the brain, as it learns to perfect an athletic skill. It also sheds light on the powerful role of the subconscious in athletics. By its very nature the subconscious is hidden from us, but psychologists believe that 90% of all functions originate in this part of the brain. In *Evolution of Consciousness,* Robert Ornstein observes (p. 216), "All judgments are made in terms of the current state of affairs in the mind–exact recorded images of the past which are an illusion. If we knew [consciously] everything that we know [subconsciously], we'd go crazy since there's so much data." We refer to the harmony between the conscious and the subconscious parts of our mental processing as the *mind/body synthesis.* I will explore this concept in more depth in Chapter 14.

In an article titled "The Mental Hazards of Golf," legendary golfer, Bobby Jones wrote (*Vanity Fair*, 1929):

> *The golf swing is a most complicated combination of muscular actions, too complex to be controlled by objective conscious mental effort. Consequently, we must rely a good deal upon the instinctive reactions acquired by long practice. It has been my experience that the more completely we can depend on this instinct–the more thoroughly we can divest the subjective mind of conscious control–the more perfectly we can execute our shots…That intense concentration upon results, to the absolute exclusion of all thoughts as to method, is the secret of a good shot. Few great shots are played when the mind is fixed on the position of the feet, the behavior of the left arm, etc.*

This explains the golf adage, *Trust your swing.* The bottom line is: think positive *before* the action, but during the action, don't think at all.

The Power of Your Instincts: A Side Trip from Sports to the Sciences

The power of intuitive thinking is often underestimated because much of its mechanisms are buried in the subconscious and are, therefore, invisible to the conscious mind. The daily observations and data that we collect are internalized in a subconscious sense that is often manifested as inspiration. What we commonly describe as "gut feeling" is really an intuitive knowledge acquired through experience but not easily quantifiable or explainable. Nevertheless, intuition is a fundamental thought process that pervades every human endeavor, its power directly related to the quality of the information stored in the unconscious database.

Instinct, the product of subconscious intuitive thought, is the prominent intellectual function in scientific research. Einstein relied heavily on his instincts and pressed his mathematical technique into service only after his intuition had hinted at a model of the universe. He asserted, "Intuition is the gift of the gods, but logic is its faithful servant." He once scribbled on his blackboard at Princeton, "Everything that counts, can't be counted, and everything that can be counted, doesn't count." For this physicist, numbers were mere vehicles to a higher order of understanding–the essence or qualitative. Logic's most powerful role lies in its capacity to validate an intuitively perceived truth.

Most of our epiphanies are innate responses to our inner knowing. They emerge from a brain that has absorbed a great deal of information and then proceeds relentlessly in a subconscious search for pattern. The results of this search suddenly explode in an instantaneous revelation or a creative vision. The more information stored in that internal databank, the more prescient the intuition. Many intellectual giants have attributed their greatness to their intuition. Bertrand Russell wrote, "The sense of certainty and revelation comes before any definite belief." Jonas Salk, the scientist who developed the polio vaccine, wrote, "It is always with excitement that I wake up in the morning wondering what my intuition will toss up to me, like gifts from the sea. I work with it and rely on it. It's my partner."

In describing the process that led to his creation of the world's first skyscraper, architect Louis Sullivan suggested, "When a design fails to materialize, get away from the drawing board. Leave the office. Take a walk. Allow your mind to roam free. It was on such a stroll that the design for the first skyscraper came to me in a flash."

Leonardo da Vinci, Charles Darwin, Nikola Tesla, Sigmund Freud and Bucky Fuller are others who used their subconscious in their creativity. In view of the pervasive role of intuitive thought in all human endeavor, it comes as no surprise that instincts play a more dominant role in athletics than conscious rational thought.

Paradoxical Intention: Trying Too Hard

The eminent German psychiatrist Viktor Frankl stumbled on the concept of *paradoxical intention* while working with impotent men in his medical practice. As long as his male patients tried, they couldn't achieve an erection. As soon as they stopped trying, performance was no problem. Paradoxical intention became central to Frankl's *logotherapy*–a type of psychotherapy that he documented in his landmark work, *In Search of Meaning* (Frankl, p. 147):

> *Logotherapy bases its technique called "paradoxical intention" on the twofold fact that fear brings about that which one is afraid of, and that hyper-intention makes impossible what one wishes.*

In another experiment, Frankl found that stuttering was no different from erection problems. When treating a young boy who stuttered when he first talked, he found that the only way the lad could stop stuttering was to stop trying not to stutter. Similarly, he showed that trying too hard to sign your name in perfect penmanship isn't possible until you just do it without thinking. These problems all derived from a subconscious quest for perfection that caused performance anxiety. In essence, Frankl's experiments revealed that you can only approach perfection by relaxing and letting your instincts guide you. Those who try to be perfect or force things to happen are setting themselves up for a potentially deflating experience–literally!

The concept of paradoxical intention is of profound significance in athletic performance. Both psychiatrists and sports psychologists have found that the harder you try, the worse you do. Any golf professional will tell you that swinging a golf club harder doesn't make the ball go farther. Most amateur golfers walk up to the tee on a par-five hole with an attitude of controlled aggression. To reach the green in as few strokes as possible, they know they must hit a long drive. Their muscles tense as they prepare to hit their longest drive of the day. They secure a death-grip on the club, lunge at the tiny white sphere with the fury of a challenged ego and inevitably hit their most embarrassing drive of the day. Why? Excessive conscious effort has interfered with the body's natural ability to function–the mental has overridden the physical. The seasoned golfer has learned that the best way to hit a long ball is not to swing hard but to swing in balance with proper body turn and rhythm. *Trying too hard causes the reverse of the intent.* This is true in sports, in playing chess, on the dance floor, or in the bedroom. Optimum success occurs in any venue when one sets a goal and focuses on the mission at hand, while allowing the instincts to guide the action.

Training the Mind to Get Out of the Way

An article in *Newsweek* (June 2, 2003, p. 14) on putting in golf blazed the headline, "Don't Think Twice–Or at All, for that Matter." The article explained that standing over a putt too long "paralyzes and proves counter-productive" to the process. Researchers at the Mayo Clinic attempted to find the cause of those mis-hit short putts that plague weekend and professional golfers alike. They came up blank because (to their surprise) golfers in lab conditions never experience the tension–known as the *yips*–that visits golfers under pressure. The yips never occurred when there was nothing at stake. In such relaxed environments, the emotions remained intact and under control. This is a dramatic example of paradoxical intention in a sports context.

Proficient athletes in any sport have practiced the game until the main skills, the sub-skills and their execution become rote. Until you can perform without thinking, you will not be exceptional. Furthermore once you've achieved this instinctive sense of a skill, you revert from feel to thought at your peril. The *Newsweek* article stated, "The better the golfer, the less the mental activity." Why would this be the case? Because muscle memory is acquired through thousands of repetitive movements that evolve and improve until the performance is perfected and internalized. Allowing the mind to interfere only detracts from the body's natural instinctual skills. In the early stages of learning a new skill, however, the conscious mind does play a role, guiding your practice of a particular movement. Until you have put enough miles on the golf clubs, skis or rackets, you have no chance of becoming good or great. Once you do reach a high level of competence, the conscious mind should no longer be part of the process. The task may then be turned over to your unconscious instinct.

The mind can interfere for many reasons. Among the most prominent is the fact that the mind knows too much of what we cannot do. These mental limitations severely impede performance especially in unknown situations. When forced to perform outside your comfort level, it is normal to stop and think. The minute that happens, you have disaster: the mind overrides what the body knows how to do. Any world-class athlete will tell you that those who are uncertain when embroiled in the heat of battle end up as casualties. Success is a function of belief, and "muscle memory" must prevail when the mind starts to question action.

Training the conscious or rational mind to get out of the way in order to enable the intuitive or subconscious to control the execution of a skill requires that the athlete assume a disposition that master coach Timothy Gallwey calls *relaxed concentration* (*The Inner Game of Golf*, p. 172):

> *What is relaxed concentration? It is simply the capacity to focus totally. It occurs when commitment, abilities, and attention can be channeled in a single direction. It is being truly conscious and free of fear, doubt and confusion. It is what enabled Ted Williams to say that sometimes he could see the ball so well "that it almost stands still for me."...Or as the master in Eugen Herrigel's* Zen and the Art of Archery *says, "A single conscious thought through the mind diverts the arrow from its course toward the target."*

There is an old fable about two centipedes, a father and son, who are walking together. The junior centipede asks, "Dad, I notice when you walk, that your 37th leg hits the ground after your 25th leg. What leg hits the ground after your 37th leg?" The senior centipede thought about the question for a minute or two and then rolled over and was incapable of walking ever again. To better understand the centipede's problem try running quickly down the stairs and thinking about each stair as you approach it!

Practice and Physical Conditioning as Prerequisites to Achieving Focus

Before athletes can rely on instinct, they need to practice the skills and sub-skills of the sport until execution is internalized. We observed in Chapter 3 how Babe Zaharias hit golf balls until her hands bled and then continued to practice until darkness closed in. Vijay Singh, rated the #1 Golfer in the World in 2004, is reported to hit more than 1000 golf balls a day to hone his skills to the level of automatic reflex. Similarly, athletes in every sport understand that incessant practice is necessary to ensure that skills peculiar to their sport can be executed correctly without conscious thought.

In sports such as soccer, boxing, cycling and marathon running, in which cardiovascular response is vital to performance, athletes must focus on building heart and lung capacity through extensive training. Similarly, in weight lifting and other strength sports, muscle power must be developed through a rigorous program of training. Practice and physical conditioning are prerequisites for outstanding athletic performance. However, most athletes at the top echelons of any sport have developed their skills and conditioning to exceptional levels. What separates the superstars from the others is their ability to achieve total focus.

Focusing on what is important is key to effective performance. During play, especially in long games like football, baseball or soccer, maintaining focus throughout is difficult. Those who keep their focus longest tend to make the fewest errors, giving them an edge. Games like golf and tennis have more breaks in play than actual play; so maintaining focus is also an issue in those sports. Distractions interfere with a focus on execution. Having a superb game plan is fine, but if it cannot be executed, it is wasted. Focus is vital in making the appropriate decision or hitting the right shot in a given situation. This is as true in the boardroom as it is in tennis or golf. "Crunch time" is no time to be thinking about what *might be* but rather what *must be* done to achieve the desired result.

Tiger Woods spoke of the focus factor extensively in *How I Play Golf*. "There's a winner's attitude to handling pressure," Tiger warned, "focus solely on what you need to accomplish." Seems trite, but it's true. Few people understand the importance of focusing on the goal at hand and the high cost of losing focus. Clutter and "psychological noise" can interfere with effective execution. Those easily distracted fall prey to such intrusions on relaxed concentration.

Achieving a Global View through Focus

Because great athletes have a global view of what is transpiring, they are better equipped to deal with the vagaries that arise as a contest unfolds. For example, the greatest boxers were not those who possessed the greatest size, the greatest strength or even the most powerful punch. Boxing fans in 1919 witnessed the crushing defeat of World Heavyweight Champion Jess Willard at 6' 6" and 245 lbs. by Jack Dempsey who was 5" shorter and 58 lbs. lighter. In 1974 the world watched Muhammad Ali outbox the bigger and stronger George Foreman in the famous "Rumble in the Jungle." Boxers must stay intensely focused on the opponent's threats and vulnerabilities, instinctively sensing when opportunity arrives and then exploding into action with lightning speed. In the dance of death between a cobra and a mongoose, the first one who blinks or loses focus has lost the battle of survival. Expertise in the execution of specific skills is crucially important, but the effective application of those skills requires focus. That is, we must be able to execute particular skills in "unconscious" fashion so that the mind is freed to respond to our instincts. This is the highest echelon of athletic performance. Athletic situations can be complex, so to deal with the complexities the mind must become lost in the moment, observing, reacting and executing at an instinctive level. This is the mental state that athletic superstars reach when in the throes of competition.

I chose to describe the role of intuition and focus in the execution of athletic skills using examples from golf because you are most likely to experience that sport first hand. However, for an example of an athlete who modeled focus and instinct, I could do no better than choose the athlete selected by the International Olympic Committee as the Athlete of the Century–Pelé. No athlete showcased the power of intuition and focus in sports better than this brilliant soccer player whose name is recognized by more people in the world than any other athlete past or present. The story of how this incredible spirit rose from impoverished beginnings in a poor Brazilian village to the status of a demi-god on the world stage has been told in four movies, including John Huston's *Escape to Victory*. However, at this point, I invite you to determine whether you are right-brain or left-brain dominant by completing the self-assessment on the opposite page.

BRAIN HEMISPHERE SELF-ASSESSMENT–Are You Right- or Left-Brain Dominant?

For each item, choose "A" or "B" to indicate which statement describes you best. The scoring key is at the bottom of the page. There are no "right" or "wrong" answers.

A	B
1. It's fun to push the limits in life.	I can live peacefully without pushing the limits.
2. I look for new ways to complete old jobs.	If the old ways work well, I don't try to change them.
3. I often have many balls in the air at once and have trouble finishing some.	I finish most jobs I begin and won't start a new one until the others are done.
4. I think in images and often see the end solutions in my mind.	I tend to think in words and prefer to work step-by-step to a solution.
5. Others see me as a person who is disorganized.	Others see me as a person who is organized with everything in its place.
6. I thrive on changes and variety in my life.	I thrive on having an orderly and well-planned life.
7. On important issues, I start with the big picture and move to the details.	On important issues, I start with specifics and build to a solution.
8. When driving in a new city, I like to find my way without a map.	Before driving in a new city, I like to use a map to plan my route.
9. My desk is usually cluttered.	I need a clean desk in order to function.
10. I prefer spacial puzzles like jig-saw or tangrams to crossword puzzles.	I prefer crossword puzzles to spacial puzzles like jig-saw or tangrams.
11. When investing, I rely mainly on my instincts and somewhat on numbers.	When investing, I trust the numbers more than my instincts.
12. Friends would more likely see me as a dreamer than as a practical person.	Friends would more likely see me as a practical person rather than a dreamer.

Instructions	Scoring Key
Count the number of "A" responses. Then use the scoring key to determine whether you are right-brain dominant, left-brain dominant or bilateral (relatively evenly balanced.)	**Number of As** 10–12: Strong right-brain dominant. 8–9: Moderate right-brain dominant. 5–7: Bilateral–balance between right- and left-brain. 3–4: Moderate left-brain dominant. 0–2: Strong left-brain dominant.

PELÉ

- The only three-time World Cup winner.

- At age 29 he scored an unprecedented 1000th goal.

- In 17 years of professional soccer, he averaged almost one goal per game.

- He led Brazil to World cup titles in 1958, 1962 and 1970.

- He scored 1281 goals in 1363 matches –over double that of any other player.

- Led the New York Cosmos to the NASL Championship in 1975; named MVP.

- Considered to be the greatest soccer player in history.

© Bettmann/CORBIS

Pelé: Sublime Instincts with Surreal Focus

For a dozen years or more, no man was so revered throughout the world as Edson Arantes do Nascimento, known to his fans as Pelé. Only Babe Ruth, Elvis Presley and Michael Jordan ever came close to the god-like reverence in which he was held and their spheres of influence did not reach as far and wide as the brilliant Brazilian's. Only Wayne Gretzky, in the sport of hockey, has rewritten the record books to the same extent as Pelé did in soccer. His world-wide impact transcended national boundaries and race and class barriers. The Shah of Iran, when at the peak of his power, waited patiently for three hours to have his picture taken with Pelé. When Pelé visited Pope

Pelé
born Oct. 23, 1940

Paul VI, the Italian newspapers reported that the Pope declared that he was more nervous of meeting Pelé than was the soccer superstar at meeting him. Queen Elizabeth II conferred an honorary knighthood on Pelé, the highest honor granted by British royalty. Pelé even engaged in an impromptu soccer kickabout in a photo op with then President of the United States, Bill Clinton.

Who is this athlete from a poor Brazilian village who rose from the depths of poverty to the highest pinnacle of the rich, the famous and the powerful? Though he possessed most of the winning characteristics described in the other chapters of this book, his most conspicuous talent was his ability to achieve a total focus by tapping into his instincts. These psychological elements contributed to Pelé's supernatural success in soccer.

Pelé's uncanny ability to sense the positions of all his teammates and his opponents enabled him to identify a scoring opportunity and execute the "killer" action in a flash. In a post-game interview, he recaptured what went through his mind during an intense moment of that crucial game, "Intuitively, at any instant, I knew the position of all the other players on the field, and saw just what each man was going to do next." Functioning in a state of relaxed concentration, Pelé was able to achieve an intense focus that gave free rein to his instincts. This remarkable ability earned him the title *Footballer of the Millennium* at the World Sports Awards of the Century ceremonies in Vienna in the year 2000.

Fellow competitors and sportscasters were effusive in their praise of Pelé's extraordinary instincts and presence of mind on the soccer field or "pitch." In describing the Brazilian victory over the reigning world champion English team in the 1970 World Cup, Pelé's biographer wrote (Harris, p. 112):

The [victory] was sealed for Brazil with a touch of genius [by Pelé] when, fourteen minutes into the second half, Tostao embarrassed Moore with a nutmeg before searching out his striking partner, Pelé. With remarkable vision, Pelé flicked the ball across to his right for Jairzinho to close in and score...In what seemed like a split-second Pelé had time to weigh up all the options. His first thought [was] about taking a shot himself, then, spotting that Banks, Labone and Cooper had moved to cover him, he instantly reassessed the situation to feed Jairzinho instead.

In an interview for the *New York Times Magazine*, Pelé spoke passionately about the "near mystical state" he entered while in the midst of action in the World Cup game against Sweden:

I felt a strange calmness...It was a type of euphoria; I felt I could run all day without tiring, that I could dribble through any of their team or all of them, that I could almost pass through them physically. I felt I could not be hurt. It was a very strange feeling and one I had never felt before. Perhaps it was merely confidence, but I have felt confident many times without that strange feeling of invincibility.

What experiences had contributed to Pelé's ability to transcend the intensity of the moment and move to a higher, more sublime state where the instincts function with greater focus? Some have suggested that Pelé was merely gifted with an innate talent, but Pelé himself sensed that it was rooted in his early imprints and his experiences. In a training manual on soccer skills, he wrote:

I don't believe there is such a thing as a born soccer player. Perhaps you are born with certain skills and talents, but quite frankly it seems impossible to me that one is actually born to be an ace soccer player. Success is no accident. It is hard work, perseverance, learning, studying, sacrifice and most of all, a love of what you are doing.

Pelé grew up with millions of soccer experiences. His database of experience was virtually overflowing by the time he reached the professional ranks. He spoke extensively about this inner sense of knowing, this automatic execution of skills that caused opponents to exclaim, "That shot was unconscious." His opponents were correct: Pelé's actions were literally unconscious because they sprang from an accumulation of past experience. The ability to focus and tap into this inner reservoir of unconscious knowledge is what allowed Pelé to score more goals than anyone in soccer history.

PELÉ'S TREK TO THE TOP

Early Imprints

Though Pelé climbed from the bottom of the social ladder to the top, we cannot say that he pulled himself up by the bootstraps, for he spent his early years without boots or shoes. In his autobiography, he described the poverty that he and his family experienced during his childhood (pp. 14–15):

> *As I grew up I began to learn what poverty is. Poverty is a curse that depresses the mind, drains the spirit and poisons life. When we didn't lack things–simple things, like enough food in the house, or the small sum that was needed to pay our rent–we were very happy...but there were many bitter arguments, virulent recriminations, [and] painful battles over the lack of necessities. [Our house] leaked like a sieve...but that leaky roof was not poverty. Poverty was having my mother worry herself sick, or upbraid [my father] for not having a job that could earn the money to pay the rent on that leaky roof...Nor was poverty wearing hand-me down clothes that seldom fit, or not having shoes...or having all of us huddled around the wood-burning stove, trying not to sleep on top of one another, and still trying to keep warm. No; poverty was wondering what would happen if we couldn't raise the money for the firewood. Poverty, in short, is being robbed of self-respect and self-reliance. Poverty is fear. Not fear of death, which though inevitable is reasonable; it is fear of life. It is a terrible fear.*

Born on October 23, 1940 in the small town of Três Corações in eastern Brazil, Edson Arantes do Nascimento, later known as Pelé, rose in three decades to the status of "best-known athlete in the world." However, his formative years were spent in the depressing squalor of a two-room shack into which were crammed 13 members of his extended family. Pelé's father Dondinho was an itinerant soccer player who had been injured and was therefore unable to play at a professional level. Unwilling or unable to train for an alternative career, he insisted on pursuing his passion for soccer though it brought little money into the household. The young Pelé absorbed his father's passion and Dondinho became his first mentor in developing the lad's soccer skills. Pelé's mother Dona Celeste was a strong-willed woman who served as the glue that bonded the family during those challenging times. Fearing that her son would become injured and penniless like his father, she made her son promise never to play the game for money.

By the time he was six, Pelé was competing in street games and on pick-up teams in the village of Baurú, where the family had moved in search of employment. He had become a street urchin who kicked anything that moved. There was no money to buy a real soccer ball, so Pelé and his friends would stuff a man's sock with rags or newspaper until it was round enough to roll. The sock that served as the outer skin of the makeshift ball was sometimes appropriated from a neighbor's clothesline and the theft was justified on the grounds that the sock served a higher purpose as a ball than as a garment. In his memoir, Pelé wrote of the thrill he derived from kicking that ball (p. 16):

> *It took skill to kick our ball, since it varied in weight depending on how lately it had been stuffed, and also whether it ran through many mud puddles as we kicked it. But it made no difference; the pleasure of kicking that ball, making it move, making it respond to an action of mine, was the greatest feeling of power I had ever had to that time.*

Every waking hour was spent exploring the nuances of kicking and controlling a moving ball. Years later, Pelé reflected, "[The streets are] where I learned the attacking style." He discovered early that focusing on a purely defensive strategy is counterproductive. A defensive style was just not the way of the streets. On the streets you go for the jugular and if that doesn't work, so be it. He carried this early lesson with him into the professional ranks and it continued throughout his life to be his mantra (Pelé, p. 244). "The object of the game of football is to score," he wrote with passion, "One cannot win games by defense; the best one can hope for with defense is not losing and not losing is not winning."

The nickname Pelé was given to him at age 9 though he was not sure of its origin. One theory was that it came from the Portuguese *pé-le*, meaning *foot*–an admonition that was given each time he accidentally touched the ball with his hands. By this time he was hooked on the game and his skills made him popular in village competitions. Then his father took him to see a professional game and the young Pelé was addicted.

When the nation of Brazil played in their first ever World Cup in 1950, Pelé was caught up in the national frenzy. As he listened to the game against Uruguay on the radio with family and friends, the air was crackling with electric excitement. Almost three decades later, recalling the pandemonium that ensued when Brazil scored the opening goal against Uruguay, Pelé said (p. 240):

> *Everyone in the house is screaming madly! Maracanã [the stadium] is exploding! The radio announcer is going insane! The house is too small to contain our joy so we run out into the street to celebrate. The neighbors are there, fireworks are going off everywhere, everyone is pounding everyone else on the back.*

However, as the game progressed, Uruguay scored a goal and then another and the game ended with Brazil losing by a score of 2–1. Pelé recalled the depth of the despair felt by a village that had so little only to lose the little that they had (Pelé, pp. 240–241):

> *It's a day I shall never forget, an emotion I shall never feel duplicated...I cry...For the first time I see adults cry...I know then that my profession has been chosen. I want to be as good as Dondinho and someday I want to avenge myself on Uruguay. Someday, I swear, I will avenge myself on Uruguay.*

Pursuing His Dream

Until he was twelve, Pelé played competitive soccer barefoot. His team was known as "The Shoeless Ones." But to play in a sanctioned league they had to wear shoes. Because the boys couldn't afford them, a sponsor was found and the team's name was changed to *Ameriquinha* (Little America). On the day that Ameriquinha won the Avalone Junior Victory Cup, 12-year-old Pelé was the *artilheiro*, the leading scorer. Soccer fans were screaming his name. Years later he recalled (Pelé, p. 93), "All I could remember was the crowd yelling my name, Pelé, Pelé–in a constantly growing chant...and my father holding me tightly and saying, 'You played a beautiful game...I couldn't have played any better myself.'"

Such *success imprints* at an early age are common experiences for many who achieve superstar status in their field of endeavor. From that moment Pelé was destined for greatness. He never shared his dream with his mother for he knew she feared he would be injured and suffer the fate of his father, unemployed and without a trade. Until he was thirteen, his mother Dona Celeste still held out hope that he would go to school to learn what she saw as a legitimate profession. However, Pelé's dream drove him to play soccer with a relentless tenacity.

When Pelé was 14, Santos, a team in Brazil's professional soccer league began to scout him. Within a year, Santos offered him a "contract-in-the-drawer" (a euphemism for a verbal contract) because Pelé was still too young to sign a legal contract. After profuse objections to her son's involvement in professional sports, Dona Celeste eventually relented. Pelé was sent halfway across Brazil to live with foster parents and play for the Santos farm team, with the understanding that he would eventually qualify for the Santos first team. At only 15, he was competing with grown men. The emerging star had to struggle for acceptance, to get playing time, to get the adult males to feed him the ball and, all the while, to avoid appearing arrogant. On two occasions, overwhelming homesickness and the fear that he would never be big enough to play on the Santos first team prompted him to give up soccer, skip camp and return to his beloved family in Baurú. Both times, a young man named Sabú, who did odd jobs around the camp, saw Pelé departing with his suitcases and persuaded him to stay and tough it out. Were it not for Sabú's interventions, Pelé's destiny might have been dramatically different.

By the time he was 16, Pelé, as the leading scorer for Santos, was selected to try out for the Brazilian national team for the World Cup, to be held in Sweden in June 1958. The fiercely contested selection process took more than a year. Brazil's national team employed a psychologist to help cull those whom he deemed psychologically ill-suited to high intensity competition. The psychologist looked over the field and saw the skinny teen as too young and too inexperienced to cope. He told coach Vincente Feola that it was premature for Pelé to participate at the world-class level, stating (Pelé, p. 38):

No, Pelé should not play. Pelé is obviously infantile. He lacks the necessary fighting spirit. He is too young to feel the aggressions and respond with the proper force to make a good forward...No, he definitely should not play.

Fortunately for the world of soccer and the Brazilian team, the coach ignored the psychologist's opinion. Pelé was selected for Brazil's national team.

The 1958 World Cup in Sweden

At the tender age of 17, Pelé traveled to Sweden. A knee injury he had suffered weeks earlier sidelined him for the first two games of the World Cup competition. Finally, the team doctors consented to his playing in the qualifying game against the USSR. In this game, Pelé hit the goal post in a spectacular scoring effort and set up one goal that contributed to a 2–0 victory over the USSR. This victory advanced the Brazilian team into the quarterfinals. In the quarterfinals, Pelé scored his first World Cup goal, leading Brazil to a 1–0 victory over Wales. He later described this as "one of the most important goals I ever scored." In the semi-finals against France, he scored three goals and his team advanced into the finals against Sweden, in Stockholm, the Swedish team's hometown.

The game against Sweden was the culmination of months of intense preparation. Brazil had never won a World Cup and had been denied victory eight years earlier in the final against Uruguay. Playing with the brilliance that was to become his trademark, Pelé scored two goals. His second goal was a spectacular show of skill that author Brian Glanville described in *The Story of the World Cup*, "Catching a high ball in the thick of the penalty area on his thigh, he [Pelé] hooked it over his head, whirled round and volleyed mightily past Svensson." That goal propelled his team to a 5–2 victory and Brazil's first World Cup. In three consecutive games, Pelé had distinguished himself as one of the greatest soccer players in the world.

When the whistle sounded to end the game and the 1958 World Cup competition, Pelé and his teammates exploded into a state of ecstasy. They cried hysterically and laughed convulsively. The cumulative pressure, building like a smoldering volcano during the months of preparation, erupted in a spontaneous release of molten human passion. In the final three games of that World Cup event, Pelé had scored an unbelievable six goals while in a kind of trance-like state that we describe today as "being in the zone." At 17 years of age, Pelé had reached the top of the world. He later observed, "Seventeen is a marvelous age, but one which unfortunately ends after a mere 365 days."

From Hero to Target

When he returned to Brazil as World Cup champion, Pelé was a media sensation and a hero in his country, his town and among his kin. He was on his way to superstardom. Having savored the sweet taste of celebrity, he was committed mentally, emotionally, physically and spiritually to becoming a soccer star. During the 1958-season he was the top scorer with a total of 58 goals in 38 games in the São Paulo league and he scored 126 goals in all the matches he played that year.

By 1962, at 21 years of age, Pelé was recognized as the best soccer player in the world. As the 1962 World Cup competition approached, the world prepared to take on the reigning champions from Brazil and Pelé in particular. However, early in the World Cup tournament held in Chile, Pelé suffered a groin injury that kept him out of the final four games. The specter of injury that had terminated his father's career began to loom on the horizon as a potential threat to Pelé's career. In spite of the absence of their brightest star, the Brazilian team went on to win the World Cup and become two-time World Cup winners. Pelé's injury continued to keep him out of the action for two months after the World Cup, but his unrelenting tenacity helped him recover to become the top scorer in the São Paulo league with 37 goals.

Pelé continued to win the title as top scorer in 1963, 1964 and 1965. However, 1966 was to be an ignominious year for the Brazilian. As the 1966 World Cup approached, Brazil, having dominated world soccer for eight years, became the target for the slings and arrows of all opposing teams. England was hosting this tournament and there was widespread feeling among the Europeans that it was about time the Old World reclaimed the Cup from the New World. In the first game of the competition, it appeared that Zhechev of Bulgaria had set out to punish and possibly injure Pelé. In his own words (Pelé, p. 194), "Zhechev did everything he could to physically cripple me…My legs ached as a result of Zhechev's constant kicking and tripping." In spite of this abuse, Pelé scored a goal and Brazil beat Bulgaria 2–0. In their attempt to preserve Pelé for the later games, the coaching staff of the Brazilian team decided to have Pelé sit out the game against Hungary who was thought to offer little challenge. However, the fierce Hungarian team scored a remarkable 3–1 upset victory against the reigning champions. Brazil was facing elimination from the World Cup competition unless it could win the next game against Portugal by a substantial score.

The abuse that Pelé had suffered in the game against Bulgaria paled in comparison to the brutal attack launched by Morais of Portugal. With Brazil trailing Portugal 2–0, Pelé took possession and moved down the pitch. Morais ran toward Pelé and knocked him to the ground in what looked like a brutal attempt to injure him. Pelé staggered to his feet and resumed play only to be savagely knocked down and jumped upon by Morais. Pelé was injured and helped from the field. Portugal subsequently won 3–1. Pelé, physically injured and emotionally demoralized, resolved never again to play in a World Cup competition. He said to the press, "I don't want to finish my life as an invalid." Pelé had experienced the ugly side of superstar status–the viciousness of lesser adversaries who would destroy what they cannot equal.

The Indomitable Spirit

Time is a great healer of the body and the soul. In the three years following the disappointing 1966 World Cup, Pelé continued to be top scorer for the Santos team, an international ambassador and widely recognized as the best soccer player in the world. As the 1960s drew to a close, he was moving toward a personal milestone–his 1000th goal. Through the fall of 1969, attendance at Santos soccer games increased as expectant fans hoped to witness this epoch-making event. On November 14, Pelé scored goal number 999 and the stage was set for a drama even greater than Babe Ruth's 700th home run. However, it was several games before the 1000th goal would materialize. Finally on November 19, 80,000 rain-soaked fans, packed into the Maracanã stadium in Rio, to witness Pelé scoring his 1000th goal on a penalty kick. Although it was not the most spectacular goal he had ever executed, its effect was electrifying. In his autobiography, Pelé described the emotional scene (pp. 218–219):

> *The roar that rose from the crowd was almost enough to hold back the rain; the photographers and reporters mobbed me at once...they were joined almost at once by hundreds upon hundreds that poured from the stands, disregarding the police and raced across the wet grass to reach for me.*

It would seem that Pelé had reached the pinnacle of his career, but he wasn't about to rest on his laurels. As top scorer on the Santos team and world celebrity, he still had much to contribute, especially when the Jules Rimet

Trophy, awarded to the World Cup champions, was currently in the possession of the English team. No nation had ever won the World Cup three times. Pelé could not resist the temptation to secure this honor for Brazil. Possessed by that vision of the ultimate prize, he eagerly prepared for the 1970 World Cup competition to take place in Mexico.

In 1970 Brazil's national team was stronger than ever. Players like Rivelino, Tostao and Jairzinho were stars in their own right and together with Pelé represented a formidable challenge to anyone who dared covet the Jules Remit Trophy. However, the English team was reputed to be even stronger than the team that four years earlier had won the World Cup at Wembley. When Brazil confronted England, the spectators witnessed the battle of the titans. In the searing 98° heat, both teams put on a remarkable display of soccer that captured all the drama of a scripted thriller. Pelé's biographer wrote (Harris, pp. 111–112):

> *In the tenth minute Jairzinho accelerated past left back Cooper and raced to the line before delivering [a cross] straight towards Pelé. Pelé hurtled over Alan Mullery, and leaped to place a perfect header towards the bottom corner of the goal...[Pelé] was already shouting "Goal!" as Banks, distorting his body like a salmon leaping up a waterfall, threw himself into the air and managed to tip the ball so that it slid over the crossbar.*

This spectacular save by the goalie Gordon Banks denied Pelé a goal, but in another spectacular play (described earlier in this chapter) Pelé set up Jairzinho for the only goal of the game that ended in a 1–0 victory for Brazil. This victory eliminated England from the World Cup and cleared the way for Brazil to proceed with their conquest. In the matches that followed, Brazil defeated Romania 3–2 and Peru 4–2. En route to the final, Brazil met Uruguay, the nation that had dealt the devastating blow to Brazil in the 1950 World Cup exactly 20 years before. Though Uruguay took an early 1–0 lead, the Brazilians rallied later in the game and won by a score of 3–1. Pelé recalled (p. 243):

> *I could picture the excitement throughout all of Brazil at the victory, and particularly I could picture the excitement in Baurú. The Uruguayan defeat of 1950 had been avenged at last, and I was very happy to have been a member of the team that did it.*

In spite of this personal triumph, the defeat of the Uruguayans and the realization of a 20-year-old dream, the real climax to the World Cup was one game away–the final against Italy.

The final game took place in Mexico City in a packed stadium of 110,000 screaming fans. A case of nerves that had overwhelmed Pelé while en route to the game had been replaced with an inner calm. He was ready to enter into the zone and respond to his instincts. And, indeed, they served him well in the next 90 minutes. At the 17-minute mark of the game, Pelé opened the scoring with a brilliant header that he delivered by leaping above the heads of the defenders and steering it above the goalkeeper. Pandemonium erupted in the stadium. But it was not long until Italy tied the score, whipping the fans into a frenzy of emotional chaos. With the score tied 1–1, the Italian team adopted the defensive-style game that had become popular in Europe. Proponents of the defensive style argued that it was best to let the opposition come to you and stay vigilant for scoring opportunities. Pelé had always railed against the defensive approach, asserting on many occasions, "Aggressive, attacking football is the best." Unlike the Italians, the Brazilian team followed an unrelenting aggressive style, focusing intensely on advancing the ball to their opponent's goal. On this day, the aggressive approach prevailed. Pelé assisted on two more goals and Brazil beat Italy by a score of 4–1 to win the 1970 World Cup! To say that the fans were ecstatic would be a gross understatement. It would be impossible to describe the raw joy and rapture experienced by the Brazilian team. As the first nation to win three World Cup competitions, Brazil was given the Jules Rimet Trophy in perpetuity. The pain that Pelé and his countrymen had suffered twenty years prior had been avenged and Pelé was now at the zenith of his playing career.

A Time to Play and a Time to Die

In justifying his decision to retire from soccer, Pelé, borrowing from the Biblical Book of Ecclesiastes, explained (Pelé, p. 262), "…There is a time to be born and a time to die…I had been born into Selection football fourteen years before; now, in a way of speaking, it was time for my playing days with the national team to die." Pelé had spent a lot of time away from his family traveling to all parts of the world. He wanted to retire while still at the top of his game and pursue other interests including higher education. And so, on July 18, 1971, he played his final game for the Brazilian Selection against the former country of Yugoslavia at the Maracanã stadium in Rio. Throughout the game, the 180,000 fans in attendance yelled "Fica! Fica," meaning "Stay! Stay!" It was an emotional scene for Pelé and his fans and yet the superstar felt that it was, indeed, the right time to hang up his spikes and move on with his life. Pelé continued to play out his contract with Santos until October 2, 1974 when he interrupted the action in his final game to fall to his knees and thank his fans for their support.

Re-entering the Cosmos

During Pelé's playing years, he earned substantial sums of money from Santos and from endorsements. He invested this money in various properties, small businesses, a dairy farm, a trucking company, a radio station and a multitude of other enterprises. He had also signed guarantees for loans that several of these companies used to support their growth. When one of the companies went broke, Pelé was required to make good on debts in excess of $1,000,000 or declare bankruptcy. Refusing to renege on his loans, Pelé considered his alternatives. The only viable choice was to lace up his boots one more time and return to the soccer pitch. His most lucrative option was the New York Cosmos soccer team who offered him $4.5 million for a three-year contract–more than he had earned in all his years with Santos. In spite of his original reluctance to continue playing soccer, Pelé realized that this was the only solution to his financial conundrum. Furthermore, it would give him the opportunity to bring a higher profile to soccer in America where *football* meant something very different from *soccer*. Though America had a soccer league, it was an insignificant part of the athletic landscape in the United States. And so, on June 11, 1975 at age 34, Pelé signed the three-year contract with Warner Communications to play for the New York Cosmos team, plus an additional three years for commercial endorsements. Pelé insisted that the agreement contain a clause that exempted him from endorsing any products, such as alcohol or tobacco, that he could not recommend in good conscience.

Many Brazilians felt betrayed by Pelé's migration to America. To protect his status with his countrymen, Warner Communications sweetened his contract by including some special benefits for Brazil. Then a representative of the United States government announced that Pelé's presence in America would enhance relations between Brazil and the United States. These declarations helped mollify the concerns of the Brazilian government and Brazilians began to take pride in Pelé's role as an unofficial ambassador of their country.

Pelé's presence on the Cosmos squad brought an immediate spike in attendance from about 8000 to 25,000 fans during exhibition games. More players from Brazil were added to the team and by the end of Pelé's second year with Cosmos, the team had 16 wins to 8 losses and Pelé won the league's Most Valuable Player award. He was also awarded a 24-carat gold-encrusted soccer boot to commemorate his 1250th goal.

During 1976 the North American Soccer League (NASL) drew over 2 million fans. Jerry Kirshenbaum of *Sports Illustrated* wrote, "Pelé is not so much promoting U.S. soccer as exposing it." In 1977, the final year of Pelé's contract, the New York Cosmos played to capacity crowds of more than 76,000 during their successful march to the NASL championship. Pelé's final appearance on the soccer pitch took place in October, 1977. An exhibition game between Santos and Cosmos was played before 75,000 cheering fans and several hundred million television viewers in 38 nations around the globe. In his classic diplomatic style, Pelé played for Cosmos in the first half and Santos in the second. The game was an emotional farewell from the greatest player in the world to the fans he wished to thank, and the tumultuous cheers from the stands returned the intensity of devotion in kind. Following the game, Muhammad Ali (who would later come second only to Pelé in the International Olympic Committee's vote for Athlete of the Century) visited Pelé's dressing room. Ali cried with emotion as he hugged the world's greatest athlete and said, "My friend. My friend. Now there are two of the greatest."

Legacy

It is impossible to assess the magnitude and extent of Pelé's impact on the world. His receipt of the Athlete of the Century Award from the International Olympic Committee places him at the top of the athletic world, but his recognition by *Time Magazine* as one of the top twenty "Heroes and icons" of the 20th century, along with Princess Diana, Mother Teresa and Che Guevara, speaks volumes of his importance beyond the realm of athletics.

Pelé was himself surprised at the reception he received in his travel throughout the world. In describing his visit to Africa, he reported (p. 203):

Everywhere I went I was looked upon and treated as a god, almost certainly because I represented to the blacks in those countries what a black man could accomplish in a country where there was little racial prejudice, as well as providing physical evidence that a black man could become rich, even in a white man's country. To these people, who had little possibility of ever escaping the crushing poverty in which they found themselves, I somehow represented a ray of hope, however faint.

In 1967 a vicious civil war was raging as the state of Biafra struggled to gain its independence from Nigeria. Deep-seated hatreds offered no promise of agreement or common ground between the belligerent parties. However, one domain in which the warring sides could reach agreement was on their mutual respect for Pelé. In a historically unprecedented move, Nigeria and Biafra agreed to a two-day truce to enable both sides to watch Pelé play in an exhibition game.

When Pelé played in the 1970 World Cup in Guadalajara, the entire city shut down. Posters everywhere announced, "No work today, we are off to see Pelé." It seemed that the arrival of Pelé in virtually any city in Central or South America was sufficient cause to declare a national holiday.

In a Presidential tribute, thanking him for raising the profile of soccer in the United States and providing a role model of the highest caliber for young children, Jimmy Carter said, "Pelé has elevated the game of soccer to heights never before attained in America. Only Pelé, with his status, incomparable talent and beloved compassion, could have accomplished such a mission."

Even in his own country, Pelé was attributed demi-god status. Before reaching his 20th birthday, he had been offered $1 million to play in Italy. The Brazilian Congress convened an emergency session declaring that Pelé was a "non-exportable national treasure." This unprecedented political intervention spoke volumes about the regard in which Pelé was held. When he left Brazil to join the New York Cosmos team almost two decades later, Pelé set a major precedent. Today, the world's best soccer players are lured by huge financial inducements to the teams of those countries that covet their special talents. Many Brazilian players are at the front of the line.

The world's most widely revered athlete modeled exceptional soccer skills, but what made him great was something much more. It was an ability to enter the state of relaxed concentration where he could look at the soccer pitch "from above the fray" and instinctively sense a scoring opportunity. In his introduction to Pelé's autobiography, Robert Fish wrote (Harris, p. ix):

It has been suggested that there is a sort of built-in computer in Pelé's head that instantly corrects itself according to the constantly changing position of the ball on the field and the ever-different location of the other players, bringing him to the right place at the right time to make the most effective play. If so...there can be no doubt that if Pelé has that sort of built-in computer, the computer has been programmed with years of hard practice, by much grueling experience, and by a life of total dedication to the constant learning of his craft.

Amen.

Chapter 6

PRINCIPLE #6: BELIEVE IN YOURSELF

I'm the greatest. I'm the King of the World
            –Muhammad Ali (after defeating Sonny Liston)

What Research Says about Confidence

A study of Nobel Prize winners published in 2001 reported that optimism was by far the most important trait contributing to the success of these academic superstars–even more important than their professional skills. Why does confidence increase the odds of success? Renowned psychiatrist David Hawkins performed hundreds of experiments in which patients performed strength exercises while thinking positively. These results were compared with their performance while thinking negatively. On the basis of these experiments, Hawkins concluded, "Muscles strengthen and weaken from positive or negative stimuli." Similar results were discovered by John Diamond in his breakthrough work in kinesiology. For years it has been standard routine for weight lifters to rehearse mentally the *successful* completion of a lift before physically hoisting a heavy weight. The mental and physical components of any athletic movement seem to work in concert.

Recent studies show that we become as we think, based on our positive or negative energy. From optimistic excitement flows positive execution, while from pessimistic thought flows error-prone negative responses. When we believe, we can; when we question, we can't. In the words of self-help writer Lynn Grabhorn (p. 305):

Every time we think of anything, we're flowing positive or negative energy. The litany never changes; as we think, we feel; as we feel, we vibrate; as we vibrate, we attract. Then we get to live the results.

Similar results are found in the field of medicine. Eminent writer Anton Wilson wrote (p. 116):

Patients fed on a high dose of optimism statistically fare somewhat better than those fed only on grim pessimism. If a doctor expects the patient to get well, this has some effect on the patient; if the doctor expects the patient to die, this also has an effect.

Self-Efficacy–The Source of Confidence

Those who believe in themselves always have an edge over those who doubt. Those who sense they will succeed are far more able to achieve. Sports psychologists claim that belief must exceed doubt by at least 50 percent, otherwise performance is reduced by tentativeness. Psychologists have long preached the importance of a positive mental demeanor, no matter the discipline. British statesman Winston Churchill summed up this all-important factor in getting to the top when he said, "A pessimist sees the difficulty in every opportunity. An optimist sees the opportunity in every difficulty."

But what is the source of confidence and optimism? Those who rise to the pinnacle of their potential always have a sense of self that is greater than that of the also-rans. This strong sense of self is called *self-efficacy*. In Chapter 3, we met Babe Zaharias whose self-efficacy was often interpreted as arrogance (Cayleff, p. 127):

> *Old Babe's aggressive self-confidence shone through despite her attempts to appear more feminine. She told one reporter, [before the U.S. Western Open] "They may as well wrap up the cup and give it to me now, for I'm going to take it."*

Oscar Wilde, the great British dramatist, once told the media after his play had failed miserably in its debut, "The play was a great success. The audience was a failure." When a reporter jokingly asked Michael Jordan if he would consider running for the Presidency of the United States, he responded, "I've always had so much self-confidence, I think I could do it." Eminent psychologist Alfred Adler observed over a century ago, "Man's opinion of self influences all his psychological processes." Adler's assertion is given further validation today by psychologist Erik Ericson who noted, "Study after study has shown that children with superior intelligence but low self-esteem do poorly in school, while the children of average intelligence but high self-esteem can be unusually successful."

The origins of self-efficacy seem often to be rooted in early imprints –those dramatic experiences that reinforce the belief that we can succeed. In the previous chapters, we observed how the early imprinting experiences became springboards to success for several superheroes. Six-year-old Wilma Rudolph resolved to outrun all her friends when they ridiculed her crippled leg. Babe Zaharias became energized and driven to win after she won a marbles competition at age seven. And Pelé at age 10 vowed to hone his soccer skills so that he could avenge Uruguay's defeat of Brazil in the 1950 World Cup competition. Our formative years are the crucible in which our dreams and self-efficacy are ignited by early imprinting experiences.

Though most easily acquired in the formative years, self-efficacy can be developed later in life by practicing positive behaviors and building an inner sense of self-worth. One of the most powerful positive behaviors involves accepting responsibility for outcomes. When things go wrong, people with low self-efficacy attempt to fix the blame rather than fixing the problem. Fearing consequences of fault, they seek external causes to which they can attribute failure. This exonerates them from responsibility and enables them to retreat to the safe world of the passive innocent victim. Those with high-self-efficacy accept a causal link between what they do and the outcomes that result. Consequently, they take credit for their successes and responsibility for their failures. The credit they give themselves deepens their self-efficacy. The responsibility they accept for their failures provides them with precious opportunities to learn and improve.

When Is Confidence "Overconfidence"?

The superstar profiled in this chapter as the model of self-efficacy is none other than the Louisville Lip, Muhammad Ali. This superstar knew above all that those who believe are destined to win even when they are deluded in their belief. In his words, "To be a great champion you must believe you are the best. If you're not, pretend you are." In spite of this assertion, Ali understood that one must not allow confidence to erode one's efforts or preparation. He told the media, "They think I'm becoming overconfident, but I will never be so overconfident that it will interfere with my training."

When we dream big, we must accept that those around us will not share in our belief that we will realize our dreams. Merely announcing our grandiose intentions will cause those around us to regard our aspirations as overconfidence or arrogance. No one would have believed that little Wilma Rudolph with the shriveled leg would become the fastest woman in the world or that shoeless little Pelé would one day be voted Athlete of the Century by the International Olympic Committee. An article in the November 16, 2001 issue of *Investors' Business Daily* reported:

More than 500 studies have been conducted on the self-fulfilling prophecy that you will win when everyone else believes [you] will fail. This research doesn't show that people feel better, it shows that confidence–even misguided confidence–helps people perform better."

Any level of confidence is justified if it is supported by the psychological characteristics, such as passion, self-efficacy and tenacity, that are embodied in the thirteen principles in this book.

What We Learn from Bluebirds, Sparrows and Crows

A generation ago, many elementary schools in the United States grouped children according to their reading and math scores. The highest performers were placed in a group called "bluebirds" and given the most challenging reading and math resources. The intermediate performers constituted the "sparrows" who basked in the comfort of less challenging instruction. The underachievers, reflecting the regard in which they were held, were designated "the crows," and routinely assigned to remedial reading and math worksheets. (The group names varied with the distribution of ornithological species in the school district.) A study reported in the *Journal for Research in Mathematics* examined the self-esteem of the members of each group. Who do you think had the highest and lowest self-esteem? Think carefully before you answer.

Surprisingly, the highest self-esteem was not found throughout the bluebird group. Those with the highest self-esteem were those at the top of each group–the top percentiles of bluebirds, sparrows *and* crows. Conversely, those with the lowest self-esteem were at the bottom of these groups. Why was this so? Why would a bottom bluebird have a lower self-esteem than a top crow? Further investigation revealed that the children assessed themselves relative to other children in their group. Our self-esteem, it seems, depends on the reference group to which we compare ourselves. In the absence of an ambitious dream, most high sparrows, content with their sense of achievement, bask in the comfort of their status within their group and do not feel compelled to strive for the lower echelons of the bluebirds.

A recent study of 20,000 Americans from 1972 to 2002 revealed that people tend to measure their level of wealth relative to their friends and colleagues of the same age. Apparently those who earned less than their friends were dissatisfied with their financial status, while those who earned more than friends their age were satisfied with their level of wealth. The researchers at Harvard and Pennsylvania State University suggested (*National Post*, August 15, 2005, p. A1), "One alternative [to striving for more wealth] would be to 'hang out' with poor people."

In his best-selling book *The Human Zoo,* anthropologist Desmond Morris described how the social classes in our adult community function in a manner similar to the classroom groups (p. 55):

The recognition of distinct [social] classes has made it possible for the members of classes below the top one to strive for a more [satisfying] dominance status at their particular class level...A man at the top of his social class may earn more money than a man at the bottom of the class above. The rewards of being dominant at his own level may be such that he has no wish to abandon his class-tribe.

However, the path to excellence in any endeavor is to rise to the top of your reference group, and then use the self-affirmation of success to move upward to a less comfortable but more challenging reference group, until eventually you are competing with the very best. Pelé began as the best soccer player among a handful of neighborhood friends and grew to become the best player on the Ameriquinha team and then the Santos team, and ultimately the best player in the world.

When Muhammad Ali was training for his fight against Sonny Liston, he woke every morning to a poster of Liston that was hanging over his bed. He would growl at the menacing picture, "I'm gonna whup you, you big ugly bear." Ali used the poster of the reigning Heavyweight Champion of the World to motivate his daily workouts. (A poster of Woody Allen would not have had the same impact.) The ladder to success is a series of rungs, each more challenging than the one before. We must resist the tendency to settle into the comfort of a rung where modest challenge does not test our abilities or threaten our self-confidence. On the contrary, climbing the ladder of success requires that we scale a sequence of increasingly demanding rungs. The energy to meet this succession of challenges and resist a multitude of naysayers must come from a very strong self-efficacy.

The self-assessment instrument on the following pages will help you determine the extent to which you have developed your level of self-efficacy. As in the other instruments in this book, there are no right or wrong answers. To determine how much you may need to enhance your self-affirmation to achieve your goals, try to respond to the questions as honestly as you can.

SELF-EFFICACY SELF-ASSESSMENT–Can You Get the Job Done?

Choose a number 1–5 (where "1" means "strongly disagree" and "5" means "strongly agree") to indicate the degree to which the statement describes you. Record for each statement the number you have chosen. The scoring key is at the bottom of the page.

There are no "right" or "wrong" answers. In making your selection, be careful to answer the questions as candidly as possible without anticipating how you will be classified. This instrument is designed to give you insights into your self-efficacy.

	Strongly Disagree				Strongly Agree
1. When I make plans, I am certain I can make them work.	1	2	3	4	5
2. One of my problems is that I cannot get down to work.	1	2	3	4	5
3. If I can't do a job at first, I keep trying until I can.	1	2	3	4	5
4. I seldom achieve the important goals I set.	1	2	3	4	5
5. I give up on things before completing them.	1	2	3	4	5
6. I like to face difficulties head-on rather than postpone them.	1	2	3	4	5
7. If something looks too complicated, I don't bother to try it.	1	2	3	4	5
8. When I have an unpleasant task, I stick to it until I finish it.	1	2	3	4	5
9. When I decide to do something, I go right to work on it.	1	2	3	4	5
10. When trying to learn something new, I soon give up if I am not initially successful.	1	2	3	4	5
11. When unexpected problems occur, I don't handle them well.	1	2	3	4	5
12. I tend to procrastinate when I face a task that I don't enjoy.	1	2	3	4	5
13. I avoid learning new things that look too difficult for me.	1	2	3	4	5
14. Failure just makes me try harder.	1	2	3	4	5
15. I feel insecure about my ability to do things.	1	2	3	4	5
16. I am a self-reliant person.	1	2	3	4	5
17. I give up easily	1	2	3	4	5
18. People think of me as a person who gets the job done.	1	2	3	4	5
19. When I delegate a job, I fear it will not be done well.	1	2	3	4	5
20. I believe I could learn a new language in a year if necessary.	1	2	3	4	5

Instructions	Scoring Key
A. Total the numbers you chose for items: #1, 3, 6, 8, 9, 14, 16, 18, 19 and 20. B. Total the numbers you chose for items: #2, 4, 5, 7, 10, 11, 12, 13, 15 and 17. Subtract the B-total from the A-total.	**30–40:** Strong self-efficacy **17–29:** Moderate self-efficacy **4–16:** Low self-efficacy **Below 4:** Build your self-efficacy by setting modest goals and achieving them.

SELF-ESTEEM SELF-ASSESSMENT–How Do You Feel about Yourself?

Choose a number 1–5 to indicate the degree to which the statement describes you. Record for each statement the number you have chosen. The scoring key is at the bottom of the page.

	Strongly Disagree				Strongly Agree
1. I often feel superior to others.	1	2	3	4	5
2. I often feel inferior to others.	1	2	3	4	5
3. I often look in the mirror and like what I see.	1	2	3	4	5
4. I seldom feel guilty when I make mistakes.	1	2	3	4	5
5. I flagellate myself over errors that I shouldn't have made.	1	2	3	4	5
6. I tend to defer decisions to others who have more money or prestige.	1	2	3	4	5
7. I believe in my decisions, even when others don't.	1	2	3	4	5
8. I am often defensive about my work.	1	2	3	4	5
9. I feel free to express love, anger, joy and hostility.	1	2	3	4	5
10. I continually compare my self-worth with those who are more talented.	1	2	3	4	5
11. I pride myself on my ability to solve problems.	1	2	3	4	5
12. I tend to boast about my achievements and possessions.	1	2	3	4	5
13. I accept compliments easily without embarrassment or obligation.	1	2	3	4	5
14. I feel comfortable among strangers.	1	2	3	4	5
15. I find new assignments intimidating.	1	2	3	4	5
16. I often blame others for my mistakes or problems.	1	2	3	4	5
17. I prefer to accept responsibilty and proceed unsupervised.	1	2	3	4	5
18. I am a perfectionist in most everything I do.	1	2	3	4	5
19. I have an intense need for confirmation of my decisions before I act.	1	2	3	4	5
20. I believe my parents are (or were) proud of who I am.	1	2	3	4	5

Instructions	Scoring Key
A. Total the numbers you chose for items: #1, 3, 4, 7, 9, 11, 13, 14, 17 and 20. B. Total the numbers you chose for items: #2, 5, 6, 8, 10, 12, 15, 16, 18 and 19. Subtract the B-total from the A-total.	**30–40:** Strong self-esteem **17–29:** Moderate self-esteem **4–16:** Low self-esteem **Below 4:** Build your self-esteem by reassessing your strengths and abilities.

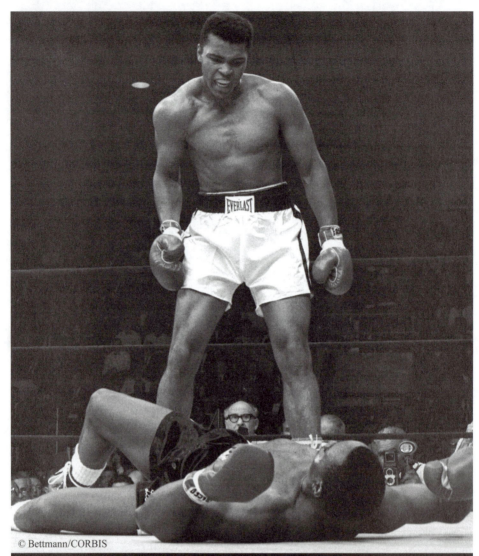

© Bettmann/CORBIS

MUHAMMAD ALI

- In 1999, named "Sportsman of the 20th Century" by *Sports Illustrated*.

- In 1988, the UN honored him with a Lifetime Achievement Award.

- In 1987, *Ring Magazine* named him "The #1 Heavyweight of all Time."

- Won the Heavyweight Championship three times: 1964, 1972 and 1978.

- Successfully defended the Heavyweight Championship 19 times.

- Won the gold medal in the 1960 Olympics in the Light-Heavyweight division.

Muhammad Ali: A Model of Self-Efficacy

Physical combat is the ultimate contest. In the animal kingdom it is the life-and-death struggle for dominance among males–a direct confrontation in which the vanquished loses the right to mate and sometimes the right to life. Boxing, its human derivative, is perhaps the only real contest of which all other competitive sports are sublimated, diluted variations. A boxer sprawled prostrate on the canvas suffers the humiliation of total defeat, witnessed by the millions who observe his

© Michael Brennan/CORBIS

Muhammad Ali
born Jan. 17, 1942

total helplessness at the hands of the victor. There are no teammates to share the shame and the loser lies impotent and nakedly alone. Muhammad Ali, boxing's greatest icon, once observed (Ali, p. 27):

> ...*when a fighter is beaten, everybody who believes in him is beaten too–his family, his friends, his children, the people who cheer him on, who give him their love, their hope, their pride...if I'm defeated I have to get up and come back again, no matter how humiliating the loss.*

It is a humiliation like no other. To risk a severe beating and possible injury takes courage. To risk both the punishment and the humiliation demands a level of courage that few possess.

When 22-year-old Cassius Clay entered the ring in the Miami Beach Convention Hall on February 25, 1964, few people believed he had even the remotest chance of lasting 15 rounds with bone-crushing Heavyweight Champion Sonny Liston. The reigning champion had demolished every opponent he encountered–most by knockouts in early rounds–and there was a growing consensus in the boxing world that Liston was unbeatable. To paraphrase a song of that era, Liston was "the baddest man in the whole damn town"–and possibly in the world. Sonny Liston was a 6-to-1 favorite and the odds were 3-to-1 that he would injure or kill his young and inexperienced challenger.

At the weigh-in ceremonies a few hours earlier, Clay had launched a verbal assault on the Champion. In a nose-to-nose confrontation that no one else would dare, he had taunted the brutal ex-convict, "I got yo' now, Sonny;

I got yo' championship now!" In an attempt to intimidate the champion, he lunged toward him yelling, "Let's git it on now!" but members of his entourage restrained him. The physical examination taken immediately after this verbal rampage revealed that Clay's blood pressure was 200/100–he was terrified and had psyched himself into a state of high anxiety for the contest of his life.

Now, just a few hours later he was entering the ring, a heavy underdog, and it was crunch time, literally. The earlier bravado had set up Cassius Clay for the greatest humiliation of his life. When the opening bell sounded, he sprung into action, dancing around the ring using his superior speed and agility to avoid Liston's deadly punches. To keep the menacing champion at bay, Clay fired quick left jabs at his head and followed with the occasional right cross. Unfazed, the champion plodded forward in a relentless attack, launching explosive punches that missed the elusive target and frustrated his attempts to land the killer blow. By the middle of the third round it was clear that the missed punches were taking a toll on the champion's energy reserve. His face showed some swelling from the challenger's left jabs and a cut had opened under his left eye. By the sixth round, Liston was showing the weariness of a cobra whose first few strikes had missed the mark. His punches were slower and his aim less controlled. Like the mongoose waiting its opportunity, Clay moved in for the kill, launching his best punches with reckless abandon. The impact of leather crashing against flesh resounded at ringside, deepening the cut under the champion's left eye and swelling the tissues of his face.

When the bell sounded for the start of the seventh round, the champion failed to respond. He had conceded. Cassius Clay leaped into the air and galloped around the ring like a man possessed, waving his arms and declaring his new status as Heavyweight Champion of the World. He screamed into the microphone at ringside, "I am the king! I am the king! King of the world!" To those who said he would lose he chided, "Eat your words! Eat your words!" He ordained himself *The Greatest*, but the media, irritated by his immodesty and self-aggrandizement, christened him with the monikers *The Louisville Lip* and *The Mouth*.

It would take almost a quarter century for the world to acknowledge that he was, indeed, the greatest. In a recent BBC poll conducted in Britain, he was voted sports personality of the century, ahead of such popular athletes as the beloved Pelé. What series of events catapulted this brash, young braggart from a poor black neighborhood in Louisville, Kentucky to the top of the athletic world where he became its most beloved icon? His story is a fascinating saga of courage, integrity and character mixed with all the dimensions of human drama. But above all, what emerges as the engine that drove his rise to the top was his deep sense of self that psychologists call self-efficacy.

Self-efficacy is not about self-promotion or personal visions of grandeur; it's about one's ability to stand alone–alone against an adversary, against public opinion, against the establishment and even against the world when those external agents conflict with one's inner beliefs. Cassius Clay, who later took the name Muhammad Ali, stood tall against white prejudice, against the mafia of the fight game, and ultimately against the U.S. Government. He was willing to suffer the consequences of his convictions and in many cases these were severe. Biographer Dr. Ferdie Pacheco observed (p. 46):

> *[Ali] emerges from any examination as a true individualist. There is only one Ali. He is unique. He is unico. If Frank Sinatra can sing "I Did It My Way," then Ali should have an opera dedicated to him. It should be entitled "The Greatest Fighter of All Time!"*

Muhammad Ali was one of the greatest fighters of all time, both inside and outside the ring. He fought for the values he held dear no matter the punishment. This is the true measure of self-efficacy. And that is why I have chosen him as the model of strong self-efficacy.

MUHAMMAD ALI'S TREK TO THE TOP

Early Imprints

Muhammad Ali entered the world as Cassius Marcellus Clay Jr. on January 17, 1942. His parents, Cassius Sr. and Odessa, provided a loving and nurturing environment for Cassius and his younger brother Rudy. Cassius Sr. was an artist who worked in paints and his mother supplemented the family income serving as a domestic for some of the wealthier families in Louisville. In that segregated society of the south, it was difficult for Cassius Sr. to get work from the wealthier white families. Consequently, money was scarce. The boys' clothes were of the second-hand variety garnered from Good Will. Ali later explained in his memoires that when there wasn't enough bus fare for both him and brother Rudy, he would race the bus to school. Rather than admit poverty, he would tell his friends that he was running to get in fight condition.

At age twelve, Cassius and childhood buddy Johnny Willis were caught in the rain. To stay dry, they parked their bikes outside and entered the Columbia Auditorium where the Louisville Home Show was under way. On their return, Cassius discovered that his new red Schwinn bike was gone. Devastated and angry, he complained to policeman Joe Martin that he was going "te whup" whoever stole his pride and joy. The officer suggested he prepare by training in the gym where aspiring boxers were working out. His first glimpse of the gym was a mesmerizing experience. His plan to avenge the bicycle theft immediately metamorphosed into a more exciting vision. Reflecting on his first impression, he said later, "I stood there, smelling the sweat and rubbing alcohol, and a feeling of awe came over me." At that moment, the passion of the young man who would become the greatest boxer in the world was ignited and a dream was in the making.

As he trained in the gym, Cassius began to idolize the local boxers who were making a name in the ring. Then, one day, on returning from a training session his dream crystallized. He wrote (p. 50):

> *I was 14 when I heard on the radio, "And still Heavyweight Champion of the World, Rocky Marciano." A cold chill shoots through my bones. I have never heard anything that affected me like those words…From that day on I want to hear that said about me.*

What followed in the next decades was a relentless dedication of time and energy that Cassius Clay committed to his climb toward the dream that gave him goose bumps.

An Early Hurdle

A psychological impediment stood between Cassius and his dream. In high school there was a bully who beat up Ali all the time and intimidated all the other kids in the neighborhood. The king of the street was Corky Baker, a tough gang leader who terrorized the neighborhood. In his autobiography Ali confessed that he always came out on the bottom in his scraps with Corky and felt that if he could beat Corky, then he could beat anyone in the world.

He knew it would be suicide to fight Corky on the streets because Corky had a "chest that burst through his T-shirt and arms like hams." In a fashion that was to become his trademark, Cassius began bragging that he could "whup" Corky if he ever got him in the ring. Predictably, Clay's boasts reached Corky who was so outraged that he had to be restrained from tearing apart his cocky adversary with his bare hands. Those who convinced Corky to save his mayhem for a confrontation in the ring were licking their chops at the prospect of collecting lucrative bets from the slaughter of a defenseless lamb.

The Cassius vs. Corky showdown had all the drama of the shootout at the O. K. Corral. It was a scheduled three-round fight, featured on *Tomorrow's Champions* and televised from the Columbia Gym, where crazed gym rats screamed for blood and salivated at the prospect of what mayhem Corky's unfettered hams could wreak on the face of the cocky youth. When the opening bell sounded, Corky rushed toward his opponent and exploded into action, throwing punches in all directions. Cassius leaned back and danced away so that Corky's powerful punches evaporated in space like misfired missiles. Then he rushed in, stung Corky with left jabs and moved back. It was in this fight that young Cassius learned the art of "dancing like a butterfly and stinging like a bee." By the second round an exhausted, frustrated and angry Corky conceded the match, claiming "It ain't fair." Years later, Ali said that this fight taught him "there is a science to making your opponent wear down."

The 1960 Olympics in Rome

Cassius Clay continued to train hard in the gym to move ever closer to attaining his dream. He strived relentlessly to build a body that could win him the Heavyweight Championship of the World. Reflecting on the thoroughbred horses he saw in his youth, he said that the sight of their beautifully sculpted muscles inspired him to train harder so his body could be in such condition.

By the time he was 18, Cassius had won 180 bouts. He captured the National Golden Gloves and the National Amateur Athletic Union titles in 1959 and again won the Golden Gloves Championship in 1960. During this period he was tall and lanky and fought as a light heavyweight. In this division he won six Kentucky State Golden Gloves titles, applying and perfecting his "float like a butterfly, sting like a bee" approach to boxing. Years later he reported that his father's loud and dramatic encouragement spurred him on and he described how his proud dad went around the neighborhood screaming, "I've got another Joe Louis!"

Cassius graduated 376 out of 391 in his class at Central High in Louisville when he was 18. Author David Remnick wrote (p. 95), "Clay's graduation was an act of generosity, the traditional debt of gratitude a school pays to its star athlete." Though never a dedicated student nor a high academic achiever, he exuded a kind of "street smart" that would enable him to survive the many horrendous challenges that lay ahead. Cassius was already a local boxing legend and about to become a celebrity on the international front at the Olympics.

When he represented the United States at the Olympic games in Rome, Cassius Clay was 18 years old and a man on a mission. Diligent training and a confident demeanor paid off handsomely and he won the Olympic gold medal in the light-heavyweight division. It was a heady time for this triumphant teenager who had fought his way out of a poor black neighborhood in the southern U.S. to the ancient center of civilization where gladiators battled for survival 2000 years earlier.

Cassius Marcellus Clay returned home to a hero's welcome. Crowds followed him everywhere he went, asking for his autograph, taking his picture and congratulating him on his success. He had become the All-American boy. The porch of his house was adorned with American flags, the steps were painted red, white and blue, and his father gathered with neighbors and sang *The Star-Spangled Banner*.

A short time after Cassius Clay had expressed this innocent patriotic emotion, racial prejudice was to rear its ugly head in a particularly odious form. Cassius and his friend Ronnie were riding their motorbikes in downtown Louisville when they decided to stop for hamburgers. Though this was a hangout for white motorcycle groups, Cassius assumed that his status as an American hero would enable them to be served. However, upon entering the restaurant, it was immediately apparent that they were in territory that was not only hostile but dangerous. A leather-jacketed motorcycle gang and their molls were spread over the booths like menacing black storm clouds. Their jackets displayed Nazi swastikas and confederate flags. The restaurant staff, anticipating trouble, beat a quiet, hasty retreat into the safety of the kitchen.

One waitress who had recognized the Olympic gold medallist was in the kitchen explaining to the boss that this customer was *the* Cassius Clay. The boss, in a loud resounding voice that reverberated through the restaurant, retorted, "I don't give a damn who he is…we don't serve niggers!" For one of the first times in his life, Cassius was speechless. Recognizing he was in a no-win situation, he resisted Ronnie's suggestion that they consider taking on the gang and instead moved toward the door. Ali said in his autobiography (p. 65), "I felt a peculiar, miserable pain in my head and stomach. The pain from punches you take without hitting back."

Once outside, Cassius and Ronnie were followed by the gang who began mounting their Harley-Davidson hogs. The gang leader with the moniker Frog called out some insults and then sent his toady named Kentucky Slim to extort tribute. The tribute was to be Cassius Clay's gold medal that he had worn around his neck since the Olympics and Frog wanted it as a "souvenir" for his girl friend. Cassius and Ronnie, refusing to comply with the request, mounted their motorbikes and departed with an insult to the purity of Frog's relationship with his mother. Reacting in a white-hot fury, fuelled by racial hatred, the gang launched a pursuit with murder in their eyes. Cassius knew that this lawless horde had previously attached black youths who had entered their neighborhood, whipping them with chains and leaving them maimed and close to death. Outnumbered and outgunned, the terrified youths fled for their lives.

What followed was a classic motorcycle chase–a flight for survival offering the fugitives the same odds as the fox in a foxhunt. Attempting to outfox his assailants, Cassius avoided the obvious escape route to the black neighborhood, pursuing a circuitous path through a labyrinth of railroad junctions and highways. His plan was to reach the Jefferson bridge that would take them from Kentucky into Indiana. The strategy seemed to work when the sound of the pursuing hogs faded and evaporated in the dismal rainy fog. However, upon approaching the bridge, they heard, Frog's girl friend cry, "There they is! There them niggers!" followed by Frog's excited exhortation, "You black bastard! We got yo' ass." As Frog's ominous machine came into view, a high-stakes race for the bridge ensued. Recognizing that Frog was preoccupied with unleashing his rage on Cassius, Ronnie told his companion to go ahead and he would follow. When Cassius reached the bridge, Ronnie was only seconds behind and Frog was closing in quickly from behind. As Frog came parallel to Ronnie, his focus and his rage were fixed exclusively on the Olympic hero. Whirling a chain above his head like a cowboy attempting to lasso a steer, he was about to unleash his fury when Ronnie jumped off his motorcycle and flung it into Frog's front wheel. In the crash that followed, Frog and his female passenger were slammed against one of the bridge's cement columns. Screams of pain were heard amidst the sounds of buckling metal and racing engines. As Frog and his girl friend lay injured and bleeding on the bridge, Kentucky Slim arrived on the scene whirling his chain in a second frontal assault. The vicious weapon missed Cassius' head, but wrapped its steel links around his shoulders. In a quick reflex action, Cassius seized the chain and yanked Frog's faithful sidekick from his motorcycle that took off into the mist like a riderless horse. Kentucky Slim came crashing to the ground. As Slim attempted to regain his upright position, the Olympic Gold Medalist launched a vicious punch that caught Slim flush in the face, sending him first to the ground and then into full retreat. Holding a switchblade to Frog's throat, Ronnie warded off the rest of the gang threatening to slit the throat of their leader unless they abandoned the struggle. A few passes of the knife through Frog's leather jacket opened cuts in the leather and in Frog that prompted him to order his gang to retreat. Following a brief tension-ridden standoff, the gang withdrew to the end of the bridge and then out of sight. Happy to escape with their lives, Frog and his girl friend struggled onto the crumpled motorcycle and fled the scene.

Once the gang had disappeared into the gray rainy evening, Cassius Clay drove his motorbike to the center of the bridge over the Ohio River. Realizing that winning the gold for America had not freed him from the tyranny of racism in his own country, he removed the ribbon with the gold medal from his neck and dropped it into the river. He said in his autobiography (p. 76):

> *The Olympic medal had been the most precious thing that had ever come to me. I worshiped it. It was proof of performance, status, a symbol of belonging, of being a part of a team, a country, a world. It was my way of redeeming myself with my teachers and schoolmates at Central High, of letting them know that although I had not won scholastic victories, there was something inside me capable of victory.*

Cassius Marcellus Clay, who had spent his youth learning techniques of boxing, was now learning about the bigger issues of life. In the process he was coming to discover who he was. Reflecting on this experience, he said, "Whatever illusions I'd built up in Rome as the All-American Boy were gone. I was back in my Old Kentucky Home."

Developing a Public Persona

Two months after the Olympics in Rome, Cassius Clay, no longer an innocent teenager from Kentucky, signed a contract with the Louisville Sponsoring Group and turned professional. Subsequently, Angelo Dundee took over as his manager and began training him for the big time. Under

Dundee, he quickly honed the fighting style that would revolutionize boxing technique. In his own words (p. 51):

I learn to put my head within hitting range, force my opponent to throw blows, then lean back and away, keeping eyes wide open so I can see everything, then sidestep, move to the right, or to the left, jab him again, then again, put my head back in hitting range. It takes a lot out of a fighter to throw punches that land in the thin air. When his best combinations hit nothing but space, it saps him.

While perfecting his fighting style, Cassius was also crafting his public persona. His overt proclamations that he was the greatest and the prettiest emerged as part of an act that was designed to build ticket sales, intimidate opponents and gain the publicity he needed to get a shot at the title. Prior to his becoming a major contender, Cassius Clay had seen the famous wrestler Gorgeous George performing in Las Vegas. He observed how this consummate showman, with his long blonde curls and outrageous self-serving claims, had whipped the fans into a frenzy. Then he watched as Gorgeous George proceeded to enter the ring and destroy his opponent to the "boos" and insults of thousands of hysterical fans yelling for his blood. Clay's biographer and ringside physician, Ferdie Pacheco, described how Gorgeous George took Cassius Clay aside after the show to give the young boxer some advice on showmanship (Pacheco, pp. 49–50):

You gotta have a gimmick, kid. You got your good looks, a great body; they tell me you can fight like a dream, and you can talk even better than you can fight. You've got your act; now you need to polish it. Always dress in white. White robe, trunks, and shoes. Especially white shoes...makes you look even faster, and it'll make the purists hate you...Now you've got a great mouth. Lots of people love your brash, cocky style, and a lot of people will pay to see someone shut your mouth with a leather glove. So, keep on bragging, keep on sassing...and always be outrageous.

The young Cassius Clay was quick to apply Gorgeous George's suggestions in the design of his own public personality. As Normal Mailer would write later, "He is America's greatest ego." Indeed, Clay was so successful in promoting this egomaniacal image that people lined up to buy tickets to see him taught a lesson in humility.

In his first two years as a professional, Cassius Clay won seventeen fights, almost all by knockouts. Normally, boxers needed to win a large number of professional fights to reach top contender status. Impatient to get a shot at the Heavyweight Champion Sonny Liston, however, Clay made outrageous claims that the champ was afraid to fight him. On one occasion he visited Liston's home in the middle of the night and woke up the neighborhood with his loud verbal challenges to the man he called "the ugly bear." He even left a large bear trap on his front lawn. The press reported the event and Clay continued to build momentum for a title fight.

To raise his profile as a heavyweight contender, Cassius was scheduled to fight Doug Jones in March 1963 in Madison Square Garden. In this Mecca of pugilism, he found his way in front of the cameras and on television, poetically predicting the round in which his opponent would meet his demise.

This served to heighten the fans' anticipation and increase the intensity of their desire to see the challenger get "whupped." Though he won the fight against Doug Jones in a split decision, it was a pyrrhic victory, because his prediction failed and sportswriters began to question whether Cassius Clay was a credible contender. Unfazed, Cassius said, "[The fans] booed me all the way to the dressing room and clutched at my robe. I had just made more enemies, and every one of them would find a way to see me fight again."

The next fight, Clay's first professional match abroad, was against British heavyweight champion Henry Cooper. On June 18, 1963, before a crowd of 55,000 screaming fans at Wembley Stadium in London, Cassius Clay adorned himself with a golden bejeweled crown and red robe that bore the inscription, "The Greatest" and was heralded by "royal" trumpets. In his usual poetic fashion, he predicted the demise of the British champion in five rounds, but nearly lost the fight in the third round when knocked down and almost out by a powerful left hook known as "Henry's hammer." He recovered to win the fight with a fifth-round victory, but had sustained another close call in his quest for a title fight. After the fight, he was visited by Sonny Liston's manager who said, "I've flown 3000 miles just to tell you Liston wants you…you've talked yourself into a title fight."

By capturing the interest of boxing fans and the media, Cassius Clay had won himself a shot at the title. However, the outrageous braggadocio that had become his external persona belied the deep inner strength and self-efficacy possessed by the young boxer. The true evidence of Cassius Clay's self-efficacy was only to emerge as his life unfolded, revealing the real character buried deep behind the mask.

A Black Muslim Heavyweight Champion

As Cassius Clay was preparing to fight for the Heavyweight Championship of the World, he met and befriended Muslim guru Elijah Muhammad. Muhammad introduced him to Malcolm X. They became fast friends, allied in their abiding hatred of the enslavement and exploitation of the black race by the whites. The message of hope for a better future through Islam claimed him and he decided to call himself Cassius X. Elijah christened him with the new name Muhammad (one worthy of praise) and Ali (most high). The transformation was complete. Cassius Clay, now Muhammad Ali, was no longer one to be controlled but one in control. Ali the Renegade was born and within a few years his views would be in conflict with those of the American Government and the majority of the American people.

The day before the championship fight that was to resolve the question once and for all as to who was world's heavyweight champion, Cassius Clay announced that he had joined the Nation of Islam and was now named Muhammad Ali. The fight promoters feared that an affiliation with a reputedly militant organization such as the Black Muslims would diminish Ali's image as the force of good against Liston's established underworld image as the force of evil. They vehemently opposed the announcement of Ali's affiliation at this time and threatened to cancel the fight that he had struggled long and hard to obtain. But Ali was prepared to risk it all and announced his conversion to the Nation of Islam, against the wishes of the fight promoters. This steadfastness in the face of such a devastating potential loss was an early indication of the strong self-efficacy that resided in the soul of this aspiring champion.

As noted earlier, Muhammad Ali shocked the world by defeating Liston in a titanic struggle that ended when Liston did not respond to the bell for round seven. Ali was less experienced, smaller and lighter but had outsmarted a stronger opponent. This would not be the last time that Ali's boxing style and instincts prevailed over the dictates of common practice. Even Ali was dumfounded at his remarkable upset victory. When commentator Howard Cosell climbed into the ring, Ali said, "I'm too fast. He was scared. I knew I had him in the first round. I shook up the world. I can't be beat." Though Liston had been regarded by the public as a thug with ties to the criminal element, Muhammad Ali now represented a more sinister threat. He was an avowed member of the Black Muslims, a religious sect associated with people like Malcolm X who preached hate and revenge against the "white oppressors." Ali's allegiance to the Black Muslims touched off a maelstrom of outrage among the American citizenry. In the good-guy/bad-guy scenario of the fight game, it appeared that there was no good guy with whom the fans could identify. Boxing was facing a crisis and the Black Muslim known as Muhammad Ali was becoming an icon for black defiance in America.

In the year following his victorious title match, Ali took advantage of a brief hiatus in his fighting schedule to flee the vitriolic controversy and visit his ancestral roots in Africa. He visited several African countries, chatting with the people and developing a sense of kinship with his contemporaries on that continent. Though Ali often had railed against the sins and atrocities of the white man against the blacks, the sect of Black Muslims to which he belonged preached pacifism rather than militancy. Muhammad Ali was apparently promoting self-efficacy for all. He was subscribing to a religion that he believed recognized the personal self-worth of all individuals, regardless of race, skin color or political affiliation. Though raised as a Christian, his disillusionment with all establishments, especially those founded by whites, had caused him to seek alternatives.

Ali's Most Formidable Adversary

As Heavyweight Champion of the World, Muhammad Ali fought many powerful contenders. In the three years after his victory in 1964, he successfully defended his title against all comers. In his rematch against Sonny Liston in May 1965, he won in a first-round knock out. But none of his adversaries was more formidable than the Government of the United States. It was early 1967 when he received a letter from Uncle Sam demanding that he appear before the draft board for induction into the army. The United States was at war with Vietnam and he was called into service.

Ali's recent conversion to the Black Muslim religion carried with it a commitment to pacifism. Though this position may have seemed inconsistent with his profession as a boxer, Ali insisted that he was not prepared to go to war for his country. He described the war in Vietnam as white men sending black men to kill yellow men. In response to public criticism for his stance on the draft, he said (Halberstam, 1999, p. 13), "The newspapers say either I go to jail or go to the Army. There is another alternative and that is justice." He told the media, "Man, I ain't got no quarrel with them Vietcong."

When Ali's comments were reported in the press, reprisals were swift and widespread. Hate mail, threats and angry telephone calls poured in. There were, however, some calls of support. One elderly gentleman who called from

England asked Muhammad Ali whether he had been quoted correctly. To the delight of the old man, Ali assured him that the quote was correct and that he was intending to stand firm. The old man chortled approval and the two established an immediate rapport. Ali suggested that he might be coming to England to fight Henry Cooper again and asked the old gentleman whom he would bet on? When the old fellow diplomatically answered, "Henry's capable, you know, but I would bet on you," Ali responded facetiously, "You're not a dumb as you look," and offered him a ringside seat if he were able to attend.

When Muhammad Ali fought Henry Cooper on May 21, 1966, the old gentleman was not at ringside to see Ali win by a knockout in the sixth round. However they continued to exchange cards and notes as pen pals separated by an ocean and two generations. A year or two after the initial contact, Ali was thumbing through a *World Book Encyclopedia* when he came upon a picture of a man with the same name as his pen pal in England. The man was described as one of the greatest mathematicians and philosophers of the 20th century. Ali was horrified to realize that this was the very person to whom he had addressed the flippant comment, "You're not as dumb as you look." He penned a quick letter of apology to which he received a response indicating that the old gentleman had enjoyed the remark. A short time later, Ali sent a letter to the old gentleman expressing the desire to visit him on a trip to England if the draft refusal did not result in a confiscation of his passport. Ali received the following response:

I have read your letter with the greatest admiration and personal respect. In the coming months there is no doubt that the men who rule Washington will try to damage you in every way open to them, but I am sure you know that you spoke for your people and for the oppressed everywhere in the courageous defiance of American power. They will try to break you because you are a symbol of a force they are unable to destroy, namely, the aroused consciousness of a whole people determined no longer to be butchered and debased with fear and oppression. You have my whole-hearted support. Call me when you come to England.

Yours sincerely,
Bertrand Russell

On April 28, 1967, Ali was ordered to appear at the draft board for induction. When he refused, he was stripped of his title and the State Athletic Commissions across the country revoked his boxing license. On May 8, he was indicted by a federal grand jury in Houston, Texas and released on $5000 bail on the condition that he not travel outside the United States. (When Ali eventually made it to England to see Russell, he was too late; the old philosopher had died.) The case went to trial the following year; Ali was convicted and given a five-year prison sentence. He managed to stay out of prison by launching an appeal, but the protracted appeals process was draining his financial resources as his precious boxing years were wasting away. Already a pariah for his Black Muslim affiliation, Ali was now regarded as unpatriotic and un-American. His refusal to be inducted had insulted those in the military as well as those who had fought in previous wars for a free America. Public outrage against him had reached gargantuan proportions and hate letters, including death threats, flooded his mailbox. Furthermore, Elijah Muhammad excommunicated Ali from the Nation of Islam for disobeying some edict of that sect. With the prison term hanging over his head, diminishing financial resources and no prospect of re-entering the ring, Muhammad Ali was approaching the nadir of his life. Surviving such an ordeal would be the ultimate test of his mettle.

Returning from Exile

As America moved from the 1960s to the 1970s, the tide of public opinion on the Vietnam War was beginning to shift. Nightly television broadcasts of brutal battles in which Vietnamese villages were torched and soldiers on both sides were seen to be suffering horrendous mutilations and death began to undermine public support for this conflict. Students protesting the war were conducting sit-ins on college campuses. The Watergate scandal had shaken American confidence in its institutions and public opinion was turning to support withdrawal from the Asian conflict. Then in June of 1970, the Supreme Court unanimously reversed its decision and Muhammad Ali became a free man–an event he regarded as his greatest victory.

Ali's enforced absence from the ring had spanned a period of more than three years–critical years when he would have been at the peak of his youth and vigor. Now those years and that vitality were lost forever. When he met the reigning champion "Smokin" Joe Frazier at Madison Square Garden on March 8, 1971, Ali was no longer the young tiger he had been. He was closing in on age 30 and his punches had lost some of their speed and power. Frazier beat him in fifteen rounds in a punishing contest that left both fighters looking as though they had been puréed in a giant blender. It was Muhammad Ali's first professional defeat. When asked how it felt to lose, he responded, "Naked...cold...It's not just the blows, it's all them witnesses. Everybody watching you. You sinking...and they roar *him* on."

After his loss to Joe Frazier, Ali realized that his climb back to supremacy, if at all possible, would be long and arduous. Age was taking a toll, but inactivity had exacted an even higher price. If he quit now, he would be remembered as a charismatic boxer who was Heavyweight Champion for three years–a boxer who had defended his title against a lot of second-rate fighters but who was untested in his ability to give or take powerful punches. Reaching from the depths of his resolve, Muhammad Ali decided to pick himself up off the canvas and once again immerse himself in the rigorous training that had brought him to the top of the world. During 1971 and 1972, he fought no fewer than 20 matches, including some exhibition fights and regularly scheduled fights against such heavyweight contenders as Jimmy Ellis, Buster Mathis, George Chuvalo, Jerry Quarry, Floyd Patterson and Joe Bugner. He won all of these bouts, most by knockouts. He was moving ever closer to a title fight when he met Ken Norton on March 31, 1973, at the Sports Arena in San Diego, California.

The fight against Norton was to be a crossroad in Ali's career. Ken Norton was a young, well-muscled ex-marine who was not considered a serious contender for the heavyweight title. This was expected to be an easy victory that would move Ali one step closer to a rematch with Joe Frazier for the title. However, Norton turned out to be a much stronger adversary than anyone had anticipated. In the second round, he unleashed a devastating blow that Ali later described in vivid detail (p. 20):

I think back to the second round when Norton got in through my guard and crashed a left up against my jaw. I know exactly when the blow came. I felt a snap and a sudden gush of blood in my throat. When I come back to my corner I ask Bundini and Angelo [his trainer] "How can you tell when your jaw is broke?"

"When you open it like this"–Bundini demonstrates–"and it clacks, it's broke."

I open it and hear the clack. A sharp pain goes around my face. I spit the blood trickling down my throat into the bucket and wash out my mouth, but more comes gushing in.

"If it's broke," Bundini is saying, "we've got to stop the fight."

But he knows I won't stop. There are thirteen more rounds to go, and I can win.

Realizing that Ali's jaw was broken, his ringside physician, Ferdie Pacheco, recommended that the fight be stopped. But Ali insisted on continuing and his manager, Herbert Muhammad acquiesced. In his biography of Muhammad Ali, Pacheco recalled (p. 114):

Ali lost a close decision in 12 rounds. His pain was excruciating. A jaw fracture is by its very nature painful; imagine being hit on the jaw by a powerful puncher for ten rounds. My admiration for Ali jumped 100 percent on that hot, painful day.

After the fight, Ali made no excuses. He accepted the defeat and graciously acknowledged, "Norton whupped me." However, the loss was devastating for him. Many of those who had believed that Ali would make a comeback were now convinced that he was a has-been. They quickly shifted their allegiance to Norton. The morning after the fight, one of Ali's entourage reported, "Howard Cosell is predicting you're finished. He's saying that three and a half years' exile took too much out of you…Only yesterday he was saying how great you are." Ali was stoic in his response. He had learned that public opinion runs with a winner and shifts its loyalty with a change in the wind. However, his sense of self was too strong to acquiesce to the judgments of others. Within six months, Ali fought a rematch against Norton. This time he was in top shape and won a 12-round decision by enough of a margin to indicate that he was back in the hunt for a title fight. There remained one man who stood between Ali and his shot at the title–his nemesis, Smokin' Joe.

On January 28, 1974, just four months after defeating Ken Norton, Ali was fighting his rematch against the only other man to have defeated him, Joe Frazier. Frazier was no longer champion, having lost his title to George Foreman–a formidable bone-crushing fighter who had won the gold medal at the 1968 Olympics in the heavyweight division. Ali had to win his rematch against Frazier if he were to retain any hope of regaining the heavyweight title. The rematch was relatively even, although it was clear that Ali out-pointed Frazier and consequently won a 12-round decision. Ali had avenged the defeats he had suffered at the hands of Norton and Frazier.

The Rumble in the Jungle

Muhammad Ali's unrelenting quest for a title fight against the reigning heavyweight champion George Foreman was now coming to fruition. In an attempt to bring the country of Zaire into the public consciousness, its President, Mobutu Sese Seko, invested $10 million in a title fight between the Heavyweight Champion George Foreman and challenger Muhammad Ali. This contest, featuring two Afro-Americans in Africa, was soon dubbed the "Rumble in the Jungle." A highly publicized affair, it captured the imagination of fans on all continents and promised to become one of the most widely watched events in the history of sport.

However, logistical problems threatened to terminate the entire event in the early stages. Posters bearing the slogan, "From the slave ship to the championship" were displayed to build solidarity between American and African blacks, but they were quickly banned by a Zaire official who stated, "We are the winners of that struggle. We sold the slaves and stayed in Africa. You were the slaves and were sent to America." The complicity of the Africans in the slave trade had been overlooked by some racist pundits in America who wished to portray the whites as the only devils of history. Ali himself came perilously close to terminating the event when he admonished reporters in the American press to take him seriously or they would be cooked and eaten by Mobutu's people when they arrived in Africa. A hostile telephone call from Zaire's Foreign Minister put a stop to all references to cannibalistic behavior.

After postponements, delays and threats of termination, the much-anticipated event finally took place on October 30, 1974 in Kinshasa, Zaire. Ali was facing the most formidable opponent of his career. The 26-year-old Foreman was bigger, stronger and younger than his 32-year-old challenger. Foreman had scored two-round knock outs against Joe Frazier and Ken Norton–the two men who had beaten Ali. In 40 professional fights spanning a period of three years, no opponent had lasted more than three rounds against him. Boxing experts and sportscasters were in general agreement that Foreman had the most powerful punch in the history of heavyweight boxing. He was not only awesome; he was virtually unbeatable.

How could Ali possibly hope to stay with him for 15 rounds? It was expected that Ali would back pedal around the ring, avoiding the champion until he tired, and then move in for the kill. However, at the opening bell Ali surprised everyone, including the champ, by rushing toward him and launching a quick left jab to his head. Then relying on his own greater speed, Ali hit and ran, hit and ran and attempted to outbox his stronger adversary. Attempting to conserve his own strength, he used the ropes to help him bounce around and avoid most of Foreman's powerful punches–a technique he later called his "rope-a-dope." By the eighth round Foreman was too tired to defend himself and Ali knocked him out. Foreman later admitted (Mann, p. 119), "Muhammad amazed me; I'll admit it. He outthought me; he outfought me. That night Ali was just the better man in the ring" Reflecting on his decision to risk a knockout punch on George Foreman, Ali said, (p. 412):

If the price of winning is to be a broken jaw, a smashed nose, a cracked skull, a disfigured face, you pay it if you want to be King of the Heavyweights. If you want to wear the crown, you can play it careful only until you meet a man who will die before he lets you win. Then you have to lay it all on the line or back down and be damned forever.

It was a modern-day version of Macbeth's last stand against the adversary who had come to slay him, "Lay on, Macduff, and damned be him who first cries, Hold! Enough!"

The Thrilla' in Manilla

With his defeat of George Foreman, Muhammad Ali had regained his title as Heavyweight Champion of the World. He was back on top–almost eight years since he was stripped of his title for refusing the draft. In the year that followed, he defended his title against Chuck Wepner and Ron Lyle whom he knocked out, and Joe Bugner against whom he won a decision. But the real test of his title was his rematch against Joe Frazier. He called it the Thrilla' in Manila, because it was situated in the capital city of the Philippines. Ali and Frazier had each won once in their two confrontations; this was to be the match to decide who was the better fighter. But it was more. Pre-fight animosity between the two fighters suggested that this was also a "grudge match." Ali had taunted and attempted to humiliate Frazier in pre-fight rhetoric and both fighters came to the match ready for war.

The fight was boxing at its most dramatic. Both fighters delivered and received crushing punishment that tested the limits of human endurance. Ali dominated in the early rounds, then Frazier dominated. Finally, Ali scored a knockout in round 14 when Frazier's blurred vision in one eye prompted his manager to throw in the towel. It was the most punishment Ali had ever sustained in a fight and he later said to his trainer, Angelo Dundee, "This is the closest I've come to dying."

While in Manila, Ali was accompanied by his mistress, Veronica Porsch. Though he was still married to second wife Belinda with whom he had four children, his feelings of invincibility had made him feel somewhat impervious to consequences. During an interview with President Marcos, the Philippine President spoke of Ali's lovely wife (referring to Veronica) on live television. A subsequent article about the Thrilla' in Manila that referred to Ali's "other wife" was the trigger that led to Belinda's suing for divorce. The strong ego that had served Ali so well in all his conflicts would also be his undoing. It is yet another example of the adage, "What makes us is often what breaks us."

The Final Round

The Thrilla' in Manila marked the peak of Muhammad Ali's career–a time when he had proved that he was a real champion and arguably the best heavyweight boxer who had ever lived. Even more, he was an icon not only for black equality but for individual freedom against the establishment. It was the ideal time for the champ to retire and use his celebrity to promote worthy causes. However, a reluctance to sit on the sidelines and a strong ego impelled Ali to postpone retirement plans for just a little longer. Through 1976 and 1977, he defended his title against several contenders, mostly of the second-rate variety. In spite of this, his victories were less decisive than in the past. Finally, his close 15-round decision against Earnie Shavers at Madison Square Garden on September 29, 1977 convinced Ali's supporters that it was time for the old pro to hang up his gloves. Resigning as Ali's physician, Ferdie Pacheco announced that Ali had suffered kidney damage from the body punches. He had also sustained serious damage to his legs a year earlier in his exhibition bout with Japanese wrestler Antonio Inoki.

In spite of all the pressure to retire, Ali pressed on. He agreed to fight Leon Spinks, a relatively undisciplined 24-year-old Olympic gold medal winner who had only five professional fights to his credit. It was not expected that he would offer much challenge to Ali, but the champ's passion for winning and maintaining a rigorous training regimen had faded. He entered the ring as a listless shadow of his former self. Spinks won the title in a 15-round decision. However, Ali's reluctance to be second to anyone led to a rematch exactly six months later, when he regained the Heavyweight title for the third time in his career–a feat never achieved before or since. Ali lost the title for the last time to his former sparring partner Larry Holmes on October 2, 1980. It had been a great run but Ali's fuel tank was running low. A year later, on December 11, 1981, Ali hung up the gloves for good after a humiliating defeat by Trevor Berbick in Nassau in the Bahamas. He was almost 40 years of age and had been a professional fighter for more than half his life.

Just five years after his last boxing bout, Ali was diagnosed with Parkinson's disease. General consensus is that the disease, sometimes referred to as "fighter's Parkinson's," is the result of cumulative damage to the middle brain from punches to the head over a prolonged period of time. Ferdie Pacheco described Ali's demeanor when the former champ was 50 years old (p. 45):

> *[Ali's] chatterbox, rapid-fire doggerel [is] no longer delivered in an electric voice, but spoken in a deep rumble, slowly and hesitantly. The animated, childlike, gleeful, mischievous face of the young champion is now round and flat, emotionless, the facial nerves no longer transmitting their rapid orders to muscles that then translate them to expression...What a ghastly price to pay for staying "on" too long, for pleasing the public, for giving it, and all of us what we wanted: the Ali Circus to ride on forever. We thought he would never grow old, would never slow down, would never stop being fun–would never stop being Ali.*

Legacy

In 1987 *Ring Magazine* ranked Ali the #1 heavyweight of all time. In 1988 the United Nations honored him with the Lifetime Achievement Award. Then in 1999 *Sports Illustrated* saw fit to name him Sportsman of the 20th Century. Muhammad Ali was to boxing what Ruth, Gretzky and Jordan were to their sports. He dominated the ring for so long that his name became synonymous with boxing.

However, Muhammad Ali has been eulogized not only for his prowess in the ring but as much for his defiance of others who might decide for him what he could or could not do. Standing alone when you are outnumbered, outgunned and outrageous demands self-efficacy of the highest order. But bragging, self-promoting and taunting non-supporters until they wish to see you pummeled to the canvas takes self-efficacy to an entirely new level.

When Howard Cosell taunted Ali about his braggadocio, he retorted, "I don't think it's bragging to say I'm something special." Indeed, he was someone very special and his recognition of this enabled him to achieve at levels beyond what most humans ever dream. The values in our culture have been strongly influenced by religious teaching that would have us believe we are unworthy and that pride is a sin. Yet pride in oneself is the cornerstone of high achievement. Great things are not achieved by those with low self-esteem. Pride only becomes a liability when it clouds our vision of reality and overrides our better judgment. It was a strong self-efficacy that enabled Muhammad Ali to challenge the establishment. When the draft board told him that he had no choice but to fight against a cause that was not his, he declined, saying, "I don't have to be who you want me to be." Did he pay a price for such audacity? You bet he did. But in the long run he became an icon for those who stand firm against institutional decree and deal with the consequences.

Muhammad Ali appeared at the right time for his role as a lightening rod of defiance against a world grown too tight and too controlling. The turbulence of the '60s proved to be his time to fight both the system and his opponents. He appeared on the scene during that era when people said no and "tuned in, turned on, and dropped out"; when Tim Leary and Fritz Perls were the darlings of rebellious intellectual set. Cassius Clay had grown up in a southern city where racial discrimination was deeply ingrained in the culture, a place where he was told where he could eat and where he could go to school. He, like millions of others, said no. He tuned in to an inner sense of his being and turned on to his own religious and cultural belief in Islam. Rejecting his name "Cassius Clay" as the slave name of his ancestors, he embraced the Black Muslim religion and took on the name Muhammad Ali. His contribution to the fight for equal rights was acknowledged by Howard Cosell (Mann, p. 85):

Muhammad Ali is transcendental to sport. He's important to the history of this country because his entire life is an index to the bigotry lodged deep within the wellspring of this nation and its people. Ali had the advantage of coming in the 1960s. That time period was incredible, and Ali understood it; he was at the heart of it; he helped shape it all.

Few athletes walk on to the field of battle with the brashness of Muhammad Ali. Long before he was the king of the ring, Ali was telling all who would listen "*I am the Greatest.*" That mentality went a long way towards beating opponents who were physically superior, or later in his career, who were years younger. Both George Foreman and Joe Frazier had superior skills but Ali believed in himself, and that belief took him beyond his limits. In his autobiography, Ali commented (p. 363):

Champions are made from something they have deep inside them–a desire, a dream, a vision. They have to have last-minute stamina, they have to be a little faster, they have to have the skill and the will. But the will must be stronger than the skill. Many fighters have lost to less skillful opponents who had the will to win, who were determined to keep going.

Chapter 7

PRINCIPLE #7: MAKE 'EM PLAY YOUR GAME

Control your destiny or have it controlled.
–Martina Navratilova

Exploit Your Opponent's Weakness

Exploit your opponent's weakness and it is less likely that yours will be exploited. That is the mantra for superior athletes. In the previous chapter, we saw how Muhammad Ali used his superior speed and conditioning to make his opponents chase him and when they tired he moved in for the kill. If you play against a tennis player like Andy Roddick who has a phenomenal forehand, it is pure insanity to hit the ball to that strength. Make him beat you with his backhand. If he does, hats off to him. He is the superior player. But allowing him to annihilate you with that forehand is inexcusable. The moral here is to always exploit an opponent's weakness and make sure you are not beaten by your own.

This principle, though applicable to all life's challenges, is particularly evident in athletics. When an athlete attacks her opponent's weakness, the opponent must either play through that weakness or lose. Amateurs and even some professional tennis players can be seen running around their backhands–their weakness–to hit a forehand. If the adversary can force them to do what they don't like or can't do, the contest is altered mentally and the outcome is weighted in favor of the aggressor.

In any business or sport it is imperative to discover your adversary's strengths and weaknesses. Focus on a weakness and attack it mercilessly. Those who do this, begin winning matches previously lost. Never go to the mat with a Sumo wrestler. If your adversary is bigger and stronger than you, your only alternative is to use your superior speed or agility to make him play your game, as Ali did with his so-called a "rope-a-dope" strategy. To make 'em play your game, use your strength to attack their weakness. This is the law of the jungle and it is paramount in the athletic and business domains.

A Strong Internal Locus of Control Is Key

A study of middle-level executives conducted in the 1990s divided the executives into two categories based on appraisals by their colleagues. Those who were seen to be successful and likely to move upward in the hierarchy were deemed "proactive." Those judged to be static and unlikely prospects for promotion were deemed to be "reactive." Both groups were given extensive questionnaires that probed their attitudes and beliefs. These revealed that the reactive group placed much greater emphasis on luck as a factor of success and believed that advancement and recognition were less correlated with competence and effort than the proactive group did. In short, those who were on the way up were much more committed to the belief that there is a causal link between effort and success, while those who were static tended to believe that success is a rather fortuitous outcome related to factors beyond individual control. Out of such psychological experiments the concept of "locus of control" has emerged. Those who believe that their success or failure is a direct consequence of their own actions are said to have a *strong internal locus of control*. Conversely, those who believe that the things that happen to them derive from circumstances beyond their control are said to have an *external locus of control*.

It is virtually impossible to achieve at a high level if you believe that the results you achieve are only loosely linked to your efforts. In fact, it may be tautological to assert that a strong internal locus of control is a necessary condition for success in the competitive arena. Charles Garfield, a Berkeley researcher in charge of training the early astronauts and Olympic athletes, wrote in *Peak Performance* (p. 29), "Peak performers have a high [internal] locus of control." Garfield found that the superstars envisioned the results they wanted and then proceeded to achieve it. He further observed (p. 144), "The one item that stands out most clearly among our peak performers is their virtually unassailable belief in the likelihood of their success. Their track records reinforce their beliefs."

Locus of Control–Are You an Internal or an External?

Many people wander through life reacting to circumstances around them without the slightest inkling that they can make things happen. They wake up in their mid-forties wondering how they ended up in a particular quandary, without having achieved any of their youthful ambitions. In many cases, they have put one foot in front of the other, day after day, satisfying the expectations of a parent, spouse, boss or coach. The fleeting days quickly rolled into weeks, months and years that soon became decades. One such victim captured this syndrome on a bumper sticker that read, "I reached middle age before I discovered that life is a do-it-yourself kit." Such people go through life in a reactive rather than a proactive stance. They tend to believe that the things that happen to them and the situations in which they find themselves are determined by external factors, i.e., factors such as luck and happenstance that are outside their control. For this reason, such people are said to have an *external locus of control* and will be referred to as *Externals*.

Others, whom I call *Internals*, generally have a proactive rather than reactive disposition. They believe that their successes and failures are very much within their control and are direct consequences of their own actions. Internals, said to have a strong *internal locus of control*, are the people who make things happen. They are highly motivated to work hard at achieving their goals because they believe that there is a causal relationship between their effort and results. Research into the behavior traits of Internals reveals that they:

• tend to postpone immediate gratification to achieve long-term goals;
• are better able to resist coercion;
• have a greater tolerance for ambiguity;
• prefer calculated risks to gambles against the odds;
• prefer games of skill to games of chance.

What Does Research Tell Us about Locus of Control?

Research has found that Internals are significantly more resistant to allowing authority figures to dictate life choices than are Externals. Renegades like Thorpe, Ruth, Zaharias, and Ali, whom we studied in earlier chapters, all had a strong internal locus of control and fought opponents and the establishment with passionate vigor. Martina Navratilova, who became the model of the consummate Internal, never allowed anyone, including the government or her lovers, to control her game or her life.

One study that investigated the concept of locus of control divided a class of elementary school students into two groups of equal number. Those perceived to be Internals were placed in one group and those perceived to be Externals in the other. All students were asked to toss beanbags through a hole in a board. Each beanbag tossed through the hole earned the student 25 points if thrown from 10 feet away and 100 points if thrown from a distance of 40 feet. The holes were of a size that made success highly probable from 10 feet but quite improbable from 40 feet. Each student was to toss beanbags until she scored a total of 300 points. The student who achieved this in the shortest time would be the winner. From what distance, 10 feet or 40 feet, do you think the Internals tossed the beanbags?

One might expect that the Internals, confident in their ability to succeed, would set themselves the greater challenge and toss the beanbags from the greater distance. However, almost all of the Internals realized that tossing a beanbag from a 40-foot distance was a low percentage proposition. Preferring to exercise maximum control, they chose to lob the beanbags in rapid succession from the closer distance, quickly accumulating a total of 300 points in 25-point increments. It was the Externals who tossed the beanbags from the greater distance, expecting that factors such as luck might win them 300 points in three 100-point bonanzas. This behavior resembled that of the person who bets everything on a long shot, hoping that good luck will bring good fortune. In short, the Internals *try* to make things happen while the Externals *hope* things will happen.

Psychologists have found that 80 percent of all great entrepreneurs, such as Bill Gates, founder of Microsoft or Jeff Bezos, founder of Amazon.com, have a strong internal locus of control. However, followers registered a locus of control that clustered near the external end of the spectrum. Their destinies are in the hands of another. When in charge, Internals take charge. Externals, on the other hand, allow others to take charge. Internals believe strongly in their ability and don't allow anxiety to undermine their progress toward their goals. Externals, on the other hand, tend to question their abilities and are often debilitated by anxiety. Many studies have shown that externals do not rebound well from adversity. Those debilitated by chaos are defeated by it.

What has locus of control got to do with athletic performance? More often than not an athlete's strength or weakness is emotional or mental rather than physical. Success in a crucial situation often depends upon whether an athlete sees herself or others in control of the situation. Some athletes choke under pressure, others get stronger as the pressure increases. When the competition gets really tough, the superstars never delegate their destiny to anyone. *They win because they believe winning lies within.*

The Mind Is Master–Just Watch the End of Any Game

It is fascinating to watch the psychosis that takes over a player in the final minutes of a game when losing is imminent. At that point, a quarterback takes a large risk, throwing a Hail Mary pass or trying a field goal from a position outside the kicker's usual range. A hockey team pulls the goalkeeper or a golfer tries to fly a water hazard from a bunker 220 yards away. It's risk all and go for broke. Such desperate measures usually fail. Had the team or athlete played with the same intensity (but less risk) throughout the game, they could have avoided the do-or-die dilemma. The moral? Play from the beginning with the passion you would bring to the dying minutes of a game and you will probably win. Play as if you have won and you will probably lose. However, playing with intensity from the very beginning requires a strong internal locus of control that focuses your mental and emotional energies at the outset. It's what athletes call "psyching-up" for the game.

But how does an athlete become "psyched-up"? We have all heard stories of superhuman feats performed by people under extraordinary stress. In a state of extreme duress, a mother has lifted two tons of automobile off a child pinned beneath its wheels. A father has wrestled and dragged ashore a shark that mauled his son. Soldiers in life-and-death situations have performed countless remarkable feats of endurance. While these are extreme examples, they tell us that we have more potential than we ever use. Great athletes are able to tap into more of this potential than the also-rans can. We recall from earlier chapters how Pelé was able to run effortlessly and without tiring when in a state of relaxed concentration and how Ali was able to draw from his reserve when he felt as if he were dying. To tap into this potential, we need to enter the fray convinced that this is the most important competition in the world and that losing it carries painful consequences. One important technique for generating this kind of motivation is to imagine that our opponent is an adversary for whom we have extreme antagonism. This is called *controlled aggression*.

Controlled Aggression–Antagonism Toward Your Opponent–Helps

Andy Macarthy, master of the Korean martial art *Jung Do* asserts, "You must imagine your opponent as subordinate to you." British behavioral scientist Rupert Sheldrake further emphasizes, "You can never allow thoughts of failure to slip into the mind, because what you perceive is what is going to happen." Such advice should be embedded in the training regimen of all aspiring world-class athletes.

Before the dissolution of the Soviet Union, Eastern Europe, including Czechoslovakia, was under the domination of the USSR. The bitter resentment of the Czechs toward the Soviets reached a flash point in international hockey games between the two nations. That hatred inspired the Czechs to play hockey as though possessed. European-style hockey is usually less physical than North American style, but the games between the Czechs and the Soviets exceeded North American standards in roughness. Elbows flew, bodychecks were vicious and the game was clearly much more than a game. The Czechs were fighting a war and it enhanced the quality of their play. They became the most formidable foe of the Soviet Red Army Team.

While growing up in Czechoslovakia under Soviet domination, Martina Navratilova developed an intense animosity toward the Russians. After she had risen to the top of the tennis world, she wrote, "My resentment against the Russians made me a better tennis player." On one occasion, she found herself playing against a Russian girl and saying to herself, "You need a tank to beat me." In her memoirs she wrote (p. 57), "I play my worst matches when I smile." Martina had discovered that empathy toward an opponent destroyed her controlled aggression and undermined her intensity.

Martina's archrival Chris Evert psyched herself up by morphing into a "bitch." Quoting from the joint autobiography of Chris Evert Lloyd and ex-husband John, biographer Adrianne Blue wrote (p. 76):

> *She would psyche herself up with a display of tantrums. "Before a match she could be a bitch," Ana Leaird says in Chris and John Lloyd's joint autobiography. "Then she would always win. Sometimes I could tell she was going to lose simply because she was being too nice."*

Muhammad Ali psyched himself up before a fight by initiating hostilities during the weigh-in ceremonies. His insults and open antagonism were intended to intimidate his opponent, stimulate publicity and, most importantly, prepare himself mentally for the conflict. His braggadocio raised the stakes by making a loss potentially more humiliating. When Ali entered the ring, he could not afford to lose; everything was on the line.

You may recall from Chapter 5 that Pelé's gentle nature off the field belied his ferocious aggressiveness on the pitch. Fellow soccer players claimed he was a master at fouling other players without being caught. Pelé had always railed against a defensive style of play and argued that the only way to win games was to play an aggressive goal-oriented style. Indeed, the superstars know that the way to take control of a match is to psyche yourself to a level where winning is everything, and then play aggressively, exploiting your opponent's weaknesses and using your strengths to dominate. Achieving this demands a strong internal locus of control.

Free enterprise is about gaining control and making others play your game. When Sam Walton pioneered the spoke-and-wheel method of distribution and introduced other cost-saving techniques, he built his single retail store into the Wal-Mart chain that under-priced the behemoth K-Mart and drove them into bankruptcy protection. Similarly, Michael Dell assembled and sold computers direct, thereby changing the rules of the game and stealing the lion's share of the personal computer market from IBM. Almost all the David and Goliath stories in business are about the young upstart creating a new game and making others play by a new set of rules.

The self-assessment instruments on the next two pages can help you to determine whether your locus of control is internal or external. Even if your locus of control is external, you can develop a more internal locus by practicing a more proactive approach to achieving your goals. First, write down your goals and your plans to achieve them. A plan should be a step-by-step sequence of tasks that leads to the achievement of each goal. Then proceed toward each goal by following these steps, revising them as necessary. When your preliminary goals are successfully achieved, repeat the process with loftier goals, continually achieving and reformulating new goals. Think big, but start small. If your goal is to break 80 on the golf course and you typically score in the 90s, your first goal should be to break 90 consistently. Your plans should involve identifying what parts of your game are costing you the most strokes: is it putting? chipping? driving? Then work on each skill in turn. It's never too late if you have the desire and commitment.

LOCUS OF CONTROL SELF-ASSESSMENT–Where Is Your Locus of Control?

For each item, choose "A" or "B" to indicate which statement describes you best. The scoring key is at the bottom of the page.

There are no "right" or "wrong" answers. In making your selection, be careful to answer the questions as candidly as possible without anticipating how you will be classified. This instrument is designed to give you insights into your sense of self.

Scale #1

A	B
1. Becoming rich is a matter of getting the right breaks.	Promotions result from much hard work and persistence on my part.
2. I have noticed a correlation between my work and my promotions.	Office politics determine who gets ahead and who doesn't.
3. White collar downsizing is intended to weed out incompetence.	The extent to which we succeed in life depends mainly upon lucky breaks.
4. It is unrealistic to think that one person can influence a large group.	I have considerable influence when I contribute good ideas to a group.
5. Promotions are more about who you know than what you know.	Capitalism is an economic system that rewards entrepreneurial enterprise.
6. I can follow if I know where we're headed, but not if I don't know.	I follow because I believe that the leaders know the way.
7. Luck has little to do with my success in school or life.	Sometimes I feel that the dice are loaded against my achieving success.
8. I can move mountains if given the opportunity.	Even though I have abilities, I can succeed only as far as society permits.
9. I believe in fate and destiny.	I believe in free will and choice.
10. Getting along with others is a skill that I practice repeatedly.	Many people are just impossible to figure out or please.

Instructions	Scoring Key	
Give yourself one point for each of the following responses:	**8–10:**	High internal locus of control.
	6–7:	Moderate internal locus of control.
1B, 2A, 3A, 4B, 5B, 6A, 7A, 8A, 9B, 10A.	**5:**	Equal internal and external control.
	3–4:	Moderate external locus of control.
Then use the scoring key to determine your locus of control.	**1–2:**	High external locus of control. You tend to believe that your destiny is outside your control.

Scale #2

Follow the same directions as for Scale #1. The scoring key is at the bottom of the page.

A	**B**
1. People generally get the rewards they work for in this world.	It's unfortunate, but most people don't get the credit they deserve in life.
2. Marks are poor indicators of what a student really knows in that subject.	School grades are good estimates of what a student knows in those subjects.
3. I place my faith in the clergy of an organized religion to distinguish between right and wrong.	I rely on my own spiritual sense or intuition to determine what is right and what is wrong.
4. Most wealthy people built their riches by ripping off the rest of us.	Most wealthy people built their riches by making sacrifices and working hard.
5. I don't have the right genes to be a very good athlete.	I could become very good at a sport of my choice if I worked hard at it.
6. By eating healthy and exercising regularly, I can extend my lifespan.	Our lifespan is pretty much determined by our genetic predisposition.
7. I drive defensively to minimize the chances that I'll be in an accident.	It doesn't matter what precautions you take, if it's your time to die, you're done.
8. When I invest, I like to purchase something with high liquidity.	When I invest, I like to buy a high-risk commodity with huge profit potential.
9. I often buy lottery tickets.	I seldom or never buy lottery tickets.
10. Losing weight is virtually impossible for people who have low metabolism.	Losing weight is more difficult for some than others.

Instructions	**Scoring Key**	
Give yourself one point for each of the following responses: 1A, 2B, 3B, 4B, 5B, 6A, 7A, 8A, 9B, 10B. Then use the scoring key to determine your locus of control.	**8–10:**	High internal locus of control.
	6–7:	Moderate internal locus of control.
	5:	Equal internal and external control.
	3–4:	Moderate external locus of control.
	1–2:	High external locus of control. You tend to believe that your destiny is outside your control.

Compare your results on scale #2 with your result on scale #1. Do you see a trend? If you find you have a moderate or high external locus of control, you are probably not utilizing your full potential. Achieving your goals is within your grasp if you're prepared to marshall your resources.

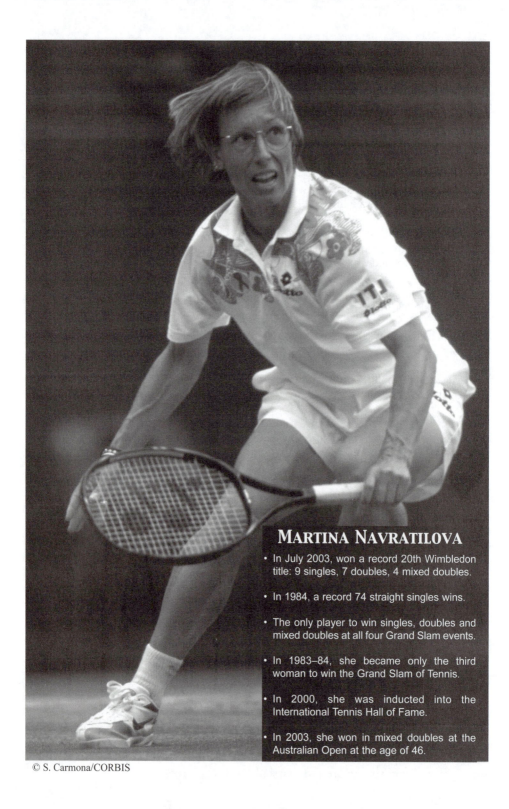

MARTINA NAVRATILOVA

- In July 2003, won a record 20th Wimbledon title: 9 singles, 7 doubles, 4 mixed doubles.

- In 1984, a record 74 straight singles wins.

- The only player to win singles, doubles and mixed doubles at all four Grand Slam events.

- In 1983–84, she became only the third woman to win the Grand Slam of Tennis.

- In 2000, she was inducted into the International Tennis Hall of Fame.

- In 2003, she won in mixed doubles at the Australian Open at the age of 46.

Martina Navratilova: Master in Making 'em Play Her Game

When Martina Navratilova was born in 1956 near Prague in Czechoslovakia (now the Czech Republic), it was a subjugated nation under the iron boot of Soviet domination. A sacrificial lamb in the World War II settlement at Yalta, Czechoslovakia had fallen under Communist domination and its citizens had become repressed as subjects of the Soviet Empire. The Soviet Union was a superpower. A powerful military was its strength; a flawed doctrine its weakness. When the Czechs attempted to free themselves from Soviet domination in 1968, the Russians played to their strength, sending tanks into Prague. The uprising was crushed. Martina Navratilova experienced the deprivation of freedom that results from domination by others–either individuals or government. When the Russian tanks rolled into Czechoslovakia, Martina was eleven. She said, "I saw my country lose its verve, lose its productivity, lose its soul." Living under Communist domination made Martina crave freedom, but it also taught her a variation of the "control-or-be-controlled" adage that translates in sports into the principle "Make 'em play your game."

© Bettmann/CORBIS

Martina Navratilova born Oct. 18, 1956

By the end of 2003, at age 47, Martina Navratilova had become the greatest female tennis player in the history of that sport. She was still active on the professional circuit and had a career total of 167 tournament wins in singles tennis–more championships than any other player in tennis history, male or female! Wimbledon became her personal playground; she won that coveted singles championship a record nine times. When she walked onto the court it was not only to win, but also to take control of the match and force the other player to play her game. As the master of the "make 'em play your game" principle, she understood that when the opponent is forced to play your game they are not playing their own. Martina's predecessors Billie Jean King, Margaret Smith Court and Chris Evert had played a defensive style of tennis, rallying from the baseline and waiting for the opponent to make an error. However, Martina was one of the first women to use the more aggressive serve-and-volley technique, moving to the net and forcing opponents to try (lower percentage) passing shots. Unable to pass Martina with consistency, the baseliners were forced to integrate serve and volley into their repertoires. When they had to serve and volley with the maestro, they were decimated.

For Martina, as for all champions, the trek to the top of the tennis world demanded courage, sacrifice and persistence. When success came, it came at a price. Pursuing her dream to play at Wimbledon required that she escape from Czechoslovakia and leave her family behind. The so-called "Cold War" between the two superpowers, the USA and the USSR, was closer to "cold fusion" than cold. Photos of bullet-riddled bodies of fugitives cut down while attempting to scale the Berlin Wall and corpses entangled in barbed wire along borders served as reminders of the gambles involved in escaping from inside the Iron Curtain. The Soviet policy was to allow their aspiring athletes to travel to international competitions on a restricted basis, as long as there was little or no chance that they might defect. To minimize the likelihood of defection, the family or spouse was not permitted to travel with the athlete. Martina was faced with a difficult decision. If she stayed in Czechoslovakia, she could say farewell to a professional career as a world-class tennis player. If she were successful in a bid for asylum in the U.S., she would have to say farewell to her family and friends–all her loved ones–to begin a new life in a foreign culture. About eight years after Muhammad Ali defied the government of one superpower, Martina defied the government of the other. On the eve of her showdown in the 1975 U.S. Open semi-finals against Chris Evert, she asked for asylum in the United States. At 18 years of age, she had crossed her Rubicon–there was no going back.

Until her citizenship was finalized six years later, Martina lived in fear of reprisals from the Soviets. In her autobiography she described the paranoia that plagued her financial manager Fred Barman as he facilitated her request for asylum (p. 144):

> *Fred was a little nervous...He was convinced that somebody was going to stuff me in a taxi, jab me with a hypodermic needle, and hustle me onto an airplane bound for Czechoslovakia. I wasn't as fearful as he was but it has happened to other people. They are sedated and jammed on a plane and you never hear from them again.*

Dealing with the fear and disquiet that accompanies defection from one's homeland is a daunting challenge, but one that wins support and sympathy from those in the adopted country. However, Martina had a further complication for which there would be little sympathy or support. In the common vernacular, Martina was gay. Former trailblazer Babe Zaharias had managed to keep her lesbian relationships secret (until after her death), using her marriage to George Zaharias as a cover. However, in Martina's case, the all-pervasive media, in their perpetual search for newsworthy soundbites, discovered the truth and publicized her lesbian liaisons. Her image as a masculine-looking gay woman set Martina in sharp contrast to the reigning queen of tennis, superstar Chris Evert, who charmed audiences with her good looks, good manners and athletic excellence. Serving as a foil for the elegant Evert, Martina served initially as the "bad guy" in women's professional tennis. As in boxing and other one-on-one sports, the existence of clearly defined good-guy/bad-guy roles enhanced the interest in women's professional tennis. It also launched one of the greatest rivalries of all time in competitive sports.

How Martina managed to emerge on top in this epic struggle for supremacy is not a story of genetic advantage, testosterone or physical skill, but rather a story of strategy–the quest for control. Both Chris and Martina dominated at different times. In the early stages of their rivalry, Martina succumbed to Chris's high-precision shots launched from the baseline. No matter how hard she tried to respond to these shots, Martina was unable to win the match point. Reacting to Chris Evert's highly tuned game moved the contest outside Martina's control and prevented her from winning. However, with help from coaches and friends, Martina eventually rediscovered what her father had taught her long ago, how to take control of the court to make Chris play her game. In her autobiography, she reflected (p. 57):

My game was rushing the net, playing aggressively, playing for fun, playing to win. My father encouraged it...I'm not exactly making that tactic into a simile for life, but there are times when I've played my life just like a tennis game. I got that directly from my father. He just wanted me to enjoy the game, to develop my attacking instincts.

MARTINA NAVRATILOVA'S TREK TO THE TOP

Early Imprints

Growing up in the stagnant void of a Communist state developed in Martina an appreciation of modern conveniences like indoor plumbing and a family car, neither of which she had as a child. She wrote, "Until I was about 12, we didn't even have hot running water and had to heat water on the coals to have a bath." The repression of Communism made an indelible mark on her impressionable psyche. She came to cherish with an uncommon intensity her independence and the right to live life as she chose. As a teenager, she knew she would escape to the West, although she didn't know when or how. Reflecting on her love of freedom, she later wrote, "I honestly believe I was born to be an American."

Martina's family culture supported and nurtured her interest in athletics. Her grandmother Agnes Semanska played tennis for the Czechoslovakian Federation prior to World War II. Her mother Jana was a ski instructor who taught Martina to ski at age three. From the time she was $4^1/2$ years old, Martina had wiled away hours hitting tennis balls against the walls of their apartment. When Martina was six her mother remarried and it changed her life. Her new stepfather Mirek Navratil spent hours with her and was her first tennis teacher. (She later took the feminine version of her stepfather's name, Navratilova.) Martina grew to worship him. Mirek encouraged her to seek her own level regardless of the consequences. In her memoirs she wrote, "I couldn't have done it without him. He was always there for me. He was great. He never questioned. He was relentless."

When Mirek took her to see a real professional tennis tournament, Martina experienced an epiphany that ignited her dream to become a great tennis player. In her autobiography, she recalled (p. 25):

An image of myself as a tennis player was formed the night my father took me to the Sparta sports center in Prague [to see] Rod Laver, the red-headed left-hander from Australia...I saw him rocketing around the court and I thought that's it, that's me, that's the player I want to be.

Not long after they began practicing, in what turned out to be a remarkably prophetic insight, Mirek told Martina, "One day you will become champion of Wimbledon...Make believe you are at Wimbledon on Centre Court holding up the trophy." Martina recalled, "I could see myself on TV doing it. I was just 7." A couple of years later she watched Billie Jean King win Wimbledon on TV and vowed, "I will win it someday." Just as Pelé's and Ali's dreams were ignited by events they heard on the radio, Martina's dream was sparked by what she saw on television. It is one more example of an early imprint that launched a life-long quest.

When Martina was 9 years old, Mirek arranged for former Czech champion George Parma to teach the young Martina the nuances of championship tennis.

Martina had a crush on the handsome, highly accomplished tennis coach who saw potential in the prepubescent youth. George spent a great deal of time helping Martina develop her game. Since she liked to move to the net to play an aggressive style, he taught her to hit a one-handed backhand instead of a two-handed backhand so that she could extend her reach by a few inches.

"By [age] 10," she later wrote, "I was playing tennis every day and soccer and ice hockey with the boys." Like Babe Zaharias, she learned that testing her skills against boys helped her with her power game and developed in her an aggressive style that may never have evolved if she had played only females. Mirek preached, "Play tennis like a boy if you want to beat the girls." She did and never regretted it.

From Amateur to Professional

It took 10 years for Martina to matriculate from bashing tennis balls against a wall to winning the tournaments throughout the Soviet bloc. By 14, she dominated tennis in Eastern Europe. However, Martina received very little acclaim for her accomplishments. In her autobiography, she described the dismal lack of encouragement of athletes behind the Iron Curtain (p. 95):

Nobody really felt appreciated under the [Communist] system...there was not enough fun or praise or rewards to go around. You'd do your job and they'd pat you on the back, but you knew you were just another wing of the state program.

At 16, Martina Navratilova won the national women's singles championship and was ranked number 2 in Czechoslovakia. This was one of the most important victories in her career in that it qualified her for international competition. Those years of hitting thousands of forehands and backhands had paid off.

The next year, 1973, Martina turned professional and started traveling outside the country for matches. Tidbits of Western culture like the music of the Beatles and the old Hollywood films that had seeped through the Iron Curtain during the 1960s had given Martina the impression that the West was "a magical place." In those capitalist nations she saw the vast divide between the quality of life in the West and her life behind the Iron Curtain. She noted in her autobiography (p. 2):

I didn't feel I belonged anywhere, until I came to America for the first time when I was sixteen…I honestly believe I was born to be American. With all due respect to my homeland, things never really felt right until the day I got off the plane in Florida to play in my first tournament in 1973. For the first time in my life, I was able to see America without the filter of a Communist education, Communist propaganda. And it felt right.

During her tournament tour in the United States, Martina was literally "a kid let out of school." Describing her binge on the American culture and fast foods, she recalled (p. 104–5):

I'd see a fast-food restaurant and I couldn't resist sampling the wares. Big Macs. Whoppers…It's a stale joke now, but people used to say I was on a "see-food" diet. Any food I could see, I'd eat.

Every time Martina returned to Czechoslovakia, she had no access to fast foods and she would return to her regular weight. In the early spring of 1975, she returned to the U.S. ready for action. She won the Virginia Slims Tournament and in the process defeated Chris Evert for the first time. However, Martina gained more than 20 lbs. during her U.S. tour. It made her feel more feminine to have curves and contours where once there had been only sinew, muscle and bone. However, the extra poundage affected her stamina and she found it difficult to recover if she lost the first set of a match. Consequently, she was beaten by scores of 6–4, 6–4 by Chris Evert in the semi-finals of the 1975 U.S. Open. Reporter Bud Collins of the *Boston Globe*, observing Martina's increased dimensions, referred to her as the "Great Wide Hope" (a play on the phrase "Great White Hope," originating during the era of boxer Jack Johnson and applied to all Muhammad Ali's white challengers during the 1970s). Martina later acknowledged that she had known relatively little about proper diet and physical training at this stage of her career.

By age 18, Martina had played in London and New York and knew she wanted to be free. The Communists were taking all her earnings and giving her a small stipend for living. She resented having the Czech government as the major beneficiary of her hard work on the courts as well as of her endorsements off the courts. Since her earliest travels outside the Soviet bloc, the Communist leaders had been issuing veiled threats to keep Martina in line. She rankled at the unrelenting bullying and control that these bureaucrats exercised to ensure that she would not become too "Americanized."

Martina Crosses Her Rubicon

In August of 1975, just two months before her 19th birthday, Martina reached her breaking point. Each time she had returned to Czechoslovakia, she wondered whether she would be allowed to leave. The bureaucrats had total control of her tennis career and her life. She decided to defect and never go back. Martina contacted her financial manager Fred Barman and asked him to help her set the wheels in motion. At the Immigration and Naturalization office in New York, she asked for asylum, telling officials, "I just want my freedom to play tennis."

The process that Martina set in motion began with a green card and would end about six years later with U.S. citizenship–provided she met all conditions satisfactorily. However, in the interim, Martina had to grapple with inner and outer demons that threatened her future as a professional tennis player. Her decision to defect had cut her off from her family and her roots–perhaps forever. Friends warned her never to consider going into an iron curtain country until she was a U.S. citizen, for without this protection, she could be apprehended by the authorities and probably never heard from again.

Two weeks after Martina had requested asylum in the U.S., the Czech tennis federation issued the following official statement about the tennis star who, earlier that year, had helped win the Federation Cup for Czechoslovakia:

> *Martina Navratilova has suffered a defeat in the face of the Czechoslovak society. Navratilova had all possibilities in Czechoslovakia to develop her talent, but she preferred a professional career and a fat bank account. She did not realize that she also needed an education.*

After her initial elation at gaining her freedom, Martina began to experience wild mood swings–a manifestation of the manic-depression that was in her family heritage. Her biological father had killed himself while in the throes of a bipolar episode. She lost herself in food and other indulgences, ballooning to 167 lbs. On the court she allowed her emotions to get in the way of her tennis. Ted Tinling attributed this bipolar behavior to her Slavic roots, writing in *World Tennis* magazine:

> *She has that Slav temperament that requires the stimulus of a crisis. She's always going to have that storm. I've always said she goes from arrogance to panic with nothing in between.*

After a humiliating defeat by Janet Newberry in the 1976 U.S. Open, Martina was devastated. This was perhaps the lowest point–the nadir–of Martina's tennis career. Fred Barman, standing in for her at the post-game interview said, "Here's a young kid who was imprisoned a year ago. She's been like a young girl in Disneyland for the first time." Peripheral distractions continued to affect Martina's game. Finally she asked her friend and former idol, Billie Jean King, for help. Billie Jean advised her to play within herself and to stop allowing her emotions to interfere with her game. But Martina's emotions were far more complicated than the public could know. Martina was beginning to discover that she was sexually attracted to some women. Having taken steps to establish her national identity, she was now struggling to determine her sexual identity.

Lesbian Liaisons

By age 18, Martina knew that she preferred the company of women. "As a kid I looked too much like a boy," she wrote (p. 2), "I was not pretty and the boys were not going to like me. Later on I didn't care." A preference for women led Martina on an emotional roller coaster of serial relationships–each characterized by torrid passion at the outset that would run its course of two or more years and climax in a vitriolic explosion, leaving both parties injured, resentful and feeling abused. At first, these emotional incidents came close to destroying her. In her autobiography she admitted, "I wear my heart on my sleeve." The vulnerability that made Martina attractive to these other women exacerbated the intensity of her pain when things went wrong. And when Martina suffered emotional pain, her tennis suffered accordingly.

Celebrity and money attracted many women to her side. The first notable love affair was with golf pro Sandra Haynie. Haynie was the LPGA Player of the Year in 1970 and winner of the U.S. Women's Open in 1974. She met Martina in April 1976, just eight months after Martina's defection, when the 19-year-old tennis star was emotionally distraught and lonely. Haynie told Martina (Blue, p. 66), "Getting there [to #1] is the easy part. Staying there's the hard part." Sandra helped her young protégé with conditioning, nutrition, and most important, mental and emotional stability. Golf had taught Sandra how to deal with anger and frustration during competition and she helped Martina control her temper on the court. During their cohabitation between 1977 and 1979, Martina rediscovered her game and began winning tournaments again.

Wimbledon

Martina's moment of truth arrived in July 1978 as she passed under the doorway that led to Centre Court at Wimbledon for the final match against Chris Evert. Inscribed over the doorway were the immortal words from Kipling's poem *If* (see p. 84). They had inspired Wilma Rudolph, 18 years earlier, as she passed through the tunnel to the Olympic track in Rome to enter an 11-second competition that would determine her future. Martina's trial would last one-and-a-half grueling hours!

From the time she was able to swing a racket, Martina's stepfather Mirek had told her that one day she would win at Wimbledon. This was the same Wimbledon that she, at age 9, had vowed to win after seeing Billie Jean King's televised victory. Here she was at last, heralded with the pomp and ceremony of English pageantry at its finest and standing on the hallowed grass courts that symbolize the rich tradition of the British gentry. Winning at Wimbledon was her dream, but it had eluded her since she had become a professional. Now at 21 she was at the center of the tennis world in Centre Court–a place whose effect she captured in her autobiography (p. 189):

> *With all the bustle of Wimbledon, the gossip, the upper-class people in the special boxes, the crowds, the importance of the tournament itself, I don't think an athlete could ever feel more onstage than you do on Centre Court. It brings out every bit of competitor, every bit of egotist, that you need to win a championship.*

In her earlier attempts at Wimbledon, Martina had been eliminated before reaching the finals. Now, she was face to face with her archrival, Chris Evert, who had won the Wimbledon Championship in 1974 and again in 1976, eliminating Martina in the semifinals. Chris had been Martina's nemesis from early on and Martina began to wonder if she would ever prevail against her. She had a love-hate relationship with Chris. On the one hand she admired Evert's tennis skill and her traditionally feminine appeal. Martina recalled with characteristic candor, "Before I even met her, she stood for everything I admired in this country: poise, ability, sportsmanship, money, style." On the other hand, there was the "hate" part of the relationship that could be more aptly described as "adversarial." In her inimitably incisive style, Martina said, "She possessed a two-handed backhand that could cut your heart out without your feeling it, and a warm smile that said, 'Nothing personal'."

Chris was standing at Centre Court between Martina and her dream as the first serve flew over the net to open the contest. Martina, suffering from a case of the jitters, struggled to free herself from the distractions of the trappings and to focus on the moment. By the time she had regained her composure, she had lost the first set 2–6. She had to win the next two sets to win the match. In the second set, Chris pulled ahead four games to two. Chris needed only two more games to win her third Wimbledon Championship. The prospects for Martina were beginning to look bleak. During her charge toward victory, Chris launched a shot that grazed Martina's temple. Martina was not hurt and later claimed that it woke her from her catatonic state. She went on to win the second set 6–4, tying the match at one set each. The third and final set would decide all.

Sandra Haynie, in her capacity as Martina's informal coach, had observed Martina's previous losses to Chris Evert and had questioned Martina's strategy against Chris. Martina recounted in her autobiography (p. 180):

> *[Sandra] couldn't understand why I camped at the baseline and played Chris's game, tournament after tournament. I always thought it would be a badge of honor to beat Chris at her own game, but Haynie told me to play my game, to get back to rushing the net.*

Whether it was Sandra's advice that took effect, or whether it was the sense of regaining control is not clear, but Martina came on more aggressively in the third set. After a close encounter with defeat that might have changed the course of her life, Martina regained control and won that set 7–5, winning the match and the Wimbledon Championship. Martina had scaled the Mount Everest of tennis. Four days later she was ranked Number 1 in the world by the Women's Tennis Association, an honor held in the four preceding years by Chris Evert. Martina had achieved her dream! But this was only the first major battle in the war with Chris Evert for the top ranking in the world of women's tennis.

Another Liaison

Oscar Wilde once observed, "In this world there are only two tragedies. One is not getting what one wants, and the other is getting it." In 1978, at age 21, Martina Navratilova had achieved the dream that had defined her purpose for as long as she could remember. But the realization of a dream seldom, if ever, matches its imagined benefits. After the initial euphoria of the Wimbledon victory faded, Martina began exploring her inner needs that she had subordinated to tennis during her quest for tennis's most cherished prize.

A month after Martina won the 1978 Wimbledon Championship, she met best-selling author and feminist Rita Mae Brown. What began as a dinner engagement quickly blossomed into a heated love affair that led eventually to the dissolution of Martina's relationship with Sandra Haynie in 1979. As the new liaison evolved, Rita introduced Martina to art, history and literature, awakening the intellectual dimension of her younger companion. During this euphoric phase of Martina's life, she continued to play well, winning at Wimbledon in 1979 by beating Chris Evert in the final. Martina retained her Number 1 ranking at the end of 1979.

However, as the 1980 season began, it was clear that Martina's interest in tennis was slowly eroding under the onslaught of Rita's denigration of tennis as "merely a game." Martina's declining motivation was accompanied by a corresponding decline in the quality of her play. She did not play in the French Open, she lost to Chris at Wimbledon and was eliminated in the U.S. Open. By the end of the 1980 season, Martina was ranked third to first-ranked Evert and second-ranked Tracy Austin.

Martina had begun to feel that Rita's unrelenting disparagement of tennis and sports in general was a veiled attempt to control how she spent her time. Recalling her attitude at the time she said (p. 213):

I'd lose a match and say, "It's not a matter of life and death," which was true, except that while you're playing it, it should feel like a matter of life and death.

When describing her antagonism toward Communist suppression, Martina had said (p. 68), "I'm against anything restrictive, people telling me what to do or what to think." But this antagonism applied not only to regimes but also to people who tried to control her life. It was inevitable that Martina would bolt for freedom; the only question was when? In April 1981, while playing a match on Amelia Island in Florida, Martina saw in the crowd a woman who was conspicuous for what Martina described as her "flaming reddish-orange hair." When they met after the match, she discovered that the woman was Nancy Lieberman, a former basketball star. This encounter was the beginning of Martina's next in her series of relationships and the end of her cohabitation with Rita Mae. The formal termination in mid-1981 was a violent scene with Rita Mae Brown that erupted when Martina announced that their relationship was over and that she had found someone else. Details of the physical confrontation that the tabloids like to call a catfight became public and fed the gossip columns for weeks.

The downward spiral in Martina's game continued through 1981 as she lost in the French Open, Wimbledon and the U.S. Open. For the second time, she ended the season ranked third behind Chris Evert and Tracy Austin. However, it would turn out that 1981 would be a watershed year for Martina. At long last, on July 20, 1981, she became a U.S. citizen and would never again fear abduction by the Communists or living as a nomad. Her affair with Rita Mae was over, and a new relationship with Nancy Lieberman had begun. The initial phase of each liaison always seemed to provide Martina with the jolt of energy and motivation she needed to push herself to peak performance. Furthermore, her new companion Nancy, herself an athlete in top condition, was able to help Martina discover the importance of proper nutrition, disciplined weight training and aerobic conditioning. Those embarrassing days when she was described as the "Great Wide Hope" were now behind her. She shed those extra pounds, dropping from a weight of 167 lbs. to 145 lbs., registering only 8.8% body fat (compared to the average of 13% for female tennis players). Since that time, Martina has had the reputation as the best-fit woman on the tour. Now that Martina had regained her sense of purpose, the stage was set for a new upward thrust in her quest for the brass ring–the Grand Slam of Tennis.

A New Era for Martina

In 1982 Martina came into her own, dominating women's tennis like no one in history. In that year she won 29 titles including an unprecedented 15 singles and 14 doubles titles. The singles titles included her third win at Wimbledon, defeating Chris Evert in the finals in three sets, 6–1, 3–6, 6–2 and regaining the number one rank in women's tennis.

The momentum she had in 1982 grew into 1983 with a win at the Australian Open and her fourth win at Wimbledon. In spite of her many victories, there were still more worlds to conquer. The "grand slam" tennis events are the four major tournaments: the French Open, Wimbledon, the U.S. Open and the Australian Open. Martina had won all of these grand-slam tournaments except the U.S. Open, having been eliminated before the finals every year from 1973 through 1982. In her own words (p. 286):

In 1983 there was a bigger goal, the last barricade. Until I won the U.S. Open, and did away with the whispers that I let Flushing Meadow [site of the U.S. Open] get on my nerves, I could not claim to be one of the greatest female players in history. Champions should win everything.

Saturday, September 10, 1983 was a steamy hot day in New York. Temperatures reached 93° as the world's two top-ranked women in tennis–Martina Navratilova and Chris Evert–took the court for the final match of the U.S. Open. The audience was treated to a spectacular display of tennis at its finest. Martina immediately implemented her aggressive strategy that she had honed with the help of her coach Mike Estep. Describing her approach, she said (p. 296):

From the start, everything went just as Mike had told me. I was charging Chris, forcing her to go for winners. Once in a while she would hit a super passing shot into the corner and the crowd would roar, thinking that Chris was finding her game. But I knew there was only a tiny patch on each side available to her, and if she could find it, more power to her.

It took 63 minutes for Martina to defeat Chris Evert in two sets, 6–1 and 6–3. She had finally won the U.S. Open on her eleventh try! Having won all the grand-slam events at least once, she joined the elite group of women who have earned what is called a "Career Grand Slam." When the 1983 season came to a close, no one was surprised that Martina was ranked number 1 in the world in women's tennis. She was the undisputed world champion. After her victory she said, "If I don't win another tournament in my life, I can still say I've done it all." It would seem that there were no more mountains to climb or worlds to conquer, but there was at least one more–*the* Grand Slam, achieved by winning all four grand-slam tournaments in the same year.

Then in early 1984, Martina, in a "take-no-prisoners" approach to tennis, defeated Chris Evert to win the French Open. This victory meant that Martina had won the four grand-slam tournaments in sequence, albeit spanning the 1983–1984 seasons. The International Tennis Federation ruled that this constituted a Grand Slam and awarded Martina the million-dollar bonus that was to accompany such an achievement. Only two other women in tennis history had achieved a Grand Slam: Maureen Connolly in 1953 and Margaret Court in 1970. (Both these women achieved their Grand Slams in a single season, regarded by purists as a *real* Grand Slam.)

From Trophies to a Trophy Wife

A few months after her victory in the 1983 U.S. Open, Martina realized that her relationship with Nancy Lieberman had lost its luster. As Nancy's career in basketball fizzled, she had channeled her energy into managing Martina's affairs. Martina felt that Nancy was becoming increasingly more controlling. Responding to her need for freedom, Martina terminated the relationship. Meanwhile, Martina was developing a friendship with Judy Nelson whom she had met in 1982 when she visited Judy's physician husband for treatment of an injury. Biographer Adrianne Blue, describing Judy as the "trophy wife," wrote (p. 114–5):

> *Judy Nelson was all that was best about White Anglo-Saxon (WASP) America. Judy was the very incarnation of respectability, not just a member of the country-club set, but also a doctor's wife...Life with Judy Nelson seemed to promise fulfillment, at last, of the American Dream. For what is that dream but fame, fortune, and a blond on your arm? In her youth, Judy had even been a beauty queen of middle rank, called Maid of Cotton.*

This torrid affair between Judy and Martina became a feeding frenzy for the media. With piranha-style ferocity, the tabloids chewed on every little detail they could discover or invent and publicized the juicy tidbits for a gossip-hungry populace. In the summer of 1984, Judy left her husband for Martina. Their domicile was established in Aspen and on February 12, 1986 the couple signed a partnership agreement–a surrogate wedding contract. This relationship ran its course and eventually ended in 1991 in a sensational court trial and tell-all book by Nelson.

Though she spoke openly in her autobiography about her gay lifestyle, Martina preferred to keep her personal life private and only wrote about it after the tabloids made it public. Martina used humor to deflect inappropriate comments or questions posed in interviews. On one such occasion, a sportswriter asked, "Martina, are you still a lesbian?" Without blinking she responded, "Are you still the alternative?"

Climax

During the early phase of her cohabitation with Judy Nelson, Martina continued to dominate women's tennis. She won Wimbledon from 1984 through 1987, the U.S. Open in 1984, 1986 and 1987, and the Australian Open in 1985, earning the number one ranking from 1982 through 1986. However, by the end of the 1988 season, it was apparent that Martina at age 32 was moving past her prime. Wimbledon was the only grand-slam tournament in which she had reached the finals, and there she lost to the new giant-killer, Steffi Graf. This rising new tennis star from Germany was an inch taller than Martina and 13 years her junior. She had intimidated the top-ranked players with her powerful serve and aggressive play. Steffi had displaced Martina as the number one ranked player in the 1987 season and proceeded to win the "purist" form of the Grand Slam in the 1988 season by winning all four of the grand-slam tournaments. Martina would never return to the number one ranking. Women's tennis had reached the end of an era.

Martina's life came crashing down in April 1989 when she suffered a crushing defeat at the hands of Gabriela Sabatini in the semi-finals of a tournament on Amelia Island. Devastated by the loss, she called her idol Billie Jean King and amid sobs of sadness and frustration, asked for help. Together, Billie Jean and coach Craig Kardon helped Martina rediscover her passion for tennis. Though Martina won no grand-slam tournaments through the rest of the 1989 season, she gradually regained her desire.

By July 1990 she was again ready for Wimbledon. Revisiting the location of her earliest dreams and eight Championships, Martina realized that she had within her grasp a record that might never be beaten. At that time, she was tied with Helen Wills Moody, who won the Wimbledon singles title for the eighth time in 1938. Another Wimbledon victory would give Martina nine victories and a record that might stand forever. When Martina reached the final at Wimbledon, her opponent was not Steffi Graf but Zina Garrison, who had defeated Steffi in the semi-finals. Playing as though her life depended upon it, Martina dispensed with Zina in two sets, 6–4, 6–1, giving her a record of nine singles wins at Wimbledon! Just three months before her 34th birthday, Martina achieved a brilliant climax to a superb career.

Denouement

In 2003, at the not so tender age of 46, Martina partnered with Russian Svetlana Kuznetsova, three decades her junior, to win the doubles in the Italian Open. Two months later she became the oldest ever to win a major championship at Wimbledon with mixed-doubles partner Leander Pae. This win, her 20th, tied her with Billie Jean King for the most victories at the All-

England Club. She told Katie Couric, "I'm older than most of the players' mothers." At an age when most super-athletes have retired and are living the good life, Martina is still competing on the World Tennis Tour. She regularly plays in the singles, doubles and mixed doubles against the likes of John McEnroe, Anna Kournikova, André Agassi and Andy Roddick. Refusing to be controlled by anyone, she is thumbing her nose at father time.

At Wimbledon, Martina told the media, "I know I don't play as well as my best 20 years ago but people don't care. I love what I do, I have a passion for tennis and a passion for life." The woman the fans once loved to hate was now an older stateswoman whom they cheered to victory. Physical fitness is a cardinal reason for Martina's success at a period in her life when most former superstars are commentating on television. In 2003 during her sudden resurgence, she told the press, "Don't let age be a deterrent to whatever you want. You can't work out sporadically. It must be a lifestyle and a constant process. It must also be fun. Don't sit on a bike in a gym watching TV and think you are getting in shape."

The former victim of communist repression has embraced the benefits of capitalism with a passion. Martina spreads her time among exotic estates in Aspen, Dallas, Antigua and the Virgin Islands. On her trips to the U.S. Open, she stays in a luxurious suite that she owns in Trump Plaza and on her trips to Aspen she skis the beautiful mountains of Colorado. Biographer Adrianne Blue reflected (p. 58):

> *By defecting, Martina could play every tournament, which was what she needed if she was to become the champion she knew she could be. Yes, she was selfish. She had to be. That very "selfishness"–a sense of self–was concomitant of her strength of character. People who line up quietly rarely arrive somewhere first.*

Legacy

When it comes to tournament wins, no one, man or woman, has won more. Navratilova won 1650 matches and 167 singles titles, including 18 Grand Slam singles titles. Once Martina had conquered her personal ghosts, not even the queen of the courts, Chris Evert, could touch her. Between 1982 and 1983 she won 176 singles matches, losing only four times. The next year she chalked up an unprecedented 74 straight victories–a winning streak that ranks with the grandest achievements in any sport, akin to Joe DiMaggio's

56-game hitting streak and Wayne Gretzky's 51-game consecutive scoring record in hockey. During a 14-month period from 1983 through 1984, Martina won six consecutive Grand Slam titles. Between 1982 and 1986, Martina had 428 victories against 14 losses and won 13 Grand Slam singles tournaments. She topped the rankings of women's tennis for all but 22 weeks of that 282-week period. Between April 1983 and July 1985, she won 109 consecutive doubles matches, including eight consecutive women's doubles titles, with partner Pam Shriver. Martina was the uncrowned queen of Wimbledon with nine singles titles. In 2003 she was still a force, winning both doubles and mixed-doubles titles. By 2003, at the remarkable age of 47, the ageless wonder had tucked in her tennis bag the Grand Slam titles shown in this table.

Martina's Victories in the Major Events

Grand Slam Event	Singles	Doubles	Mixed	Total
Australian Open	3	8	1	12
French Open	2	7	2	11
Wimbledon	9	7	4	20
U.S. Open	4	9	2	15
Totals	18	31	9	58

Billie Jean told reporters, "She'll be remembered as the best ever." *Sports Illustrated* writer Curry Kirkpatrick wrote on June 18, 1984, "Navratilova is simply too good for her sport." Friend and fellow combatant Chris Evert told *Sports Illustrated* (1999), "Martina revolutionized the game by her superb athleticism and aggressiveness, not to mention her outspokenness and candor. She was never afraid to say what she really thought." Martina spoke openly about her renegade behavior, saying (p. 69),"I never did fit the mold…In a country where people played a clay-court style of life, just to survive [in Czechoslovakia], I was the serve-and-volley kid."

The Grande Dame of Tennis's true strength was forcing others like Chris Evert to play her game or suffer the consequences. If they refused to come to the net, she put the ball away. Tennis experts will tell you that those who control the net control the game. Occasionally they are passed but more often they slam the ball home. An opponent forced out of their game plan is highly vulnerable. That axiom prevails in all racket sports. "Just being aggressive," Martina wrote in her memoir, "I could win my share of matches on the tour." What was she saying? Attacking the net when most female players were playing at the baseline placed her in control. For Martina offense was the weapon of choice. It made her one of the most intimidating forces in the history of tennis.

Explaining the theory behind her aggressive approach, Martina stated (p. 289), "There are two theories in tennis: work on your weakness or work on your strength. [My coach] subscribed to the latter." The idea underpinning the "work on your strength" approach is that if your strengths are well honed, you can force your opponent to play to your strengths and your weaknesses will seldom be exploited. This principle is particularly applicable in sports involving direct confrontation such as combat sports, racket sports, and most team sports.

Martina reads voraciously and has five books in print. Her books have titles in synch with her style–*Tennis My Way*, *Martina*, *The Total Zone*, *Breaking Point* and *Killer Instinct*. In *Breaking Point* (1996) she wrote, "And tennis is often more mental than physical, especially at the championship level when both players have so many gifts." The secret of Martina's monumental success was the mastery of herself that led to the mastery of her adversaries. In Martina's words, "You have to keep a positive attitude. You have to remember you have no control over anything but your attitude."

Chapter 8

I had to be physically and mentally prepared to do a dive. I had to be able to see it in my head.

–Greg Louganis

Success Begins with a Vision

Do you have a clear vision of your goals? If so, how vividly and in what detail can you visualize them? Those who can't envision success can't achieve it. All success begins with seeing and believing. Superb athletic performance is all about an athlete's ability to visualize doing what is difficult. Conversely, failure haunts the athlete who envisions failure. Those who self-flagellate after hitting a bad golf shot, exclaiming "you idiot" or "you bum, you can't do anything," suffer the consequences of a self-fulfilling prophecy. Winners see a positive outcome in their mind's eye and this positive image more often than not yields a positive result. Syber Vision, a California-based company, that published a series of taped interviews with high achievers from all walks of life, reported, "Visualization was considered to be the most important aspect these achievers had in common. They sensed with the greatest possible clarity the successful performance of their ambition." Ralph Vernacchia states (pp. 35–6):

[Visualization] helps us get the "feeling" for a desired performance. For an athlete this means both the kinesthetic or "body" feeling and the "emotional" feel for a performance. Thought precedes action, but there is an intermediate step in this process, that is, thoughts create images that stimulate feeling and feelings that result in action...Athletes who perform effectively will often comment that they are "feeling it," and when they comment on their performance they say that it "felt" great, not that it "thought" great.

Imagination Is the Launch Pad for Visualization

In his book *Peak Performance,* Charles Garfield reflected on his experience in training Olympic athletes and future astronauts, observing, "Sustainable high performance begins with an internal decision to excel." Garfield went on to analyze what he found in the minds and hearts of the winning athletes, "Great accomplishments are always the result of imagination. Almost all world-class athletes, astronauts and other peak performers are visualizers. They see it, feel it and experience it before they actually do it."

Dr. Christiaan Barnard, the surgeon who achieved the world's first successful heart transplant, said he believed humans could achieve anything within the scope of their imagination. The imagination triggers the visualization process. The superathlete first imagines a desired result–the path of a long putt that ends in the cup or the trajectory of a tennis return that sizzles with topspin into the far corner of the court. Then the athlete begins to execute in unconscious fashion the action that has been internalized from thousands of hours of conscious practice and mental rehearsal. Whether the action is a slow and deliberate putt in golf or a lightning fast return in tennis, the process is the same. Execution is merely a reflex action that has been programmed through prolonged mental and physical experience. There is no way to consciously decide how to execute an action; it has to be automatic and, as Vernacchia observed, it has to be felt rather than thought.

Visualization and Mental Imagery

In the current literature on athletic performance, the terms visualization and mental imagery are used interchangeably to describe the technique that encompasses at least three mental processes: imagining desired results, mental rehearsal and relaxed concentration.

Imagining desired results is only the first step in the visualization process. The next step, often described as mental rehearsal, is imagining the full execution of the action down to the minutest detail. It is particularly important that the mental rehearsal be multi-sensorial and contain vivid images. As the athlete visualizes the execution of the movement, she must imagine the sounds, scents and particularly the feel of that action–a process described by sports psychologist Terry Orlick as *feelization*. Once "feelization" is achieved, the athlete is able to trust the body to perform the skill instinctively, that is, without the intrusion of rational thought. This is the focus that was described in Chapter 5 as relaxed concentration. When this state is reached, the athlete is able to perform in a fashion that is sometimes described as "unconscious."

VISUALIZATION PROCESSES

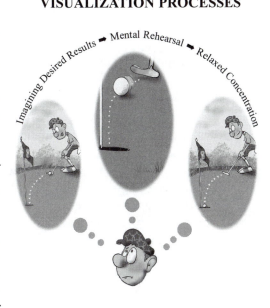

One of the most dramatic examples of the power of visualization in enhancing performance is the fascinating story of Major James Nesmeth. As a prisoner of war in Vietnam for seven years, he spent a major portion of his confinement in a small cell that resembled a cage. Deprived of companionship and the freedom of movement, Major Nesmeth resolved to preserve his sanity by using mental imagery. Unleashing his vivid imagination, he transported himself to his favorite hometown golf course where he could see in his mind's eye the rich green fairways, the sandy brown bunkers and the white puffy clouds that floated freely across an azure blue sky. He could hear the cacophony of birdcalls and smell the fragrance of the spring flowers. In the sanctuary of this idyllic environment, he teed his ball on the first hole and unleashed a powerful tee shot, "feeling" the exhilaration of the club head sliding through the ball and visualizing the flight of the white sphere as it launched skyward. As the ball vanished into the distant horizon, Major Nesmeth would sling his clubs over his shoulder and proceed to his next shot–all while physically confined in a cruel cage! Transcending the ugly reality of his confinement, he would play an entire round of golf, imagining each shot with meticulous focus on method and outcome. Day in and day out, Major Nesmeth played a round of golf in his head, preserving his sanity for the duration of his imprisonment.

When the War ended and he regained his freedom, Major Nesmeth seized the opportunity to play yet another game of golf on that old familiar course, but this time it was real. He visualized every shot prior to its execution just as he had during the countless days of his imprisonment. At the end of 18 holes, he discovered that he had scored 74–about 20 strokes better than his best score prior to his incarceration!

Why Does Visualization (Mental Imagery) Work?

Major Nesmeth's story is a strong testimonial to the power of mental imagery. But why does it work? Sports psychologists, kinesiologists and neurologists offer several explanations. The psycho-neuromuscular explanation asserts that imagery strengthens the neural pathways for certain movements by "grooving" a sequence of muscle contractions that predispose the body to execute the contractions in that sequence. For example, power lifters who visualize the sequence of muscle contractions prior to executing a heavy bench press pre-program those muscles to fire in the rehearsed sequence during the actual lift. A second explanation, related to the first, is that imagery may enable the brain to internalize the action in a way that makes the action less conscious and more automatic. In effect, the imagery serves as a mental rehearsal that has a similar effect to physical practice, transferring the image into a "feel." Bio-Informational Theory offers a third explanation, suggesting that the mind, muscles and emotions work collaboratively in the performance of any action and that imagery, if sufficiently vivid and representative of the real action, helps to prepare the central nervous system for the performance of the envisioned action. In essence by simulating the attitudes and emotions associated with the successful execution of a particular movement, the imagery creates a mind-set that predisposes the body to execute successfully and attain the envisioned emotional and attitudinal states.

How Do the Athletic Superstars Use Visualization?

As noted above, visualization as practiced by the super-athlete embodies three processes: imagining desired results, mental rehearsal and relaxed con-centration. Mental rehearsal usually follows and is guided by a visual image of the perfect execution of an action. Describing how he always visualized the perfect shot before initiating his swing, Jack Nicklaus wrote (p. 79):

I never hit a shot, even in practice, without having a very sharp, in-focus picture of it in my head. It's like a color movie. First I "see" the ball where I want it to finish, nice and white and sitting up high on the bright green grass. Then the scene quickly changes and I "see" the ball going there: its path, trajectory, and shape, even its behavior on landing. Then there's sort of a fade-out, and the next scene shows me making the kind of swing that will turn the previous images into reality. Only at the end of this short, private, Hollywood spectacular do I select a club and step up to the ball.

But what is the source of this mental image? Often the athlete is imitating the action he has seen as performed by the very best. Arnold Palmer, in his quest to develop the classic swing of Sam Snead, once described his own use of imagery (Hemery, pp. 106–7):

I could watch a good player like Sam Snead, who had a great golf swing, and could go and concentrate on what he was doing, and then in my own mind, maybe not in yours, but in my mind I could go and swing the club just like that. And that was all I needed. It didn't matter whether I was doing it but I could imagine that I was doing it and I'd get the results I wanted.

Palmer's observation that "it didn't matter whether I was doing it" is particularly important in suggesting that the benefits from such imagery may emanate more from the consistency it yields than from the accuracy of the imitation. In other words, the imagery helps us perform the action in the same way every time, even if it does not accurately reproduce the action we're trying to imitate.

Throughout this chapter, we have taken a number of our examples of visualization from golf because it is the sport to which many readers can relate. However, visualization is widely practiced in virtually every sport. Terry Orlick explains (p. 109):

Many athletes find it helpful to imagine and feel themselves performing skills perfectly immediately before competitive performances. High jumpers feel their ideal jumps, divers their perfect dives, skiers their best runs, gymnasts their perfect routines; archers follow their arrows to the center of the target. Team sport athletes run through key offensive moves, quick transitions, and great defensive moves. This process strengthens confidence by calling up the feeling of a best performance, and focuses full attention on the task at hand. It serves as a last-minute reminder of the focus and feeling you want to carry into the game or performance.

Sylvie Bernier, former Olympic champion in springboard diving, described how she uses imagery to perfect her dives before a competition:

I did my dives in my head all the time...I started with a front dive, the first one that I had to do at the Olympics, and I did everything as if I was actually there. I saw myself in the pool at the Olympics doing my dives. If the dive was wrong, I went back and started over again. For me it was better than a workout.

In his autobiography, superstar Bill Russell, who led the Boston Celtics to 11 NBA championships, describes imagery he used while sitting on the bench watching basketball great McKelvey retrieving rebounds and moving on the hoop (p. 73–74):

Something happened that night that opened my eyes and chilled my spine. I was sitting on the bench watching Treu and McKelvey the way I always did. Every time one of them would make one of the moves I liked, I'd close my eyes just afterward and try to see the play in my mind. In other words, I'd try to create an instant replay on the inside of my eyelids. Usually I'd catch only part of a particular move the first time I tried this; I'd miss the headwork or the way the ball was carried or maybe the sequence of steps. But the next time I saw the move I'd catch a little more of it, so that soon I could call up a complete picture.

In remarkably similar fashion Wayne Gretzky, generally regarded as the greatest hockey player of all time, described his use of mental imagery:

We taped a lot of famous pictures on the locker-room door: Bobby Orr, Potvin, Beliveau, all holding the Stanley Cup. We'd stand back and look at them and envision ourselves doing it. I really believe if you can visualize yourself doing something, you can make that image come true...I must have rehearsed it ten thousand times. And when it came true it was like an electric jolt went up my spine.

Imagery, when used as mental rehearsal of a particular action or skill, helps to refine technique and build consistency. However, imagery is also used to establish a proper mind-set for intense competition. When used in this way, it is sometimes referred to as "emotional imagery." Former tennis great John Newcombe described how he used imagery to reduce tension and prepare himself mentally for his matches at Wimbledon (Hemery, p. 117):

Let's say I had to play on the Centre Court: before I left Wimbledon the night before, I would walk up to the back of the stands and look down on the court and I'd close my eyes and have a mental picture of the court and myself being one–familiarity, so that when I came out to play there I felt right at home.

Through emotional imagery, athletes familiarize themselves with the battlefield environment and rehearse their reactions to potentially challenging situations that may unexpectedly appear during the heat of battle. Mental and emotional imagery are part of virtually every athlete's repertoire of preparation practices. Shane Murphy, President of the Division of Exercise and Sport Psychology of the American Psychological Society contends, "It's almost impossible to find an [outstanding] athlete who does not use imagery or visualization."

Of all the super-athletes profiled in this book, none described the use of imagery more vividly than the world's greatest diver, Greg Louganis. In the face of monumental challenges that drove him to attempt suicide several times, he rose to the top of the Olympic diving platform and the top of the world of diving. However, before diving into the remarkable story of Greg Louganis, the master of visualization, you may want to assess your own visualization skills using the instrument on the following pages. If you score low in mental imagery and visualization skills, you are in an excellent position to greatly improve your success in sports and in life. With practice, you will find visualization progressively easier to do until it eventually becomes an automatic part of your approach to achieving your goals.

VISUALIZATION SELF-ASSESSMENT–Can You Visualize Success?

This visualization assessment is set in a golfing context because that is the most common experience of most readers. However, if you are not a golfer, I invite you to adapt this assessment to your favorite sport by identifying four specific skills on which you would like to focus. Then modify the questions below to correspond to those skills.

Choose a number between 1 and 5 to indicate the extent to which you can visualize the scenario described in each item. Select "1" if you have no visual image, "2" if the image is vague, "3" if moderately clear, "4" if clear and distinct and "5" if clear and vivid. Record for each statement the number you have chosen. The scoring key is at the bottom of the next page.

Driving

	No Image				Vivid Image

1. Close your eyes and visualize your favorite professional golfer launching a 300-yard drive. It's a fluid execution seen in slow motion. How vividly can you see this image?   1 2 3 4 5

2. Close your eyes and imagine yourself executing a powerful drive. It's a smooth rhythmic swing as your weight transfers fluidly and your body finishes in balance with a full follow-through. How vividly can you see this image?   1 2 3 4 5

3. Visualize the image described in item #2. How deeply can you feel the execution of this powerful movement?   1 2 3 4 5

4. Imagine that all your friends are gathered at the first tee as you launch a 300-yard drive that soars skyward and lands in the center of the fairway and rolls out of sight. The gallery cheers. How clearly can you capture your mood?   1 2 3 4 5

Pitching

5. Visualize your favorite professional golfer executing a sensational pitch to the green. It's a smooth execution with a complete follow-through. How vividly can you see this image?   1 2 3 4 5

6. Imagine yourself executing a long pitch to the green. It's a smooth fluid swing with a full follow-through that carries your hands above your head. The ball bounces on the green and rolls up to the pin. How vividly can you see this image?   1 2 3 4 5

7. Visualize the image described in item #6. How deeply can you feel the execution of this "poetry in motion"?   1 2 3 4 5

8. You need to get up and down in two strokes to save par. Imagine that your clubhead passes deftly under the ball, sending it skyward onto the green where it lands softly and rolls up close to the pin. Your friends cheer and announce "it's a gimme." How deeply can you recapture how you feel?   1 2 3 4 5

Chipping

9. Visualize your favorite professional golfer making a difficult chip over a bunker onto a green. The ball comes out hot from the heavy fringe and then checks up quickly, coming to rest near the pin. How vividly can you see this image?

    1 2 3 4 5

10. Imagine yourself executing a chip as described in item #9. The ball runs toward the cup coming to rest just below the pin. How vividly can you see this image?

    1 2 3 4 5

11. Visualize the image described in item #10. How deeply can you feel the execution of this fine-touch shot?

    1 2 3 4 5

12. Imagine that all your friends are watching as you chip the ball over the bunker and roll it up to the pin. Your golfing partners groan sympathically as the ball comes to rest on the edge of the cup. How vividly can you feel your emotional response to this shot?

    1 2 3 4 5

Putting

13. Visualize your favorite professional golfer executing a sensational putt that rolls along a serpentine path, breaks toward the hole and teeters on the lip for a split second before toppling into the cup. How vividly can you see this image?

    1 2 3 4 5

14. Imagine yourself executing a long putt over an undulating green that breaks left and then right, gradually slowing until it dies in the cup. How vividly can you see this image?

    1 2 3 4 5

15. Visualize the image described in item #14. How deeply can you feel in your hands the smooth velvet touch of the putter rolling the ball along the contour of the green?

    1 2 3 4 5

16. Imagine that your foursome is watching as your ball spirals over the undulating green and rolls into the cup for a birdie, winning the match for your team. How vividly can you imagine how you feel?

    1 2 3 4 5

Scoring Key: Visual Imagery	Scoring Keys: Kinesthetic & Emotional Imagery
Total the numbers you chose for items: #1, 2, 5, 6, 9, 10, 13 and 14.	Total the numbers you chose for items: #3, 7, 11 and 15. Use the scoring key below to assess your skill in kinesthetic imagery.
Use the scoring key below to assess your skill in visual imagery.	Total the numbers you chose for items #4, 8, 12 and 16. Use the scoring key below to assess your skill in emotional imagery.
33–40: Excellent visual imagery. **25–32:** Good visual imagery. **17–24:** Need more practice. **Below 17:** Need to learn visualization.	**17–20:** Excellent imagery skills. **13–16:** Good imagery skills. **9–12:** Fair imagery skills. **Below 9:** Need to learn imagery skills.

GREG LOUGANIS

- In 1984, voted the "Outstanding Amateur Athlete in the United States" by the AAU.

- In 1984 and 1988 Olympics, he won gold medals in springboard and platform diving.

- Won gold medals in Pan American Games in 1979, 1983 and 1987.

- Five-time World Champion: springboard in 1982, 1986; platform in 1978, 1982 and 1986.

- Won 47 US national diving titles–a record.

- In 1985, elected to the US Olympic Hall of Fame.

Greg Louganis: Master of Mental Imagery

Visualize yourself in your swimsuit standing on a wet platform the height of a two-story home, overlooking an Olympic pool more than 30 feet below. It's your final of ten dives that will determine how the rest of your life will unfold. Not only is it your last dive, it's also the most treacherous. This reverse three-and-a-half pike has a frightening 3.4 degree of difficulty and is considered the most difficult dive in the sport. It requires that you jump high and away from the platform and then spin backward toward it. As your head passes perilously close to the platform, you must bring your knees up to your chest and execute three somersaults in rapid

© Neal Preston/CORBIS

**Greg Louganis
born Jan. 29, 1960**

succession. Coming out of your third somersault, you must straighten your body in a fraction of a second so that as you impact the surface of the water at 32 mph you make no splash. Failure to execute the dive with perfect or near-perfect form will cost you the gold medal and the realization of a dream to which you have dedicated 20 years of your life.

Close your eyes and hear the cacophony of more than 10,000 excited spectators at poolside below. Several hundred million television sets throughout the world are focused on your every move as you approach the end of the slippery surface. A nation of almost 300 million people have pinned their hopes for Olympic gold on you and how you perform this most dangerous feat. It's all or nothing at all. What goes through your mind as you attempt to focus on the dive? How do you block out the memory of the pain and shame you felt when you hit your head on the diving board just a few days earlier attempting that very dive? The springboard only cut you for a few stitches, but the inflexible platform could snap your neck and render you a quadriplegic or kill you as it did Russian Olympic diver Sergei Shalibashvili just five years earlier.

When Greg Louganis climbed to the top of the Olympic platform to attempt the most difficult dive of his life, he entered a semi-hypnotic state in which he visualized the dive he was about to perform. For Greg it was all about removing himself from the noise, the fears and the taunts to allow his body to do what it did best. In his autobiography, he described his state of mind as he approached his moment of truth (p. 208–9):

This time I had to narrow my focus and shut everything out. I had to go into my own world: just the pool, the board, and me and Ron [his coach]. I had to be intensely aware of my body and my timing to make sure that everything was in sync. I couldn't afford to be distracted by the audience...I clasped my hands in front of me and closed my eyes, as if in prayer. A lot of people thought I was praying, but I was actually trying to get focused...I took a deep breath, and as I exhaled, I said to myself, "Breathe, relax, get your arms through."

Before executing this all-important dive, Greg Louganis had attained a state of relaxed concentration, the final stage in the visualization process. The earlier stages in the visualization process, i.e., imagining desired results and mental rehearsal, had been practiced the night before and throughout his diving practices. In describing how he learned the difficult reverse three-and-a-half, he said (p. 113–4):

...The new dives weren't easy to learn, and before I did each one, I had to be able to visualize it, which meant that I had to see somebody else do it before I'd give it a try. When I visualized the dive in my head, it would take about three seconds to go through the dive, but I would see it in slow motion. I don't know how I did that, but because I could see it in slow motion, I was able to take the dive apart and memorize it step by step.

Greg's ability to apply mental imagery in all its forms enabled him to rise above all others and dominate the diving scene over a 12-year period that spanned four Olympic games. But the story of Greg Louganis is not just an engaging account of exceptional athletic achievement. It's a story about a young child who was abandoned by his teen-aged parents, mocked by his classmates for a reading impairment that resulted from dyslexia, and scorned by his adoptive father for his homosexuality. It's a real-life drama about a suicidal boy who found within himself the resources needed to push through ridicule, abusive relationships, addiction, painfully low self-esteem, homosexual orientation and HIV infection to rise to the top of the world and discover who he is.

GREG LOUGANIS'S TREK TO THE TOP

Early Imprints

Life for Greg Louganis began on January 29, 1960. From the outset, it was a struggle. His Samoan father and Scandinavian mother were mere children themselves–15 years old and unmarried. Lacking the financial resources to provide a home for their child, they decided to put Greg up for adoption. At the age of 9 months, he was adopted by Peter and Francis Louganis who lived in a suburb of San Diego, California. Peter was of Greek origin and Frances was a Texas farm girl of northern Irish ancestry.

Though his mixed heritage would later turn out to be an advantage, Greg's olive complexion made him a target for abuse by his white-skinned schoolmates who called him "nigger" and "retard." The latter insult resulted from Greg's reading difficulties that were later attributed to dyslexia. Ridicule from his peers and a sense of rejection by his biological parents caused Greg to have low self-esteem and feelings of isolation at school. When his adoptive mother Frances started him in dance and gymnastics classes at age three, Greg found a niche into which he could escape. Natural body awareness proved an advantage in both activities.

From age three until eleven, he spent each weekend in dance competitions leaving little time for a normal childhood. However, the 1960s was a time when real men didn't eat quiche and real boys didn't take dance lessons. Dancing was regarded as an activity for girls, and a boy who participated in dance was often considered effeminate or a sissy. Peter Louganis was an old-style authoritarian Greek immigrant, a tough taskmaster who was incapable of relating to a highly sensitive boy, especially one who violated his definition of manhood. Life in the Louganis household became for Greg a fruitless quest to please an unreceptive, judgmental parent. Though a loving mother, Francis was submissive and reluctant to stand up to her domineering husband.

On one occasion, when Greg was 10 years old, an older classmate told Greg to meet him at the bus stop after school. When Greg arrived, the older student punched him and slammed his head into the pavement. His head was cut and his shirt torn as a cheering cluster of onlookers celebrated his humiliation. During the assault, Greg felt that the bully's rage and contempt were merely a manifestation of his father's inner feelings toward him. In his autobiography he reflected (p. 37):

During the fight, I remember it felt like my father was the one throwing the punches. For years after, I had this awful feeling that Dad thought I deserved to get beat up, that he thought I was a sissy, and that he agreed with all the things the kids at school said about me.

Years later Frances shared a chilling revelation with Greg. On that afternoon, she explained, someone had told her there was going to be a fight at the bus stop and that Greg was going to be beaten up. She rushed down to the bus stop and to her horror saw her husband and her cousin in the crowd of spectators. Feeling powerless to stop the fight, she ran home crying rather than witness the cruel battering of her son. On hearing this, Greg realized that he had, indeed, seen his father in the crowd, but was so horrified at the time that he had blocked it from his memory until the moment his mother recounted the incident.

Although Greg had been involved in gymnastics and dance from age three, it wasn't until he was nine that he took his first diving lesson. Within three years, he was diving in earnest. His early success in this sport provided him with a therapeutic escape from the negativity that he associated with his school and home environments. *Psychology Today* asserted in July 1999, "The opposite of play is not work. It's depression." Greg seemed to sense that diving was his play and his only antidote to the dark moods and depression that increasingly threatened his survival. He explained (p. 38):

Being beat up at elementary school–like being beaten by my dad–proved to be a big motivator. The name-calling and the humiliation pushed me to strive to be better than everyone. It made me angry, and I learned to focus most of that angry energy on my acrobatics and diving.

However, as Greg entered his teens, the taunting classmates had added the terms "fag" and "queer" to their repertoire of insults. The continual barrage of verbal abuse seriously undermined Greg's self-worth. Whether he would eventually succumb and self-destruct, or use the abuse as a motivational springboard, was anyone's guess. In fact, Greg would spend the next decade of his life walking the razor's edge between the abyss of breakdown and the ecstasy of breakthrough.

Ladders to Climb and Snakes to Avoid

Before Greg could climb to the top of the Olympic platform, he would have to scale many ladders and avoid many snakes in his personal and professional life. Like most of California in the 1970s, San Diego was at the forefront of the counter-culture revolution. Marijuana was considered "cool" and some pundits were touting dangerous hallucinogenic drugs, such as LSD, as "mind-expanding." By the seventh grade, Greg had discovered that smoking pot made him more socially in tune with his peers. It also offered the added bonus of a momentary escape from depression. His use of pot increased during his years in junior high and eventually he "graduated" to the amphetamine speed. Alcohol also became one of the feel-good drugs he used to cope. In the Jungian typology, Greg Louganis would be classified as a "feeling" personality type, a personality that is also prone to addiction. Though he did not develop a full-scale addiction, he did develop an emotional dependence that exacerbated his mood swings and his depression.

When he reached the age of 12, Greg was already an accomplished dancer and acrobat. But the incessant pounding on concrete floors had taken a toll on his knees. Physicians informed his mother that he had to quit gymnastics and dancing or chance ruining his legs. Greg was devastated. The prognosis almost destroyed him and led to his first suicide attempt. In describing this traumatic event, he wrote (p. 40):

> At twelve years old, I decided that I would kill myself. I went into my parents' medicine cabinet and took a bunch of different pills, mostly aspirin and Ex-Lax. Then I took a razor blade out of the cabinet and started playing with it over my wrist. I started to bleed, but I didn't go deep enough to cut any veins or arteries. It also turned out that I didn't take enough of anything from the medicine cabinet to do myself harm.

Masquerading at first as a major setback, Greg's prohibition from dancing turned out to be a blessing in disguise. His need to perform had been evident from a very young age, so when he couldn't dance, he channeled all his energies into diving. Little did he realize that almost ten years of practicing summersaults, elegant flips and acrobatic moves would yield handsome dividends in his performance on the high board. The chaos he experienced at age 12 was morphing into the success he was beginning to enjoy in his early teens.

In the summer of 1973, Greg entered the diving competitions at the Junior Olympics in Colorado Springs and represented the United States at the World Age Group Championships in Luxembourg. In the following year, his coach John Anders encouraged him to spend the summer in Tucson, Arizona to work with coach Charlie Silber who had access to a diving platform where he could practice. Greg continued to improve his diving skills. After returning home in the fall, he began to work with Olympic coach, Dr. Sammy Lee. Dr. Lee helped him develop the killer instinct that had been antithetical to Greg's nature. Describing Lee's coaching style, Greg recalled (p. 49):

Diving with Dr. Lee, however, was not fun. He was hard-nosed and inflexible, and like with my father, it was his way or no way. His approach was very aggressive: Go for it; get killed; get up; go for it again; get killed again...Dr. Lee told me that I didn't have a killer instinct, that it wasn't in my nature to fight...Part of his training was to toughen me up, which I needed...He taught me to push through those difficult workouts when all I wanted to do was crawl into bed and pull the sheets over my head. Despite his telling me I wasn't a fighter, however, Dr. Lee often expressed how much faith he had in me, which gave me the confidence I needed to compete.

In the summer of 1975, on Dr. Lee's suggestion, Greg traveled to Ron O'Brien's diving camp in Decator, Alabama. One of the top coaches in the United States, O'Brien helped Greg hone the execution of his twists and somersaults by practicing on a trampoline. O'Brien's coaching style matched Greg's learning style. Commenting on Ron O'Brien's approach, Greg observed (p. 51):

Ron really understood me. He knew I needed help with both the technical and the mental aspects of my diving. I wasn't the kind of diver who did a dive because I wanted to be a daredevil. I had to be physically and mentally prepared to do it. I had to be able to see it in my head.

In January 1976, Greg moved in with Dr. Lee and his family who lived just a few hours north of San Diego. This enabled him to train every day and receive coaching from Dr. Lee while he continued to attend high school. His mentor worked tirelessly with Greg, grooming him for the summer Olympics later that year in Montreal, Canada. To everyone's surprise, including Greg's, he came first in both the springboard and the 10-m platform events in the qualifying round held a month before the Olympics. Here he was, a boy of 16, about to represent the United States at the Olympics and compete against men twice his age!

The Montreal Olympics in 1976

Greg came to the Olympics with high expectations. From an early age he had identified winning with acceptance. Receiving a score of 10 on a dive was one of the only things that brought the approval he craved from his father. As he saw it, the only way to be worthy of love was to achieve perfection. Consequently, when he placed sixth in the springboard competition at the Olympics, he was humiliated and couldn't face his parents at poolside; he merely headed for the Olympic Village and went straight to bed.

However, the platform competition was a different story. Greg rose to the top, matching the reigning Olympic champion Klaus Dibiasi dive for dive. When it was time for the ninth dive, the two divers were alone in their bid for gold. Dibiasi had won the gold medal for Italy in this event at the 1968 and 1972 Olympics. Only two other males had won two Olympic gold medals in the platform dives, and one of them was Dr. Sammy Lee in 1948 and 1952. If Klaus Dibiasi were to win the gold this time, he would surpass Dr. Lee and become the only male diver to win three gold medals in the platform event. Dr. Lee had more than one reason to want Greg to win the gold in this event.

As Greg Louganis completed his difficult front-three-and-a-half pike and entered the water, he knew that he was past vertical and that the gold medal had slipped from his grasp. The disappointed and angry Dr. Lee chastised him in front of the gallery as he emerged from the pool. Greg later reported that he felt worthless and incapable of responding to Dr. Lee's attack. When he completed his tenth and final dive to win the silver, he wept with the shame of having let down his coach and those who expected him to win gold. In his autobiography, he noted, p. 62, "It would be many years and another two trips to the Olympics before I could hold that silver medal in my hand and feel anything other than revulsion." When his father put his arm around Greg and whispered in his ear, "I'm very proud of you," Greg thought his dad was merely trying to mollify his pain. After all, he had failed to win the gold.

Up to this point in his life, Greg had used diving to show the world he was normal, but he was not; he was different in many ways. And those differences enabled him to perform abnormal feats. One difference that caused him great emotional pain was his sexual orientation. While in his teens, he first came to the realization that he preferred the company of boys rather than girls. However, it was not until the Montreal Olympics when he came to terms with his homosexuality. He recalled in his autobiography (p. 71):

> *Montreal was where I remember telling someone for the first time that I was gay, where I fell in love for the first time…I don't really know how I knew what a gay person was, but by the time I got to the Olympics, I had no doubt that I was one.*

The object of Greg's infatuation was one of the male Russian divers whom Greg described as "absolutely beautiful." Apparently, the admiration was mutual and Greg experienced his first homosexual relationship. He later described this tryst as his "rite of passage"–it was the first of several gay relationships that would define his life in the decade to come. Although Greg had finally acknowledged within himself his homosexuality, he was not yet ready to "come out of the closet."

In Search of an Identity

After winning silver at the Olympics, Greg was surprised at the approval and adulation that poured from all sources. The pilot on his flight home announced Greg's presence to the passengers, and the airline staff regaled him and his family with free food and drinks for the entire flight. When they disembarked, there was a media frenzy–television and newspaper reporters descending en masse to get a sound bite, a quote or a picture. He was invited to appear on talk shows and at gala occasions, including a special invitation to meet with President Gerald Ford at the White House. Overnight he became a hero at Valhalla High School in San Diego where, in his own words, he "left as an invisible person and returned as a hero." He experienced ambivalent reactions from his schoolmates, similar to those Wilma Rudolph had described exactly 20 years earlier: most students wanted to "touch the robe of greatness" while others, assuming he had become a snob, snubbed him. Greg Louganis was a celebrity whose life was irrevocably changed, though inside he remained an insecure teenager troubled by low self-esteem. At a time when most teens were competing for dates, this high-school sophomore was an international star, yet he was unable to reconcile the public acclaim with his feelings of inadequacy. He later commented (p. 68):

I didn't see myself the way other people saw me. To them I was this sexy Olympic icon, an image the newspapers seemed to encourage when they described me as having a "muscular, brown, supple body." I may have been all those things to others, but at sixteen, when I looked in the mirror I didn't see anyone different from the skinny, dark-skinned sissy I'd been before I went to the Olympics.

This was not false modesty. Greg Louganis was exhibiting the same perceptual distortion that causes the anorexic to look in the mirror and see a fat person. The elation that followed his triumph in Montreal would inevitably be followed by a let down—the kind of mild depression that all humans are hardwired to experience as the emotional hangover after an emotional high. However, the deep depression that had plagued Greg in his pre-Olympic days returned with a vengeance. A back injury he sustained in the fall of 1976 when practicing a dive restricted his practice sessions and he began to believe he might never again participate in Olympic diving. At the same time, his homosexuality was undermining his sense of self-worth and increasing his sense of isolation. In the fall of 1977, Greg reached the depths of despair and once more attempted suicide with an overdose of pills. Fortunately, this second suicide attempt was unsuccessful.

What lifted Greg from his chronic depression was not mental therapy but diving. As his back injury healed, he found that he could perform like his old self. Having accumulated extra credits for coaching, Greg graduated from high school in January 1978 and focused entirely on his diving. Then in May of that year, Ron O'Brien, the diving coach with whom Greg had trained four years earlier, came to coach at Mission Viejo, just an hour north of Greg's home. This was a watershed event in Greg's diving career as he weaned himself from Dr. Lee and adopted Ron O'Brien as his new mentor. While Dr. Lee's tough coaching style had helped Greg develop some toughness and competitive verve, Ron O'Brien's positive and encouraging style that Greg described as "nurturing" was a better fit with the temperamental diver's personality. O'Brien seemed to know when to stroke Greg's ego and when to apply the prod. They built a trusting mentor-protégé relationship that would take them to the next two Olympic Games.

In the fall of 1979, Greg went to the University of Miami on an athletic scholarship. Majoring in drama, he split his time among social activities, diving, and taking acting and dance lessons. In his dance lessons he found himself dancing with male partners, some of whom were also gay. For the first time in his life he was becoming comfortable with his sexual orientation. He later recalled, "Suddenly there were all these other people like me out there. It was such a relief to know I wasn't the only one." However, his elation would be short-lived. He entered a gay relationship that he described as "his first real relationship," but when it came crashing down, he went with it. A third unsuccessful suicide attempt followed. Once again, with a little help from friends, he recovered from the overdose of drugs and life's adversities.

The Moscow Olympics in 1980

At the end of his freshman year at the University of Miami, Greg returned to California and coach Ron O'Brien to prepare for the 1980 Olympics in Moscow. By the time of the Olympic trials in Austin, Texas in June 1980, Greg Louganis was head and shoulders above all the other male divers in the United States. He took first place in both the springboard and platform events. On his seventh dive in the springboard competition, the reverse two-and-a-half pike, he received six 10s and a 9.5, virtually a perfect score. His performance in the platform competition was even more impressive: he scored several 10s and beat the second-place diver by 65 points! Subsequently, the other divers referred to him as GL, for God Louganis.

However, it was all for naught. To punish the Soviet Union for their invasion of Afghanistan in December 1979, President Carter and the United States government boycotted the Olympic games. The American athletes who had trained so hard for four years would have to wait another four years to compete for an Olympic medal. To all members of the U.S. team, especially those who would be too old to compete in 1984, this was devastating news. However, Greg was still young and had several prime years still ahead.

In December 1980, Greg transferred to the University of California in Irvine on an athletic scholarship. To help him psyche up for the 1984 Olympics, Ron O'Brien encouraged him to formulate and visualize short and long-term goals. One goal was to set the record for the most national championships for a male diver, so O'Brien scheduled Greg into about 20 diving competitions per year up to 1984. Louganis achieved this goal with a total of 18 national championships by the end of 1981. However, as the 1984 Olympics approached, Greg discovered that he was being beaten in national meets by a rising star, Bruce Kimball. Recognizing that Kimball's consistently impeccable mechanics were virtually unbeatable, Greg decided to include more difficult dives in his repertoire. Scoring in diving usually involves collecting scores from seven judges on a scale from 1 to 10, tossing out the highest and lowest scores, adding the five remaining scores together, multiplying by the degree of difficulty, and then multiplying by 0.6 (this last factor is applied to keep the scores historically comparable to earlier scores which involved only five judges). By performing more difficult dives, Greg could achieve higher scores with a slightly lower quality of execution. Furthermore, to compete with Louganis, other competitors would be forced to attempt harder dives that might exceed their strength or agility capabilities. This strategy was Greg's application of the principle "Make 'em play your game" that I presented in the previous chapter.

To master the difficult dives, Greg applied the visualization techniques that enabled him to transcend the purely physical and enter a state of higher consciousness. As Michael Murphy described in *The Psychic Side of Sports*, "Sports are one of the commonest ways in which people experience altered states of consciousness–there is an element of extrasensory perception." Greg Louganis knew how to learn dives in this way and he was prepared to press this advantage.

Preparing for the Los Angeles Olympics in 1984

Greg's strategy and rigorous practice routines paid off at the world championships in Ecuador in 1982. Prior to that event, he had been training 5 to 6 hours per day, 6 days a week, and he was now nearing the peak of his diving potential. In the springboard event he beat Soviet Aleksandr Portnov, the gold medalist at the Moscow Olympics, by a substantial margin of 126 points. Bruce Kimball came in third. A significant contribution to Greg's runaway victory was the near-perfect score of 92.07 points that he received in the very difficult front three-and-a-half pike–the highest score ever achieved in the history of springboard diving. Greg also won the platform event, beating Vladimir Alenik of the Soviet Union by less than five points. This victory resulted from his perfect execution (seven 10's) of an inward one-and-a-half pike. By late 1982, as he approached his 23rd birthday, it was clear that Greg Louganis was becoming the dominant force in international diving.

Greg graduated from college in early 1983, enabling him to devote himself full time to preparing for the '84 Olympics in Los Angeles. If he could win two gold medals in Los Angeles, he would be only the third man in the history of diving to reach this pinnacle. As 1984 approached, the media were already billing him as "the Baryshnikov of diving" and a sure bet for two gold medals. As the pressure mounted, Greg became obsessed and trained furiously. O'Brien weighed the divers regularly, insisting that they reach extremely low levels of body fat. A test by the sports psychologists at UC Irvine showed he had a body fat level of 6%. That is extremely low, even for a world-class athlete. In another test, his higher-than normal fast-twitch muscle system was first documented. Greg's quadriceps muscles came in at 75% fast-twitch, compared to one of the female members of the team who registered 30% fast-twitch. The researchers who tested Greg attributed his elegant explosions off the diving board to this "fast-twitch" muscularity. Those with a high percent of fast-twitch muscle are quicker and tend to excel in short-burst sports like basketball, racquetball, squash, sprinting and diving. This is one factor in which genetics plays a role, but it was not the dominant factor in Greg's success as a diver. It was Greg's capacity to visualize a dive in slow motion and see its component parts that enabled him to master the difficult dives. This use of mental imagery combined with his ability to reach a state of relaxed concentration, enabled Greg to achieve consistently flawless execution of these complex movements.

The Los Angeles Olympics in 1984

Qualifying for the '84 Olympics was not a slam-dunk. Bruce Kimball had beaten Greg in six of the previous 11 national events and Greg would have to get past him to get to the Olympics. Invoking the "Make 'em play your game" principle, Greg perfected the difficult dives that he had learned for the world championships in Ecuador two years earlier. At the Olympic trials in Indianapolis, Bruce Kimball proved to be extremely tough competition, staying within 10 points of Greg–a miniscule margin–up to the tenth dive. Finally on the tenth dive of the platform competition, Greg executed, with near perfect form, a dive with a difficulty of 3.4 compared to Kimball's 2.9. Greg's strategy had paid off and he was off to the Olympics.

It had been eight years since Greg had won the silver medal at the Montreal Olympics and it had haunted him ever since. For most, it would have been acceptable to come in second, but not the obsessively driven Louganis. For eight long years, he waited to have a shot at not one but two gold medals. In his first event, the springboard, he took his dives one at a time, focusing on that dive and avoiding distracting thoughts about winning. Each time he walked onto the springboard, encouraging cheers of "Greg! Greg!" rose up from 12,000 screaming fans, most of whom waved American flags in a hopeful transference of energy and triumph. He surfaced after each dive to the deafening applause of admiring aficionados. It was clear that Greg was in the zone, executing each dive with the skill and panache more often associated with ballet than diving. In his memoir, he spoke often about how he would enter into a kind of metaphysical state prior to each dive. It was a euphoric state that drove out all negative energy that was inside. Later he explained, "If you have to think, it's over. It's reflex, so you must have it within, or you have already hit the water." When he completed his final dive, he had won the gold medal by more than 92 points, achieving a record 754.41 points for this event. Only one other diver in the history of Olympic springboard had ever scored more than 700 points and that was Alexandr Portnov, whom Greg had soundly defeated two years earlier. Greg was finally an Olympic gold medalist!

His chance for a second gold medal came in the platform event. With one gold to his credit, the pressure to win was slightly reduced. However, as he progressed through his dives, it became apparent that he had a chance to break the elusive 700-point barrier and a good chance of winning a second gold. At this point, the fear of failure began to creep in, threatening to break his concentration and bring disaster. By the time he reached his final dive, Greg had accumulated just over 618 points. He would need 82 points on his final dive to break the 700-point barrier. However, this final dive was the infamous reverse three-and-a-half that had killed Sergei Shalibashvili one year before. Not only would Greg have to avoid hitting the platform, but to execute the dive with perfect or near-perfect form, he would have to have his head pass close to it. To settle his nerves and regain his focus, Greg envisioned the perfect dive as he climbed to the top of the platform, reciting the words from the musical, *The Wiz*, "Believe in yourself right from the start. Believe in the magic that's inside your heart." Gathering his internal resources, he exploded up and out from the platform, flipped backward toward it, and passed within inches of it as he spun toward the water. A tumultuous cheer signaled a near-perfect dive that earned him 92.82 points, a total of more than 710 points and his second gold medal! Greg Louganis was on top of the world.

Two weeks after the Olympics, Greg won in the U.S. Nationals, giving him a total of 29 national titles and breaking the record held by Cynthia Potter. In the wake of Greg's Olympic victory, this achievement was an anticlimax, but it represented the successful completion of a goal he had formulated years earlier. Greg began to wonder whether it was time to retire. Were there more worlds to conquer? He had won two Olympic gold medals in diving, but this was not a record. However, no male diver had ever won four Olympic gold medals; was it time to formulate a new goal?

What Next?

The roller coaster ride that was Greg's life was poised to take another sharp dive into near chaotic oblivion. Shortly after the Olympics, Greg moved in with his lover–a sinister manipulator who knew how to exploit Greg's vulnerability to his own ends. Recognizing Greg's lack of interest in financial matters, he persuaded him to sign a contract making himself Greg's manager and in charge of his finances. The course of the next few years followed a script that is typical of an abusive relationship. The male companion bullied and punished Greg who, lacking in self-esteem, accepted the punishment as his due. Early in their affair, his partner established physical dominance by forcibly raping Greg. Preying on Greg's need to be loved, the lover proceeded to gain his trust and then control his life. By screening all Greg's communications, he was able to isolate him from his friends and then his family. When the relationship ended four years later, Greg discovered that he had been bilked of all his earnings from his numerous endorsements and media appearances. He also discovered that his former lover was a con-man who had been investigated by police for petty and grand theft as well as insurance fraud.

In 1988, Greg discovered he was HIV positive. At that time, the HIV virus and AIDS were just appearing on the radar screen of the public conscious as something that infected mainly gay white males. The prognosis was dismal. As the HIV virus mushroomed into full-blown AIDS, it systematically destroyed the immune system, leaving its victim defenseless against infection. AIDS victims were seen in the late stages of the disease as thin, wasted ghosts of their former selves. The once robust movie idol, Rock Hudson, appeared on television in 1985 as a ravaged skeleton. He died soon after. Before the development of drugs to arrest the progression of the disease, being diagnosed HIV positive was tantamount to a death sentence. In the absence of comprehensive scientific data on the contagiousness of HIV, the American public became paranoid about associating with those who were infected. Dentists and doctors began wearing plastic gloves and those in contact sports became conscious of the dangers of contracting the virus through cuts. There was considerable controversy about the need to test professional athletes for the virus and the possible exclusion of those infected.

Being HIV positive was a stigma and those infected were perceived as a danger to everyone else.

When Greg finally summoned the courage to leave his lover in late 1988, he would discover the truly insidious nature of his male companion. Greg's HIV positive status, though confided to his lover, was a secret that Greg felt he could not afford to share with the world. However, his lover was also HIV positive. It was never clear if one had transmitted it to the other or whether they were both were infected prior to their relationship. However, it was clear that if Greg's HIV status were made public, his career could come to an abrupt end. Of course, this opportunity was not lost on his unscrupulous companion who used the threat of public exposure to blackmail Greg. A settlement was arranged and Greg regained his freedom. The exploitive ex-lover died from AIDS within two years, while Louganis continued his life under the foreboding specter of an imminent and painful death.

The Seoul Olympics in 1988

As the Seoul Olympics approached, Greg began to gear up for his quest to become the first male diver to win four Olympic gold medals. However, in the four years since his previous Olympic gold, he had progressed from being one of the younger competitors to one of its veterans. His strongest competitor in the platform event would be the young Xiong Ni of China who was about half Greg's age. Greg reported that some of the divers referred to him as Grandpa. Furthermore, he had become bulkier as he matured, and his heavy schedule of celebrity appearances prevented him from training as rigorously as in 1984. Added to this was his HIV-positive status that required doses of AZT medication every four hours plus regular injections of gamma globulin.

As expected, Greg sailed through the Olympic trials with first-place finishes in both events by a substantial margin. The Olympic drug screening that he feared might eliminate him from the competition did not test for HIV. He was now able to focus undistracted on the Olympic contest. Within six weeks, he was in Seoul, Korea, dazzling the poolside gallery as he always had in the past. By the time he finished his first eight of the eleven preliminary dives on the springboard, he had a substantial lead. There was little doubt that he would make the finals scheduled for the next day.

However, on what would become his infamous ninth dive, a reverse two-and-a-half pike, Greg hit his head on the board. It was a thud that was heard half way around the world. The horrified spectators rose to their feet as Greg surfaced, embarrassed and badly shaken. Blood was oozing from a deep gash in his head, but only Greg and Ron knew that the blood contained the HIV virus. It would appear that Greg's hopes for qualifying for tomorrow's finals had suddenly evaporated. He was rushed to the medical station where the doctor determined that he would need four stitches to close the gash in his head. But he still had two more dives to perform. There was no time for anesthetic if he were to continue competing. He had strived all his life for this elusive gold and he wasn't about to wimp out now. Greg chose to have the stitches without anesthetic and a few minutes later, he returned to the board and ripped (entered the water without a splash) one of the toughest dives performed in the Olympic games. The thunderous applause was deafening. The ecstatic patrons showed their appreciation of his courage and verve. The final dive, though the toughest and most dangerous of all, was performed well, but its impact was anticlimactic. The finals in the springboard were also somewhat anticlimactic. Greg performed the same dives as in the preliminaries, only this time there were no glitches and he won the gold medal with a score of 730.80. He was within one gold medal of achieving his ultimate goal–the most career golds won in Olympic diving competition.

During the three-day hiatus between the springboard and platform events, Greg resumed his rigorous practice schedule. From the 10-meter platform, the body accelerates to a speed of approximately 32 mph before it impacts the water. When the hands precede the head on entry, the impact is substantial but tolerable. When the hands aren't quite together, and the head has fresh stitches, it's a different story. In Greg's words, "The few times I missed, my ears were ringing from the pain." As Greg prepared for the platform event, he had to focus beyond the pain and beyond the ever-present danger. His accident on the springboard a few days earlier was a grim reminder of the competition in Tbilisi in 1979 when he hit his head on the platform while performing a reverse pike and was knocked unconscious for 20 minutes. The platform is less forgiving than the springboard and the potential for a fatal accident is much greater. Greg would have to rely more heavily than ever on his visualizing techniques to block out his fears and establish a focus.

The finals in the Olympic platform event were a spectacular blend of esthetics and athleticism. Sports analysts characterized Greg as a dancer pirouetting through the air. His rhythmical movement as he twisted and turned gracefully, while suspended high above the poolside spectators, was an elegant ballet in a weightless space. But this competition would not be a slam-dunk. In the four years between the 1984 and the 1988 Olympics, the Chinese divers had improved substantially. They had studied Greg's dives in the '84 Olympics and had mastered the difficult dives, wiping out Greg's strategic advantage. He knew that the Chinese had closed the gap and that he was in for the fight of his life.

When Xiong Ni of China approached his final dive, he was 3 points ahead of Greg Louganis. Ni stood on the platform, preparing for his inward three-and-a-half dive, a dive with a 3.2 degree of difficulty. Meanwhile Greg was getting ready to climb the ladder, attempting to focus by visualizing the perfect dive and reciting the words from *The Wiz*, "Believe in yourself." Then he heard Ni enter the water without a splash. Ni had ripped his final dive. The crowd went wild in their thunderous applause for Ni's near-perfect performance. The posted scores were all 8.5s and 9s. Greg knew that this was his last hurrah. It was the only chance he would have to win a fourth Olympic gold medal and establish a new record. If he lost this opportunity, it would be lost forever. He later described what went through his head in these final moments (p. 206):

> *Most of the time I looked at my diving as a performance. Part of me was a competitor but mostly I felt like I was a performer. But on this dive I was 90 percent competitor and 10 percent performer. I had to be a competitor because it was going to be very close.*

Greg climbed the steps to attempt the infamous reverse three-and-a-half with a 3.4 degree of difficulty. Putting his hands together as if in prayer, he visualized the perfect dive. Then, having achieved a single-minded focus, he leapt up and out, flipping back toward the board, as close as he dared for maximum height and optimal form. As he completed his third rotation, he kicked his legs upward and stretched out his body. A minor splash as he entered the water told him that he was a little short of vertical. Greg emerged from the water, looked up at the scoreboard and knew he had won. Though the last dive of his competitive career was not perfect, it was near enough to give him a final score of 638.61 and win the gold by 1.14 points. Greg Louganis had become the first man in history to win four Olympic gold medals in diving! He looked at his coach and mentor Ron O'Brien and both broke down with emotion. The two friends embraced. Later at the team banquet, Greg came to the podium, turned to Ron and said (p. 213):

Ron, I couldn't have gotten through this without you. It took all ten years of our experience together, and a lot of love and trust, to get through a very difficult week. Nobody will ever know what we went through, nobody.

Indeed, Ron was one of the only people who knew that Greg was afflicted with a terminal condition and was wondering just how long before he would die. Greg broke down in tears, went to Ron's table and they both wept.

Legacy

Greg Louganis left the world of diving with a level of expertise that will be almost impossible to beat. At age 16 he won a silver medal in the 1976 Olympics, following that with double gold medals in the 1984 and 1988 Olympics in the springboard and platform events. These four Olympic gold medals were unprecedented achievements in the annals of diving. In total, Greg had 47 U.S. national diving titles, more than anyone else in history. Louganis was also world champion in springboard in 1982 and 1986 and in platform in 1978, 1982 and 1986, and won gold medals in the Pan American Games in 1979, 1983 and 1987. His honors include membership in both the U.S. Swimming Hall of Fame and the Olympic Hall of Fame. He was the AAU Outstanding Amateur Athlete in the U.S. in 1984. However, his trek to the top was a precarious journey. Until he learned how to master his internal turmoil and the fears that plagued him from age twelve, he was a very fragile athlete.

The Louganis journey, like those of the other superstars profiled in this book, provides valuable insight into the motivation that underlies high achievement. Zaharias struggled against gender discrimination and Rudolph and Ali against racial discrimination. Both Greg Louganis and Navratilova had to battle discrimination against gays. In all these cases, the strength to achieve beyond personal limits grew out of a tortured psyche, the way a pearl grows out of the irritation in an oyster. No irritation, no pearl. Both adversity and insecurity are a *petri dish* for the breeding of achievement and success. Those with a mortal fear of failure are poised to overachieve.

Ted Turner once observed, "You will hardly ever find a super-achiever anywhere who isn't motivated at least partially by a sense of insecurity." Fear of failure is arguably the strongest of all motivators for success. Overachievers often try harder not to fail than to win. On recalling his fears before his final difficult dive at the 1988 Olympics, Louganis said, "I wasn't at all afraid of hitting my head. I was afraid of not doing the dive well enough to win." Ironically, the more he felt lost in the game of life, the more he dominated in the sport of diving. In his memoir he wrote with passionate honesty, "My whole life I couldn't fit in, because I was stupid, because I had dark skin, because I was adopted, because I was gay, because I was HIV positive." The closer he came to the precipice with drugs, drink and suicide attempts, the better he seemed to perform. Crisis appears to have fueled his athletic prowess. For Greg, life was a continuous battle between breakdown and breakthrough, but the breakdowns contributed to his breakthroughs. He walked the razor's edge between achieving and surviving and this led to his becoming the greatest diver in history. You will learn more about using breakdown as a springboard to breakthrough in Chapter 12.

Visualization was Greg's method of learning the difficult dives and reaching the level of relaxed concentration that enabled him to focus. He pictured the perfect dive in slow motion, sensing each movement step by step. He wrote (p. 18):

I would do every step over and over in my head until I visualized getting it right...By practicing over and over in my head, I stopped worrying about going blank. I had the routine so deeply memorized that I could feel it. Dancers call it kinetic memory.

Describing his pre-dive ritual before the final dive of his competitive career, Greg said (p. 3):

As I waited at the bottom of the ladder for my turn, I went through the dive in my mind, visualizing each step and playing music in my head to the beat of the dive. Most of the time I dove to "If You Believe" from The Wiz, *because of its message: If you believe within your heart you'll know / That no one can change the path that you must go. Believe what you feel, and know you're right / Because the time will come around when you'll say it's yours.*

Today, as a trainer and breeder of Harlequin Great Danes, Greg is now pursuing his life's passion. In 1999, he co-authored a book with Betsy Sikora Siino titled *For the Life of Your Dog: A Complete Guide to Having a Dog in Your Life, From Adoption and Birth Through Sickness and Health.* New advances in medicine have enabled him to keep AIDS at bay and to visualize a fulfilling life.

Chapter 9

PRINCIPLE #9: THINK HOLISTICALLY TO ANTICIPATE OUTCOMES

I don't skate to where the puck is. I skate to where it is going to be.
                                                                    –Wayne Gretzky

The Gestalt and Holistic Thinking

The world's great visionaries are those who see beyond conventional horizons. While most people focus on the individual tiles in a mosaic, the visionary sees the picture that they compose. This "big" picture is what cognitive psychologists call the *gestalt*–the whole. Seeing the picture rather than the tiles is thinking *holistically*, and such thinking begins with a far-reaching perspective. Visionaries peer outward in space and look forward in time, imagining what others would dismiss as impossible. In their seminal publication *The Limits to Growth*, the authors observe (Meadows *et al.*, p. 24):

> *The majority of the world's people are concerned with matters that affect only family or friends over a short period of time. Others look further ahead in time or over a larger area–a city or a nation. Only a very few people have a global perspective that extends far into the future.*

Envisioning a car for the masses, Henry Ford introduced the moving assembly line to produce his Model T and doubled the wages of his employees, thereby creating a middle class in America. When Tim Berners-Lee envisioned an electronic superhighway that would connect the world through a series of "hyperlinks," he developed a communication network that became the World Wide Web. The world's greatest advances in business and technology have come from visionaries whose far-reaching perspectives have enabled them to think holistically, see patterns and anticipate change.

A chess master contemplating the next move does not focus on an individual piece, but on the relative positions of the pieces. In the patterns that the pieces form on the full expanse of the chessboard, the master sees predicaments and opportunities. A sequential analysis of all possible moves and countermoves for each chess piece beyond the next two moves is unmanageable. However, by thinking holistically, the master can envision configurations that can evolve three or more moves ahead. While the amateur's focus is local and specific, the master's focus is global and holistic. Those who can't see it can't master it.

Holistic Thinking in Athletics Is Key to Anticipation

Athletic superstars, like great entrepreneurs, operate ahead of the action. Like eminent chess masters, they subordinate the action at hand to focus on where it will be two or three moves later. Superstars are master strategists who rely on their instincts to guide their course of action–especially when in a chaotic environment. Intuition allows the superstar to sense where to go prior to what transpires–to anticipate future action. In his research on the role of conscious activity in athletics, Robert Ornstein noted (p. 146), "We cannot consciously control our actions and still function at peak. Virtuoso performances and quick reactions are below consciousness." In short, muscle-memory has stored neurologically what works best.

Superstars, such as Pelé, Thorpe and Gretzky, anticipate the unfolding of events and respond to these visions. Hinting at the importance of anticipation, Gretzky once asserted, "I don't skate to where the puck is. I skate to where it's going to be." Athletic superstars see the action holistically. Like the commentator in the press box situated high above the fray, they view the action from the omniscient perspective of someone removed from it. Only by being mentally or physically removed from the action can one see the inter-action. That is the reason why generals like Hannibal and Napoleon viewed the battlefield from a distance.

At times, the superstar's anticipation seems surreal–the athlete materializes from nowhere, suddenly appearing in front of the goal or net and scoring. Such exceptional athletes appear to have a sixth sense of *knowing*. They operate in a kind of ethereal zone beyond the pale of others. It sets them apart, puzzling coaches and bewildering opponents. In the words of former New York Knicks player Walt Frazier, "Sometimes Bill Bradley has passed the ball [to where I intend to be] before I've taken the first step. It's like telepathy." Tennis players, anticipating their opponent's response, stand at the net waiting for the return. Basketball players drive to the basket, waiting for the ball to be thrown. Similarly, racquetball and squash superstars, having little time to react, merely anticipate where the next shot will appear and go to that spot.

To the spectator, this magical anticipation is often perceived as a genetically acquired mystical power. In reality, the superstar has been observing the game from a global perspective and trusting his instinct to anticipate opportunities. But what is the origin of this instinct? If it were genetic, we would expect it to be an inherited trait. However, anticipatory talent is not observed to run in families. A more plausible explanation for exceptional anticipatory ability and its roots in instinct can be found in neurophysiology and neuropsychology.

Revisiting the Findings of Brain Research

You may recall our discussion in Chapter 5 of some recent findings in brain research. The left hemisphere, which stores and records data, is the main center of activity in sequential thinking, logic and language. The right hemisphere is the domain of holistic thinking, imagination and spatial awareness. While the left brain helps us behave rationally, the right brain allows us to chase fantasies. Together they are a magical combination that enables us to perceive situations in their local and global perspectives. Ornstein explains (p. 134), "The left brain controls things that happen sequentially, the right controls things that happen all at once."

Research has shown that women tend to be more intuitive than men. Why? Females have more interconnections between the two brain hemispheres than males do. This means that the intuitive right brain is more strongly integrated with the rational left, allowing greater communication between the two. UCLA researcher Melissa Hines asserted, "Women's brains are paragons of holism and men's are paragons of specificity. This allows females to have better access to both sides of the brain and therefore makes it easier for a woman to express emotions than a man."

Intuition is what made Golda Meir, then Prime Minister of Israel, call a cabinet meeting a few days before the Yom Kippur War in 1973 to express her concerns that war was pending. Her cabinet said she was being too female, and should go on vacation. But Golda had sensed that troop movement dispatches she had seen were a harbinger of imminent danger. By trusting her instincts, she anticipated the war several days before it started. Her cabinet's reluctance to trust her instincts almost cost the Israeli state its existence.

The imagination, centered in the right brain, generates spontaneous images of possibilities through a curious and apparently arbitrary composition of data retrieved from the subconscious. What is possible competes with what is practical in a struggle for dominance in the decision-making process. By trusting their instincts, visionaries are able to harmonize these two apparently conflicting cognitive processes, melding new and unconventional visions with practical methods of execution. The ability to adapt to spontaneous situations is the root of supernatural performance in any endeavor.

Anticipation–A Derivative of Instinct

Anticipation in athletics is all about seeing the game holistically and acting instinctively. This is only possible after hundreds of thousands of experiential inputs that make anticipation an unconscious synthesis of past experiences. Great anticipators know what will probably happen before it happens. After experiencing a given play thousands of times, the seasoned player knows that it will likely happen again in a similar fashion. Experienced tennis players know that hitting the ball deep to the right will probably result in a cross-court return (down the line is far too difficult and dangerous), so charging the net will yield a significant advantage. Your opponent is back so you should be at the net waiting to execute the killer blow. Similar situations emerge in every sport. The mind records and internalizes these sequences, developing an intuitive sense of what will transpire in similar situations. Superstars know instinctively where the ball will go after it is hit or thrown.

But this is only part of anticipation. The rest is an internal sense of the probability that one event will predictably follow another, based on variables such as the score, time remaining, situation and a myriad of other factors. Anticipation is not about certainty but about an instinct for probabilities–the kind of instinct that is internalized through extensive experience.

Thus, the "promised land of winning" resides in spontaneous, instinctive and minimally conscious action. There is always a chance that instinct will fail you, but that is preferable to ignoring your instincts and blocking access to your most valuable database of information. When a blackjack dealer turns up a six, the odds are in your favor. Fear of losing should not prevent you from betting when the odds give you a competitive edge. Over-thinking can cause you to lose in sports just as it can at the blackjack table. Supporting

Yogi Berra's assertion that ninety percent of baseball is half mental, neuroscientists have recently concluded that baseball is 90 percent mental and only 10 percent physical. I believe this is true of all athletic competition.

Linear vs. Non-Linear Thinking

Tapping into your imagination is important whether you are chasing hot stocks or moving balls. As we observed in the previous chapter, visualization begins with imagination. It is the imagination (emanating from the right brain) that enables us to break out of old paradigms and conceive entirely new possibilities. Albert Einstein, who revolutionized physics, understood this when he wrote, "Imagination is more important than knowledge." His imagination enabled him to envision how time could flow at different rates in different universes and how light could bend in a gravitational field. By juxtaposing concepts in random ways, as in a dream that conjures strange images and happenings, the imagination explores possibilities that the left brain can accept as useful or reject as nonsense. The strong presence of imagination and right-brain activity in the thought process is known as *non-linear thinking*. Thought that involves mainly sequential brain processes is generally referred to as *linear thinking*.

Have you ever known anyone who seems to be "lucky" in his or her investments–not just once or twice, but more often than not? This person invests in real estate that suddenly skyrockets in value, buys a stock just before it appreciates five-fold, or sells an equity before its value plummets. What appears as arbitrary and lucky is often the result of good instincts and non-linear thinking. Non-linear thinkers are open to life's possibilities, relying to a large extent on their "gut feelings." They seem to be able to anticipate market swings and social trends even though they may not appear to have a particularly high IQ or an academic pedigree. Linear thinkers, on the other hand, are often snagged in what is called "analysis-paralysis." They focus on the details rather than taking a global perspective and tapping into their instincts. Linear thinkers are usually those who follow the trends, entering a hot market before it crashes or selling a property just before its value climbs into the stratosphere. Such people lament that they sometimes lose even when they bet on a "sure thing." Why does this happen so often to the linear thinker?

Consider someone who is seeking an investment that will appreciate substantially over 20 years. A linear approach might involve researching mutual funds to determine which have returned the greatest yield during the past decade and investing in that particular fund or family of funds. The research may be thorough, but the investor has assumed that past performance is a valid indicator of future performance–in itself a poor assumption. An equally serious omission is that the investor has not tapped into his or her own instincts about those investments from a global perspective. A non-linear thinker might take into consideration a broader range of factors such as international trade, demographic changes, or trends in consumer purchasing for housing or entertainment. This approach might also involve looking at foreign markets to anticipate inflation, population flows and the implications of new technological breakthroughs. Assessing the importance of these factors in a quantitative manner is a formidable task because mathematical models require many assumptions, any one of which, if flawed, can invalidate the conclusion. In most cases the non-linear thinker will trust a gut-level instinct that derives from the database of information stored in the subconscious. While there is no guarantee that the visionary's investment will outperform that of the linear thinker, history has taught us that the odds favor the visionary, particularly if this non-linear thinker is constantly reading and absorbing information. The "luck" of non-linear thinkers is preordained by a willingness to trust their subconscious instincts.

The greatest player in the history of hockey attributed his success to his ability to see what was going to happen before it happened. He was the prototype of the classic non-linear thinker in athletics. Wayne Gretzky typically skated to where the puck might be after two passes. This was a radical departure from standard playing procedure during his era. It made him special. In 1994, after Russian coach Tarasov watched Gretzky play, he told the press, "He is the only player who can play the game above the ice level. He sees things before they happen. If he were playing chess he would be a grand master." Among all athletes, none is better known for his ability to anticipate than Wayne Gretzky, and for that reason, I have chosen to profile him as the model for Principle #9: *Think holistically to anticipate outcomes.* To assess your own decision-making processes, try the assessment instrument on the opposite page.

DECISION-MAKING SELF-ASSESSMENT–Rational or Intuitive?

Choose a number 1–5, with 1 the lowest and 5 the highest, to indicate the degree to which you believe the statement describes you or how you feel. Record for each statement the number you have chosen. The scoring key is at the bottom of the page.

There are no "right" or "wrong" answers. In making your selection, answer the questions as candidly as possible without anticipating how you will be classified.

	Strongly Disagree			Strongly Agree	
1. I make decisions based on facts rather than gut instinct.	1	2	3	4	5
2. It's more important that my decision feel right than that it can be supported by a logical reason.	1	2	3	4	5
3. When assembling something, I prefer to read the directions first.	1	2	3	4	5
4. When I am confused about an investment decision, I go with my instinct rather than attempt to get more data.	1	2	3	4	5
5. I prefer receiving verbal directions to a location, instead of receiving a map.	1	2	3	4	5
6. When faced with a difficult decision, I sometimes prefer to "sleep on it" rather than make the decision right away.	1	2	3	4	5
7. When I drive in an urban area, I pay closer attention to the traffic and pedestrians than to the road signs.	1	2	3	4	5
8. Before choosing a house or apartment, I check for signs of water damage, infestation and other structural defects.	1	2	3	4	5
9. I often write down the pros and cons when I have to make tough decisions.	1	2	3	4	5
10. Before signing a contract with a person, I prefer to see them face-to-face.	1	2	3	4	5
11. The best decisions I make are based on a detailed analysis of factual information.	1	2	3	4	5
12. I believe that in every decision-making situation, there is a right choice and a wrong choice.	1	2	3	4	5

Instructions	Scoring Key	
A. Total the numbers you chose for items: #1, 3, 5, 8, 9, 11 and 12.	**24–30:**	Decision-making is highly rational.
	17–23:	Decisions mainly rational, some intuition.
B. Total the numbers you chose for items: #2, 4, 6, 7 and 10.	**9–16:**	Balance between rational and intuitive.
	0–8:	Tend toward intuitive decision-making.
Subtract the B-total from the A-total. Use the scoring key to interpret your score.	**Below 0:**	Decision-making based mostly on intuition.

WAYNE GRETZKY

- In 1997, voted the "greatest ever NHL player" by *The Hockey News*.

- Holds record for most career goals (894), assists (1963) and points (2,857).

- In 1986, he set the record for the most assists (163) and most points (215) in a season.

- Won the Hart Trophy for Most Valuable Player nine times

- Played in 208 playoff games in which he scored 122 goals and 260 assists (382 points).

- Led the Edmonton Oilers to become Stanley Cup champions in 1984, 1985, 1987, 1988.

- Helped Canada win the Canada Cup Championship in 1987.

- Averaged over 200 points for six consecutive seasons.

- Won the Art Ross Trophy 10 times as the NHL scoring leader.

Wayne Gretzky: The Great Anticipator

Sir Winston Churchill once described Russia as "a riddle wrapped in a mystery inside an enigma." Such a description could aptly describe the anticipatory ability of the greatest hockey player of all time–Wayne Gretzky–a Canadian of Russian and Polish descent. This quiet, unassuming, self-effacing superstar was an excellent skater, but not the best in the league; he had a hard wrist shot, but it wasn't overpowering, and his slight build prompted some sportswriters to predict that he wouldn't survive the physical punishment of professional hockey. Yet this mild-mannered legend broke virtually every record in the annals of professional hockey, setting the record for records broken. He was described by sportswriter Steve Dryden as "the most statistically dominant athlete in the history of North American professional sport."

© Reuters/CORBIS

Wayne Gretzky born Jan. 26, 1961

Intrigued by this clandestine phenomenon, Canadian sports physiologists and psychologists wanted to find out what made him so exceptional that he dominated the game of hockey for two decades. In one examination, Dr. Art Quinney, Dean of the Physical Education Department at the University of Alberta, tested Wayne and concluded, "Wayne is not gifted physically in any particular way." Dr. Cam O'Donnell also examined the enigmatic superstar in depth, and reported, "His reaction time was no faster than any other player, nor was his short-term memory." None of the tests could account for Gretzky's exceptionality. (If you've read the previous chapters, you may not be surprised. Jim Thorpe, Babe Zaharias and Pelé also registered "no exceptionalities" in physiological tests.) The researchers overlooked what really made Gretzky "The Great One": it was not physical, but mental.

Peter Gzowski, a writer who had been a close acquaintance of Wayne's from early in the hockey star's career, wrote about his research-based theory on what made Gretzky exceptional (*Total Gretzky*, p. 10):

At the core of my discoveries...was the realization that what set Wayne apart from his peers, and indeed, perhaps even from the dominant players who had preceded him, was not his physical gifts...and not even his visual talents–or not as we usually understand that phrase.

Instead, his mastery was a matter of perception...Where most players saw an assortment of individuals, both teammates and opponents, Wayne saw situations...[Like a grand master of chess], Wayne was a grand master of hockey: one glance around and his mind told him not only where people were but what they were likely to do next. That's why, I figured from my studies, he always made so many passes to apparently open spaces only to have a teammate suddenly appear in position to gather them in.

What Gzowski described was a holistic perspective that enabled Wayne to anticipate the moves of his teammates and opponents. Among the many opponents who attempted to describe the moves of the elusive enigma was goalie Mike Liut, who faced Gretzky in many games over a 14-year period. Reporting on a particular occasion, Liut said (*Total Gretzky*, p. 88):

Everyone knows [Gretzky] had unnatural hockey sense, but it was driven home when I lived it, when I was victimized by it...I remember him one night standing to my left below the goal line as the puck was fired into his corner. Our defenseman rushed at him. Wayne never looked back; he felt him coming. Just as the puck reached Wayne's stick...he fired it on his forehand off the end boards. The defenseman missed it. Wayne spun clockwise and emerged in front of the goal line with the puck on his stick. My pulse shot up like a champagne cork. I wanted to applaud...I never had any more respect for him than at that moment.

Denis Potvin, three-time winner of the Norris Trophy as best defenseman in the NHL, reported (*Total Gretzky*, p. 89):

Hitting Gretzky was like wrapping your arms around fog. You saw him, but when you reached out to grab him your hands felt nothing, maybe just a chill. He had the strongest danger radar of anyone on the ice. I think he could sense me coming, the way you can sometimes look ahead and sense somebody watching you from behind...I can't remember one time in my career when I got a good piece of him.

These animated descriptions, by those who were often victims of Wayne Gretzky's incredible talent for anticipation, paint a vivid picture of the holistic mind working in harmony with the body at the highest level. Sportswriters and sports psychologists are virtually unanimous in ascribing Gretzky's exceptional prowess to his holistic approach to hockey: seeing situations, identifying patterns and anticipating outcomes. By functioning at this level, he operated on the horizons of the visionary, looking beyond the immediate to the imminent. But how did Wayne Gretzky acquire this penchant for holistic thinking that gave him such anticipatory powers? The story of his life and particularly the experiences in his formative years provide some hints.

WAYNE GRETZKY'S TREK TO THE TOP

Early Imprints

In 1961, Brantford was a mid-size town, population approximately 74,000, located about 60 miles southwest of Toronto, Canada. Before Wayne Gretzky appeared on the world stage as *The Great One*, Brantford was best known as the home of Alexander Graham Bell, inventor of the telephone. Today it is more widely known as the place where hockey's greatest superstar was born (January 26, 1961) and, shortly after, laced up his first pair of hockey skates that became his main mode of transport for the next 40 years of his life.

Wayne began skating at age two on the frozen Nith River that flowed through his grandparents' farm. However, it was on the backyard ice rink built by his father, Walter Gretzky, where he honed the skills that led him to the National Hockey League (NHL). Explaining why he made this ice rink, later dubbed "Wally Coliseum," the proud father said, "I didn't flood the backyard to build a hockey star. I flooded it so I could watch from the kitchen, where it was warm." Walter Gretzky had tired of the countless frigid winter nights, shivering on the peripheries of public outdoor rinks to accommodate Wayne's pleas for just a few more minutes of ice time. Direct access to the Wally Coliseum through the back door at 42 Varadi Avenue enabled young Wayne to live his first winters on skates, eat his meals without removing his skates, and return to the ice without missing a shot. A backyard light, supported by another in the neighbor's yard, extended the ice time into the late evening. Plastic Javex bleach containers served as pylons around which Wayne could skate with the puck to develop his stick-handling skills. Wally Coliseum seemed to be the focal point of Varadi Avenue where all the neighborhood boys acted out their fantasies of playing in the NHL and winning the Stanley Cup before millions of cheering fans. Canadians have always embraced hockey as part of their identity and hockey superstars as their royalty.

The Gretzkys were a typical hockey family in their dedication to the game, though their sacrifices may have been a magnitude or two greater than the average. Walter Gretzky had been a competent player in Junior B hockey and coached his four sons on the fundamental skills. More importantly, he had an instinct for coaching. As sportswriter Roy MacGregor observed (*Total Gretzky,* p. 20):

> *Walter's greatest gift...was to nurture a craving, an itch for the game, and to provide the space to play and the time to experiment, and then to pass on the small things that he himself had learned while playing so that his son's own creativity could one day take them for his own.*

Wayne's mother, Phyllis, was strongly committed to her role as "hockey mom" adding her support by surrendering the house to hockey equipment clutter, skate marks on the floor and the continuous army of children marching through the house to the rink.

Eight Years of Minor Hockey

In his 1990 autobiography, Wayne spoke candidly about his early passion for hockey (Dryden, p. 21), "I'd get up in the morning, skate from 7:00 to 8:30, go to school, come home at 3:30, stay on the ice until my mom insisted I come in for dinner, eat in my skates, then go back out until 9:00" This was a ritual virtually every day of his young life. By the time Wayne reached six years of age, he had spent most of his life on skates with a stick and a puck and was desperate for a chance to play organized hockey. Since there were no leagues in the Brantford area for children in that age group, Walter took his eager eldest child to try out for the Nadrofsky Steelers of the Brantford Atom League where he would be competing against 10-year-olds. Wayne made the team, but in his first year with the Steelers managed to score only one goal. However, as the table shows, after his initial season, Wayne's scoring statistics rose exponentially, until by age ten, he had become a scoring machine with 378 goals in a season of 69 games.

Gretzky's Goals in His First 10 Seasons As an Amateur		
Year	**Division**	**Goals**
1967–68	Novice	1
1968–69	Novice	27
1969–70	Novice	104
1970–71	Novice	196
1971–72	Novice	378
1972–73	Peewee	105
1973–74	Peewee	196
1974–75	Bantam	90
1975–76	Junior B	27
1976–77	Junior B	36
Total Goals		1,160

Word of this rising new star blew across the Canadian landscape like an ice storm. A *Toronto Telegram* article on October 28, 1971, early in Wayne's final season with the Nadrofsky Steelers, wrote of this "phenom" who might one day become a superstar. The article quoted the 4-foot-10-inch, 70-pound prodigy, "Now Gordie Howe is my kind of player. He had so many tricks around the net no wonder he scored so many goals...I'd like to be just like him." Wayne Gretzky at ten years of age had already formulated a goal to be like his idol, Gordie Howe, known to all as "Mr. Hockey." Within a year, Wayne was sitting at the head table at the Kiwanis "Great Men of Sports" Dinner beside his hero. A mentor-protégé connection sparked between the 44-year-old icon and the 11-year-old phenom, blossoming into a strong friendship through the years as Wayne strived ever harder to best Gordie's records, always insisting on wearing jersey #9–Gordie's number.

Wayne's growing celebrity, as one might expect, was a double-edged sword. He was featured during an intermission segment of *Hockey Night in Canada* and profiled in the April 1972 issue of *Canadian Magazine* while still a pre-teen. This brought him to the attention of people in the hockey enterprise who could further his career, but it also made him a target on and off the ice. Players on opposing teams looked for opportunities to put the slightly built youth out of commission, while some of the parents of players on his team spewed even more virulent venom. They complained that Gretzky was scoring so many goals only because the coach played him longer than their offspring. Some brought stopwatches to the games to clock his total ice time and even attempted to have the coach removed for alleged preferential treatment.

Negativity from those who saw him as a threat seemed to fuel Wayne's resolve to excel. In fact, sportswriter Roy MacGregor, later offering a prescient insight into what made Gretzky tick, commented (*Total Gretzky*, p. 23):

Sensitivity [to criticism] drove him on toward ever-greater success, and it would be folly to ignore this personality trait in trying to understand what made the Great One great. As Gretzky himself conceded to [Hockey News writer] Bob McKenzie, "It made me a better player."

In the fall of 1972, after five years with the Nadrofsky Steelers, Wayne moved up to the peewee league and joined the team sponsored by Turkstra Lumber. In his two seasons with that team, he continued his stellar performance, scoring 105 goals in the first year and 196 goals in the second. For the 1975–76 season, Wayne joined the Charcon Chargers, for whom he scored 90 goals. As Wayne's reputation outside Brantford continued to grow, the resentment toward him from within the community seemed also to escalate. The intensity of this hostility appeared to reach a climax on Brantford Day, February 2, 1975, when the Brantford hockey teams from all age levels were invited to Maple Leaf Gardens in Toronto to perform for the parents. When 14-year-old Wayne skated onto the ice, a boisterous segment of the Brantford community booed. The self-effacing teen, who aspired to excellence, was confused and devastated. Referring to the nastiness arising from such petty jealousies, the normally sanguine Gretzky commented years later, "I had seen adults at their best and their worst. I learned that jealousy is the worst disease in life…and I decided I wanted to get out of that town."

Three Years in Junior Hockey

Both Walter and Wayne knew it was time for Wayne to leave Brantford if his game was to reach the next level. At age 14, the budding superstar enrolled at West Humber Collegiate in Toronto and lived with foster parents Bill and Rita Cornish, in order to play in the Young Nationals Hockey organization. However, residency requirements precluded his playing in the minor hockey league, so he joined the Vaughan Nationals of the Junior B League that was outside the authority of Ontario minor hockey. Once again, Wayne, at 14 and 135 pounds, was forced to play with a much older and bigger cohort–this time, 20-year-olds. Moving away from home molded Wayne in a number of ways. He was forced to grow up fast and to learn how to deal with opponents who were stronger and more experienced. Almost overnight, his maturity and sense of self developed well beyond his years.

In his first year of Junior B hockey, Wayne scored 27 goals and 33 assists and won the Rookie-of-the-Year award. In his second year, he scored 36 goals and 26 assists. Then in a move that surprised everyone including Walter, the Soo Greyhounds of the Junior A League drafted Wayne. The fact that the Greyhounds played out of Sault Ste. Marie, a town located 500 miles north of Brantford, initially prompted Wally to oppose the move, but he eventually capitulated after extensive negotiations. Wayne insisted that he would play if he could have the number 9 on his hockey sweater because that was the number worn by his idol Gordie Howe. However, that number had already been worn by Brian Gualazzi during the previous three years. Wayne's insistence on the number 9 and Gualazzi's reluctance to relinquish it seemed to present an impasse. Then coach Muzz MacPherson stumbled upon an ingenious compromise. The following day when he brought Wayne to his office, a Greyhounds hockey sweater with the name Gretzky and the number 99 was hanging on the door. "There's your new number. If you can't wear one 9, wear two," he exclaimed. The rest is history.

Revealing the fierce competitive spirit that characterized his play, Wayne asked MacPherson at the first practice how many points the league scoring champion had earned the previous season. When the coach reported that it was 170, Wayne asserted confidently, "No problem, I'll break that." Indeed, Wayne was as good as his word. By the end of the season, he had scored 70 goals and 112 assists for a total of 182 points. Coach MacPherson became one of Wayne's greatest fans. Effusive in his praise of Gretzky's abilities, he remarked, "Great anticipation, great puck sense. He'll tell you something he's going to do in a game–like Babe Ruth–and he'll go right out and do it." Further extolling the virtues of his superstar, MacPherson later described an incident in which he benched Wayne because the team was losing 4–1 and he wanted to save him from injury in a lost cause. Describing Wayne's reaction, he explained (Taylor, p. 43):

> *I told him this one is over and he wouldn't be playing much in the third. He's hot. "You think this is my fault?" he asks.*
>
> *But I sit him out until about seven minutes left. It's still 4–1, but one of their guys gets a spearing penalty and we're on the power play, so I tap Wayne on the shoulder and say go.*
>
> *He's still ticked off at being benched. "You want me to win it, or tie it?" he says, kind of sarcastic.*
>
> *"A tie would be lovely," I say.*
>
> *So he goes out and scores three goals and we get a tie. So he's coming off the ice and one of our kids looks at me.*
>
> *"You made a mistake, coach," he says. "You should have told him to win it."*

As the Gretzky reputation grew, sportswriters dug into their thesauruses for more superlatives to describe this emerging wonder. The frequently used phrase "The Great Gretzky" first emerged in an article in December 1977, when Wayne was 16 years old, and within a short time it morphed into the moniker, "The Great One."

Turning Professional

In the spring of 1978, it was rumored that the World Hockey Association (WHA) was about to draft under-age juniors. This generated speculation that if the rumor were true, Wayne might turn professional. Highly respected and outspoken hockey analyst Howie Meeker was quoted in the *Brantford Expositor* on May 4, 1978, "[Being drafted] would retard his development. He's still a boy...He's not mature physically yet...I know he can outthink and outsmart the others and his skating is not that bad–But turn pro at 17–he'd get killed."

In the summer of 1978, war broke out between the WHA and the NHL. The owners of WHA teams began signing under-age players from the Junior A League. Nelson Skalbania, owner of several sports franchises including the WHA Indianapolis Racers, offered Wayne Gretzky a four-year contract worth $825,000. Wayne's agent Gus Badali encouraged the signing because, as he later explained (Taylor, p. 52):

I thought he'd be safer in the pros than staying in the Junior A. He'd been so dominant that first year [in the Junior A League], I was truly concerned that he wouldn't survive a second. He barely survived the first one. The number of goons taking swings at him illegally was incredible...I'd seen a game in Hamilton in Junior B when he'd literally beaten the other team by himself, and two 20-year-olds pummeled him. They definitely would have been in jail if it had happened in the street...I felt that in his second year, somebody would gun him down.

Delighted at the opportunity to become a professional and earn an income commensurate with his skills, Wayne signed the contract, dated June 10, 1978. Walter Gretzky had to co-sign because 17-year-old Wayne was not yet of legal age. Some believed that he would be demolished if he remained in the Junior A League, while others believed he would meet his demise if he entered the professional ranks. The frail-looking teenager from Brantford was about to escape the pursuit of the headhunters to enter the realm of the so-called enforcers.

Wayne's debut with the Indianapolis Racers was less than stellar. In a town known for its racing, the Racers were unknown. In his first eight games, Wayne had scored a total of three goals and three assists. Skalbania, who was suffering financial hardship, offered to sell Wayne's contract to the Winnipeg Jets but the offer was rejected on the basis that Gretzky "was too small and wasn't worth the money because he would never make it." Ultimately, Peter Pocklington, owner of the Edmonton Oilers, purchased the contract from Skalbania and Wayne Gretzky on November 2, 1978 became an Edmonton Oiler.

When Wayne joined the Oilers, he was fortunate to have a young coach who was not steeped in rigor or control. Glen Sather allowed his young tigers the freedom to explore and find their niche, as well as to err–the key to developing superstars. As sportswriter Steve Dryden observed (p. 27), "In Edmonton Wayne was operating with few rules and allowed to try new moves, make mistakes and learn from them." Mark Messier, a burgeoning superstar soon to be recruited for the Oiler squad, would later say, "Well, chemistry is good-quality people with talent working towards the same goals. Glen gathered the talent and let us play our way." These comments speak volumes to those who aspire to coaching and add further credence to recent research findings that the parents of creative geniuses allow freedom and have few rules.

Another dimension of Wayne's growth and success was his positive demeanor and love of the game of hockey. Negativity was never part of his life. He told *Sports Illustrated*, "I go to the rink happy and I leave happy." Psychologists acknowledge that happy people always outperform unhappy people. The positive environment and the esprit de corps of the young Oiler team was the petri dish in which a new brand of hockey was incubating.

A Dynasty in the Making

In his first season with the Edmonton Oilers (1978–79), Wayne once again proved the skeptics wrong. He not only survived the physical abuse hurled at him, but he finished the season with 43 goals and 61 assists for a total of 104 points! This, together with the points he scored in Indianapolis, placed him third in WHA scoring and won him the Rookie-of-the-Year award at the age of 18. Furthermore, he was now old enough to sign a contract. Recognizing Gretzky's tremendous potential, Peter Pocklington signed Wayne to a 21-year contract worth approximately $5 million.

Meanwhile, rumors of a merger between the WHA and the NHL became a reality in the summer of 1979 when the NHL expanded to include four WHA teams, including the Edmonton Oilers. In the 1979 draft, Glen Sather acquired Mark Messier, Kevin Lowe and Glenn Anderson, three young players with remarkable potential. As the 1979–80 season unfolded, it was becoming clear that Sather's uncanny ability to identify and nurture talent would eventually pay dividends. Wayne Gretzky scored 51 goals and 86 assists for a total of 137 points. His line-mate Blair McDonald scored 46 goals and 48 assists (94 points). By the time their first NHL season ended, the Oilers were one of the nine teams in the NHL that had scored more than 300 goals. They had proved themselves worthy of their NHL franchise. However, few were yet aware that a dynasty was in the making. It wasn't just a strong hockey team that was evolving, but rather a new phenomenon–a team that would revolutionize the way hockey was played. The old defensive style of hockey–that involved dumping the puck over the blueline and chasing it into the opponent's zone, trapping the puck against the boards to freeze play, and man-on-man coverage–would soon be challenged by a new, more offensive style of play involving rink-wide passing, teamwork and carrying the puck across the blueline toward the opponent's goal. Gretzky was changing hockey the way Babe Ruth transformed baseball and Pelé redefined soccer.

Wayne's rookie year in the NHL was an unparalleled success. Though the youngest player in the league, he won the Hart Trophy as the league's most valuable player and the Lady Byng Trophy for combining a high standard of ability with sportsmanship and gentlemanly conduct. His 137 points tied him with Marcel Dionne as the league's leading scorer. However, the Art Ross Trophy, awarded to the leading point scorer, was given to Dionne because he had scored two more goals. Furthermore, Wayne was denied the Calder Trophy awarded to the rookie of the year because it was ruled that his season in the WHA had been his rookie year as a professional hockey player. (This ruling was inconsistent with the fact that his goals and assists acquired in the WHA were ruled ineligible for inclusion in the NHL statistics.) In his NHL rookie year, Wayne Gretzky had come within a whisker of making a clean sweep of all the trophies available to a center forward in a regular season. His spectacular performance not only proved he was NHL caliber, but also that he was headed for superstardom. On March 31, 1980, reporting that he had been offered $2 million for Wayne Gretzky, owner Peter Pocklington commented, "There is no price on greatness. They'd have my head [in Edmonton] if I sold him." It was a statement of the "read-my-lips" variety that would come back to haunt the outspoken owner before the end of the decade.

During their inaugural season in the NHL, the Oilers had built some credibility in the league, but many skeptics still dismissed their performance as a flash in the pan. Continuing to build for the future, Glen Sather added more youth and ability to the lineup by drafting Paul Coffey, Jarri Kurri and Andy Moog. However, the team was still evolving and ended the season with an unimpressive 29-35-16 record. Wayne himself increased his scoring over the previous year to 164 points, including 55 goals and 109 assists. This won him his first Art Ross Trophy and second Hart Trophy, and a position on the First All-Star Team. During this watershed year, Wayne Gretzky continued to hone his holistic style of play, observing the positions of his teammates from behind the opponent's goal and anticipating opportunities as they emerged. This location would eventually be dubbed "Gretzky's office."

Wayne's next learning experience occurred during September 1981 when he played for Team Canada in the International Canada Cup. Although Wayne led the tournament in scoring, Canada lost to the Soviet team in the final game by a humiliating score of 8–1. Wayne assumed much of the responsibility for the loss saying, "I played so badly that they should have sent me to Siberia." Reflecting on his performance in that series, he reached the conclusion that the Soviets had exploited his tendency to pass rather than shoot, so he resolved to capitalize on his scoring opportunities by shooting more often. As he later observed, "You miss 100% of the shots that you don't take."

Honing his holistic view from Gretzky's office and implementing his shoot-more-often strategy paid significant dividends in the 1981–82 season. In this, his third season in the NHL, Wayne led the Edmonton Oilers to a very strong 48–17–15 season and a remarkable total of 417 goals. Wayne himself enjoyed his most spectacular season so far by shattering records at an astounding rate. On December 30, 1981, he scored five goals against the Philadelphia Flyers, achieving 50 goals in 39 games–a record that few believe will ever be broken! By the end of the season, he had accumulated an astronomical 212 points, composed of 92 goals and 120 assists, making him the only player to have scored more than 200 points in a season! The runner-up in the scoring was Mike Bossey with 147 points. There was no contest for the Art Ross and the Hart Trophies that year and all the skeptics were forced to hide or admit they were wrong. It was a season in which Wayne not only smashed many NHL records, but also set a new one by renegotiating his contract to $20 million, spread over 15 years. The Great One had finally proved himself a superstar beyond a shadow of a doubt. The only alternative left to the naysayers was to assert that records and awards don't count as much as the ultimate achievement–winning the Stanley Cup. When the Oilers lost in the playoffs to the Los Angeles Kings, some critics said that Edmonton lacked the depth to win the Stanley Cup. They could concede that Gretzky was "The Great One," but they doubted that he could lead the team to the ultimate prize.

As the 1982–83 season opened, the pressure was mounting on Glen Sather and the Oilers to prove themselves to be Stanley Cup material and silence the critics once and for all. The Edmonton squad, and Gretzky in particular, wanted the silver chalice so much that they could almost taste the champagne from it. As the season progressed, the players began to anticipate each other's moves, making the Oilers a well-oiled machine. Sather attempted to build depth into the team by reducing the time that Wayne's line was on the ice and strengthening the other lines to share the scoring burdens. The Oilers finished first in their division. In post-season play, they showed their power in steamrolling over all the opposition until they reached the finals against the reigning Stanley Cup Champions, the New York Islanders. The Oilers were a young, energetic and talented team, but their easy skate through the season and the playoffs had not prepared them for the physically brutal and punishing style of the seasoned Islanders–a team who had scrapped their way to the top. When all else is equal, tenacity and sheer desire determines who will win. In the second game of the finals, as Gretzky moved near the net, he was cut down by the goalie Bill Smith, who received a five-minute major penalty for slashing. Though not seriously injured, Wayne was unable to score on Smith during the remainder of the series and New York renewed their status as Stanley Cup Champions in a four-game sweep.

Though the Oilers had been denied in their quest for the Holy Grail of hockey in 1983, Wayne Gretzky himself had achieved another banner year. He scored 71 goals and 125 assists for a total of 196 points, besting runner-up Peter Stastny by a huge 72 points! Wayne was moving from hockey superstar to celebrity. His blonde good looks and charismatic persona caught the public attention, quickly transforming him into a media darling. Playing out of character as a bad guy, Wayne had a brief stint on the afternoon television soap opera, *The Young and the Restless*. As requests for endorsements poured in from various commercial enterprises, Wayne accepted enough of these to make his image ubiquitous. His hockey income seemed irrelevant.

On October 4, 1983, Lee Fogolin removed the "C" that identified him as captain of the Oilers and presented it to Wayne Gretzky, saying, "I don't think there's anyone more deserving or prouder to take it than Wayne because he does so much for us on the ice." Deflecting attention from himself in characteristic fashion, Wayne accepted the honor saying, "We have one goal and one goal only–and that's to win the Stanley Cup." Resolutely determined to win the ultimate prize at the end of the 1983–84 season, the Oilers strived throughout the year with a tenacity and intensity that had been lacking in prior seasons. Edmonton came roaring out of the gate at the beginning of the season. Leading the charge was the new captain who set a pace never seen before or since by scoring at least one point per game in the first 51 games of the season. During that scoring streak, The Great One racked up a total of 61 goals and 91 assists for an average of 3 points per game. It was a remarkable run, compared by the sportswriters to Joe Dimaggio's 56-game hitting streak. En route to scoring 87 goals and 118 assists that season, Wayne set several more NHL records including the most shorthanded goals (12) and the most consecutive games with an assist (17).

While all sorts of individual accolades and awards were accruing to The Great One, the trophy he coveted most was within reach. The Oilers finished the season with a record of 57-18-5 and headed into the Stanley Cup playoffs loaded for bear. They annihilated the Jets in a three-game sweep, barely defeated the Calgary Flames in a seven-game struggle, and skated past Minnesota in the semi-finals. As many had predicted, they once again came face-to-face in the Stanley Cup finals with the reigning champions–the tough New York Islanders. The first game, on New York's home ice, was a hard-fought, hard-hitting contest in which each team attempted to intimidate the other. Edmonton came out on top, squeaking out a 1–0 victory. However, the second game began to look like déjà vu when the Islanders routed the Oilers 6–1. Following this devastating loss, Wayne shared with the press the personal pressure he felt to win the silver cup. "I've had pressure since I came to this organization. I know there is no in-between for Wayne Gretzky. I'll be one of the heroes or I'll be the goat." This intense pressure felt by the captain diffused through the team, creating a pressure-cooker intensity that exploded on the ice into two decisive 7–2 victories for Edmonton on their home ice. Edmonton was leading the series 3 games to 1 coming into the fifth and potentially deciding game of the Stanley Cup finals. At the beginning of the third period they had a comfortable 4–0 lead–just 20 minutes away from their first Stanley Cup. Then Pat LaFontaine of the Islanders scored two quick goals in the first minute of the period, and New York was back in the race. The Oilers held off the attack, and when the Islanders pulled the goalie in the dying moments of the game, Edmonton scored into an empty net, winning their first Stanley Cup! For Gretzky, it was the realization of a dream he had formed early in life. After his retirement in 1999 he commented, "The biggest thrill of my career? It's no comparison. My first Stanley Cup in Edmonton."

Indeed, the Stanley Cup victory of May 1984 was the Oilers' first, but it wasn't the last. They won again in 1985, 1987, 1988 and 1990. During the early 1980s, Glen Sather had built and nurtured a team around The Great One and in the process created a dynasty that not only dominated hockey through the rest of the decade but changed the way the game is played.

The Trade that Shook a Nation

It is no secret that Canadians are known for their hockey. In a climate where ponds are frozen for four months a year, the Canucks learn to skate as youngsters and develop a devotion to hockey as both participants and spectators. International hockey competitions like the Canada Cup Tournaments are a matter of national pride and anything less than winning is interpreted by every Canadian as a personal embarrassment. As a Canadian icon, Wayne saw international hockey as a challenge and an opportunity to prove Canada's supremacy in its national sport. When Wayne was asked what game in his entire career represented his best performance, he surprised few by naming the second game of the three-game final of the Canada Cup between Team Canada and the Soviets, played on September 13, 1987. In that contest, The Great One set up five of the six Canadian goals and Canada defeated the Soviets 6–5. The dramatic winning goal, scored in overtime by Mario Lemieux on what has been described as an unbelievable pass from Gretzky, gave Team Canada their second consecutive Canada Cup victory (the previous one in 1984). It is no wonder that Canadians claimed Gretzky as their national treasure.

In many ways, the fair-skinned, blue-eyed, Canadian hockey star was like the dark-skinned, black-eyed, Brazilian soccer icon, Pelé. Both exuded a self-effacing charm that belied the ferociously competitive spirit within. Both demonstrated an ability to achieve a state of relaxed concentration that enabled them to transcend the field of battle and anticipate the play ahead. Both rewrote the record books in their sport like no other. And both superstars railed against a defensive style of play, advocating instead an aggressive offense to overpower opponents. Pelé's supremacy in soccer was so great that in 1960, the Brazilian Congress declared Pelé a *national treasure* to prevent his trade to any team outside Brazil. Canadians didn't propose such measures, though Nelson Riis, then House Leader for the NDP political party, lamented from the floor of Parliament, "Wayne Gretzky is a national symbol, like the Beaver. How can we allow the sale of our national symbols? The Edmonton Oilers without Wayne Gretzky is like...*Wheel of Fortune* without Vanna White." Everyone knew that Wayne Gretzky *was* a part of the Canadian identity, eh? It was inconceivable that he or anyone else would contemplate his playing for any team outside Canada. Wasn't that why owner Peter Pocklington had flatly refused all previous trade offers for the Great One? However, on August 9, 1988, just 24 days after his marriage to actress Janet Jones, Wayne stunned and dumfounded a nation of hockey aficionados. Appearing at a jammed press conference, eyes tearing and voice choking with emotion, he announced "I'm disappointed to leave Edmonton...I promised 'Mess' [Mark Messier] I wouldn't do this." Described as the biggest trade in professional sport, the deal involved the transfer of Gretzky and two other Oilers to the Los Angeles Kings in exchange for five excellent players and $15 million. Canada, and particularly the city of Edmonton, went into mourning. It was as though a national disaster had befallen the country.

The Los Angeles Kings

Gretzky's arrival in Tinseltown catapulted hockey into the realm of respectability as a professional sport across America. Off the ice, Gretzky became a celebrity to the celebrities in the entertainment industry. On the ice, his stellar performances continued to delight fans who were discovering that hockey was perhaps the most exciting of all spectator sports. In the 1988–89 season, his first with the Kings, he helped the team get from 18th to 4th place in the NHL standings. Then the Kings defeated the Oilers in the Smythe division playoffs but lost to the Calgary Flames in that division final. Wayne himself scored 168 points (54 goals and 114 assists).

As the first decade of his professional career came to a close, Gretzky had shattered most of the "single-season" records. Then, as he entered his second decade, he began to smash the cumulative or "career" records. On October 15, 1989, barely a decade after his entry into the NHL, he was playing against the Oilers in Edmonton, the city where he had been loved and revered, then vilified. At 4:32 of the first period, Wayne assisted on a goal, tying Gordie Howe's career scoring record of 1850 points. Then at 19:07 of the third period, Wayne scored the tying goal in the game and his 1851st point, eclipsing Howe's record. Play was halted as Howe and some NHL VIPs conducted a brief ceremony honoring Gretzky's achievement. A thunderous ovation from the Edmonton fans echoed loudly and clearly that all was forgiven–a forgiveness that survived the final insult when Wayne scored the winning goal over Edmonton at 3 minutes and 24 seconds into overtime. The prodigal son had returned home and had been warmly welcomed. When Mr. Hockey was asked how he felt about having his record broken, he commented, "The fact that the record was broken by someone who's such a great person takes away any sense of loss I might have." Both Wayne Gretzky and his idol Gordie Howe remain class acts both on and off the ice.

During his second and third seasons with the Kings (1989–90, 1990–91), Wayne once again silenced the skeptics by winning the Art Ross Trophy as the leading scorer in the NHL. On completing his first decade as the most dominant player in the NHL, Gretzky the icon was morphing into Gretzky the legend. Superstars are defined by outstanding performance over several years, while legends are defined by dominance over decades. In 1990, the Associated Press voted Wayne Gretzky *Athlete of the Decade* for the eighties, an honor transcending hockey and encompassing athletics in general.

The fall of 1991 was to become one of the most traumatic periods of Gretzky's life. On September 14, 1991, he was playing in the first game of the two-game Canada Cup final against the United States when he was checked into the boards from behind. A back injury resulting from that impact sidelined him for the remainder of the tournament, which Team Canada subsequently won in two games. Though he had been the top scorer in the Tournament prior to his injury, it was beginning to look as if The Great One was moving beyond his peak performance years. In the first few games of the 1991–92 season, Gretzky was kept off the score sheet and appeared to be struggling to maintain his high standard of play. Then on October 16, he received the devastating news that his father and lifelong mentor had suffered a brain aneurysm and was close to death. Wayne rushed to his father's side to be with him during a life-saving operation that ultimately restored Walter's mental processing skills, but left significant gaps in his memory.

On his return to regular season action, Wayne's performance gradually improved, though it was too late to help the Kings. They ended the season with an unimpressive 35–31–14 record, and lost to the Oilers in the playoffs. Prospects for 1992–93 seemed even more dismal when Gretzky had to sit out the fall season on account of a diagnosed herniated thoracic disc. Concerned that his injury may prevent him from playing without pain, Wayne began to talk about retirement. He appeared to be reaching the nadir of his career, and the sportswriters renewed their prediction that he would never take the Kings to the Stanley Cup.

However, when Gretzky returned on January 6, 1993, the team began to gather a momentum that carried into the playoffs. The Kings got past Calgary and the Canucks, winning both series four games to two, and reached the semi-finals against the Toronto Maple Leafs. The series with Toronto was a close contest, and after four games it was tied at two games apiece. Gretzky had only one goal and four assists in those four games and had been described as a series "no-show" on account of his lackluster performance to that point. The Great One usually came alive at Maple Leaf Gardens, so when Gretzky and the Kings came to Toronto for game five, hopes were high that sparks would fly. However, Wayne's play was short of spectacular and he was held scoreless as the Kings lost to Toronto, falling behind in the series 3–2. Sportswriter Bob McKenzie, reporting in the *Toronto Star* that Wayne Gretzky was "skating with a piano on his back" expressed the general disappointment over Gretzky's uninspiring performance. The tone of the article suggested to some that Gretzky was past his prime at 32. Ever sensitive to criticism, the Great One resolved once again to prove the pundits wrong, muttering, "This is one piano that has another tune to play."

On their return to Los Angeles for game 6, the Kings were facing elimination. Fighting for survival, they fought the Leafs to a tie by the end of regulation time. Then, in sudden death overtime, the piano sounded another note and Gretzky scored the winner, forcing the series to a seventh game. The Kings packed their gear and flew to Toronto for the deciding contest on May 29, 1993. And what a game it was! With all the drama of spectacular rink-wide passes, fast skating and smooth stick-handling, the Great Gretzky morphed into a maestro to lead his team to a 5–4 victory. In this virtuoso performance, he contributed three goals and one assist. Years later, Wayne described this as his best performance ever in an NHL game. In reaching the zenith in his standard of hockey, Gretzky brought the Los Angeles Kings to the Stanley Cup finals and in so doing silenced the naysayers once again. Although the Kings lost the Stanley Cup to Montreal in five games, they had finally achieved legitimacy as a franchise, and hockey had taken root in California.

Traveling to New York via St. Louis

Though the Kings floundered in the next three seasons, 1993 through 1996, Wayne continued to pile up points, pushing career records ever higher and beyond the reach of generations of players to follow. However, these years were plagued with a labor dispute that became a lockout, a scandal involving Bruce McNall (one of the owners of the Kings), and a general disintegration of morale in the Los Angeles organization. Realizing that his chances of being on a Stanley Cup team were waning, Wayne asked to be traded. On February 27, 1996, he was traded to the St. Louis Blues where he was greeted with much fanfare and high expectations.

In his second game with the Blues, Gretzky was knocked out, suffering a mild concussion. Additional injuries to his back in subsequent games ultimately began to take a toll on his performance. When St. Louis was eliminated by Detroit in the second round of the playoffs, the coach assigned much of the blame to Gretzky for not covering his man. On July 21, 1996, just five months after joining the Blues, Wayne exercised his free agency and signed with the New York Rangers. Like Pelé two decades earlier, Gretzky decided to play out his final years in New York.

During his tenure with the New York Rangers it was clear that Wayne's awe-inspiring performances were behind him. He turned 36 during his first year with the Rangers. Although he still possessed his remarkable anticipatory sense and extraordinary passing skills, he had lost some of the speed and agility that gave him that extra stride advantage over the others during his prime. In spite of this, he was the top scorer on the Rangers team with 25 goals and 72 assists, sharing the league lead in assists with Mario Lemieux during the 1996-97 season and making the Second All-Star Team. That year the Rangers got as far as the third round in the playoffs before they were eliminated by Philadelphia. However, in the two seasons that followed, the Rangers did not make the playoffs, even though Gretzky continued to set new career records. On October 26, 1997, he got his 1851st assist, exceeding in assists Howe's *total point* record of 1850. The Great One owned almost every record in the book and few challenges remained. As the end of the millennium approached, Wayne was nearing his fortieth year. He was in the sunset of his playing years and retirement was looming on the horizon, but when? The hockey world, like Hamlet anticipating the ultimate end, was gradually coming to acknowledge, "If it be not now, yet it will come: the readiness is all."

The Last Hurrah?

The end of an era sometimes hits like a bomb–an unexpected shock reminding us of our mortality and the years that have passed in the running current of time. In other instances, the end is preceded by a growing body of rumors that swell with a tone of inevitability, bringing the bittersweet feelings of happy memories mixed with the pain of finality. Wayne Gretzky's retirement was of the latter variety. On April 10, 1999, commentator John Davidson announced to the hockey world on *Hockey Night in Canada* that The Great One might retire after the final game of the regular season in New York on Sunday, April 18. For Gretzky's penultimate game in Ottawa on Thursday, April 15, Canadian fans crammed into the Corel Centre to pay tribute and celebrate the career of a Canadian legend. Ubiquitous posters displaying entreaties like, "Say it ain't so, Wayne," and "Wayne, please don't leave us," revealed the depth of the bond that Gretzky had forged with the hockey public and with Canadians in particular. Gretzky's hometown of Brantford had long since embraced him as their favored son, overriding the earlier disapproval of a vocal minority. Not since Pelé had a nation lamented so fervently the end of an era.

The contest that night between the Ottawa Senators and the New York Rangers was an anticlimax to the post-game ceremonies and press conference that followed. At the end of the game, the players on both teams lined up to shake hands with the colleague they had all revered as The Great One, recognizing that hockey would not be as exciting without him. In a special tribute, he was named as the only star in the usual three-star selection ritual. At the press conference following the game, it was clear that his decision to retire had been the most difficult of his life. Surrounded by his family and closest friends and choking with emotion, he said, "It's an emotional time for me; it's an experience I'll never forget tonight." The formal announcement of Gretzky's retirement was made at a press conference in Madison Square Garden the next day. The pomp and pageantry preceding and following his final game was a cross between the coronation and the funeral rites of a great monarch. Some cheered while others, including his wife Janet, wept. Then NHL Commissioner Gary Bettman announced (Dryden, p. 106):

When you take off your jersey after today's game, you will be the last player in the NHL to ever wear 99. You always have been and you always will be The Great One and there will never be another. On behalf of all your fans, we miss you and we thank you.

Gretzky's number, 99, was the only number in the history of hockey to be retired by every NHL team. The only other athlete so honored in professional sport had been baseball's Jackie Robinson.

Retiring from active play enabled Wayne to spend more time with his wife Janet and their children Paulina, Emma, Ty, Trevor and Tristan. However, hockey is in his blood and he will remain intimately involved in the game until his final days. In the 2002 Olympics in Salt Lake City, he served as general manager of Team Canada and helped lead them to a gold medal in hockey–their first in 50 years! Shortly after retiring, he bought into the Phoenix Coyotes and in 2005 he signed on as their head coach. It will not be the last of the contributions he will make to sports in the decades ahead.

Legacy

By the time Wayne was 21 he owned twice the scoring records of his closest rival. By his mid-twenties he had annihilated the record book, averaging over 200 points for six consecutive seasons. To put this in perspective, consider that no other player in the history of the NHL has ever scored 200 points in one season. *Sports* magazine wrote, "Wayne Gretzky is the best player in any sport." During his first decade in the NHL, The Great One won the Hart Trophy nine times as the League's most valuable player. In only his second season he won the Art Ross Trophy as the NHL's leading scorer and during his 20 years in the NHL won that trophy ten times. His total points of 2857 exceed by more than 1000 the previous record held by his childhood hero Gordie Howe. These numbers will probably never be equaled. His 894 total career goals exceed Howe's by 93. But even more impressive than these records is that he holds more scoring records than all the other players in the NHL together–a total of 61 in all! During Wayne's assault on the record books, the Associated Press and United Press International named him Athlete of the Decade for the 1980s. Later, the Associated Press named him Hockey Player of the 20th Century. In 1997, *The Hockey News* voted him the "greatest ever" player in the NHL. If eminence is a measure of performance relative to one's peers, then Gretzky is super-eminent.

Though The Great One will be forever remembered by statistics in the record books, one of his most valuable contributions to hockey is the role model he provided for hockey fans, young and old. Always gracious and self-effacing off the ice and a sportsman of the highest order on ice, he projected an understated persona that is especially refreshing in a sport characterized by aggressive and often hostile behavior. From his youth, Wayne was confident but never cocky, choosing to let his stick and the puck speak eloquently on his behalf. Like his friend and hockey icon Gordie Howe, he oozed the kind of class that brings dignity and perspective to sport. Though his scoring set him apart from the rest, his focus was always on the team effort, raising the performances of his teammates by orchestrating surreal scoring opportunities. As the consummate team player, he lead the upstart Edmonton Oilers to five Stanley Cups during their first 11 years in the NHL and brought the Kings to the Stanley Cup finals.

While there is unanimous agreement that he was the greatest player in hockey, there is endless speculation and conjecture about what made The Great One great. *USA Today's* Kevin Allen commented (April 19, 1999):

Nothing scares us more than something we don't understand, and no one has ever completely understood why Gretzky seems to be everywhere and nowhere at the same time. Gretzky was stealth before most of us understood what stealth was...[He] was a player who used all his senses to dominate his sport. It was obvious to me that Gretzky was to hockey what Albert Einstein was to physics. Gretzky looked at the sport in ways most simply can't comprehend. He thought, heard, saw, felt, smelled and experienced the game differently from everyone else.

Reflecting on what made Gretzky special, Orr and Tracz of the University of Toronto observed (p. 38):

It often appeared as if he had been dropped on the ice from another planet; he seemed to just know what was happening, and likely to happen, on the ice at all times. It made him seem supernatural, with powers of anticipation that no other player possessed.

While most agreed that Wayne Gretzky's supremacy was somehow associated with his surreal ability to anticipate the play, the action and the opportunities while in the midst of the fray, most assumed this ability was a genetic gift. However, Wayne's father begged to differ, explaining (*Total Gretzky*, p. 20):

People say you can't teach anticipation. I'm not so sure. I used to get them out on the ice and I'd shoot the puck down the boards toward a corner and I'd say, "Chase that." Well, they'd go right into the end after it. Then I'd say, "Wait, watch me." I'd shoot it in again, and let it roll around the net. Instead of following it around the boards I'd cut across to where it was rolling. "There," I'd say. "You've got to know where it's going to go."

Wayne himself gave evidence supporting his father's assertion (Orr and Tracz, p. 38):

My dad drilled into me nonstop not to go where the puck is now but to where it was going to be, just to think quickly about the situation in front of me and what the guy with the puck is likely to do with it. That was befuddling at first because, like all kids, I wanted to chase the puck, get it and hang on to it. But he never eased up on encouraging me to try to read the play and react to what was most likely to happen.

I know his insistence about it helped me later on. Driving home after games we had watched or I had played in, he would grill me about specific plays and get me to tell him what every player on the ice had done. We did that over and over until I could analyze just about every play in a game and where players were and where they should have been.

Through his career in hockey, Wayne Gretzky has provided us with excitement and entertainment. In the process, he has changed the way the game is played and the way it is seen and interpreted. Biographer Steve Dryden opined (p. 23):

It was in his brilliant location passes, his sense of players yet to arrive–perhaps anticipating their role in the larger play long before they themselves did–that he changed, forever, the manner in which this evolving game is played.

In essence, Gretzky's power was his ability to play within himself and above the ice. It was his prescient sense–of where to go and when–that coaches call *anticipation*. Psychologists call it holistic thinking and a sense of the gestalt.

Chapter 10

PRINCIPLE #10: IGNITE YOUR COMPETITIVE ZEAL

If you're not going to compete, I'm going to dominate you.
                                                    –Michael Jordan

Competitive Zeal

W hy do some people rise to the top in the competition for power, prestige, money or achievement while so many others languish unfulfilled and undistinguished? Studies of great entrepreneurs, inventors, scientists and athletic superstars reveal one characteristic that is common to virtually all over-achievers–competitive zeal. Though related to passion, competitive zeal is distinguishable by its focus on winning the struggle for dominance by triumphing over others. Since the "others" who lose this struggle form the majority in society, competitive zeal is often maligned as self-serving ambition. It is also considered selfish and hostile. Indeed, competitive zeal is all of those things, but without it there is no reaching the top. If winning is your goal, then no personal characteristic is more important than a powerful competitive zeal that can help you push past the pain, endure setbacks, and persevere when all others have abandoned the struggle. Even within the context of a team sport, individual competitive zeal serves to energize the team in the pursuit of a common goal, as long as the zeal is not perceived to be motivated by personal ambition–but more about that later.

In this chapter, I will provide you with some insights and techniques to help you ignite your competitive zeal. However, before delving into specific techniques, we must review some background information, some of which you may already know, that will shed light on how the competitive instinct became such a vital part of the human psyche.

Competition and Survival of the Fittest

Competition is vital to survival. Plant and animal species compete for space on this planet and the species that win the competition are the ones that survive and reproduce. Even within a given species, the competition for food and mating privileges is fierce. Only the strongest are able to survive and procreate. This is the basis of Darwin's "survival of the fittest" principle. It's nature's way of "weeding out" the species that cannot adapt well to the environment and pruning the members within a species so that only the strongest reproduce.

Understanding the origin and nature of competitive instincts in humans comes, in part, from studies of competition among and within various animal species. The struggle for dominance within the human race mirrors the behaviors we observe across a wide spectrum of animals, including gorillas, wolves, lions, deer and even chickens. Young males (and often females) of these animal species engage in physical contests that help them test their speed and strength against siblings and other individuals. Through these simulated fights, they develop combat skills, honing both their attack and defense techniques. These physical contests serve a very important social function: establishing a hierarchy or "pecking order" (a term derived from bird behavior). Sitting at the top of the pecking order is the so-called *alpha male*[1] to whom all others pay homage. Occasionally, a subordinate decides to challenge for the top spot. This challenge can be the ultimate contest for both combatants who risk physical harm or death to gain or maintain the ultimate prize: mating privileges.

What Makes an Alpha Male?

What characteristics determine which individuals emerge as the alpha males? Naturally, size and strength play a critical role among animals. Larger individuals often intimidate others into submission merely by expanding to their full height, puffing out plumage or fur or snarling to show a menacing row of teeth. These mock displays serve to establish a hierarchy without the violence that could injure or maim individuals and weaken the group. However, when two contenders for mating privileges are close in size and strength, neither is sufficiently intimidated to concede and a physical contest ensues. It is then that tenacity and intensity come into play and the victor is the individual who craves the mating rights the most, i.e., the individual with the greater sexual energy (what psychologists call *psycho-sexual* or *libidinal energy*). Sexual energy, as the product of a chemical interaction between the body and the brain, can be observed only indirectly through its appearance as *competitive zeal*. In the animal kingdom, when two combatants are relatively equal in size and strength, competitive zeal is the deciding factor in the struggle for dominance.

---

[1] In almost all animal species the alpha male is actually a male, although there are some species in which the alpha male is female.

In human societies, the struggle for dominance is not necessarily evident as a struggle for mating privileges. It is sometimes sublimated into a struggle for power, wealth or self-actualization. In such cases, size and strength are of little or no importance in the struggle for dominance, and large physical stature is not a significant advantage. Clearly, alpha male status in a prison environment calls for a different set of characteristics than alpha male status in a university faculty or a large corporation. Intelligence, risk-taking propensity, ruthlessness and leadership skills have different levels of importance in each culture as the skill set required to win alpha male status. However, one characteristic is prerequisite to alpha male status in virtually every culture: competitive zeal. The link between dominance and competitive zeal, so evident in the animal kingdom, remains a powerful dynamic in the human species.

How Is Competitive Zeal Affected by Success and Failure?

An interesting aspect of the Darwinian principle operating in the animal kingdom is observed in many species such as walruses, where the alpha male has a harem consisting of all the females in that colony. Any male wishing to mate must challenge the alpha male. If the challenger loses, he becomes sexually impotent and unable to procreate. Similarly in the mandrill (a species of primates), male individuals who lose these early contests never develop the mature male characteristics and facial coloring that are necessary for participating in the mating

The Mandrill

ritual. It's nature's way of preventing the genes of the weaker individuals from entering the gene pool of the next generation. In such animal species, the loss of one or more conflicts can result in permanently low sexual energy or impotence.

The diagram on the following page shows how sexual energy, and hence competitive zeal, are linked to the struggle for dominance. Defeat, whether suffered through intimidation or actual conflict, results in a reduced sexual energy for the vanquished, moving that individual downward in the hierarchy and diminishing his sexual energy. The victor, on the other hand, receives sexual gratification and/or positive reinforcement that serve to increase his sexual energy and competitive zeal.

Animal Struggle for Dominance Feedback Loop

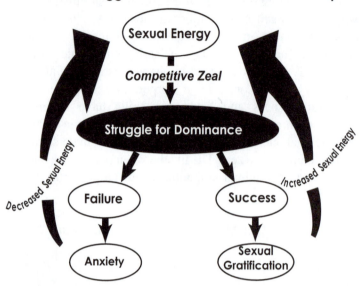

We also observe among humans a link between competitive zeal and success or failure in the competition for dominance. Males who suffer setbacks in their business or financial affairs often feel emasculated, suffering anxiety and even sexual impotence. Conversely, males who experience success in the struggle for dominance are sometimes described as drowning in testosterone and are seen to exude big T (T for testosterone) personalities. In *Sex and Power*, Michael Hutchison wrote, "The testosterone levels of winning male tennis players and Harvard wrestling team winners were higher than the losers." In his best-selling book *Liar's Poker*, Michael Lewis described the hierarchy among the Wall Street bond traders during the bull market in the late 1980s. In that culture, the alpha male was the broker who generated the greatest profits and was dubbed "a Big Swinging Dick." Describing the ethos surrounding this epithet, Lewis wrote (p. 46):

To this day the phrase brings to my mind the image of an elephant's trunk swaying from side to side. Swish. Swash. Nothing in the jungle got in the way of a Big Swinging Dick...That was the prize we all coveted...Everyone wanted to be a Big Swinging Dick, even the women.

Human Struggle for Dominance Feedback Loop

In *Entrepreneurial Genius: The Power of Passion*, I profiled a dozen of the greatest entrepreneurs of the 20th century, including Henry Ford, J. Paul Getty, Donald Trump, Martha Stewart and Richard Branson. Without exception, all were Big T personalities who exuded extreme competitive zeal in their quest for dominance. This who's who of entrepreneurial genius included Coco Chanel, founder of the perfume empire that bears her name–a beautiful woman whose high sexual energy rivaled that of her male counterparts. J. Paul Getty's quest to become the richest man in the world was fueled by a highly active libido that also earned him a reputation as a prolific womanizer. All of these Big T personality types became alpha males in their dominance of others within their sphere of influence. Their sexual energy fostered their success and, conversely, their success fuelled their sexual energy and competitive zeal. In his classic book *Think and Grow Rich*, Napoleon Hill asserted, "Sex energy is the creative energy of all geniuses."

In Chapter 2, I related stories about Babe Ruth's famed sexual energy, which was strongly linked to his fierce competitive instinct that drove him to hit more home runs in a season than most entire teams. After smashing a colossal game-winning home run out of the stadium in St. Louis, he strutted into a brothel, threw down a wad of bills and proclaimed, "Close down. They are all mine," and he proceeded to fulfill his ultimate fantasy. His libidinal energy was as legendary as his baseball prowess. Wilt Chamberlain, an alpha male who dominated basketball for nearly a decade, once bragged that he had sex with more than twenty thousand different women. Though this estimate may be exaggerated, it suggests that he too possessed a high level of sexual energy.

In human societies, the link between competitive zeal and success or failure is more complex than the corresponding link for animals because the struggle for dominance is often a quest for ego gratification rather than sexual gratification–what Sigmund Freud called *sublimation* (see p. 55). Hence the feedback loop connecting competitive zeal to success or failure has two alternative outcomes that are absent in the feedback loop for animals. As shown in the diagram on the preceding page, when the human struggle for dominance results in a successful outcome for an individual, the reward may be sexual gratification, ego gratification or both, but in all cases this outcome feeds confidence and enhances sexual energy and competitive zeal. On the other hand, a failure in the struggle for dominance has two possible outcomes: acceptance of defeat along with decreased competitive zeal, or a challenge response that *stimulates* competitive zeal. It is the mindset of the individual that determines which of these responses prevails. Champions respond to failure with renewed vigor and increased competitive zeal. Others respond to repeated failure with passive resignation and acceptance of defeat.

Gaining the Competitive Edge

The Human Struggle for Dominance Feedback Loop offers important lessons for those who wish to gain the competitive edge. To prevail in the struggle for dominance, one must never accept or become resigned to defeat. Like a vanquished bantam in a cockfight, anyone accepting defeat is relegated to a lower position in the pecking order. For centuries, class structures, caste systems and political structures have disenfranchised segments of the population by preventing or discouraging them from aspiring to education, wealth or any form of self-improvement. Once an individual accepts an inferior position in the hierarchy, he becomes the greatest impediment to his own success. What is the alternative to accepting defeat when confronted with failure?

The answer is shown in the Human Struggle for Dominance Feedback Loop as the "challenge" alternative. Any individual who hopes to win the struggle for dominance must interpret a setback or failure as an opportunity to learn. Bill Gates, an alpha male in the world of computer software, explained, "I always learned more from my failures than my successes." By interpreting a failure or setback as a challenge, the superstar in business or in sports is energized and returns to the struggle with renewed vigor and enhanced competitive zeal.

I described in Chapter 7 how Martina Navratilova, passing under the archway on the way to Centre Court at Wimbledon, noticed the inscription from Rudyard Kipling's poem *If.* In their depiction of disaster as a masquerade for potential triumph, these lines capture the response of all great athletes to failure. Rather than allowing a setback to deplete their competitive zeal, sports superstars understand that the difference between triumph and disaster is a matter of perception. A humiliating loss or negative criticism typically ignites their competitive zeal with an explosive spark. In the previous chapter, I related how Wayne Gretzky had his greatest NHL performance following an article in the *Toronto Star* that criticized his play and suggested that he was "skating with a piano on his back." The Great One, indignant and challenged, asserted, "This is one piano that has another tune to play." Then he responded by scoring the winning goal in overtime in the next game and racking up three goals and one assist in a 5–4 victory over Toronto, knocking them out of the race for the Stanley Cup. Sportswriters wax eloquent about the dramatic motivational power that highly competitive people derive from negative criticism.

During the 1997 season, Knick's coach Jeff Van Gundy told the New York press that Michael Jordan was a con man for befriending Knick players in order to beat them. That night in Madison Square Garden, Michael scored a remarkable 51 points, as if to say, "Don't tug on Superman's cape." Van Gundy learned the dangers of antagonizing a superstar of MJ's magnitude.

Those who use setbacks, adversity and criticism to ignite their competitive zeal soon discover that they are able to transform their defeats into victories that, in turn, generate more zeal and more victories. This process of energy regeneration is captured in the adage: "nothing succeeds like success."

The Pros and Cons of Competitive Zeal

Psychiatrist John Diamond, the father of behavioral kinesiology, discovered in his neurological research that positive people, i.e., optimistic people with high competitive zeal, influence those around them by infusing them with more energy. Testing people for positive and negative energy, he discovered that the thymus gland is the funnel for *life energy* in each of us. He reported (p. 60):

> *The thymus gland regulates energy flow in the body. When stressed it shrinks. In death it atrophies. It is the link between mind and body. Muscles are energy pumps for the thymus which monitors and rebalances our life energy.*

When those with high negative energy, i.e., pessimistic people and naysayers, were placed among the positive energy types, the positive types became weaker and the negative types became stronger. Diamond used the phrase *reciprocal thymus relationships* to describe this interaction. Building on the idea of energy flow from one individual to another, he wrote (p. 107), "If our life energy [competitive zeal] is high, others will benefit from close contact with us; if it is low our relationships with others become part of the problem."

Diamond's findings are supported by a growing body of evidence showing that great athletes enhance the performance of those around them. We observed in the previous chapter how Gretzky's skills and competitive zeal ignited the performance of his teammates, culminating in four Stanley Cups for the Oilers and Stanley Cup contention for the Kings. Offering insight into the effect of competitive zeal and positive mental energy on athletic performance, Diamond explained, "Your thoughts have the power to alter the physiological response of your muscles." In his study of professional football players, he found that most journeyman players receiving a pass were somewhat distracted by the prospect of the impact that would follow. Superstars, however, were undistracted and entirely focused on catching the football. Tests on both groups as they thought about receiving a pass revealed that journeyman players suffered significant stress and tested weak and with much lower energy flow than the superstars who suffered little stress and tested stronger. In short, self-doubt and anxiety reduce strength in a physical struggle.

Competitive zeal is a double-edged sword. Though it is vital to reaching a position of dominance in a social milieu, it can generate a variety of restraining forces that oppose its goals. When the competitive zeal of an individual is perceived by members of the group to be directed toward the group's goals, the competitive instincts it arouses are supportive. However when the competitive zeal of an individual is perceived as self-serving, the competitive instincts it excites are hostile and adversarial. World-renowned psychologist Rollo May observed:

Individual competitive success is both the dominant goal in our culture and the most pervasive occasion for anxiety. This anxiety arises out of the interpersonal isolation and alienation from others that inheres in a pattern in which self-validation depends on triumphing over others.

Babe Zaharias, the superstar we visited in Chapter 3, was famous for an overt competitive zeal that bordered on arrogance and alienated her fellow women golfers. Prior to the final round of a prestigious tournament, she entered the locker room where her competitors were gathered and chided them in her east Texas drawl, "Hi girls! Ya gonna stick around and see who'll finish second this week?" When she attempted to penetrate the country-club circuit, Babe was disparaged as a "truck driver's daughter," shunned by the establishment and banned from amateur golf.

In the previous chapter, we observed that when Wayne Gretzky's competitive zeal as an adolescent brought him to the top of the league in scoring, he faced the petty jealousies and competitive instincts of teammates who were threatened by his personal ambitions. In spite of his self-effacing demeanor, he was vilified and accused of pursuing his own success at the expense of others. To avoid these restraining forces, many athletes, senior executives and politicians with strong ambitions learn to align their personal goals with those of their team, corporation or country so that their competitive zeal is perceived as beneficial to the group and therefore supported. However, an individual wishing to gain the competitive edge can never afford to reduce his or her competitive zeal because it's the fuel that is vital to winning. Good manners demand that displays of personal ambition be muted, but winning the struggle for dominance demands that ambition burn intensely beneath the surface.

The Origins of Competitive Zeal

Competitive zeal is not something you're born with[2]. It's something that often germinates deep in the psyche in youth and is kindled by experiences that excite and nurture its growth. Research has not yet identified the precise

---

[2]However, libidinal energy, the propensity for competitive zeal, has a genetic component.

nature of these experiences, but studies of the early years of people like Michael Jordan reveal a few small successes that follow a number of failed attempts. Each success seems to reinforce in the individual the belief that challenges can be overcome by merely expending more effort. As these positive early imprints accumulate, the individual develops a tolerance for failure, i.e., an ability to continue to struggle in the face of repeated setbacks or defeats.

The study of competitive zeal is particularly important because an understanding of its origin and effects provides invaluable insights beyond athletics, to every domain of human endeavor. Research in mathematics reveals that the greatest problem-solvers have a high tolerance for failure and are energized rather than discouraged by failure.

For over 20 years, Professor Andrew Wiles of Princeton University struggled to prove a conjecture called *Fermat's Last Theorem* that had eluded the greatest mathematical minds for over 350 years. Mathematical societies had posted large financial prizes for its solution, but no proof was forthcoming and some mathematicians began to believe that the conjecture could not be proved. After countless failed attempts, on June 23, 1993, Dr. Wiles sent a shock-wave through the mathematical world, announcing that he had a proof. Subsequent investigation revealed a flaw that invalidated his proof and the goal of his life's work. Though devastated at first, he picked through the ashes of yet another failed attempt in a renewed quest to repair the flawed proof. Within three years, he had discovered a way to resolve the difficulty. His revised proof was subsequently validated and celebrated throughout the world mathematics community. At the heart of success in any endeavor is a fierce competitive zeal that interprets failure as a challenge to which it responds with a renewed vigor.

Cooperation

Survival in nature is based on a delicate balance between competition and cooperation. Sometimes the survival of a species or a group of individuals is contingent upon cooperation. In such cases, the competitive instincts of the individual must be subordinated to the survival needs of the collective. For example, the survival of many insect species such as ants, bees and termites involves a complex social cooperative involving hierarchies and the division of labor. In other animal species, including *Homo sapiens*, two parents usually share the burdens of providing the necessities of life for themselves and their offspring and, in so doing, perpetuate the existence of the family. Similarly, a particular culture or nation attempts to ensure its survival through cooperative entities like a military unit, a police force or a government body.

Team sports offer an ideal medium for studying the interaction of competition and cooperation. The teams in a league all compete with one another, but competition at the highest level requires that all the team members cooperate so that the team functions as a unit. The different positions on a hockey, soccer, football, basketball or baseball team represent a division of labor with each player having a distinct role description. The effectiveness of the team is contingent on the degree of harmony and cooperation among those in these different roles. Many of the sportswriters quoted in the previous chapter described how Gretzky's team orientation was evident in his brilliant playmaking and spectacular passes that "fed" his teammates, enabling the Oilers to compete favorably against the other teams and dominate the league. Clearly, cooperation is important and unbridled competitive zeal in an individual can be detrimental to the goals of a team and undermine its ability to function productively. However, anyone wishing to reach the top must never allow the demands of a cooperative effort to diminish their competitive zeal, for when the flame of passion flickers, the intensity of the performance cools.

What is the measure of your competitive zeal? How do you respond to setbacks? Do you become discouraged or challenged by failure? The assessment on the following page is designed to help you determine how you respond to failure so that you can improve your ability to transform negative results into challenges that ignite your competitive instincts. When you have finished the assessment, I invite you to read the profile of Michael Jordan–an alpha male of the first magnitude whose competitive zeal propelled him to the top in the struggle for dominance.

COMPETITIVE ZEAL SELF-ASSESSMENT–Are You Competitive?

Choose a number 1–5, with 1 the lowest and 5 the highest, to indicate the degree to which you believe the statement describes you or how you feel. Record for each statement the number you have chosen. The scoring key is given below.

There are no "right" or "wrong" answers. In making your selection, answer the questions as candidly as possible without anticipating how you will be classified.

	Seldom			Usually	
1. Prior to any competition, I experience anxiety.	1	2	3	4	5
2. I prefer playing games for rewards than for fun.	1	2	3	4	5
3. The more physical the game, the more I like it.	1	2	3	4	5
4. I prefer individual sports to team sports.	1	2	3	4	5
5. I do not sleep well the night before a big athletic contest.	1	2	3	4	5
6. I get butterflies and/or my heart races when I'm watching a closely contested game.	1	2	3	4	5
7. When I play sports, winning is more important to me than having fun.	1	2	3	4	5
8. When people put me down, I become more motivated to achieve.	1	2	3	4	5
9. I hate to lose and when I do, it bothers me for some time.	1	2	3	4	5
10. I worry about my performance prior to a game.	1	2	3	4	5
11. I am aggressive in pick-up games.	1	2	3	4	5
12. I feel somewhat hostile toward people who beat me in sports.	1	2	3	4	5
13. I analyze my competition to find a weakness in their game or methods.	1	2	3	4	5
14. I get butterflies in my stomach when beginning a contest.	1	2	3	4	5
15. I tend to feel that people are more competitive against me than against others.	1	2	3	4	5
16. I pride myself on my athletic abilities.	1	2	3	4	5
17. Others say that I am very competitive.	1	2	3	4	5
18. I feel inclined to race any driver who challenges me at a stoplight.	1	2	3	4	5

	Seldom				Usually
19. Winning isn't important to me, it's imperative.	1	2	3	4	5
20. When I lose, I feel a little inferior to those who beat me.	1	2	3	4	5
21. If faced with losing, I'm prepared to cheat in order to win.	1	2	3	4	5
22. I use strategies and tricks to gain advantages in competition.	1	2	3	4	5
23. I tend to play against highly competent people rather than those of lesser competence.	1	2	3	4	5
24. When playing in a team situation, I get angry at my teammate (or teammates) if they cause us to lose.	1	2	3	4	5
25. I am impatient with teammates who do not put a full effort into winning.	1	2	3	4	5

Scoring Key

Total the numbers you chose for all the items.
Then use the scoring key to determine how competitive you are.

Total Score	**Level of Competitiveness**
100 – 125	You are very competitive
75 – 99	You are moderately competitive.
50 – 74	You are not very competitive.
Below 50	Time to get those juices going.

MICHAEL JORDAN

- Universally acclaimed as the best basketball player of all time.

- Led the Chicago Bulls to 6 NBA championships in 1991–1993 and 1996–1998.

- Won a record 10 NBA scoring titles with regular season and playoff points per game averages of 31.5 and 33.4.

- Most league (5) and playoff (6) MVP awards.

- Selected to 14 All-Star teams.

- Ranked #1 in 2001, 2002 and 2003 as the US Fans' Favorite Athlete.

Michael Jordan: Competitive Zeal Personified

When conversing with Wayne Gretzky, an interviewer from *Esquire* magazine attempted to draw a parallel between Gretzky and Michael Jordan as stars of comparable magnitude. Gretzky, interjecting with characteristic humility, asserted, "When people talk about me as the Michael Jordan of hockey I just want to laugh. No one belongs in the same breath as Michael. That's not modest. That's just fact." What a tribute from The Great One–the man who demolished the hockey record book! Yet such tributes to Michael Jordan, affectionately known as MJ, have poured in

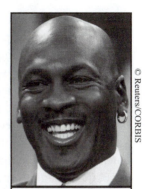

© Reuters/CORBIS

**Michael Jordan
born Feb. 17, 1963**

from all sources within and outside the world of basketball. Descriptions of Michael Jordan's status as the athlete of all athletes challenge a sportswriter's vocabulary of superlatives. Author Scott Turow, an avid Bull's fan, wrote, "Jordan plays basketball better than anyone else has ever done anything." Is there a higher testimonial of achievement? What could be the source of such supremacy—supremacy that earned this athlete the highest magnitude of respect from the greatest superstars in all sports?

As an NBA rookie, Michael Jordan wanted to display his dominance over every center in the league by leaping into the air, floating to the basket, reaching over the head of the defending center and slam-dunking the ball through the hoop. Scoring in this way is basketball's equivalent of a struggle for dominance in the animal kingdom. It's dramatic, conclusive and an unequivocal display of unfettered power over another. Michael Jordan's most dramatic slam-dunks over the head of an opponent were often captured on posters featuring Michael and his hapless victim who was said to have been "posterized." Some commentators suggested that the centers he wished to humiliate in this way included not only those on the opposing teams, but also those on his own team. Such competitive zeal emanates from a psyche raging with energy and passion. When directed outward toward opponents, this competitive zeal energizes all members of the team, but if it spills inward toward teammates, it generates antagonism and feeds hostile feelings. MJ's fierce competitive zeal aroused both reactions.

During his unprecedented run in the NBA, Jordan's intensity was off the scale. His hyperkineticity and sizzling competitive spirit infused his teammates with passion and intimidated his opponents. Jordan's competitive rage helped transform NBA basketball from an Olympic-style game involving systematic plays and positional strategies into a fierce struggle for dominance featuring trash-talking, in-fighting and a variety of other intimidation techniques. The goal was not merely to win, but to humiliate the opposition and relegate them to a lower position in the hierarchy.

Like Gretzky and other athletic superstars, MJ was most intense when challenged or criticized. In a game against the Utah Jazz in 1988, *Air Jordan*, as he became known for his virtual levitations, stole the ball and thundered down the court, dunking the ball aggressively over six-foot John Stockton. As the 6' 6" Jordan returned up the court, Larry Miller, owner of the Utah Jazz, sitting at courtside, screamed at him, "Why don't you pick on someone your own size?" In his inimitable fashion, MJ came roaring back down the court with fire in his eyes and skied over seven-foot center Mel Turpin. After slamming the ball through the hoop, Jordan ran back down the court and, confronting the flabbergasted Miller, demanded, "He big enough for you?" Biographer David Halberstam spoke of Jordan's "unmatched will to excel, an inner competitive rage," and "a passion unmatched by anyone else in the game."

The competitive zeal of an athlete is most strongly felt by those who compete against him in the struggle for dominance. Providing a scary insight into the intensity of Jordan's burning desire to win, former NBA player Rolando Blackman described his struggle against MJ (Krugel, pp. 182–183):

> *Playing against MJ was like going in search of the great white shark. You wanted to find it and destroy it, but you needed a shark cage so that you wouldn't be destroyed in the process. And you had better have a strong team around you or MJ would devour you and move on to the next thing in his way.*

Former NBA player Olden Polynice offered another testimonial revealing the lethal nature of MJ's competitive zeal (as quoted in Williams, p. 90):

> *MJ was so friendly before the game. A great sportsman. He'd come over to shake hands and chat with you. You'd think, "MJ said hi to me! I can't wait to get home to call my mom and tell her. Wow, what a nice guy." Then you'd have to refocus because MJ was lulling you to sleep. He was thinking about attacking you and how badly he was going to kill you.*

Even Michael's college coach admitted, "MJ was the nicest guy in the world, but once he got on the court he was a barracuda." It was no accident that Jordan's opponents and colleagues frequently compared the struggle against Michael Jordan on the basketball court to a struggle for survival in the animal world. They sensed by his intensity that in every game he was fighting for his life.

Michael Jordan's life offers a powerful lesson for anyone who seeks the key to success in any competitive endeavor. Talent, ability and physical stature play a role in the struggle for dominance in athletics, but its a minor role. Success is rooted much more deeply in the mindset that interprets failure as opportunity and uses it to ignite the competitive instinct. As in the animal kingdom, competitive zeal in any struggle is a major factor in determining the victor and the vanquished. But how does one acquire the mindset that arouses competitive zeal? The life of MJ is an engaging story that models winning behaviors while unlocking some of the secrets of competitive dominance.

MICHAEL JORDAN'S TREK TO THE TOP

Early Imprints

The person who would eventually be known to the world as Air Jordan was born on February 17, 1963, in Brooklyn, New York, and rooted shortly after in Wilmington, North Carolina. His parents, James and Deloris Jordan, were imbued with strong religious and moral values and served as character models for young Michael as he entered his formative years. Later expressing his indebtedness to his parents, MJ said (as quoted in Williams, 2004, p. 98):

When you see me, you see a combination of both [parents]. My father liked to joke, have fun, and enjoy life. The business side of MJ comes from my mother. Without my parents I couldn't be a complete person and wouldn't be in the position that I'm in today.

Michael's first love was baseball. During the summers of his youth, it was the focus of his life and the outlet for his unbridled energy. Friends nicknamed him "rabbit" because he seemed to be in perpetual motion. (Recall that Wilma Rudolph's boundless energy earned her the nickname "Skeeter.") At the age of twelve, Michael pitched a two-hitter for the Wilmington team in the Little League World Series of the Babe Ruth League. Years later he recalled (Smith, p. 204):

My greatest accomplishment really is the MVP award I got when my Babe Ruth League team won the state baseball championship. That was the first big thing I accomplished in my life, and you always remember the first.

In describing his early approach to batting, MJ reported, "I was the kind of kid who always went for the home run. Why go for the base hit when you can go for all four bases?" His was a mindset that visualized lofty goals, which he chased relentlessly in an ever-escalating spiral of challenge and achievement.

During those very years when Walter Gretzky's backyard rink was serving as the "field of dreams" for Wayne and his siblings, James Jordan's backyard basketball court began to serve the same purpose for Michael and his brothers. Throughout his childhood, Michael honed his basketball skills against older brother Larry, who held an edge in height, weight and experience. These highly competitive siblings engaged in titanic one-on-one battles on their backyard court–battles that Michael consistently lost in what we might call the early struggle for dominance. His interminable losses in this struggle served only to intensify Michael's determination to win. MJ later recalled (Krugel, p. 34), "As soon as I grew taller than him [brother Larry], I vowed to never lose to him again." Describing how Jordan's compulsion to win had emerged from these formative experiences, biographer Halberstam reported (p. 100), "…teammates came to realize that he was driven by an almost unparalleled desire–or need–to win. The ghost of losing to his brother Larry in backyard contests still lived."

In Michael Jordan's case, his early successes in baseball helped him build a tolerance for his repeated losses to older brother Larry in the one-on-one drills in basketball. MJ once reported (Sachare, p. 171):

Those backyard games really helped me become the player I am today in a lot of ways. Larry would never give me any slack, never took it easy on me. He'd rather beat me up than have me beat him in a game. I learned a lot about being competitive from him.

Rather than allowing the incessant defeats to discourage him, Michael built up an inner rage like a volcano preparing to blow. He vowed that once he beat Larry, he would never lose again. Years later, when he walked on the basketball court, his pent-up energy exploded and the world watched in wonder at the fury that poured forth. Manifest as competitive zeal, this energy was the fuel that carried Michael Jordan to the top in the struggle for dominance. Michael Jordan and Babe Zaharias are prime examples of athletic superstars who hated to lose at anything and responded to every defeat and setback as a motivating challenge.

As shown in the competitive instinct feedback loop, defeats can lead to acceptance and decreased energy levels, or to a perceived challenge that increases energy output. The decision resides with the individual and Michael consistently chose the latter. As the Chinese philosopher Confucius observed over two thousand years ago, "Our greatest glory is not in never falling, but in rising every time we fall." It was as if the young warrior had an intuitive understanding of this ancient wisdom. Those early wars for dominance on the backyard tarmac in Wilmington groomed Michael for competition at the highest level, in the same way that shinny in Wally's coliseum prepared Wayne for superstar performance. Excited by the competitive arena offered by one-on-one contests, Jordan gradually abandoned the pursuit of his baseball dreams and embarked on a new voyage that would carry him to the top of the basketball world, and, in the eyes of many, raise him to the status of "greatest living athlete."

When Michael entered the tenth grade at Laney High School, he tried out for the Laney High Buccaneers varsity team. However, his skills did not sufficiently impress coach Clifton Herring who dropped him from the roster. On learning that he had been cut from the team, Michael was so distraught that he ran home, went to his room, broke down and cried inconsolably. Years later as he reflected on that traumatic event in his life, MJ said, "Getting cut was good, because it made me know what disappointment felt like, and I knew I never wanted to have that feeling, ever again…that taste in my mouth, that hole in my stomach."

As I explained in some depth in Chapter 4, breakdown can lead to breakthrough–hitting bottom can serve as a springboard to reaching the top. For the next three years Michael was picked up at 6 a.m. by coach Herring who delivered him to the gym and put him through dribbling and shooting drills designed to make him a high-school star. The intensely driven teenager was dedicated to ensuring he would make the varsity team. In the process, he learned that the world belongs to whomever wants it enough to pay the price and endure the pain.

By his junior year, Michael had reached a height of 6' 2". His improved skills won him an invitation to the Five Star Summer Basketball Camp in

Pittsburgh. Only the best young players in the country were considered for this camp, where college coaches helped emerging stars and chose the outstanding participants for scholarships. On returning to Laney High School, Michael was ready for the court wars. He made the All-State team and led Laney to the State Championship, scoring 27.8 points per game. By the time he finished his senior year, 6' 4"–tall MJ, a power forward, had learned how to play the post-up game with his back to the basket.

The North Carolina Tar Heels

After winning All-State honors, Michael Jordan was recruited by legendary coach Dean Smith to play for the North Carolina Tar Heels. Smith was a team-oriented coach who was known for his reluctance to recruit the so-called "hot dog" players or those with superstar potential, for fear their personal quests for dominance would detract from team play. However, he made an exception in Michael's case and, acting on pure instinct, offered him a scholarship. Coach Smith's instincts served him well in his selection of this passionate warrior whose burning need to dominate drove him to practice like a man obsessed.

Traditionally, freshmen at North Carolina didn't make it into the starting lineup, but again Smith broke his own rules and put Jordan on the starting team. Since he was a freshman playing with two seniors, Sam Perkins and James Worthy (who would later win All-American honors and become NBA stars), Jordan was made the third option on plays.

At the end of his freshman year in 1982, Michael was named National Collegiate Athletic Association (NCAA) Player of the Year. In this, his inaugural season, the name "Jordan" became indelibly etched in the history of Tar Heel Blue as this intensely competitive 19-year-old gave the first glimmer of the supernova that was about to explode into the world of basketball. With 32 seconds remaining in the NCAA Championship game, the Tar Heels were trailing Georgetown 62–61. Coach John Thompson of Georgetown called a time out. The savvy Smith, knowing that Thompson would expect the ball to go to Worthy or Perkins, called a play to set up Jordan. Shortly after the action resumed, Jordan broke into the clear and snapped up a pass as his defender came thundering toward him. With 17 seconds remaining on the clock, he launched an 18-foot jump shot that ripped the net, rescuing victory from the jaws of defeat! Not only did Michael help Smith win his first NCAA Championship, but he also hit the so-called "winning shot that was heard around the basketball world." That monumental field goal instantly catapulted Jordan into superstardom. "My career started after that shot," he told the media later, "I was fearless." That incident also ignited MJ's passion for winning in the dying minutes of crucial games–a ritual that would become a defining signature throughout his career.

Hitting that winning shot won Jordan the attention of the NBA. Through the 1982–83 and 1983–84 seasons at North Carolina, he continued to surpass expectations and at the Olympic games in 1984, he added a gold medal to his accomplishments, topping off his career as an amateur. By the end of his junior year at North Carolina, he was courted by the NBA and had to decide whether to return to college for his senior year or turn professional. His mother wanted him to finish school but his father preferred that he seize the opportunity and turn professional immediately. Michael chose the latter option, though he eventually heeded his mother's wishes and completed his degree.

Professional Basketball: The Making of a Superstar 1984–89

Though regarded by the NBA as a player with substantial potential, Jordan turned professional in a year when a great depth of talent was emerging from the college ranks. In the 1984 NBA draft, the Houston Rockets selected center Akeem Olajuwon as their number 1 draft choice. Then the Portland Trail Blazers bypassed Michael Jordan and selected center Sam Bowie. (This choice would later haunt the Portland coaching staff.) The Chicago Bulls, a weak franchise at that time, were given the next choice and they selected Jordan. Though it cost them $6.3 million for a seven-year contract (the third largest ever given to a rookie), this decision would turn out to be their resurrection from mediocrity.

In the sneaker business, Nike was second to Reebok. Nike recognized Jordan's star quality as a potential promoter of their products and signed him to a five-year contract, at approximately $1 million per year, to endorse their basketball sneakers to be named "Air Jordans." It was an investment that would yield Nike revenues of $130 million within four years and catapult them to the number one rank in sneaker sales. This Jordan-Nike endorsement also ushered in a new era linking corporate America to the NBA.

As a professional basketball player, Michael wasted no time initiating his program of intimidation–not only the intimidation of the opposing teams, but also the intimidation of his teammates. As he explained (Krugel, p. 38):

I used to have a hell of a practice. I thought practice was my proving ground to my teammates, where I had to prove to them, "Hey, I was the third pick in the draft, and I was worth it. I was the highest paid player on the team, and I was worth it."

Indeed, Michael worked harder than anyone in practice to show his dominance. Coach Doug Collins said, "Practice is what made him go. Every day he had this need to show he was the best." In the 1984–85 season, his first with the Bulls, MJ averaged 28 points per game and was named NBA Rookie of the Year. A broken foot caused him to miss most of his second season but his performance in the playoffs against the Boston Celtics served as a harbinger of what was to come. In the first playoff game at the Boston Garden, Jordan scored 49 points against the all-powerful Celtics. Though impressive, it paled in comparison with his virtuoso performance in the following game. On April 20, 1986, Air Jordan poured in 63 points against the Celtics and superstar Larry Bird. In a post-game interview, an incredulous Larry Bird opined, "I think he's God disguised as Michael Jordan." Although 63 points was a new record for a playoff game, it was MJ's dazzling array of moves that astounded the basketball world. However, Michael was not ebullient in his post-game interview. Noting that the Bulls had lost 135–131, he told reporters, "I'd give all the points back if we could have won the game. I wanted to win so badly." In the next game of the playoffs, the Celtics changed their defense, double-teaming Jordan so that he would have difficulty getting the ball. The strategy worked. Boston won 122–104, eliminating the Bulls, and then went on to win the NBA Championship.

MJ carried the momentum from those playoffs into the 1986–87 season. On opening night against the New York Knicks, Michael scored 50 points. A few weeks later, he led the Bulls to a 101–99 victory over the Knicks by scoring his team's last 18 points. That victory was rescued by MJ in a solo effort that saw him dribble the length of the court and rip a 10-foot jump shot with one second remaining in the game! In that year, his third with the Bulls, he averaged 37 points per game and won his first of ten NBA scoring titles. In each of the six years that followed, he would win the scoring title, tying Wilt Chamberlain's record of seven consecutive scoring titles.

During the mid- to late-1980s, MJ continued to provide the fans with dramatic displays of fierce competitive play, awe-inspiring athleticism and dramatic leaps, prompting some fans to ask if he could fly. As Orr and Tracz observed (p. 46):

On the court, the most famous maneuver in the Jordan repertoire was his gravity-defying flight to the basket for a slam-dunk in which he appeared to bypass the laws of physics. Just when it seemed that he had reached the apex of his leap, Jordan found a way to go even higher. Those dazzling takeoffs would see him switch the ball from one hand to the other while seeming to walk on air, leaving witnesses shaking their heads in amazement. That move, of course, led to the "Air Jordan" nickname and the shoe of the same name.

The Jordan Rules

At the end of the 1987–88 season, Michael was voted the NBA's Most Valuable Player. There was also a growing consensus that MJ was the greatest basketball player of all time. He was difficult, if not impossible, to defend. Every team grappled endlessly with the question, "How do you guard MJ?" Biographer Krugel explained (pp. 123–24):

[Rolando] Blackman knew why it was so hard to guard Jordan. The man could take off from the foul line, hold the ball in his right hand, extend it, then switch the ball to his left hand while still rising, and flip an underhanded shot off the backboard and into the basket. The man could dart toward the basket on an angle, face the basket head on and turn his back on it at the last minute, and flip a shot over his head and in–with a defender hanging on both arms.

Attempts to double or triple-team Jordan failed because it left other Chicago players open to scoring. Eventually Chuck Daly, coach of the NBA Champion Detroit Pistons, formulated a plan to stop MJ. Called the "Jordan Rules," this strategy was designed to enlist the entire team to force Michael into the center lane where they would punish him physically. A forearm shoved into his back, a stiff body shot as he slashed to the basket, and other creatively robust bumps and thumps were designed to wear him down and drain his energy. This physical assault stimulated Jordan's competitive zeal, prompting him to drive even harder into the opposition to show he could blast through their physical abuse.

As the Jordan Rules were applied with increasing intensity by Detroit and in modified forms by other teams, MJ realized that he needed to develop more muscle mass to survive the physical onslaught. Enlisting the services of personal trainer Tim Grover, he gradually increased his body weight from 195 to 215 pounds, adding inches to his chest, shoulders, arms and back. His increased size enabled him to drive down the middle, take the punishment, and still score more than 40 points in a game.

Our Greatest Strength Is Our Greatest Weakness

In spite of Jordan's stellar performances, the Chicago Bulls were not winning championships. As in the case of Wayne Gretzky and the building of the Oiler dynasty, it would take the Bulls a few years to put together a starring cast around their superstar. In the 1987–88 season, Scottie Pippen and Horace Grant joined the Bulls. These strong players, combined with John Paxon and Bill Cartwright, rounded out a team that would eventually make a bid for the NBA Championship. However, through the mid-1980s, Jordan, as Chicago's lone superstar, had become the central focus of their offense. As the shooting guard, he controlled the ball, took most of the shots and accounted for most of the Bulls' points. In fact, in the 1987–88 season, he won virtually all the individual awards including MVP, Defensive Player of the Year and All-Star MVP. In the 1988–89 season he was the NBA scoring leader, averaging 32.5 points per game, while contributing a career-high eight assists and eight rebounds per game. Believing that the strength of the team resided solely in his scoring prowess, Michael was reluctant to pass to his teammates. Chicago's point guard John Paxon, who typically spoke well of Jordan, commented sardonically that playing offense on Jordan's team meant increasing the number of spectators in the arena by four. Jordan's greatest strength, his competitive zeal, had become his greatest weakness. Opposing teams were prepared to concede 40 or 50 points to Jordan in any game if they could force him to take most of the shots, thereby preventing the other members of the Bulls from scoring in the double digits. It was becoming clear that in spite of his remarkable scoring ability, MJ's obsessive need to dominate was impairing the team's ability to win. Meanwhile Coach Doug Collins was reluctant to curtail Jordan's dominance for fear it would inhibit his productivity and hurt the team performance.

Phil Jackson became the coach of the Bulls in the 1989–90 season. He later said, "The greatness of Michael Jordan is his competitive drive. The weakness of Michael Jordan is his competitive drive." Recognizing that the Bulls needed to make optimal use of the talents of all the members of the team, Jackson introduced plays that used Jordan as a decoy, drawing two and three-man coverage of Jordan and freeing other players to score. He implemented the triangle or triple-post offense to move the ball among three players until one of those players saw an opening and exploited it. At first, the new strategy had limited success because it didn't permit MJ to dominate the play as he had. However as Phil Jackson continued to pressure Jordan into working the system, results began to emerge. The Bulls finished the season with 55 wins vs. 27 losses–their best record in almost two decades. He encouraged Jordan's team play by telling him that 10 assists on his part were worth 30 points to the team.

Jackson was well aware that scoring leaders don't win championships. In fact, since 1950, the only scoring leader who was also on an NBA Championship team was Kareem Abdul-Jabbar. It's a tribute to Phil Jackson that he was able to wrest from Jordan a larger measure of control of the Bulls and transform the team into a more cooperative effort that exploited the talents of a star-studded lineup. In the words of Halberstam (p. 47), "Jackson had to maximize Jordan's vast abilities, without letting him suck the oxygen from his teammates." At the beginning of the 1990s, it was clear that the Bulls were becoming a complete team and serious contenders for an NBA Championship.

A Dynasty in the Making: 1990–93

Phil Jackson's continuing attempts to encourage Jordan to rely on his teammates did not prevent Michael from delivering game-winning exploits. In the 1989 playoffs, Jordan eliminated the Cleveland Cavaliers with a jump shot from the top of the key that swished the net and, with all the drama of a Hollywood movie, stole the game as the final buzzer sounded. On March 28, 1990, almost a year after this stinging defeat of the Cavs, Michael found himself back in Richfield Coliseum facing a hostile crowd, still embittered by their earlier humiliation. Motivated by the cacophony of jeering and booing in the packed arena, he almost single-handedly defeated the Cavaliers, in what he later described as his "best game ever by far." He piled up points by slashing to the basket, displaying dramatic slam-dunks and ripping jump shots from outside. As the final buzzer sounded he repeated the insult of the previous year by sinking the tying basket that sent the game into overtime. The Bulls subsequently defeated the Cavs 117–113 in an overtime cliffhanger that denied the Cleveland fans the revenge they had sought. When the dust settled, the record showed that MJ had scored 69 points–a career high.

MJ's heroic performance continued into the 1990–91 season. With an average of 31.5 points per game during the regular season, he led the Bulls to the NBA finals against the Los Angeles Lakers. In the third quarter of the third game of the series, the Bulls were trailing the Lakers by 15 points and it looked as if the Lakers would go ahead two games to one in the series. Then Michael launched an offensive that closed the spread and put the Bulls in the lead by a point. With only 9.8 seconds remaining, the Lakers scored a basket, apparently sealing the fate of the Bulls. However, MJ once again rose like a phoenix from the ashes of imminent defeat and, charging the length of the court, sank a 10-foot jump shot, tied the score, and sent the game into overtime. Chicago subsequently won that game and then shut out the Lakers for the remainder of the series, earning their first NBA Championship in the history of their franchise. Jordan, who had played the key role in Chicago's climb to the top of the world of basketball, was named the Most Valuable Player in the finals. As if to prove that this was no fluke, the Bulls went on to win the championship in the next two seasons, earning what was dubbed a "three-peat." To no one's surprise, MJ won the MVP honors in both final series. It was clear that a new dynasty had emerged under the leadership of Phil Jackson, the coach, and Michael Jordan, the player.

Retirement

En route to reaching the highest pinnacle in the world of basketball, MJ broke old records and transformed NBA basketball into a more aggressive, more combative and more exciting spectator sport. Shortly before the Bulls won their third NBA Championship, he confided (Krugel, p. 1), "I just can't wait for the playoffs to start. The championships now are the only reason I'm playing. I still want to win championships. There's still a burning flame in here." But once the third NBA Championship was won, his flame for basketball flickered out. Once Promethean superstars conquer a goal, they need other motivations to keep their fires alight.

Like Alexander the Great lamenting that there were no more worlds to conquer, Michael looked for greater challenges beyond the horizons of basketball–beyond the domains that he had already conquered. Such is often the quest of the greatest athletic superstars when they reach the pinnacle in their sport. Thorpe and Zaharias moved from their triumphs in track and field into other sports where they quickly rose to the top. Jack Nicklaus, on reaching the zenith in golf, mused about the possibilities of competing on the tennis court. When the adrenaline rush that feeds the fiercely competitive athlete begins to fade, the quest begins for new sources of excitement to feed the endorphin addiction. So it was with Michael Jordan during the summer of 1993 as he looked outward toward the horizon from the top of basketball's Mount Olympus and contemplated his future at the age of 30. His original dream had been to play professional baseball, but that had been moved to the back burner when his passion for basketball was ignited.

On August 13, 1993, America was stunned by the news that a body found in a creek near McColl, South Carolina, had been identified as James Jordan, Michael's father. His red Lexus, a present from Michael, had been stripped and left by the side of Highway 74 just 50 miles north of McColl. The autopsy revealed that James Jordan had been shot in the chest. It was conjectured that Mr. Jordan had pulled off the highway to rest when set upon by his assassins. On hearing the news, Michael was devastated. He and "Pops" were not only father and son, but they shared a powerful bond similar to that enjoyed by Wayne and Walter Gretzky. If Michael had been undecided about his future plans, this traumatic event helped him reach a decision. After announcing his retirement at an NBA press conference on October 6, 1993, he said, "Being an optimistic person, the best thing I can say about my father's passing is that he got to see me play my last game."

Charismatic Appeal

Jordan always had the ultimate Q rating, the media rating for star-draw that sells products through endorsements. Gatorade jumped on the Michael bandwagon, attempting to exploit his image as a "cool," clean-cut, athletic superstar. Those '90s Gatorade commercials told the world to *Be Like Mike*. But the Air Jordans with the Nike label were even more successful. Kids from both the ghetto and the country club demanded nothing but what Jordan wore.

A remarkable indication of his popularity is the fact that one-third of the television viewer ratings for the 1993 NBA Finals was attributed to Michael Jordan's presence on the court. Dick Ebersol of NBC extensively analyzed that particular series to find out why, for the first time in history, the NBA had surpassed the World Series. That year the NBA Finals had a 17.9 rating, or approximately 27.2 million viewers. Basketball had come of age, and most of it was attributable to the Jordan mystique.

Off the court, Michael Jordan was as brilliant as he was on it, bringing the same competitive zeal to the sneaker wars that he brought to the court wars.

His fight to protect his corporate persona was as intense as his struggle to protect the Bulls' basket. When black activist Harvey Gantt, a Democrat, solicited MJ's endorsement for a Senate seat in North Carolina, Michael refused, explaining, "Republicans buy sneakers too." An article in *USA Today* (Sept. 27, 2001, p. 3C) portrayed him as "the most successful of a new and amazing breed of modern day corporate jocks."

During his first 14 years with Nike, Michael received $150 million from his endorsements. This was a drop in the bucket compared with the billions that Nike had earned from their association with MJ. In 1998, *Fortune* magazine studied the influence of various athletes on their sport and estimated that Jordan's worth to the game of basketball through his playing, his endorsements and his products was $10 billion. Such numbers were hitherto attributable to saviors and governments rather than athletes.

The Dark Side of Competitive Zeal

Jordan has a big T personality (see Chapter 2)–a personality associated with high levels of testosterone accompanied by a penchant for thrill-seeking. Big Ts are more aggressive than others; they thrive on adventure, sleep sparingly, love to test limits, opt for the new rather than the conventional, and tend to get more than their share of speeding tickets. One teammate told *Sports Illustrated*, "This guy is a killer. He's the most viciously competitive player I've ever seen." Biographer Sam Smith observed (p. 159):

Jordan doesn't bear idleness well. This is not uncommon among great athletes, one thing that explains their desire to drive fast. Charles Barkley has always told friends he expects to die someday going 150 miles per hour down the road, and friends who have driven with Jordan are amazed he has avoided such a fate. He would come screeching to a halt in front of the Chicago Stadium parking lot after going 70 miles per hour down the side streets, and observers would say they'd often see Jordan gunning through stop signs at intersections, almost testing whether his reflexes were fast enough to get him past approaching cars. Athletes of such ability, it seems, need constant challenge.

Jordan's high risk-taking propensity found an outlet in gambling. In February 1992, two checks totaling $108,000 and signed by Michael Jordan were found in the briefcase of a murdered man, Eddie Dow. Though Jordan claimed these were business loans, it was later revealed that they were payments of gambling debts incurred in high-stakes golf games. Money for its own sake was never important to Michael. He had more than he would ever spend, but he wagered whenever the opportunity arose, often betting $1000 on sinking a shot from half-court after practice. Journalists wrote extensively on his infamous gambling soirees in golf and in casinos. In his 1993 book, titled *Michael and Me, Our Gambling Addiction, My Cry for Help*, golf hustler Richard Esquinas told of winning $1.25 million from Michael in a ten-day golfing spree and $100,000 on a single putt. When the press asked Michael's father whether his son had a gambling problem, he responded, "Michael doesn't have a gambling problem, he has a competitiveness problem." Meanwhile, the NBA was concerned about the negative publicity and warned Michael to cease his high-profile gambling antics.

Pursuing a Lost Love

When Zen master coach Phil Jackson learned that Jordan was contemplating retirement from the basketball court to chase an unfulfilled dream on the baseball diamond, he cautioned his protégé (Halberstam p. 9), "pure genius is something very, very rare and if you are blessed enough to possess it, you want to think a long time before you walk away from using it." Baseball had been MJ's first love. Jilted in early youth, she now beckoned him back with the promise of a new challenge and closure on an unfulfilled affair. The challenge of a career in baseball was an itch that Michael had to scratch. Fortuitously, the owner of the Chicago Bulls, who also had controlling interest in the Chicago White Sox, was able to help Jordan link up with the Sox affiliate, the Birmingham Barons, in the class AA Southern League.

Throughout the 1994 baseball season, MJ rediscovered the drudgery of traveling from town to town for inconsequential games in insignificant towns where the stakes are small and the rewards are smaller. There was not enough stimulus to ignite Jordan's competitive zeal and his baseball performance failed when he discovered he couldn't hit a curve ball thrown by the pros. When a labor dispute loomed on the horizon prior to the 1995 Major League Baseball season, he came out of retirement with the simple pronouncement, "I'm back." Michael rejoined the Bulls late in the 1994–95 season, playing the last 17 regular season games and averaging 27 points per game.

A Career Resurrected: 1995–1999

On his return from retirement, Michael discovered that he had lost his fine-tuned conditioning. Now approaching 33 years of age, he was not as fast as a decade earlier, and posterizing opponents with his slam-dunks was harder to achieve. Never willing to concede anything to an opponent, he developed his fadeaway jump shot that enabled him to launch a shot from three-point distance as he fell back and away from a defender. This new weapon in his arsenal made him even more difficult to cover. Describing how criticism had motivated him to add new techniques to his offensive attack, Michael said (Krugel, p. 42):

> I read what I couldn't do and I learned from that. I read that I couldn't go to my left, I practiced that and they stopped saying that. Then they said I couldn't hit the jump shot consistently. I practiced my jump shot and eventually they didn't know where I was going or what I was going to do and that became the most lethal part of my game.

This new element in his offensive repertoire played a vital role in some of his most dramatic last-minute wins in the seasons that followed. Just six games into the 1995–96 season, Jordan tallied a total of 55 points against the Knicks at Madison Square Garden, in a thriller that saw him feed Bill Wennington for the game-winning basket in the Bulls' last-minute, 113–111 victory. On April 16, 1996, the Bulls became the first team in NBA history to win 70 games, and they topped off the season by winning their fourth NBA Championship. Jordan won the NBA scoring title with an average of 30.4 points per game and was named the MVP for the season, the finals and the All-Star Game.

In the 1996–97 season, Jordan continued to dazzle millions of spectators. One of his most memorable performances occurred in Game 5 of the 1997 NBA Finals against the Utah Jazz. On the morning of that game, Jordan's bodyguards found him in bed "deathly ill and curled up in a fetal position." He had suffered severe nausea all night and had not slept. No one expected him to suit up, let alone play that night. Though his body was spent and fighting a high fever, Jordan's unyielding competitive spirit would not let him cave in to this ultimate challenge. As he walked onto the basketball court that evening, the media commented how his normally dark skin was tinted an eerie grayish pallor and how his hollowed eyes revealed the depth of his exhaustion. Like a dazed prize fighter rising on the count of nine and refusing to accept defeat, he pressed through his fatigue and managed to score a remarkable 21 points in the first half. Teammates were mesmerized. As the second half began, commentator Marv Albert told the viewing audience. "Look at the body language of Michael Jordan. He has difficulty just standing up." Somehow Jordan reached down deep and elevated his body above illness. His will took over and in the final quarter of a game that he shouldn't have played, MJ scored 15 points, giving him a total of 38 for the game. Included in this Herculean effort was a three-point jumper that put the Bulls ahead 88–85 with 25 seconds remaining on the clock, paving the way to the Chicago 90–88 win. That night, millions of viewers got a first-hand look at the stuff of which exceptional athletes are made. The Bulls went on to win the series in Game 6 and become the NBA Champions for the fifth time.

On June 14, 1998, in a playoff game against the Portland Trailblazers, Jordan began dropping in three-point shots from all over the court. In his trance-like state of relaxed concentration he felt invincible–a feeling that Pelé had so clearly described about his own ethereal moments. Performing in the zone as never before, he ran down the court after sinking a low-percentage shot and, looking over at the announcers, shrugged his shoulders in disbelief. His scoring was "unconscious." Coach Phil Jackson said:

Michael had attained a quality of mind few Zen students ever achieve. His ability to stay relaxed and intensely focused in the midst of chaos is unsurpassed. He loves being in the center of a storm. While everyone else is spinning out of control, he moves effortlessly across the floor, enveloped by a great stillness.

It was fitting for a superstar of Jordan's magnitude that his last game with the Chicago Bulls, Game 6 of the 1998 NBA Finals, would showcase one of his most dramatic performances. As in the previous year, the Bulls were facing the Utah Jazz in the NBA Finals. After five games, the Bulls were leading 3–2 and on the verge of winning their sixth NBA Championship. The game had all the drama of a scripted thriller, with both teams displaying periods of brilliance and alternately taking the lead. With about a minute left on the clock and Chicago trailing Utah 83–81, MJ slashed toward the basket, but was fouled. He scored both free throws to tie the score. However, Utah came back and scored a three-point shot with only 41.9 seconds remaining. A three-point deficit with only 41.9 seconds left seemed an insurmountable gap when suddenly, Michael dribbled down the right side of the court and drove to the basket for a lay-up shot that reduced Utah's lead to a single point. With

18.9 seconds left, Utah had the ball and the opportunity to run out the clock, when the ubiquitous Jordan appeared from nowhere, stole the ball and headed up court. Only one man, Bryon Russell, stood between him and the NBA Championship. Jordan faked a drive to the basket, throwing Russell off stride. Then he levitated for what seemed like suspended time as he released a high, looping jump shot. The audience rose to their feet in what would become a photographic classic, depicting faces of exuberance and horror as the ball swished through the hoop. It was Chicago's sixth NBA Championship and the swan song of basketball's greatest player.

Labor negotiations delayed the beginning of the 1998–1999 NBA season, but when the season resumed, MJ was absent. On January 13, 1999, Michael Jordan announced his retirement for the second time. At almost 36 years of age, he had won all the prizes and awards to be had, including six NBA Championship rings and the highest all-time scoring average of 31.5 points per game. It was the right time to leave.

The Washington Wizards

Unable to stay away from the game he loved so much, MJ purchased a minority share in the dismal Washington Wizards basketball team in 2000. He served as an executive to help raise the sagging fortunes of that franchise. Though his presence was intended as a stimulus to the team, the Wizards finished the 2000–01 season with a disastrous 19–63 win-loss record.

On September 25, 2001, Jordan came out of retirement for the second time, signing a two-year contract with the Wizards. Attendances soared as fans crowded into coliseums to see a legend, always wondering what MJ might do next. Every home game was sold out during the 2002–2003 season, despite the fact the team never achieved .500 ball or made the playoffs. In fact, the Wizards led the league in attendance with 1,597,596 fans coming solely to witness Jordan's on-court wizardry.

One February night in 2003, Michael added one more record by scoring 42 points just a few weeks after his fortieth birthday–becoming the first player of that age to achieve such a feat. When the media interviewed him after the game he merely explained, "I don't feel 40, I feel good."

Prior to retiring for the last time, Michael wrote an editorial (*Los Angeles Times*, April 20, 2003, p. D13): his final farewell to a sport that defined his life. Only the opening and closing lines are reprinted here, but they provide insight into the passion that made Michael Jordan one of the greatest athletes in history.

Dear Basketball:

It's been almost 28 years since the first day I met you in the back of our garage. 28 years since my parents introduced us...I love you, Basketball. I love everything about you and I always will. My playing days in the NBA are definitely over, but our relationship will never end.
Much Love and respect,
Michael Jordan

Legacy

The sculpture adorning the entrance to Chicago's United Center depicts Michael Jordan flying through the air with a demeanor of pure grace, elegance and power. The inscription tells it all. "The best there ever was. The best there ever will be." Sports psychologist Steve Lerch wrote, "Fans worship Michael Jordan with the same intensity as they worship religious figures." *Maclean's* magazine characterized Michael as "Baryshnikov with a jump shot." His famed moves are legend.

Indeed, many sportswriters and basketball aficionados have been effusive in their descriptions of Michael Jordan's dominance in basketball and in athletics. Orr and Tracz, in *The Dominators*, make a strong case for MJ as the "greatest athlete ever" (p. 45):

When ability, accomplishment, style, income, respect, and worldwide recognition are included in the tally, the strongest case can be made for Michael Jordan...a combination of factors–basketball's worldwide explosion, and the extension of instantaneous communication to all corners of the planet in the 1990s, Jordan's excellence in six NBA championships with the Chicago Bulls, the marketability of his shiny bald head, and the globalization that made many of the products he endorsed available everywhere–put "His Airness" solidly in the number one position.

After his final retirement, Michael Jordan wrote his autobiography *For the Love of the Game: My Story*. He wrote his own legacy in the self-effacing style that endeared him to fans and the media:

There is no such thing as a perfect basketball player, and I don't believe there is only one greatest player either. Everyone plays in different eras. I built my talents on the shoulders of someone else's talent. I believe greatness is an evolutionary process that changes and evolves era to era.

Chapter 11

PRINCIPLE #11: FOCUS YOUR TYPE A TENDENCIES

Sometimes you have to be super aggressive if you're going to win.
–Jeff Gordon

The Discovery of Type A Behavior

Are you always in a hurry? Do you get impatient when stuck in traffic or waiting in line at the supermarket? Are there never enough hours in the day for you to get things done? If you answered "yes" to all of these questions, then you may be a *Type A personality*. The assessment at the end of this section will help you find out. Before we explore the classification of personalities into Type A and Type B categories, I will share with you the story of how Drs. Friedman and Rosenman stumbled upon this concept with the help of an upholsterer.

While serving as Director of the Harold Brunn Institute for Cardio-vascular Research in San Francisco, Dr. Meyer Friedman conducted groundbreaking research into the physiological causes of heart disease. In particular, he examined the connection between heart disease and cholesterol, and discovered that the liver is the chief source of cholesterol not derived from food. In his private practice, he treated patients with heart problems. One day, the upholsterer who maintained the furniture in his waiting room commented that the fronts of the seats and the chair arms in his waiting room seemed to wear out much more quickly than similar furniture in the waiting rooms of other physicians. Dr. Friedman asked himself why heart patients would cause more wear and tear on the furniture than patients with other ailments. Perhaps there was a link between personality and heart problems. He conjectured that stress, evidenced by high motility or hyperkineticity, might be a factor contributing to the onset of atherosclerosis and myocardial infarctions.

Investigating this connection, Dr. Friedman and his colleague Dr. Ray Rosenman recorded the cholesterol levels of 40 accountants over one year and found that their cholesterol levels increased substantially during tax time. These results suggested that negative emotions did prompt the increased production of cholesterol and the buildup of arterial plaque that leads to heart problems. When the two physicians applied for a grant to study the connection between emotional stress and heart problems, they were informed that to be eligible for a grant in the field of psychology, they would have to associate "visible signs of stress" with a behavior. Friedman and Rosenman chose the generic term "Type A behavior" for their submission and their grant application was approved.

In their funded study, the two researchers developed criteria for identifying stress-oriented or "Type A" behavior. Then, using these criteria in a study of 3154 men, they demonstrated that those who displayed Type A behavior had a significantly greater risk of developing myocardial infarctions. In a subsequent study, they showed how behavior could be modified to reduce such risks. The research of Friedman and Rosenman became a foundation for understanding the effects of stress on the cardiovascular system and led to the modern preventive treatment of heart disease.

Type A and Type B Personalities

Several types of behavior are identified as Type A behaviors, and people who display most of these are said to have a Type A personality. All others are said to have a Type B personality. The classification of all humans as either Type A or Type B is only definitive at the extremes of the spectrum, because most people display a combination of Type A and Type B behaviors. According to a 1959 paper by Friedman and Rosenman, an individual with a Type A personality:

- has a chronic sense of time urgency called "hurry sickness."
- has a quick, staccato style of speech, often interrupting others.
- is very competitive–even in non-competitive situations.
- is achievement-oriented, hard driving and status-conscious.
- carries a rolling anger and is frequently hostile and aggressive.

The popular image of a classic Type A personality is an angry, hard-driving, highly stressed executive who berates and bullies his subordinates to squeeze from them one last ounce of work and penny of profit. His rolling anger explodes into a tirade at the least provocation, driving his blood pressure off the scale and sending his blood pulsating into the veins in his head. He is aggressive, hostile and impatient with anything that impedes his progress. However, a Type A personality does not necessarily show all aspects of this description. Some Type As are quite calm, exude charm and display an open, responsive demeanor. Yet they are fiercely competitive, highly achievement-oriented and ever vigilant in the efficient use of their time. Michael Jordan is a Type A personality who displayed on the court a fiercely competitive instinct, a hard-driving nature and an aggressive behavior that bordered on hostility. And yet, in television interviews, he would flash a warm friendly smile, ooze charm and convey an aura of inner tranquility. Wayne Gretzky, also a Type A personality, shows less hostility than Jordan yet he is just as intensely driven, fiercely competitive and achievement-oriented.

In contrast to the image of the Type A person, the Type B person is seen as a phlegmatic, laid-back individual who is happy-go-lucky and content to allow others to lead the charge. Type Bs are slow to anger, sometimes lethargic and generally happy to "go with the flow" rather than make waves. Because such people are not achievement-oriented, they are not represented among the athletic superstars in this book. However, as the "silent majority," the Type Bs are responsible for maintaining the stability of our society by accepting the status quo and abiding by the social norms. Most of the characters depicted in television sitcoms are Type B personalities because viewers relate better to people who are engaged in coping with the daily vicissitudes of life than to people who are struggling to conquer new worlds.

The Pros and Cons of the Type A Personality

Research into heart disease has revealed that Type A males are two to three times more likely to suffer angina or heart attacks than Type B males. Type A behavior at its most negative is like driving a car with one foot on the accelerator and the other foot on the brake. The high psychic energy is driving the body to achieve, while fear-induced negative emotions are dissipating the psychic energy and causing internal conflict. The system eventually consumes itself and burns out.

With such a potentially disastrous downside to the Type A personality, why would anyone want to be anything but a Type B? Because our society values and rewards the Type A personality. We celebrate achievement and honor those who make breakthroughs in science, engineering, sports and business–almost always the product of Type A behaviors. In the warp-speed computer world in which it is said there are only the quick and the dead, there is a high premium on being first with a new idea, first to market and first in sales. Those who live with a perpetual sense of urgency have the competitive edge over those who ruminate over decisions or take a slower, but more secure path.

Studies have found that about 30% of successful entrepreneurs are hypomanic compared with 1% of the general population. Furthermore, most successful entrepreneurs have Type A personalities. Jeff Bezos, founder of Amazon.com, left a million-dollar-a-year job to risk all his time and resources on building a bookstore in cyberspace before the giant competitor Barnes and Noble could react. He hardly slept until he had established his company as the preeminent on-line bookseller in the world. Dana Brown, head of ordering at Amazon.com, often worked through the night. When the orders were finally transmitted at 4:30 in the morning, no one else was there except Jeff. Although Dana herself worked 15 to 18 hours a day, she said, "Jeff was always there. I never saw him go home." Nick Hanauer, a close friend of Jeff in the early years, said (Spector, p. 230):

> *[He is] the most single-mindedly focused person I've ever met–to his detriment; it's all he cares about. He lives, eats, breathes Amazon.com. It occupies virtually his every waking moment. He is maniacally focused. I worry about his health. I worry about what he's going to be like when he's 50.*

Similar testimonials have been made about Martha Stewart, who is reported to sleep only a few hours a night and is famous for multi-tasking in her attempts to juggle her multi-media empire. Donald Trump, Ted Turner, Bill Gates and most other business moguls are strong Type A personalities. It is not surprising that all the athletic superstars profiled in this book are Type A personalities. Without competitive zeal, fiercely aggressive behavior and a strong passion to achieve, such brilliant achievements are highly unlikely or impossible.

Given the research on the link between the Type A personality and heart problems, why is it that few of these great overachievers fall victim to angina or myocardial infarctions? The answer lies in recent research that suggests that only some Type A behaviors are correlated with heart problems. A study reported in the *Journal of the American Medical Association* (October 22/29,

2003) investigated the link between various Type A behaviors and the development of high blood pressure. Collecting information on more than 3000 individuals over 15 years, the researchers concluded that the Type A behaviors associated with high impatience, anger and hostility substantially increased the likelihood of high blood pressure. However, no such causal link could be attributed to the competitive behavior. In essence, the negative forms of Type A behavior (free-floating anger and hostility) seem to be linked to heart problems, while hurry sickness and competitive drive, if accompanied by positive feelings of excitement, are not harmful and may, in fact, be healthful. Dr. Hans Selye, who pioneered the concept of stress as an emotional force on the body, referred to stress that produced positive feelings and the release of endorphins as *eustress*. Dr. Selye suggested that optimum health resulted not from the absence of stress, but from the existence of challenge and excitement that generates eustress. Thus, it seems, if we wish to achieve at a high level, we must focus on our *positive* Type A behaviors, including competitive instinct, goal-orientation and sense of urgency, while eliminating the dissipative behaviors such as undue impatience, anger and frustration. Not only does the minimization of these negative behaviors reduce the likelihood of acquiring stress-related diseases, but it also preserves energy for achieving our goals.

The Origins or Causes of the Type A Personality

Is the Type A personality inherited or acquired? To the extent that libidinal energy is metabolic, it is inherited. However, as we observed in the struggle for dominance feedback loop in the previous chapter, some or most of our competitive instinct may derive from early imprinting experiences. Psychologists believe that Type A personalities equate achievement with self-worth. The relentless struggle to achieve is tied to a subconscious need to feel worthy or to achieve the love of a parent. Mozart was driven to write music at a frenetic pace to please a demanding father. When Ted Turner reached the pinnacle of his stature as a media mogul, he looked skyward and asked his deceased father whether he was at last satisfied by his achievements. Both Wayne Gretzky and Michael Jordan strived hard to perform for fathers who were both supportive and demanding of their best efforts. Both Gretzky and Jordan glanced into the audience for parental approval when they executed spectacular plays, and both felt as though the gallery was empty when their fathers were absent.

If the quest for love or self-worth is at the heart of the Type A personality, it is the irritation in the oyster of life that creates the pearl of achievement. The enslavement of the Type A personality to the quest for achievement yields products of human enterprise that enhance everyone's quality of life. While seeking resolution of their needs, Type A individuals become benefactors of human society. That is, most Type A's confuse self-worth with achievement.

How to Make Your Type A Behaviors Work for You

The Human Struggle for Dominance Feedback Loop, on page 249, showed you how an individual can interpret a setback in two different ways: as a defeat or as a challenge. Those who register a setback as a defeat suffer a loss of competitive zeal, while those who register it as a challenge are energized and display increased competitive zeal. Similarly, some individuals react to a situation as stressful while another may find it exciting. The American Heart Association (at www.americanheart.org) explains:

> *Stress is your body's response to change. It's a very individual thing. A situation that one person finds stressful may not bother someone else. For example, one person may become tense when driving; another person may find driving a source of relaxation and joy. Something that causes fear in some people, such as rock climbing, may be fun for others. There's no way to say that one thing is "bad" or "stressful" because everyone's different.*

Describing ways to cope with stress, the American Heart Association asserts, "Remember that it's not the outside force, but how you react to it inside that's important." This message contains a key idea: a strong achievement-oriented, aggressive and highly competitive approach to reaching your goals does not have to be stressful. The secret is to channel your Type A behaviors into positive experiences. Look upon obstacles as exciting challenges that, when achieved, will give you the competitive edge over others. Instead of reacting with anger when you shank a shot in golf, try to determine how to hit a shank shot. Once you discover how, you will learn how to avoid one in the future. Interpret deadlines as incentives rather than as threats; stimulate your competitive instincts by attempting to complete tasks more quickly and efficiently than you have in the past. When you become proficient at focusing your Type A behaviors, you will find that you are happier, you enjoy the journey to the top and you have much more energy to achieve your goals. In the long run, you will also be much healthier than if you allow stress to become a daily companion.

Try the assessment on the following pages to determine the extent to which you are a Type A personality. If you discover that you have a Type A personality, you have an advantage in achieving at a high level. However, you must learn how to focus your energy and exploit any obsessions you may have. Many Type As are consumed by their restlessness and fail to capitalize on the emotional highs that come from setting goals and striving to achieve them. Pursuing goals is a productive way to invest the energy and emotional fervor that emerges from your Type A personality. However, if this energy is not productively focused, it can turn inward, generating stress and frustration. These negative emotions, if unchecked, can lead to stress-related illness such as coronary disease that results when adrenaline combines with other ingredients to form plaque within the blood vessels. Some extreme Type As develop addictions through substance abuse. Identify which of your Type A behaviors are positive and which are negative. Set goals for yourself and strive to reach these goals. Formulate strategies for avoiding the negative and exploiting the positive Type A behaviors, tapping into whatever activity or enterprise gives you goose bumps. Once you have implemented these strategies, you will find that you are more successful in achieving your goals and will derive more joy in their pursuit.

Following the assessment, I profile an athletic superstar who thrives on what others find extremely stressful–high-speed, high-density traffic on life's superhighway–a tarmac where anarchy reigns, where there are no rules of the road, and where the specter of death is ever-present.

TYPE A/B PERSONALITY SELF-ASSESSMENT–Are You Type A or B?

Choose a number 1–5, with 1 the lowest and 5 the highest, to indicate the degree to which you believe the statement describes you or how you feel. Record for each statement the number you have chosen. The scoring key is on the next page.

There are no "right" or "wrong" answers. In making your selection, be careful to answer the questions as candidly as possible without anticipating how you will be classified. This instrument is designed to give you insights into your personality and personal orientations.

Scale #1

	Seldom			Usually	
1. I'm on time for appointments.	1	2	3	4	5
2. I interrupt or finish other people's sentences.	1	2	3	4	5
3. I tend to do several things at once.	1	2	3	4	5
4. I get impatient if forced to wait in line at a bank or movie.	1	2	3	4	5
5. I feel rushed in my work.	1	2	3	4	5
6. I become angry when stuck in traffic.	1	2	3	4	5
7. Work causes me to skip meals.	1	2	3	4	5
8. I find it difficult to control my temper.	1	2	3	4	5
9. I tend to walk fast, talk fast and eat fast.	1	2	3	4	5
10. When I go to a mall, I get what I want and leave without window shopping.	1	2	3	4	5

Scale #2

	Seldom			Usually	
11. I enjoy job-related activities more than leisure-time activities.	1	2	3	4	5
12. I end each workday thinking I could have achieved more than I did.	1	2	3	4	5
13. My friends call me a workaholic.	1	2	3	4	5
14. I strive hard to complete tasks and feel unresolved until a job is completed.	1	2	3	4	5
15. My most satisfying times are when I'm completing work in my profession or job.	1	2	3	4	5
16. Most of my friends are colleagues from work.	1	2	3	4	5

Scale #2 (cont'd)

		Seldom			Usually	
17.	I'd rather work than take a vacation.	1	2	3	4	5
18.	I work more than 8 hours per day.	1	2	3	4	5
19.	I am told by my friends (or spouse) that they feel they are in competition with my work for my attention.	1	2	3	4	5
20.	I bring work home that I have to complete after dinner or on weekends.	1	2	3	4	5

Scale #3

		Seldom			Usually	
21.	Friends describe me as "hard-driving."	1	2	3	4	5
22.	Recognition and achievement are very important to me and govern my behavior.	1	2	3	4	5
23.	I suffer stress when trying to finish an important project.	1	2	3	4	5
24.	When playing games like cards or chess, the pleasure is in winning more than in the social interaction.	1	2	3	4	5
25.	I'm not happy unless I'm busy.	1	2	3	4	5
26.	I take tea or coffee to drink in the car on my way to work.	1	2	3	4	5
27.	I use my cell phone in public places like golf courses and restaurants.	1	2	3	4	5
28.	I check my telephone and/or email messages more than three times a day.	1	2	3	4	5
29.	I go to work when I have a cold or the flu.	1	2	3	4	5
30.	At the end of the year, I have unused vacation days.	1	2	3	4	5

Instructions	**Scoring Key for All Scales Combined**
A. For each scale total the numbers you chose for the 10 items.	Total your three scores from Scales 1, 2 and 3. Then use the key below to interpret your results.
Scale #1: Over 45 is hyper. Under 20 is patient. **Scale #2:** Over 45 is workaholic. Under 25 indicates balance. **Scale #3:** Over 45 is a driven person. Under 20 is laid back.	**135–150:** Hard-core Type A personality. **120–134:** Strong Type A tendencies. **100–119:** Type A tendencies, somewhat competitive. **80–99:** Bilateral Type A and Type B. **60–79:** Moderate Type B **Below 60:** Content with life in the slow lane.

JEFF GORDON

- Won 35 races by age 6 and 82 races by age 7.

- At age 8, he won 52 races including the National Championship in Denver.

- At age 14, he won his first sprint-car race in Chillicothe, Ohio.

- At age 17, he won the USAC Rookie-of-the-Year Award.

- At age 18, he was the 1990 National Midget Champion.

- At age 20, he won the Grand National Rookie Title in Stock Cars.

- At age 23, he became the youngest to win on the NASCAR circuit.

- In 1998 he had an unprecedented 13 wins (5 consecutive) and 17 top-five finishes.

- In 1999, he established the Jeff Gordon Foundation to help children with cancer.

- Won the prestigious Winston/Nextel Cup in 1995, 1997, 1998 and 2001.

- By 34 years of age had won the Daytona 500 three times–only five others have won three or more times.

Jeff Gordon: A Type A+ Personality

When I hear the words "Gentlemen, start your engines," I hit the start switch. The distributor sends power to the engine, and the rumble of a finely tuned racing engine reverberates through my ears…When forty-three drivers start their engines at the same time, it sounds like thunder. I think it's the sweetest sound in the world.

**Jeff Gordon
born Aug. 4, 1971**

These are the words of NASCAR Wonderboy Jeff Gordon describing his exhilaration as his adrenaline rush heralds the beginning of another death-defying contest among men and machines. During the next three intensely focused hours, his body will flow a river of adrenaline as it experiences all the natural physiological reactions to severe stress. It's a lifetime of high anxiety and survival response, compressed into a single afternoon, as vividly described in Jeff's autobiography (p. 80):

A five-hundred-mile race is exhausting. Think of the last time you got in a tight situation on the interstate. You probably sat a little straighter in the seat, tightened your grip on the wheel, and put all your senses on high alert. When you got out of the situation, which probably happened in a minute or less, you realized how tense you had gotten. Now, imagine sustaining that level of intensity for five hundred miles at speeds exceeding 190 miles per hour. That's what we go through every week. It is grueling.

People like Jeff Gordon live life on the edge. They thrive on the adrenaline rush that flows from challenge and risk, especially when the stakes are high. Only a Type A+ personality would describe such an experience as both "sweet" and "grueling." Years later his mother said, "He was hyperactive and couldn't sit still, not even to watch television. He just wanted to do!"

NASCAR is a Type A sport run in a Type A environment by Type A drivers. In fact, racing glorifies all the components of the Type A personality. It demands hurry sickness, it rewards aggressive competitiveness, and it is literally hard driving. Those not so inclined had better find a different venue to display their talents. If speed isn't in their blood, then racing isn't their calling.

Stock cars come equipped with 750-horsepower engines that catapult a metal missile through and around the opposition. These cars travel at 220 miles per hour on straightaways and average 190 mph in a typical race. Hitting a wall or another car at such a speed can be deadly. In fact, Dale Earnhardt, the Intimidator and one of the giants of NASCAR, was killed in February 2001 in the Daytona 500 race. The crash stunned millions of fans and sent a shock wave through competitive car racing.

With the front tires rotating at 43 revolutions per second, the average race car moves the length of a football field in one second. It accelerates from 0 to 100 miles per hour in less than three seconds. Such power demands a driver who thrives on danger and speed. Jeff Gordon found early in life that he was stimulated, rather than intimidated, by both.

JEFF GORDON'S TREK TO THE TOP

Early Imprints

Jeff Gordon was born on August 4, 1971 in Vallejo, California. When barely a year old, he and his older sister Kim, accompanied their mother Carol (who was single at the time) on a date with John Bickford. A racing enthusiast who had met Carol at the auto parts firm where she worked, John had invited her to a car race at Vallejo Speedway. Their courtship led to marriage when Jeff was four and John Bickford became Jeff's father and mentor. When John purchased a BMX racing bike for Jeff's fourth birthday, the child took to it like a fish to water. Within a year, Jeff was racing against older boys with a competitive zeal that would soon become a raging, all-consuming passion.

When Jeff's mother expressed fears that racing a two-wheel bicycle was too dangerous for a five-year-old, John bought him a quarter-midget race car. Apparently, John had convinced Carol that the gas-propelled race car was safer because it had four wheels rather than two and a roll cage around the driver who was protected by a helmet. At the age of five, before he had learned to read or write, Jeff was racing competitively and winning quarter-midget events throughout California.

In the months and years that followed, Carol and John Bickford sacrificed their time and resources to indulge Jeff's passion for racing. To help him acquire the reflexes needed for the competitions ahead, Carol raced against him when he was five, cutting him off and forcing him to react instantaneously. As Jeff later commented in his autobiography (pp. 24–25):

Looking back on those days, it's hard to fathom the commitment my mom and dad made when I was five, six, seven, and eight years old. We traveled and raced every single weekend for more than two straight years. Every spare penny was poured into parts for the car, entry fees to races, travel, lodging, meals, gasoline, whatever we needed for me to race.

By the time Jeff Gordon was six he had won 35 races. By age seven he had won 82. This wunderkind set speed records on five different tracks. At age eight he won 52 events including the Grand National Championship at Denver. By the time he was nine he was beating college students and at ten he won a second national title. By eleven he had won the quarter-midget Nationals and by twelve, he had won over 200 races. It was clear that this boy among men had a high-speed dream of silver trophies that he would chase for the rest of his life. In his autobiography, he wrote (p. 37), "Winning is what has always driven me. If I never won, I would give up racing and move on to something else where I could be competitive."

From Quarter Midgets to Speedway Karts to Sprint Cars

By age twelve, Jeff had won all the awards available in quarter-midget racing. It was time for a greater challenge. John moved him into speedway karts, which are faster and require more driving skill. Jeff continued to win kart races, but his increasing success brought a diminished challenge. As he moved into adolescence, his boredom with racing increased and he began to hang out with friends who were destined for trouble. Sensing that their son was headed down the wrong road, John and Carol realized that he needed to channel his interests in a more productive direction.

It was at this watershed moment in his life that Jeff read an article in a racing magazine about Sport Allen, a thirteen-year-old who was racing sprint cars. Jeff told his parents that the prospect of racing these open-wheel powerhouses excited him. Ever committed to accommodating their son's dreams, John took Jeff to Jamestown, Indiana, one of the centers of open-wheel racing, where they met with Lee Osborne, a builder of sprint cars. At that time, sprint car motors had 700 horsepower and cost about $40,000–well beyond John Bickford's budget. However, since John owned an auto parts shop, he offered Osborne free auto parts in exchange for building a special sprint car chassis so that Jeff could reach the pedals and see over the hood. By selling his boat, John raised the money to buy a used motor. Personal sacrifice and ingenuity enabled John to provide Jeff with a custom-made racing sprint car. Overnight, the thirteen-year-old had graduated from a quarter-midget race car with a 2.85-horsepower engine, to a go-kart with a 10-horsepower engine and finally to a sprint car with a 700-horsepower engine that could accelerate from a standing start to 60 miles per hour in less than three seconds.

Jeff had his racing sprint car, but there was a major problem. Racing full-size cars in California required a driving license, thereby excluding anyone under the age of sixteen from participating in formal racing competition. To prepare Jeff for the next level in racing, John took him out of school in California, where he was in the eighth grade. They drove 2500 miles east to Jacksonville, Florida, where All-Star sprint car races had no minimum age requirements. As Jeff later explained to the press (Brinster, p. 19), "Nobody was fool enough to drive that young, so they didn't think they needed an age rule." Registering Jeff for the Speedweeks competitions in February 1985 presented yet another challenge. The organizers of the races were at first dumfounded and then outraged at the prospect that a father would enter his thirteen-year-old son in such a dangerous sport against seasoned professionals. Some onlookers suggested that John was guilty of child abuse. Ignoring their comments, John once again used his persuasive talents. By signing a waiver, releasing the organizers of all legal liability, he was permitted to enter Jeff into the competition.

Jeff had very little experience driving his new sprint car, let alone racing it. He explained the trauma of his first experience in his autobiography (p. 33):

> When the lights went green, I felt like I was trapped in a Star Wars video game. Guys were flying by me faster than anything I'd ever seen. My whole body shook as those cars sped by me. It scared me to death; this wasn't go-karts anymore.

Jeff was on the track with men twice his age. The men looked at this baby-faced boy in amazement, thinking "this kid is crazy; he'll be seriously injured or killed." However, within three nights of racing, Jeff was becoming comfortable in his new sprint car and beginning to focus on winning. By the end of the week, he had won $300 and, more importantly, came to the attention of ESPN who featured him on their *Speedweeks* program. Racing against more experienced men developed in Jeff a steely internal strength that would enable him to respond fearlessly to the life-threatening situations that he would confront in the years ahead. It was now clear that car racing would be Jeff's life-long passion.

Open-Wheel Racing

Later that year, continuing in their total support of Jeff's career, the family pulled up stakes in California and moved to a town near Indianapolis where open-wheel racing is the state sport. Leaving their family auto parts manufacturing business in California was a financial hardship for John and Carol. Years later, in an interview with *Newsweek*, John recalled, "We slept in pick-up trucks and made our own parts. That's why I think Jeff is misunderstood by people who think he was born to rich parents and had a silver spoon in his mouth."

Once in Indiana, Jeff perfected his skills in open-wheel racing by driving sprint cars and midgets–the latter being open-wheel 600-horsepower race cars usually run on dirt tracks. He raced every weekend and won his first open-wheel championship at age 14 in Chillicothe, Ohio. While attending Tri-West High School, Jeff joined the cross-country track team to get in shape for racing. (Few realize that race car drivers are among the fittest athletes of any sport.) His good looks and agreeable personality (that won him "prom king" honors in his senior year) offered future promise of huge commercial endorsements if he ever reached the top of the car-racing world. Though still a long way from the top, by the time Jeff graduated in 1989, he had won over 100 open-wheel races. Then in 1990, at age 19, he became the youngest winner of the USAC Midget Championship.

NASCAR Busch Grand National Competition

Having won the USAC Midget Championship, Jeff reacted in typical Type-A fashion by searching for another challenge in car racing. The two possibilities he considered were Formula One Racing and NASCAR. The former, being international, would require racing throughout the world, especially in Europe. Preferring to stay in America, Jeff opted for NASCAR.

The sport of NASCAR was born on the back roads of tobacco country a century ago as moonshiners frequently tried to outrun the tax men to avoid paying tax on their illegal corn liquor. The winner earned bragging rights in the bar. This epic struggle between the so-called revenuers and the speed merchants was played out in the 1990 movie *Days of Thunder* starring Tom Cruise. Several scenes depict daredevil driving on dirt roads as supercharged stock cars outrun and outwit the local authorities.

The genesis of today's National Association of Stock Car Auto Racing (NASCAR) occurred during the Great Depression when Bill France Sr. headed to Florida to find work. While en route to Miami, he came across Daytona–at that time a small beach town. Each year during a period called Speedweek, speed enthusiasts from all over the world would congregate to challenge land speed records along Daytona's 20-mile stretch of beach. One of the minor attractions was a stock car race, also held on the beach. When the land speed trials moved from Daytona to Utah's Bonneville Salt Flats in 1936, Bill France Sr. sponsored the stock car race in Daytona, charging 50 cents admission and awarding a bottle of rum to each lap leader, a case of oil for the pole winner (fastest time in the qualifying round), and a box of cigars for drivers who showed up sober.

The annual race, held on July 4, was an outstanding success and the Daytona stock car races drew increasingly large crowds. In 1948, Bill France Sr. founded the National Association for Stock Car Auto Racing. Races were held throughout the south on rented dirt tracks. The first sanctioned race was run at Darlington, South Carolina, in 1950 before 25,000 fans. In 1958, Bill built the Daytona International Speedway where he held the first Daytona 500 the following year. The Daytona 500 was an immediate success, attracting 42,000 fans in its first year and 72,000 fans in 1960. It eventually became the Wimbledon of NASCAR racing.

When Winston, the cigarette company, took over sponsorship, NASCAR grew until it was among the top three most popular sports in America. Five million screaming fans show up at tracks each year urging drivers for more and more speed. Disaster lurks around every turn as cars traveling at 220 miles per hour cover distances in reaction times that exceed the driver's range of vision. By the time a driver sees a foreign object on the track or a collision ahead, it is too late to avoid it.

In exchange for being featured as a student in an ESPN clip, Jeff jumped at the offer of free tuition at the famous Buck Baker driving school (for stock cars) in North Carolina. The stock cars were more than twice the weight of the open-wheel vehicles, and the high-banked tracks enabled them to negotiate high-speed turns more smoothly than their open-wheel counterparts. Overwrought with excitement and exhilaration after his first day in Baker's driving school, he paced back and forth, waving his arms and exclaiming to his mother (p. 43), "Mom, I've found it. This is it. This is what I want to do the rest of my life." On his final day at the driving school, Jeff persuaded his mother to accompany him in a test ride of his first full-size race car. As the seatbelt snapped shut and the thundering engine revved up, Carol's initial reluctance was transformed into fear. Then as the car accelerated to 150 miles per hour, her fear approached panic and she screamed, "Oh, God, Jeff, slow down!" However, slow was not a gear in Jeff's emotional transmission. He had been molded for life in the fast lane, where you run at top speed until you see a checkered flag. Both Jeff and his family were in for the ride of their lives and would see many checkered flags in the decades ahead.

Though Jeff was a quick study, his venture into NASCAR racing required considerable adjustment and familiarization. The wheelbases, balance and aerodynamics of Busch Grand National race cars (a type of NASCAR) are significantly different from open-wheel cars and require different handling skills. While the lighter open-wheel car offers a chance of recovery from fishtailing on a high-speed turn, the greater momentum of the Busch car makes recovery unlikely. Furthermore open-wheel cars have no fenders, so drivers avoid contact between vehicles. However, rubbing fenders to jockey for position is considered fair game in NASCAR racing. In 1990, Jeff entered three NASCAR events, but he did not drive well enough to qualify in any of them. It was a period of learning and transition.

In 1991, Jeff Gordon hit the big time, landing a contract to drive the Carolina Ford Dealers' car in the 1991 Busch Grand National series. Though he didn't win a race that year, he was in the top five finishes on five occasions and won the Busch Grand National Rookie of the Year award at the age of 20. The following year, Jeff recruited Ray Evernham as his crew chief. Playing a vital role in communicating with the driver during a race, the crew chief alerts him to cars approaching from the rear, solicits information about how the car is handling, and suggests when to make pit stops and change or inflate tires. He also leads the entire maintenance crew, inspiring them to minimize the time spent in pit stops during races and repairing and fine-tuning the car between races. The choice of Evernham for this role would prove to be crucial in the development of Jeff Gordon's NASCAR driving skills.

Working with Ray Evernham and driving a car sponsored by the Baby Ruth candy bar company in 1992, Jeff set a NASCAR record by winning eleven pole positions (registering the fastest time in the qualifying rounds of eleven different races). However, his most important triumph was his first NASCAR win–a first place finish in the Atlanta 300. In a stroke of good fortune, Rick Hendrick, a preeminent car owner on the (NASCAR) Winston Cup circuit, saw Jeff Gordon's remarkable win that afternoon. Reflecting on his impressions, he said (p. 59):

> *I turned around and saw this car coming around turn four. I saw the haze coming off the tires that happens when a car's loose [fishtailing]...Atlanta is a fast track, so I assumed he was going to get out of the throttle [take his foot off the gas]. The car wiggled a bit, but he kept pressing it through the turn. I turned to my friends and said, "Let's watch this guy a minute. He's about to bust his butt." But he never did. We watched him run another ten laps and he did the same thing every time. I asked one of my guys, "Who is that?" And he said, "That's Jeff Gordon."*

The NASCAR Winston (Nextel) Cup Competition

That fateful event would begin Jeff Gordon's move up to the highest level in NASCAR–the Winston Cup circuit. Hendrick hired Jeff as his race car driver, providing him with the best engineers, a top crew and generous financial support. Jeff later commented (p. 65):

> *I realized that if I was going to win a lot of championships, I had to align myself with the best. Rick was that guy. He loved winning as much as I did, and I loved it more than food and water.*

Jeff raced the 1993 season in the Winston Cup circuit under contract with Hendrick Motorsports. His Dupont 24 Chevy Lumina was a dramatically conspicuous, multi-colored machine that led to Jeff's moniker, "Rainbow Warrior." It was clear that this would be a spectacular season for the rainbow warrior when he won the Gatorade 125–the first race of the season–and qualified for the Daytona 500. (At this race, he also met Brooke Sealy, the Miss Winston beauty queen who presented the checks and trophies and whom he would marry the following year.) He then got the attention of the racing world by placing fifth in the Daytona 500. In his first season on the Winston Cup circuit, Jeff finished fourteenth in points and won the Maxx Race Cards Rookie of the Year award.

The promise that Jeff Gordon showed in his rookie year was surpassed in the years that followed. At the beginning of the 1994 season, crew chief Ray

Evernham continued to inspire the crew with slogans that he posted on the walls. One of the posters displayed (Gordon, p. 85):

From Nobody to Upstart
From Upstart to Contender
From Contender to Winner
From Winner to Champion
From Champion to Dynasty

He checked off the first two categories in the list, indicating that the team had reached the contender level and that this would be the season for their first win. Ray's prediction materialized in Charlotte, North Carolina, when Jeff was welcomed by the checkered flag at the end of NASCAR's longest race, the Coca Cola 600. Millions of viewers saw Jeff weeping as he entered the winner's circle and announced, "This is the happiest day of my life. This is a memory and a feeling I'll never forget." Then in August, Jeff had his second NASCAR victory, winning the inaugural Brickyard 400 at Indianapolis.

With a miscue in the pit during the Daytona 500, resulting in a damaged car and a disappointing finish, the 1995 season was off to a bad start for the Jeff Gordon team. However, a string of wins began a week later with a victory in the Goodwrench 500, followed by a victory in the Purolator 500. Jeff continued building momentum as the year unfolded and entered a neck-and-neck race with Dale Earnhardt for the Winston Cup. This trophy is the holy grail of the NASCAR circuit, awarded to the driver who accumulates the most points throughout the racing season, based on finishing positions and laps in the lead. As the season progressed, a rivalry emerged between Earnhardt, seven-time winner of the Winston Cup, and Gordon, the pretender to the throne. Earnhardt had been nicknamed "the Intimidator" on account of his threatening presence on the track, his rough-hewn demeanor and the sinister-looking black car that enhanced his bad-boy image. Earnhardt nicknamed Jeff "Wonderboy" because of Jeff's young, clean-cut image. Jeff was the youthful challenger to some and a mere upstart to others, particularly to the Earnhardt fans. Though fans may have thought them adversaries, each respected the talents of the other. When Jeff first appeared on the NASCAR circuit as a fresh but confident driver, Dale Earnhardt took notice and told the media (Zeller, p. 35):

He has that competitive nature. You can see it in everything he does. I don't care whether it's racing or computer games, he's competitive, and that's why he's a winner. He goes that extra mile.

Just as Arnie's Army three decades before had resented Jack Nicklaus in his challenge for the alpha male status in golf, so also the followers of Dale Earnhardt resented the challenge of 23-year-old Jeff Gordon for the top spot in NASCAR. This resentment even took the form of posters displaying epithets like "Gordon Sucks" and "Anyone but Gordon," and loud boos following Jeff's loud-speaker introductions at the race tracks. Ray Evernham later offered insight into why Jeff was booed (Stewart, p. 37), "He's good looking, a gazillionaire, has his own jet, a beautiful wife and has won more races than anybody. If I weren't his best buddy, I'd be booing him too."

The Earnhardt vs. Gordon rivalry heightened the drama of NASCAR as if it had been scripted in Hollywood. The competition for the Winston Cup was fierce–Gordon needed his first win to move him from contender to champion and Earnhardt needed his eighth Winston Cup to move him ahead of Richard Petty, co-holder of the record for the most Winston Cups at seven. When the 1995 season ended, youth had been served. Jeff Gordon edged out Dale Earnhardt by 34 points in one of the closest races in Winston Cup history. At the age of 24, Jeff had reached the pinnacle of NASCAR driving. He could now check off the category, "From Winner to Champion." Only one more unchecked category remained on the poster.

From Champion to Dynasty

After his first Winston Cup, Jeff Gordon became a national celebrity and a valuable commodity for commercial endorsements. He appeared on *The Late Show with David Letterman* and on *Good Morning America*. As he became a household name, he was deluged with offers to endorse products. With this universal recognition came the downside of fame–constant harassment by fans for autographs, photos and various requests. Recognizing that the fans are the source of revenue, Jeff was able to handle his newfound celebrity with affable compliance. He also hired a business man to handle Jeff Gordon Inc. and that avalanche of requests.

Gordon's new status as an icon of NASCAR didn't interfere with his racing, however. In fact, in the years that followed his first Winston Cup he continued to accumulate awards, win races and establish new records. In 1996, Jeff won a phenomenal ten races, but some poor finishes related to mechanical failings caused him to miss winning his second Winston Cup by 37 points. However, in the next season (1997), he hit the top with a bang heard throughout the racing world. Wonderboy won 10 races on 10 different types of tracks. He won on a 2.5-mile speedway, a two-mile speedway, a 1.5-mile speedway, a one-mile speedway, a one-mile banked speedway and the "lady in black" track at Darlington. He also won the prestigious Daytona 500 on February 16, 1997, making him at 25 the youngest winner in the history of that event. He capped it all off with his second Winston Cup.

By 1998, Jeff Gordon was everywhere in the media. Pepsi featured him in their Super Bowl commercial and another guest appearance on *The Late Show with David Letterman* kept him in the public eye. On the track, Jeff had a breakout year, winning 13 races including five consecutive wins. He finished with 26 top-five finishes, earning him his third Winston Cup in four years. Dale Jarrett, whom Jeff had edged out by 14 points for the Cup, gave Wonderboy the ultimate tribute when he told the press, "It should be illegal to be that young, that good looking and that talented." In the 1998 season, Jeff won over $9 million. By age 30, he was number two in all-time money winnings and was second only to Richard Petty for the most career stock car wins. Jeff admitted to *Sports Illustrated*, "My life has been a blur ever since I can remember."

The ultimate showdown between Dale Earnhardt and Jeff Gordon came in 1999. The Intimidator, who had won his first Daytona 500 in 1998, and Wonderboy, who had won his first the year before, were matched in the 1999 Daytona 500. Jeff's fastest time in the qualifiers had won him the pole position in NASCAR's most prestigious race and he was ready for the challenge of his life. However, the NASCAR officials imposed a 15-second penalty on him for having too many crew in the pit. This penalty put Jeff at the tail end during the first lap and it appeared that he was beaten before he began. However, he dropped in behind some of the cars ahead and gained speed by riding in their slipstream–a technique known as "drafting." With only 11 laps to go, Jeff had managed to work himself into fourth place. Waiting patiently for his opportunity, Jeff noticed that there was just enough space to squeeze between the inside border of the track and the car ahead. He throttled the car on the curve, sliding slightly below the car ahead and missing it by a couple of inches. He was now on the inside lane, driving beside two other cars.

A quick glance in his rear-view mirror presented the specter of a black car rocketing forward like Darth Vader in a Star Wars attack. Dale Earnhardt was tailgating so closely that Jeff couldn't see the Goodwrench logo on the hood of Dale's car in his mirror. Wonderboy knew it was now or never. As they approached a turn, a space opened that was barely the width of a car. Jeff surged ahead, threatening to scrape the paint off both sides of his car as he shoehorned himself between the other two race cars at a speed that brought the crowd to its feet. But Earnhardt followed in his slipstream and stayed on his tail.

Jeff gained on the straightaway but Dale closed in on the turns and the two cars rubbed against each other as they jockeyed for the lead. But Jeff succeeded in blocking Dale Earnhardt from gaining the lead through the final turn. When he reached the finish line with Dale in hot pursuit, Jeff realized he had won the battle of the titans in a final showdown, and with it his second Daytona 500 victory in three years! In those moments of elation, Jeff couldn't have imagined that two years later, his competitor, colleague and friend, Dale Earnhardt, would die in a brutal crash while striving for his second win in the Daytona 500.

The first year of the new millennium was a rebuilding year for Jeff Gordon and his team. Ray Evernham and some of the crew left and Jeff brought in Robbie Loomis as the new crew chief. Together they recruited and trained a new crew, but it was clear that it would take some time to develop the team into a smooth functioning unit. Consequently, Jeff finished the 2000 season with only three wins and 11 top-five finishes. However, in the 2001 season, the members of the team began to mesh and Jeff improved his performance to six wins and 18 top-five finishes. This was enough to earn Jeff his fourth Winston Cup at the tender age of 30.

So often when our professional lives are at the zenith, our personal lives enter a period of great challenge. And so it was with Jeff Gordon. In March 2002, Brooke Gordon filed for divorce. From the first signs of trouble in paradise, the media swooped in, reporting every detail, both real and fictional, and playing on the high drama of American royalty in conflict. The $15-million settlement with Brooke included a palatial mansion in Palm Beach, Florida. She and Jeff had accumulated a fleet of high-speed boats, 17 fast sports cars, various motor homes, and mansions in North Carolina and on the West Coast. In an interview with Regis Philbin, Jeff admitted that the divorce had significantly affected his performance in 2002, with three wins and 13 top-five finishes. Jeff performed little better in the 2003 season, with three wins and 15 top-five finishes. He finished fourth in the running for the Winston Cup. (On June 19, 2003, NASCAR announced the signing of a 10-year contract with Nextel, replacing Winston as the sponsors of its top series of racing competitions. Beginning with the 2004 season, the former NASCAR Winston Cup Series was renamed the NASCAR Nextel Cup Series.)

In the 2004 season, it was clear that Jeff had put his personal problems behind him as he regained the intense focus that was his hallmark. Though he did not win his fifth Winston/Nextel Cup, he was in contention for the trophy down to the bitter end and finished the season with five wins, 16 top-five finishes and winnings of over $8 million. Before the dust had settled on that season, Jeff catapulted out of the starting gate with a dramatic win in the 2005 Daytona 500 on February 20. It was his third win in that prestigious race, placing him in the elite group of five who have won that event three times or more. It also signaled the end of what some had been calling a slump. Although this victory brought him $1.4 million in winnings, he commented in an interview with the Associated Press:

You know, I learned quite a while ago that it's not racing that I love, it's winning…I would say that we enjoy the victories that we have these days more than ever, partly because we recognize just how special they are and how hard it is to win in Nextel Cup.

At the time of writing, Jeff is only 34 years old. With four Winston/Nextel Cups under his belt, Jeff is preparing to check off the final category on Ray's list as he and his team move from champion to dynasty. He is already the highest money winner in the history of his sport.

Legacy

NASCAR drivers epitomize the Type A personality. Rushing through life, as though transporting illegal whiskey with the revenuers in hot pursuit, they are perpetually impatient to progress from one thrill to the next. Preoccupied with speed, they think fast, walk fast, talk fast, eat fast and drive fast. This prevailing sense of urgency pervades all aspects of NASCAR. Even the time allotted to pit stops has decreased exponentially over the years. In 1950 a pit stop took four minutes. By 1990 it had dropped to 35 seconds and by 2000 to under 20 seconds. Now if the crew doesn't get the car out in less than 14 seconds, they are putting their driver at a serious disadvantage.

Even amongst a field of Type A personalities, Jeff is perceived as more extreme in his competitive instinct and his aggression. In an interview following the 1999 Daytona 500 showdown between Gordon and Earnhardt, driver Rusty Wallace, who tried unsuccessfully to block Gordon's move into the lead, said that Gordon's death-defying slide between the two cars was unnecessarily aggressive. To this Gordon responded, "I was aggressive, but those are the moves you have to make to win in that situation."

Though Jeff Gordon exuded fierce competitiveness, impatience, aggressiveness and an obsession for winning and achievement–the classic Type A behaviors–he seldom showed anger or hostility. Instead, he focused his Type A tendencies toward motivating his performance and achieving his goals. To date, they have earned him the status of an icon in NASCAR, along with fabulous wealth and the ultimate prize, self-actualization. After winning the Daytona 500 in 2005, Jeff Gordon hosted a party on board his 106-foot yacht, the *24 Karat*. He later told reporters:

Walking onto that boat was similar to being in Victory Lane. I was screaming, yelling, high-fiving and enjoying the moment as much as I could...[After this party] I want to focus on wins...and do what we can to win the championship.

Through his commercial endorsements, Jeff has given NASCAR a public face. His pleasant, self-effacing and charming persona endears him to television audiences, contributing to the burgeoning popularity of this relatively new sport. As he observed in his autobiography (p. xiii), "In recent years NASCAR has become more popular than Major League Baseball, PGA Tour golf, ATP tennis and the NBA." But Jeff's contributions are not limited to sports. In 1999, he established the Jeff Gordon Foundation, an organization dedicated to helping children suffering from cancer. Among the charities it supports are the Leukemia and Lymphoma Society, the Make-A-Wish Foundation, the Hendrick Bone Marrow Foundation and the Riley Hospital for Children in Indianapolis. As one of NASCAR's most generous contributors to charities, Jeff Gordon has served as a role model to other athletes in sharing the fruits of his lucrative career with others who are less fortunate. Looking back on his hectic life on the tarmac to date, Jeff said (p. 218):

One thing I'd learned from my past struggles was that you never know when your next win is going to come, so you need to appreciate the moment. I'd also been reminded that we aren't promised tomorrow. You need to live every moment of life to its fullest.

Jeff Gordon is living proof that a Type A Personality, if properly focused, can bring all the rewards of a full life, even if you have to re-upholster your furniture twice as often as everyone else.

Chapter 12

PRINCIPLE #12: SEE AN OBSTACLE AS AN OPPORTUNITY

Make an obstacle an opportunity, make a negative a positive.
                    –Linda Armstrong (Lance's mother)

In 1913, Henry Ford's Model T was widely acclaimed as the "people's car." However, it sold for $500, and the typical factory worker, earning $2.34 per day, could not afford to buy one. Furthermore, Ford had just introduced the revolutionary moving assembly line. His employees, disgruntled over the hectic pace of the new mass production process, were leaving Ford faster than he could replace them. Raising his workers' wages would require a further price hike to remain profitable, but a rise in the price of the Model T would make it even less affordable, causing sales to decline. Henry was caught between a vanishing workforce and a gaggle of angry stockholders who opposed increasing wages.

An inspiration from Emerson's *Self Reliance* moved Henry to pursue an impossible dream–to build a car for the masses, a car that even his production workers could afford, and simultaneously increase their wages. Quoted in the *Detroit Journal*, he promised, "We will produce ten thousand cars a month at $400 apiece." Few believed him, but they listened. Then, Ford turned his promise into a reality.

Within a year of his inspiration, Ford more than doubled his workers' wages to $5 per day, reduced the workday from nine hours to eight, and dropped the price of his Model T from $400 to $340. This led to one of the most fascinating stories in the annals of economic history. Ford's competitors did not understand how a reasonable man could drop the price of a car below cost when the factory was already at full production. The stockholders, fearing that such drastic measures would drive their company into bankruptcy, launched lawsuits. They claimed that Henry had gone mad; no longer competent to run the company he founded. However, with the increased wages, men lined up to work at Ford. By reducing the length of the workday, Henry could run two shifts. Reducing it further meant three shifts. The newly implemented rotating shifts enabled Henry to fully utilize his plant 24 hours a day, lowering his unit production costs. As production costs fell, Ford could reduce the price of his Model T. In fact, between 1908 and 1916 Henry dropped his prices by 58 percent, causing sales and profits to rise exponentially. Henry Ford had discovered a model for production (shown in the flow chart) that is now embedded in a sub-discipline of economics called *price-elasticity theory*. Within a short time, Ford was building half the automobiles in the world. What had appeared to be an insurmountable obstacle turned out to be an opportunity to revolutionize the workweek and increase wages substantially, thereby creating a middle class in America. What could have broken him made him a tycoon!

Ford's Industrial Model for Production

Henry Ford's triumph in snatching victory from the jaws of defeat is only one of numerous stories of business triumphs resurrected by captains of industry from what appeared to be hopeless messes. Where most people see problems and insurmountable obstacles, the winners in business, sports and life see opportunities. The Mandarin word for "problem" is the same as the word for "opportunity," indicating that the Chinese have recognized for millennia that obstacle and opportunity are two sides of the same coin. Without problems, there are few opportunities.

Breakdown is the Stimulus for Breakthrough

In his study of creativity in the arts, Richard Tansey, former professor at UC San José, theorized that abstraction begins when our progress is blocked. That is, the creative process begins when we confront an obstacle that forces us to move into an abstract or problem-solving mode. Thomas Kuhn, in his seminal work *The Structure of Scientific Revolutions*, described a similar pattern in the creation of new paradigms in the sciences. Scientific theories are continuously modified and revised until an observation that contradicts the theory causes the entire structure to collapse. This collapse becomes the stimulus for an entirely new formulation of the theory that encompasses both the old and the new observations. In short, most (if not all) of civilization's greatest innovations and discoveries have been stimulated by obstacles or problems. When problems arise, opportunities abound.

In 1977, Ilya Prigogine won the Nobel Prize in Chemistry for his work in dissipative structures. His investigation of the Second Law of Thermodynamics led him to assert, "It is out of chaos, turmoil and disorder that higher levels of order and wisdom emerge." Explaining why the emotional system, like a fractured bone, is stronger after healing than it was before a breakdown, he said, "Psychological suffering, anxiety and collapse lead to new emotional, intellectual and spiritual strengths...Many systems of breakdown are actually harbingers of breakthrough."

Obstacles Provide the Opportunity for a Competitive Edge

Those who are highly competitive in business or sports realize that the obstacles they face are the same ones that confront their competitors. Surmounting these obstacles gives them a competitive advantage over an adversary who is defeated by them. While the faint of heart see obstacles as reasons not to compete, the fierce competitor sees these same obstacles as allies. Why is it that the greatest golfers want to play tournaments on highly challenging courses? Quite simply, their competitive advantage comes from their superior ability in dealing with the toughest challenges, such as narrow fairways, cavernous sand traps and undulating greens. It is the obstacles in any competition that separate the "sheep" from the "goats," enabling the superiors to distinguish themselves. When the course is too easy, the leader board is crowded with golfers tied for the top spot, but when the course is tough, the field is spread more widely, with the preeminent golfers at or near the top. For the same reason, most companies survive and flourish in a thriving economy, but a recession annihilates weak companies, leaving the strong to survive and thrive. Michael Dell proved this in the world of personal computers. To surpass IBM, he customized his product and sold it directly, reducing the cost and increasing its features. The rest is history.

Our Ability to Win Comes from the Habit of Overcoming Obstacles

Reflect for a moment on the athletic superstars profiled in the previous chapters of this book. Each one was confronted with significant obstacles, especially in their early years, that they had to overcome to survive. Jim Thorpe, a member of the Sac and Fox Indian tribe, overcame abuse and prejudice in the "white man's" schools to become Olympic champion and "the greatest athlete in the world." Babe Ruth grew up in an orphanage. Babe Zaharias came from poor east-Texas beginnings and struggled first against gender discrimination and then later against social class discrimination by the country club set. Wilma Rudolph had to endure racial and gender prejudice as she persevered through a physical disability to become the fastest woman in the world. Muhammad Ali also had to struggle against racism, while Martina Navratilova and Greg Louganis fought discrimination against homosexuality. Wayne Gretzky and Jeff Gordon had to compete against much older people and contend with the petty jealousies aroused by their stellar achievements. Yet all of these pre-eminent athletes rose to the top of the world of sports–not in spite of these obstacles, but because of them. Overcoming these obstacles made them strong. Persevering and prevailing against adversity is what forged in them the resolve to go on, even as the pain became unbearable and abandoning the struggle became ever more appealing.

Bodybuilding provides a dramatic example of a sport in which the ability to push through the pain is paramount. In fact, the slogan "no pain, no gain" emerged out of the sweaty grunt-and-grind gyms of the bodybuilding world. Pain is the obstacle bodybuilders push against to build and sculpt their muscles. As the muscles perform successive repetitions of an exercise, the pain builds to an unbearable intensity that has the bodybuilder begging for release. Agonizing routines lasting four or five hours a day, six days per week, involve blitzing and blasting muscles to the point of total fatigue. Only by exhausting the muscle in this way, causing micro damage to its fibers in a process known as *fiber hypertrophy*, can the bodybuilder make it grow larger and stronger. Arnold Schwarzenegger, Governor of California and seven-time winner of Mr. Olympiad (the highest honor in that sport), reported in his *New Encyclopedia of Modern Bodybuilding* (p. xxi), "What made me stand out from my peers…was a deep, deep desire to build muscle and the intense commitment to let nothing stop me."

Health Clubs and Weight-Loss Clinics Live by Statistics

The economic survival of health clubs and weight-loss clinics is based on the fact that only a small percentage of our population is able to suffer through the obstacles to reach their goals. Burning with the fire of good intentions and excited by the prospects of a new body image, the new member signs on for a year or more, paying an up-front retainer. However, as the exigencies of life intrude on available time, and the benefits of the workouts (and/or diet) seem to be slower than anticipated, the resolve begins to weaken and the dream begins to fade. The new member misses one workout and then another. As one disenchanted member leaves the gym for the last time, another excited neophyte enters the gym, eager to sign up and shell out. Only the small fraction of the population who anticipate and value the pain as an important and inevitable means to achieving their goals are able to endure the short-term misery in exchange for long-term gains.

The Greatest Obstacle to Success

The most formidable obstacle in any quest is the demand for energy and time that stands between the competitor and the prize. Those wishing to reach the top of any human endeavor must resolve to make that enterprise the center of their lives. Those unwilling to make that sacrifice will lose out to the others. The idea that talent can substitute for effort is a myth. The allegory of the *Hare and the Tortoise* has played out over and over again in the annals of sports, business and life, and continues to reassert its truth to all who care to observe. Schwarzenegger, who also had a successful career in acting, asserted (p. xxii), "I know I can succeed in anything I choose, and I know this because I understand what it takes to sacrifice, struggle, persist, and eventually overcome an obstacle." He went on to say (p. 242), "When the going gets tough, it is always the mind that fails first, not the body." In this observation, Arnold has captured what separates the pre-eminent from the also-rans: the ability to persevere and retain an unrelenting commitment to your goals when pain, tedium or other obstacles threaten to defeat you. Viewed from a competitive perspective, these obstacles are your allies. If you wish to gain the competitive edge, you must embrace them as opportunities.

The Mind, Not the Body, Is the Dominant Factor in Achieving Success

The ability to see obstacles as opportunities is probably the most important prerequisite to achieving success. Only by anticipating the obstacles and embracing them as allies can we push through the barriers and distinguish ourselves. In this chapter, I have chosen to profile Lance Armstrong, seven-time winner of the Tour de France cycling competition, as the athlete who most dramatically models my Principle #12: *See an obstacle as an opportunity*. Armstrong embraced the agony of the grueling three-week ordeal around the perimeter and through the mountains of France as a chance to out-suffer the competition and win the ultimate conquest in cycling. In his autobiography, he explained (p. 23):

What makes a great endurance athlete is the ability to...suffer without complaint. I was discovering that if it was a matter of gritting my teeth, not caring how it looked, and outlasting everybody else, I won. It didn't seem to matter what the sport was—in a straight-ahead, long-distance race, I could beat anybody. If it was a suffer-fest, I was good at it.

Lance Armstrong is the living validation of Dr. Ilya Prigogine's insight into how trauma can lead to either greater adversity or increased empowerment. When individuals hit the wall, they either crawl unceremoniously into a bottle and self-destruct, or reemerge stronger and more determined to succeed than before. Describing this critical juncture as the *bifurcation point*, Prigogine asserts, "All dissipative structures are teetering perpetually between self-destruction and reorganization." Others have subsequently validated Prigogine's findings. Psychotherapist Stephen Wolinsky, in *The Tao of Chaos*, wrote:

A personality is born of chaos and resistance to chaos can only beget more chaos and resistance. Chaos is no longer an enemy, but a friend. Trying to get rid of chaos is folly; use it for growth. In order to be free, one must ride the rapids of chaos.

Armstrong agrees. After his successful battle with cancer, he explained, "Cancer knocked down a wall in me. Without the cancer, I wouldn't have won even one Tour." In a vivid illustration of Prigogine's concept of a bifurcation point, Lance reflected (p. 269):

There is a point in every race when a rider encounters his real opponent and understands that it's himself. In my most painful moments on the bike, I am at my most curious, and I wonder each and every time how I will respond. Will I discover my innermost weakness, or will I seek out my innermost strength?

To what extent are you able to push through pain to achieve your goals? Do you tend to embrace obstacles as opportunities, or do they tend to discourage you? The tenacity self-assessment on the opposite page is designed to help you determine how you react to adversity. Compare the results of this assessment with the results you obtained in the resilience test in Chapter 4. Did you discover similar results? Why?

TENACITY SELF-ASSESSMENT–How Do You React to Setbacks?

Choose a number 1–5, with 1 the lowest and 5 the highest, to indicate the degree to which you believe the statement describes you or how you feel. Record for each statement the number you have chosen. The scoring key is given below.

There are no "right" or "wrong" answers. In making your selection, answer the questions as candidly as possible without anticipating how you will be classified.

	Seldom			Usually	
1. I learn from my mistakes and attempt not to repeat them.	1	2	3	4	5
2. I view adversity as an opportunity.	1	2	3	4	5
3. When I fail to solve a puzzle, I redouble my efforts to solve it.	1	2	3	4	5
4. Obstacles for me are temporary roadblocks to the top.	1	2	3	4	5
5. When I suffer a major setback, I become discouraged.	1	2	3	4	5
6. I tend to avoid pessimists and people who are negative.	1	2	3	4	5
7. I look on failure as a learning process.	1	2	3	4	5
8. When people put me down, I become more motivated to achieve.	1	2	3	4	5
9. I feel that life is an endless array of problems to be endured.	1	2	3	4	5
10. I believe that success is rarely possible without hard work.	1	2	3	4	5
11. To get my body in shape, I do physical training.	1	2	3	4	5
12. People who are more talented than I outperform me.	1	2	3	4	5
13. I avoid trying to sell an idea or a product to anyone who is unreceptive.	1	2	3	4	5
14. I complete tasks that I undertake.	1	2	3	4	5
15. I avoid trying to develop skills in areas for which I lack talent.	1	2	3	4	5
16. I am able to stick to a diet to lose weight or improve health.	1	2	3	4	5

Instructions	Scoring Key
A. Total the numbers you chose for items: #1, 2, 3, 4, 6, 7, 8, 10, 11, 14, 16. B. Total the numbers you chose for items: #5, 9, 12, 13, 15 Subtract the total in B from the total in A.	**40–50:** Persistent & tenacious beyond the norm. **30–39:** Strong persevering tendencies. **20–29:** Can be buoyed or destroyed by failure. **10–19:** Tend to give up when things go wrong. **Below 10:** Need to develop tenacity.

LANCE ARMSTRONG

- At 15, Texas Triathlete Rookie of the Year.

- At 16, Winner of the Iron Kids Triathlon.

- At 21, wins the World Championship in Oslo, Norway to become world's top cyclist.

- At 25, diagnosed with cancer. Eradicates cancer with aggressive chemotherapy.

- Wins the Tour de France every year from 1999 through 2005—a record-setting 7 times.

- In 1997, established the Lance Armstrong Foundation to raise money for cancer.

© Tim De Waele/CORBIS

Lance Armstrong: The Indomitable Spirit

The most feared statement in the English language is just three words: "You have cancer." These words send a shock wave shuddering down the spine of even the bravest individuals. The immediate reaction is denial–there must be a mistake–especially when you're a successful young athlete with high potential and higher aspirations. When the tests reveal that you have testicular cancer that will require surgery, leaving you sterile, and that the cancer has spread to your lungs and your brain, the next reaction is acceptance–how much time do I have? This devastating news was given to Lance Armstrong on October 2, 1996 when he was just 25 years of age. It was a death sentence without appeal–it was virtually hopeless.

Lance Armstrong born Sept. 18, 1971

Lance Armstrong's reaction to the devastating news was different. From early in his life, his mother Linda had always impressed upon him the importance of struggling through adversity, saying (Armstrong, 2001, p. 37), "Make an obstacle an opportunity, make a negative a positive." He learned this lesson well, for after he recovered from the initial shock, Lance decided to treat the cancer as a challenge–an obstacle against which he would launch all of his energy and the totality of his inner fury. To motivate his struggle, he spoke to the disease as he would any other insidious intruder, asserting, "You picked the wrong guy. When you looked around for a body to try to live in, you made a big mistake when you chose mine." After surgery to remove the tumors from his brain and testicles, he embarked on a brutally aggressive program of chemotherapy, involving four cycles of chemo treatments over a three-month period. Refusing to give in to a pessimistic prognosis, he stayed the course in his grueling battle against the devastating disease, suffering the pain, the nausea, and the misery of chemotherapy. In the end, he was triumphant, routing the cancer and returning to the peak of health. It was the ultimate ordeal, but one that taught him how to push through pain to reach his goals. Lance Armstrong modeled Principle #4: *Transform breakdown into breakthrough.*

In the months following his cancer treatments, he founded the Lance Armstrong Foundation dedicated to providing help for victims of cancer. He explained (Armstrong, 2001, p. 158):

One of the redeeming things about being an athlete–one of the real services we can perform–is to redefine what's humanly possible. We cause people to reconsider their limits, to see that what looks like a wall may really just be an obstacle in the mind. Illness was not unlike athletic performance in that respect: there is so much we don't know about human capacity, and I felt it was important to spread the message.

Less than three years after he was diagnosed with terminal cancer, Lance Armstrong was training for the 1999 Tour de France–the epitome of cycling. Before cancer had entered his life, he hated cycling in cold rain and strong headwinds. On one occasion, he had dropped out of a race in disgust at the level of misery he was expected to endure. However, after his triumph over cancer, he welcomed the misery as a challenge, explaining (Armstrong, 2001, p. 196), "What had cracked me in Paris were the cold, wet conditions, but now I took satisfaction in riding through them."

On the eve of the 100th anniversary of the Tour de France, *USA Today* (July 3, 2003) wrote, "Lance will win. His near obsessive attention to detail will prevent small mistakes that can cost precious minutes." Lance did win the 2003 Tour, becoming only the second person ever to win The Tour for five consecutive years, tying Spain's Miguel Indurain. The media subsequently called it the "Tour de Lance." The story of how he won the 2003 Tour de France captures all the elements that combine to make competitive sport so exciting. But even more exciting is what Lance Armstrong's triumph over cancer taught him about competition in sport and performance in life. He mused (p. 68):

I learned what it means to ride the Tour de France. It's not about the bike. It's a metaphor for life, not only the longest race in the world but also the most exalting and heartbreaking and potentially tragic...It is a test. It tests you physically, it tests you mentally, and it even tests you morally.

Translating the lessons learned from cancer into athletic performance enabled Lance to tap into his inner strengths and transform himself from an excellent cyclist to the pre-eminent cyclist of his era. He wrote (Armstrong, 2001, pp. 113–14):

Without belief [in ourselves], we would be left with nothing but an overwhelming doom, every single day. And it will beat you. I didn't fully see, until the cancer, how we fight every day against the creeping negatives of the world, how we struggle daily against the slow lapping of cynicism. Dispiritedness and disappointment, these were the real perils of life, not some sudden illness or cataclysmic millennium doomsday. I knew now why people fear cancer: because it is a slow and inevitable death, it is the very definition of cynicism and loss of spirit. So I believed.

LANCE ARMSTRONG'S TREK TO THE TOP

Early Imprints

On September 18, 1971, seventeen-year-old Linda Gunderson (née Mooneyham) gave birth to a 9-pound-12-ounce baby who decades later would become an international icon for survival. Linda's frequently expressed motto, "Make every obstacle an opportunity," eventually became the mantra of her son Lance. By the time Lance was two, Linda and her husband had separated and she and her son embarked on a struggle for survival captured in the lyrics of the song of that era, *You and Me Against the World*. She and Lance started out in a rundown public housing project in Dallas. Linda lied about her age to land an after-school job as a server in the local Kentucky Fried Chicken franchise to pay for her session at Kilgore Rangerette drill team camp. Then she worked as a cashier at Kroger's grocery store and a file clerk in the post office, earning enough to provide for them both while putting herself through school. Each time she obtained a job with better pay, she and Lance upgraded to better living conditions. Lance explained in an interview (*USA Today*, April 5, 2005, p. 13C), "My mom moved us from one ratty apartment to another every time she changed jobs, which was often. It gets hot in Dallas in the summertime, and we never had air conditioning."

Though Lance never knew his biological father, his feelings of abandonment created in him a latent anger that he would later convert into controlled aggression. His mother was his emotional salvation, providing him with the love that would sustain him through the trials that lay ahead. She stimulated his mind by reading to him every night. She became his pal, mentor, role model and parent. She adored him and doted on him, but trained her only child to be independent and self-sufficient. Her unrelenting efforts to improve their living conditions eventually landed Linda a full-time job as a secretary. Enjoying a higher level of affluence, she and Lance moved from a poor suburb of Dallas to the more affluent suburb of Plano.

When Lance was three, Linda met and married Terry Armstrong who subsequently adopted Lance. In his autobiography, Lance described his relationship with his new stepfather (Armstrong, 2001, p. 20):

The paddle was the preferred method of discipline. If I came home late, out would come the paddle. Whack.. If I smarted off, I got the paddle. Whack. It didn't hurt just physically, but also emotionally. So I didn't like Terry Armstrong.

At age seven, Lance got his first bike, a Schwinn Mag Scrambler that gave him a sense of "liberation and independence." This freedom to "roam without rules and without adults" would prove to be his emotional and mental escape–the same kind of inner peace that Jim Thorpe enjoyed when he ran into the woods to commune with nature. Armstrong later commented (p. 21), "Back then I was just a kid with about four chips on his shoulder, thinking, *maybe if I ride my bike on this road long enough it will take me out of here.*" The bike became Lance's constant companion and a symbol of his freedom, but his first experience with racing was not on a bicycle, but in a foot race. When in the fifth grade, Lance came first in a race sponsored by his elementary school. This piqued his interest in competition, an interest that would evolve into a passion and then an obsession.

When he entered Plano East High School, Lance discovered that the student body was mainly upper middle class. The only way for a working class boy to earn status was to excel at football. However, his experiences on the gridiron turned out to be short-lived. He explained (p. 21), "I had no coordination. When it came to anything that involved moving from side to side, or hand-eye coordination–when it came to anything involving a ball, in fact–I was no good."

A few months later, he attempted to gain acceptance among his peers by joining the City of Plano Swim Club, but his deficient swimming skills landed 12-year-old Lance in a class with the seven-year-olds. He later commented, "I went from not being any good at football to not being any good at swimming." However, it was at this point that Lance Armstrong's inner resolve began to emerge. The swim coach set up a rigorous training schedule of workouts from 5:30 to 7:00 every morning and within a year,

Lance was fourth in the state in the 1,500-meter freestyle. Every day before school the 13-year-old rode his bike ten miles to swim practice, and then swam laps for two-and-one-half miles. After school, he swam another three-and-one-half miles in the pool and then cycled home–altogether six miles of swimming and 20 miles of cycling! When he saw a poster advertising a junior triathlon competition called Iron Kids, he signed on immediately. The triathlon combined biking, swimming and running, three athletic events in which he had demonstrated some ability. Always supportive, Linda bought Lance a triathlon outfit that was made of a fast-drying material to enable the hyperactive teenager to move from one event to the next without stopping to change. She also bought him his first racing bike, a Mercier, on which he cycled to victory in a local triathlon and then another in Houston. Armed with the self-confidence that comes with repeated victories, Lance was thirsting for greater challenges. Winning gave him an adrenaline rush like nothing else–a rush that he relentlessly pursued in triathlons across the state.

Like Wayne Gretzky, Jeff Gordon, Tiger Woods and other athletic superstars, Lance cut his competitive teeth with older, more experienced athletes, entering the 1987 President's Triathlon in Lake Lavon at the tender age of 15. When he finished 32nd, people were astounded that a young person could complete such a grueling ordeal. During an interview with the press, he confidently asserted, "I think in a few years I'll be right near the top, and within ten years I'll be the best." The next year, he finished fifth. The prize money from triathlons became Lance's main source of income. By age 16, Lance was sponsored by the Richardson Bike Mart, training with men in their late 20s and earning close to $20,000 annually. He was also national rookie of the year in sprint triathlons, and began to dream of Olympic competition. Supporting her son's lofty ambitions, Linda bought him a key chain engraved "1988"–the year of the up-coming summer Olympics.

The fascination with speed and acceleration that obsessed Babe Ruth, Michael Jordan and Jeff Gordon was first evident in Lance Armstrong during his teen years. Exuding the typical Type A personality, Lance purchased a Camaro IROC Z28 monster that he raced at night at speeds up to 120 mph on roads with 45-mph speed limits. Drag racing with his school friends gave him some social cachet, though he never felt part of the "in crowd" at Plano East High School. The sports he played were not the glamour sports and the clothes he wore were not the status brands. He later reflected (Armstrong, 2001, p. 33):

Some of my more social friends would say things like, "If I were you, I'd be embarrassed to wear those Lycra shorts." I shrugged. There was an unwritten dress code; the socially acceptable people all wore uniforms with Polo labels on them...It was total conformity, and everything I was against.

It was clear from early in his life that Lance Armstrong, like all the super-stars profiled in this book, was an individualist, one who had learned to value his uniqueness. By his senior year at Plano East, he cared little about accept-ance in his peer group and focused on his future as an athlete. When he was invited by the U.S. Cycling Federation to train with the junior U.S. national team and travel to Moscow for the 1990 Junior World Championships, the school administrators would not excuse his absence from school. Ignoring the threat that he might not be allowed to graduate, he traveled to Moscow any-way, and participated in the championships. Meanwhile, Linda arranged to have Lance's credits transferred to a private school, Bending Oaks, where Lance completed a couple of make-up courses in time to graduate. He later reported (p. 36), "At the graduation ceremony, all of my classmates had maroon tassels on their caps, while mine was Plano East gold, but I was not embarrassed." After graduation, Lance Armstrong was ready to leave home and launch into a career in international competitive cycling.

International Racing: Cycle Carefully Down the Hill and Pass 'em All

There's an old joke that contrasts impetuous youth and sagacious maturity. According to the story, a young bull and an old bull look down from the top of a hill to a field of cattle. The young bull, raging with testosterone says, "Let's charge down the hill and hump one of them cows!" The old bull, casually surveying the landscape below responds, "No, let's walk *slowly* down the hill and hump 'em all." Marathon racing is about pacing yourself, establishing a rhythm that expends your energy reserves in the most efficient manner. The vigor of youth tempts the neophyte to shoot his bolt early and exhaust his energy before the race is finished–a common mistake that cyclists call "bonking." When Lance Armstrong entered the international cycling competitions in Europe, he was a young bull. In fact, the Spanish press would later name him *Toro de Texas*, on account of his brash, impulsive approach to cycling. He also resembled the young bull in his approach to women. As he explained (Armstrong, 2001, p. 80), "My teammates teasingly named me

FedEx for the speed with which I changed girlfriends. The FedEx slogan was *When you absolutely, positively have to have it–overnight.*"

As he approached his 19th birthday, Lance Armstrong entered the 1990 amateur World Championships in Utsunomiya, Japan, as a member of the U.S. national cycling team. The team coach, Chris Carmichael, instructed Lance to hold back during the early part of the 115-mile race and ride in the wind-protected back draft behind the other team members (a practice known in cycling and car racing as *drafting*). This would enable him to conserve his energy until Carmichael signaled him to go. However, Lance's aggressiveness prompted him to ignore the coach's instructions and he exploded into action, passing the other cyclists as if they were going backward. However, as he neared the halfway mark in the race, he began to fade. Other cyclists passed him as he struggled to keep pedaling. Sheer courage, grit and pride enabled him to finish in 11th place, but he realized he had cost the team an opportunity to win a medal. Lance Armstrong had bonked.

After a disappointing 14th-place finish in the 1992 Olympic Games in Barcelona, Lance turned professional. One of the pioneers of American cycling, Jim Ochowicz, signed him to a contract with a team sponsored by Motorola. When Ochowicz asked the aspiring cyclist about his ambitions, Lance responded, "I want to be the best rider there is. I want to go to Europe and be a pro. I don't want to be just good at it. I want to be the best."

Armstrong's first professional race was the Clásica San Sebastián in San Sebastián, Spain. It was a cold, rainy, miserable morning as the cyclists set out on the one-day tortuous competition over a bumpy course that stretched for more than 100 miles. As the day wore on and the misery index climbed, rider after rider abandoned the struggle and pulled off to the side of the road, exhausted and cursing the elements. Though close to joining the quitters, Lance persisted through the pain and finished the race in last place behind 111 other competitors. Some of the Spanish spectators laughed and jeered at this weary competitor as he crawled across the finish line, almost half an hour behind the winner. Once again, Lance had bonked. Experiences such as this prompted him to write, "Cycling is a sport that embarrasses youth."

After his humiliating performance, Lance Armstrong, like Pelé and other athletic superstars in their early years, began to doubt whether his ambitions were realistic. However, reassurance from Chris Carmichael prompted him to compete in the Championship of Zurich. With little strategic planning but a lot of desire and energy, Lance astounded the world of cycling with a second-place finish, convincing him that he was, indeed, capable of achieving his lofty ambitions.

In the months that followed, the peaks and valleys of Lance's performance resembled the undulating roads that snaked through the mountain cycling courses in Europe. Though his roughly hewn, brash style had earned him some enmity among the cyclists and some bad press in Europe, he was becoming a force to be reckoned with.

In early 1993, Thrifty Drugs posted a $1-million prize for anyone who could win the Triple Crown of Cycling, consisting of a one-day race in Pittsburgh, a six-day race in West Virginia and a 156-mile one-day road race through Philadelphia. By June, Lance had won the first two legs of the Triple Crown and traveled to Philadelphia in hopes of winning the third and final leg and the $1 million. This time, there was too much on the line to risk a loss. Lance applied the lessons he had learned about conserving his energy and pacing himself. He restrained his impulse to surge ahead until he was within 20 miles of the finish line, and then he let loose on one of the steepest inclines on the course. Describing his intensity, he later reported (Armstrong, 2001, p. 59):

> *I was almost in a rage. I don't know what happened–all I know is that I leaped out of the seat and hammered down on the pedals, and as I did so I screamed for five full seconds...I crossed the finish line with the biggest winning margin in race history. I dismounted in a swarm of reporters, but I broke away from them and went straight to my mom, and we put our faces in each other's shoulder and cried.*

The Tour de France

Lance returned to Europe that summer and entered the Tour de France–the ultimate contest in cycling. Considered by many as the most grueling sporting event in the world, it involves three weeks of self-inflicted torture that tests the mind, body and soul. Each day, the cyclists cover approximately 70 to 90 miles and burn about 9000 calories. They travel at high speed both up and down mountain roads, sometimes in 100-degree heat and sometimes in rain-soaked misery. The Tour often begins north of Paris, traverses to the perimeter of France from the heartland, through the Alps, down to the Mediterranean and back up through Eastern wine country to end at the Arc de Triomphe–a total of more than 2100 torturous miles over uncertain terrain. The race consists of 20 segments (called stages) spread over the three-week period. Seven stages feature steep mountain climbs that exhaust the body's resources and cause the mind to question the logic of competing. In these Alpine stages, climbs of 7000 or 8000 feet are common and cyclists reach speeds of up to 70 mph on the descents. The cyclist with the shortest time in completing a stage is said to have "won that Tour stage."

In the 1993 Tour de France, Lance Armstrong sprinted past all the riders in the 114-mile stage from Châlons-sur-Marne to Verdun, becoming at 21 the youngest cyclist to win a Tour stage. However, two days later, Lance bonked and withdrew from the Tour, exhausted and beaten by the steep inclines and the cold rainy weather. As Lance himself later observed (p. 60), "I just couldn't seem to get it through my head that in order to win I had to ride more slowly at first. It took some time for me to reconcile myself to the notion that being patient was different from being weak."

In the following year, as Yogi Berra would say, it was déjà vu all over again. Although performing well on several stages in the 1994 Tour, Lance eventually ran out of steam and dropped out of the race. Completing the Tour de France was a goal that continuously eluded him, though he worked relentlessly on his pacing, striving to acquire the self-discipline that defines the mature athlete. Then, during the 1995 Tour de France, Lance experienced the kind of tragedy that deepens one's resolve and focus. His teammate Fabio Casartelli, gold medallist in the 1992 Olympics, was killed in a high-speed descent when his bike hit a curb and he landed on his head, fracturing his neck and skull. The team was devastated and considered dropping out of the race. However, Fabio's wife persuaded them that her husband would have wished them to continue. It had been Fabio's dream to win the next stage of the Tour from Bordeaux to Limoges. As a tribute to his friend and teammate, Lance decided to win that stage on Fabio's behalf. When 25 miles outside Limoges, he launched an aggressive attack, reaching dangerously high speeds on the downhills. Somehow the energy lacking in his previous attempts to complete the Tour was now available in abundance and Lance sped past the competition, winning that stage by more than a full minute. He subsequently went on to complete the Tour de France for the first time, placing a respectable 36th out of approximately 200 starters. More important than this achievement was his realization that he had within himself a deep reservoir of energy and power that had hitherto been untapped. It took Fabio's inspiration to awaken in Lance the awareness of his own potential. Reflecting on that experience, he said (Armstrong, 2001, p. 69), "There were no shortcuts, I realized...I wouldn't be able to win a Tour de France until I had enough iron in my legs, and lungs, and brain, and heart."

The Ultimate Obstacle

At the age of 25, Lance was on top of the world. His opulent mansion, flashy Porsche and vivacious girlfriend projected a lifestyle of the rich and famous. He was becoming an international celebrity and his $2.5-million contract with the Cofidis racing team promised continued wealth and recognition. Furthermore, he appeared to have found the resolve to dig deeper into himself for the energy to win the Tour de France, However, when everything seems at its best, the chaotic vagaries of life often turn things toward the worst. And so it was with Lance Armstrong.

In the 1996 Tour de France, Lance expected to improve on his 36th-place finish of the previous year. However, he surprised the cycling world by bonking once again and dropping out of the race. The next month he was the American favorite to win a medal at the 1996 Olympics in Atlanta. However, his performance was sluggish and he finished a disappointing 6th in the time trial and 12th in the road race. He later said that he felt as if he were dragging a manhole cover. On October 2, 1996, Lance Armstrong discovered that the invisible manhole cover was actually a dozen tumors in his lungs. X-rays and blood tests revealed that he had an aggressive form of testicular cancer that had spread to the lymph glands in his abdomen and into his lungs. The cancer had already progressed to stage 3, and his chances of survival were considered minimal.

After the cancer was diagnosed, Lance went to the highly respected center for cancer in Houston, Texas to plan his future. The oncologists there told him they could almost certainly guarantee his life, but he would probably never ride or walk again. Seeking a second opinion, Lance contacted an oncology group in Indiana. There, Dr. Craig Nichols presented him with a high-risk option: a radical system of chemotherapy and non-traditional treatment that could not guarantee his life, but if successful, would possibly permit him to ride and walk. Unwilling to live a lower quality of life, Lance Armstrong said, "I don't want to live if I can't ride or walk. Give it all to me doc."

Recognizing that time was of the essence, the doctors scheduled surgery for the next morning and a program of chemotherapy to begin the following week. Warned that chemotherapy often leads to permanent sterility in such cases, Lance banked his sperm, and immersed himself in reading everything he could about cancer and cancer treatments. He began his chemotherapy just five days after the original diagnosis, encouraged in the hope that a rigorous attack on the cancer, combined with an understanding of the processes occurring in his body, might have a successful outcome. Lance was in desperate need of good news, but it was not to be. Just days into his chemo treatments, he learned that his insurance coverage was withdrawn on the grounds that his cancer was deemed a predisposition. When doctors suspected that the cancer might have spread to his brain, they suggested he submit to an MRI scan. Exactly one week after his surgery for testicular cancer, the doctors informed Lance that the cancer was in his brain and that they would have to cut into his skull to remove the cancerous lesions. In seven days, Lance Armstrong had plummeted from the top of the world into the darkest depths of despair. Fate had tossed him the ultimate challenge–the challenge of survival against all odds.

The inspirational story of how Lance Armstrong summoned his courage and endured the endless torments of four aggressive chemotherapy treatments that brought him to death's doorstep is well-documented in his best-selling autobiography, *It's Not About the Bike: My Journey Back to Life*. It reveals not only the horror that one faces when confronted with imminent death, but more importantly, the capacity that each of us has to triumph against what appears to be formidable odds. Through it all, Lance had the support of doctors, nurses and friends. But most of all, his mother Linda was at his side, encouraging him through every step of the ordeal. In an interview with *USA Today*, Linda described the magic moment when Lance awakened from his brain surgery and whispered without opening his eyes, "I love you, Mom. I love my life…and you gave it to me…and I love you so much for that."

As 1996 drew to a close, Lance finished his chemotherapy treatments and won his fight for survival. Like the Tour de France, filled with days of agony, misery and fear, this struggle spanned three months, not three weeks, and the prize was life itself. Though sports psychologists have told the media that the Tour is the most physically demanding event in the world, Lance subsequently assured us that it pales in comparison to the struggle to beat cancer.

In fact, winning the ultimate contest had a short-term downside for him. After that struggle, all other challenges seemed trivial. Suddenly, Lance Armstrong discovered that he had lost interest in cycling. It took him a year of rethinking his life and bumming around in a pseudo-retired state before he regained his passion for cycling. But when it returned, it returned with a vengeance. For the ex-cancer patient, no obstacle would be too tough, no adversary too strong, no loss too debilitating, no mountain too high or road too steep.

Tour de France, 1999

In late 1997, just one year after his cancer ordeal, Lance began training again. In January 1998 he returned to Europe and competitive racing. Cancer had changed his physique. He was now 15 pounds lighter than before, which gave him a decided advantage when pedaling his weight up the mountains. In May 1998, Lance interrupted his rigorous training program to fly to Santa Barbara where he married Kristin Richard, a woman he had met and lived with shortly after his bout with cancer. After a brief honeymoon, during which he trained on the bike every day, he returned to Austin, Texas. From there he went to the U.S. Pro Championships where he came in fourth. He skipped the 1998 Tour de France in July, because he knew he was still not ready to compete at the highest level. To prepare himself for the 1999 Tour, he entered the Vuelta a España, a 2348-mile tour through Spain spanning 23 days. He finished in fourth place, only two minutes and eighteen seconds behind the winner. Lance knew that he was back in top form and now better able than ever to win marathon races.

When the cyclists gathered at the start line for the 1999 Tour de France, few people regarded Lance Armstrong as a serious contender. However, in a preemptive strike, Lance captured the attention of the cycling world when he won the first stage of the Tour, a short 5-mile time trial known as the *Prologue*. This put him in the lead and earned him the prestigious *maillot jaune*–a yellow jersey worn by the leading cyclist in the Tour de France. The maillot jaune is a status symbol that identifies the leader as the man to beat. (In time trials, the riders start at different times, so the time leader is not always at the front of the pack or *peloton*.) He wore the maillot jaune proudly as he set out on July 4th for the next stage of the Tour. Running through the flat plains of eastern France, this part of the course gave an advantage to the sprinters rather than the climbers. The peloton moved swiftly across monotonous roads, as the fiercely competitive cyclists bumped each other and jostled for position. The maturity that Lance had acquired during his struggle with cancer enabled him to hold back during the stages through the plains, avoiding collisions and conserving his energy for the mountainous regions in the later stages. He sacrificed the maillot jaune for several days, intending to recapture it in the mountain climbs.

When they reached Metz, the starting place for the next time trial, Lance knew it was now or never. This time trial covered a distance of 35 miles and included two major inclines: one that was one mile long and another that was two-and-one-half miles. It required both strength and stamina to mount these steep inclines at top speed and into strong headwinds. In a dramatic display of power, stamina and pacing, Lance managed to complete the stage in 1:08:36 (1 hr., 8 min., 36 sec.) and reclaim the maillot jaune.

However, the most grueling part of the race was still ahead. The next part of the Tour consisted of the Alpine stages–those uphill roads that rewarded powerful climbers and destroyed those lacking in stamina or resolve. Lance knew that his maillot jaune would make him a target of his competitors. To protect his slender lead of only two minutes and 20 seconds, he would have to draft behind his team to conserve his energy and to avoid a collision that could cost him precious time. Through the help of his teammates and the judicious use of strategic drafting, he survived the Alpine stages with the yellow jersey still in his possession. The Alps and the Pyrenees were behind him. He had traveled 2200 miles in 86:46:20, and was 6 minutes and 15 seconds ahead of Escartin who was in second place.

The penultimate stage of the Tour was a time trial, about 35 miles long, over west-central France. It required cycling at top speed for over an hour. With his commanding lead, winning the Tour would be inevitable, provided Lance rode conservatively and merely avoided accidents. However, Lance was cycling to the tune of a different drummer. Only three riders in the history of the Tour had ever swept all the time trials and Lance needed to win this stage to join that elite group. Throwing caution to the winds, he went flat out for 68 minutes and 17 seconds to sweep the time trials and earn a place in the record books. By the eve of the final stage, he had increased his lead to 7 minutes and 37 seconds, making his Tour victory a *fait accompli*. The final stage, a ceremonial ride of 89 miles into Paris, though anticlimactic, was the apex of a long climb from the bottom of life to the top. Resplendent in the maillot jaune of victory, Lance Armstrong rode at the head of the US Postal-sponsored team onto the Champs-Elysées, leading the peloton through Paris like a conquering army. Lance was only the second American to win the Tour de France in almost a century of its existence.

The Tour de France, 2000 and 2001

Lance Armstrong's victory in the 1999 Tour de France took the cycling world by surprise. Merely three years earlier, this non-European upstart had been struggling with terminal cancer that had ravaged his body and now he had beaten the most highly conditioned cyclists in the world. The 1998 Tour had been beset by a drug scandal that saw many of the top riders banned from participation in the '99 Tour. Lance's superb performance in the 1999 Tour had stimulated speculation in journals *L'Equipe* and *Le Monde* that the drugs he took in his cancer treatments were a dominant factor in his 1999 victory. Others attributed his victory to the absence of the banned cyclists. Still others said that Armstrong's victory was merely a fluke, something that could not happen again. If Lance Armstrong were to silence these naysayers, he would have to do it all over again–the training, the suffering, the anguish, the sacrifice and the victory.

In the 2000 Tour de France, all the cycling superstars were back in the competition. The 1997 winner Jan Ullrich and the 1998 winner Mario Pantani would be part of the peloton whose sole aim was to dethrone the man who had paraded down the Champs-Elysées in the maillot jaune a year earlier. Describing his motivation for enduring the pain of another Tour de France challenge, Lance Armstrong said (p. 270):

> *Every year that I get back on the bike and try to win another Tour de France is another year that I've survived the illness. Maybe that's why winning a second Tour de France was so important to me–because to me, cycling is the same as living. I intended to win another Tour, and the reason I intended to was because nobody thought I could. They figured that my comeback of 1999 was miracle enough. But I no longer viewed my cycling career as a comeback, I view it as a confirmation and a continuation of what I've done as a cancer survivor.*

The Tour de France in 2000 was even more punishing than in the previous year, but in the end, Lance Armstrong finished with the maillot jaune and his second Tour de France victory by a margin of more than six minutes. Drug tests taken throughout the race were always negative, leaving the skeptics with no alternative but to accept that Lance Armstrong was indeed the top cyclist in the Tour de France format. It was clear that he would be the target for all other cyclists in the next year's torture test.

During the Tour de France in 2001, the powerful German rider Jan Ullrich, the unrelenting Spaniard Joseba Beloki, the Kazakh Andreï Kivilev and the French rider François Simon challenged Armstrong throughout the race, threatening at any unguarded moment to capture and run away to Paris with the maillot jaune. When Lance Armstrong and the US Postal team reached the end of the eighth stage at the foothills of the Alps, they were trailing François Simon by a frightening margin of 35 minutes. Armstrong was in 24th place and in danger of falling hopelessly behind. The first mountain stage would test the mettle of all riders and be a major factor in determining the winner. Spanning a distance of 130 miles and ascending more than 6000 feet over three mountains that were rated "beyond category" (*hors de catégorie*) in difficulty, this stage would present the most grueling challenge of the Tour. The third of these menacing peaks, the Alpe d'Huez, had a steep 12-mile incline. Deemed the Mount Everest of cycling, this horrendous peak would provide the ultimate test.

As Lance and the US Postal team scaled the first peak, it was clear that the arduous climb was beginning to take its toll. Nearing the top, the riders heaved with oxygen deprivation and struggled to maintain their rhythm; some merely pulled off the road and quit. Lance was draped over his handlebars in the posture of a spent and beaten competitor as he labored at the back of the peloton. The television coverage of his travails was dramatic, one commentator announcing, "Armstrong looking in a spot of trouble." Not only the world, but even the other members of the peloton who were in communication with their TV-equipped follow cars, were aware that Armstrong was suffering greatly and in danger of abandoning the struggle.

Seizing the opportunity to increase their lead to an insurmountable margin while Lance was failing, the Telekom team (led by Jan Ullrich) went on the attack. They moved rapidly to the front of the peloton, cycling at a higher cadence. Mile after mile, they hammered the pedals, climbing the inclines and blitzing down the declines. By the time the peloton approached the Alpe d'Huez, it seemed clear that Armstrong and the Postal team were all but finished. But as he approached the foot of the Alpe d'Huez, Lance decided that he had played possum long enough. As he had hoped, the Telekom team had expended a considerable amount of their energy speeding over the first two peaks. They would have trouble sustaining their cadence over the largest mountain of all. Like a cavalry bugler sounding the charge, Lance yelled to his teammate Chechu, *"Vollebak"* meaning "full gas." Then Lance began the sprint that shocked the world, a sprint that saw Lance speed to the front of the peloton, past Ullrich, to win that critical stage of the Tour de France.

However, the Tour was still far from over. François Simon was still wearing the maillot jaune with a 13-minute lead over Lance as they approached the Pyrenees. But Simon began to fade during these mountain climbs and Lance continued to press forward, through the agony, with a tenacity that the other riders couldn't match. He won the stage following the conquest of the Alpe d'Huez and two days later claimed the maillot jaune.

Lance Armstrong crossed the finish line on the Champs-Elysées on July 21, 2001 having won the Tour de France for the third time, having cycled 2150 miles in 86 hours, 17 minutes and 28 seconds!

On July 28, 2002, Lance Armstrong rode into Paris for his fourth time sporting the maillot jaune and winning the Tour de France. His superb performance in the mountain climbs left the other riders in the dust, establishing once and for all his (and the US Postal team's) superiority in the Tour de France. Their margin of 7 minutes and 17 seconds was substantial. The French newspaper *Le Parisien* graciously acknowledged the American victory with the headline, *Merci Jaja…Bravo Armstrong*–a joint tribute to the leader of the French team, Laurent Jalabert and to Lance Armstrong. It looked as if the French had finally accepted the brash Texan as a true champion.

The Tour de France in 2003–The Centennial Year

In 2003, the Tour de France was celebrating its centennial. The inaugural event in 1903 began as a challenge issued by the newspaper *L'Auto*. The original course was much shorter with no mountain stages. Since the bicycle was a relatively new invention, the technology was rather crude. The bikes had only two gears and the absence of brakes meant that the rider dragged his feet to slow down or stop. Within seven years, brakes were developed and the mountain stages were added. A century later, the cyclists were riding on virtually weightless bicycles while communicating with their follow cars via two-way radios. They monitored their wattages, speed, caloric expenditure and heart rate through computers fixed to their bikes. The Tour de France had evolved from a simple sport into a science, but the fundamental requirements were still speed, endurance, strategy and tenacity.

During the first hundred years of its existence, the Tour de France had evolved from a local challenge into a huge media event, broadcast around the world to hundreds of millions of fans. With such global exposure came sponsorships, television contracts and huge revenues to the sport, the hosts, the media and all those involved. Winning the Tour brought instant celebrity and substantial monetary rewards. Inevitably, as the rewards increased, the competition became fierce. Having won the Tour four times, Lance Armstrong was now recognized as the front-runner. Everyone expected him to win again, and by a significant margin. As he explained in *Every Second Counts* (p. 232), "When you hear that all the time, it gets to you, and you feel that there isn't much to race for. You can only lose." Being the favorite also made him the focus and the target.

When he came seventh in the Prologue at the beginning of the 2003 Tour, Lance began to feel that this setback was a harbinger of things to come. Then in the very first stage of the race, 176 cyclists in the peloton collided in a chain reaction that sent riders skidding and tumbling in all directions. Though several sustained injuries, Lance escaped with bruises and friction burns.

The racing stages through the relatively flat heartland of France in 100-degree temperatures constituted the next obstacle. With the help of his team-mates who rode in front, enabling him to draft and conserve his strength, Lance was able to survive the first week of the Tour and move from twelfth to second place by the time the peloton reached the Alpine stages. By the steep incline at Galibier, Lance was suffering extreme fatigue. At the top of the climb, he looked down and discovered his brakes had been partially engaged the whole time up the mountain! He released the brakes, but the climb had drained his energy resources.

Emotional breakdown occurs when a rider "hits the wall." It is then that the will takes over or the race is over. As the peloton approached the formidable Alpe d'Huez, Lance was overcome by dehydration from the 100-degree heat and a stomach ailment that had been with him from the start of the race. He would later tell the press, "I had to come to grips with the fact that it may be over for me." Armstrong's longtime friend and coach Chris Carmichael had told the media, "He and his family have sacrificed too much for him to give in at any point. That's not in his personality. If he's behind, he will attack all the way to Paris. It will be World War III." Carmichael's words proved prophetic. Toughing it out was not new to Armstrong. He struggled against the pain and misery and, though four minutes slower than in 2001, he managed to place fourth in that stage and reclaim the maillot jaune.

The next leg of the race presented a challenge of a different kind. While flying down an incline at 50 mph, Joseba Beloki skidded on the greasy tar that was melting in the 100-degree heat, tossing both the bike and the rider across the slippery pavement. Right behind, Lance hit his brakes and swerved to avoid a collision. His bike became airborne and he left the road, hurtling across a field of tractor furrows, still seated on his runaway cycle. Mimicking the antics of a Hollywood stuntman in a slapstick comedy, he performed a series of gymnastic maneuvers that returned him miraculously to a position further up the road. His quick thinking had averted a disaster that could have cost him the race.

Two days later, in a crucial time trial, Lance became overheated. He drank water in copious quantities, until he discovered, to his horror, that he had consumed it all. Rules prevent getting help during a time trial, so he would have to press on without water. Dehydration set in as Lance's body depleted its fluids, leaving a white ring of salt deposits around his mouth. Minute by minute he slowed as his body consumed itself and the competitors closed the gap in his lead. When he reached the end of that stage, Lance had lost almost six quarts of fluids (15 pounds) and one minute and 36 seconds to Jan Ullrich, his closest competitor. Though he still held the maillot jaune, his lead had been cut to only 34 seconds.

The dehydration left Armstrong weakened. In the next stages he lost more time to Ullrich, who whittled his lead to a mere 15 seconds. As they entered the final stages of the race, members of the peloton speculated that Lance was failing and was about to be surpassed. Then in the penultimate mountain stage, to Luz-Ardiden, Lance hammered on the pedals at top speed, trying to make up for lost time when a Tour souvenir bag that a child spectator was swinging snagged on his handlebars, flipping the bike and slamming Lance onto the pavement. Giving vent to every cuss word in his repertoire, Lance got up, put his chain back on his bike and began to ride like a man possessed. Though he thought the race was lost, his anger and adrenaline drove him relentlessly and he went on to win that stage in dramatic fashion. In a feature article for *USA Today*, his wife Kristin, wrote (July 25, 2003):

When he crashed I was so scared, and yet I saw it happening, the spirit of the underdog being unleashed. He was on fire. I knew no one would catch him. When the odds are stacked against him, he stacks himself against the odds.

The next few days of the race were comparatively uneventful, with rivals Armstrong and Ullrich pacing each other and saving themselves for the final time trial from Nantes. It would be the deciding stage before the final celebratory ride into Paris. Lance awoke at 6:30 a.m. in Nantes to a driving rainstorm. Always the careful planner, he cruised on his bike in the rain to study the locations of the corners, the manholes and the train tracks where his bike might skid. Meanwhile, his archrival Jan Ullrich studied a videotape of the road rather than test it himself. That would prove to be a serious mistake. While making a corner at a speed that was too fast for the road, Ullrich's bike skidded out from under him and he slid across the pavement into bales of hay. The precious seconds he lost in mounting his bicycle and accelerating to the speed of the peloton put him too far behind to recover. When Lance Armstrong rode triumphantly up the Champs-Elysées in his yellow jersey for the fifth consecutive time, just 61 seconds ahead of everyone else, he joined the ranks of the elite. Only four other cyclists had ever won the Tour de France five times. And no one had won it six times.

Tour de Lance: 2004

The temptation to go for a record-breaking six Tour de France victories was irresistible. Navratilova had won Wimbledon six times in a row; Michael Jordan had won seven scoring titles; and Wayne Gretzky had won eight. It's what the athletic superstars do to challenge themselves. They set goals and then pursue them with a vengeance. That's what Lance Armstrong did when he entered the Tour de France in 2004.

This time, the complacence that nearly cost him the 2003 Tour victory was replaced by an intense focus and will to win. Now at age 32, he had become an old bull, a master of strategy who knew how to pace himself to get maximum output from minimum effort. Hanging back in the early stages, he lost the Prologue and wore the yellow jersey only once in the first 14 stages. Rumblings began to circulate that he was past his prime and that it would be unlikely that he could come from behind and win. However in the 15th stage, a mountainous portion of the race to Villard de Lans, he cycled over 100 miles in remarkable time and captured the maillot jaune. Then he won three of the five remaining stages, never again surrendering it. As he rode triumphantly to the Arc de Triomphe for the sixth time, the world recognized his supremacy. Some suggested the Tour be renamed "The Tour de Lance."

Tour de Lance 2005

When Lance Armstrong completed his sixth victory in the Tour de France in 2004, his teammates held up six fingers in celebration of a new benchmark in the sport of cycling. But Lance displayed seven fingers as he looked ahead to 2005, already formulating the dream to win an unprecedented seven Tour victories, and setting the bar high above the reach of successive generations. In the eleven months between the 2004 victory and the start of the 2005 race, Lance trained hard, preparing for what would be his final entry into the Tour de France and his career swan song. Winning his seventh Tour de France would be the ultimate jewel in his crown as cycling's preeminent icon. It would enable him to leave his sport while on top, a feat that all champions strive to achieve. However, as he approached his 34th birthday and the 2005 Tour, Lance announced, "Time is not on my side...I'm nervous about the opening stage in the mountains." Armstrong was referring to stage 10, the first alpine stage–a gruelling climb through the Alps that begins at Grenoble and ends with a 13.8-mile climb to the ski station of Courchevel. The steep mountain challenges the very best and exacts a level of punishment that thins the peleton to the few who can successfully suffer life's greatest agonies.

The 21 Stages of the 2005 Tour de France

The circled numbers indicate each of the 21 stages of the race. The race began on July 2, 2005 and ended at the Arc de Triomphe, in Paris, on July 24, 2005. The stages took place on consecutive days, except for days of rest on July 11 and July 19. The cyclists covered a total distance of 3593 km (2232 miles).

The first stage of the 2005 Tour was a 19-km time trial from Fromentine to Noirmoutier-en-l'île on the Atlantic coast of France. Though a relatively short stage of the Tour, it was designed to test the riders' ability to sustain high speeds over a prolonged period. Lance rocketed out of the chute, determined to win the maillot jaune and serve notice on all his competitors. Averaging a speed of 54.59 km/h (33.9 mph), he gained 51 seconds on his closest rival Alexandre Vinokourov and 1:06 (1 min., 6 sec.) on the 1997 Tour winner, Jan Ullrich. However, this effort was not enough to win Armstrong the yellow jersey. That honor was reserved for 26-year-old David Zabriskie who edged out Lance by two seconds, establishing a time trial record of 54.676 km/h (33.95 mph). Though Zabriskie was not considered a potential threat in the later mountain stages, some people wondered if this was a harbinger of things to come. Would this be the year when youth would be served?

In stages 2 and 3 as the peloton raced through the relatively flat plains of northern France, Armstrong stayed patient, keeping a steady pace and looking for opportunities to sprint ahead of the pack, but he was unable to capture the maillot jaune. Then in the fourth stage, the peloton set out from Tours under scowling skies and raging headwinds. They traversed the terrain of the Loire River valley, graced on both sides by medieval castles and Renaissance architecture. But the rich history of the region was lost on Lance who was suffering to make a history of his own. Within 2 km of the end of the 67.5 km team time trial, David Zabriskie, wearing the maillot jaune, missed a turn and crashed into a barricade. Meanwhile, Lance Armstrong came hurtling across the finish line, capturing the yellow jersey and leading the pack by 1:26.

On completion of stage 7 in Karlsruhe, Germany on July 8, Armstrong's lead had been whittled to 55 seconds. Competition became more intense the following day as the Peleton scaled the long uphill climbs from Pforzheim, Germany to Gérardmer in Northeast France. As the day wore on and the uphill pace quickened, Lance's teammates collapsed, leaving him to battle alone against his strongest rivals. The eighth stage would become known as the day the Discovery Channel team bonked. However, through it all, Lance prevailed, retaining the maillot jaune that he had held since stage 5.

Finally, in the ninth stage, a 171-kilometer route involving six climbs, Germany's Jens Voigt, in a dramatic tour de force, completed the stage in 4:11:24 and captured the maillot jaune. Armstrong, who had fallen into third place, now trailed Voigt by 2:18. If the contenders for the 2005 Tour de France victory were to make a bid for the coveted prize, this was the time. After a day of rest, they would enter the first Alpine stage–the dreaded tenth stage that

Lance Armstrong had previously said "made him nervous." As one of the toughest stages in the 2005 Tour, it would present three ascents in quick succession, culminating in the *hors catégorie* mountain Col du Calibier that reaches 2645 m (8678 ft.) above sea level–the highest point in the Tour.

Embracing the philosophy that his mother had ingrained in his psyche, Armstrong saw these horrendous obstacles as opportunities to distance himself from his main contenders. He launched into the tenth stage with an aggressive pace that left his rivals grimacing in pain. His teammates rallied with him, facilitating his fast-paced charge to the top. By the time he finished the 13.8-mile climb to the ski station at Courchevel, Lance had regained the maillot jaune with a lead of 38 seconds. It was a lead that he maintained through the remaining Alpine stages, enabling him to wear the yellow jersey into the Pyrenees.

The 15th stage of the 2005 Tour represented the last serious challenge to Lance Armstrong's bid for a seventh Tour victory. Regarded by many as the most difficult stage, it spans a distance of 205.5 km (127.7 miles) and involves six climbs totalling almost 16,000 feet. While the steep inclines punish beyond belief, the steeper descents offer much greater dangers as cyclists reach speeds over 110 km/h (70 mph). It was on this route that Fabio Casartelli, the gold medalist in the 1992 Olympics was killed almost exactly 10 years earlier in the 1995 Tour de France. Paying tribute to their fallen colleague, many of the riders set out on the 15th stage wearing armbands inscribed with "Fabio."

The heat was searing in the south of France as the peloton made its way through the final mountain stage of the Tour. Armstrong and his Discovery Channel team set an aggressive early pace. It was Lance's last opportunity to increase significantly his lead over his rivals and ensure a seventh victory. Not to be denied, several contenders launched heavy attacks, breaking away from the peloton when only 29 km (18 miles) out of the starting gate. The renegade breakaway group continued their assault on the torturous climbs, increasing their lead over the peloton to 14 minutes by the time they had reached the summit of the first climb, the Portet d'Aspet. The mountains exacted a heavy toll on the dozen cyclists in the breakaway group and by the time they reached the top of their fourth ascent, only six competitors remained and their lead over the peloton had shrunk to 12 minutes. Meanwhile, Lance Armstrong, remembering the bonking experiences of his early years, was maintaining his aggressive pace at the head of the peloton, but significantly behind the renegade group. (Since none of the top contenders was in the renegade group, Armstrong's lead was not in jeopardy.) Suddenly his top rival and foremost contender, Ivan Basso of Italy, fired his afterburners in a last gasp attempt to close in on Armstrong's small overall lead. Armstrong responded, clamping down on the pedals and leaving the rest of the peloton in the dust.

By the time the breakaway group was 4 km from the top of the final ascent, the Pla d'Adet, it contained only two members, George Hincapie of the Discovery Channel team and Oscar Pereiro of Spain. In a dramatic gladiatorial contest between the two fierce competitors, Hincapie prevailed by a margin of 6 seconds to win that Tour stage. Armstrong and Basso crossed the finish line 5 minutes later in a dead heat, enabling Armstrong to retain his margin of 2:46 over Basso and the yellow jersey.

With the last daunting mountain stage of the 2005 Tour behind, victory for Lance Armstrong was, barring collisions or mishaps, a *fait accompli*. When he rode triumphantly to the Arc de Triomphe exactly one week later, he had won the Tour de France for an unprecedented seventh time, edging out Ivan Basso by 4:40. Accolades poured in. The Tour organizers broke precedence by allowing Lance to address the audience of 500,000 aficiondos who braved the rain and the humid heat to hear from the preeminent icon of cycling. The celebrations that followed were not just celebrations of a sporting event, but more importantly a celebration of the human spirit–the unyielding resilience that enables someone to rise from the depths of despair to the highest levels of achievement. It was a celebration of what we all have deep within us. Talk show host David Letterman put a humorous spin on the test and ordeal when he listed his *Top Ten Signs that Lance Armstrong Is Getting Cocky*. Among these was the indicator, "Lance is only giving 109%."

Legacy

Any list of the greatest athletes of modern age contains the name Lance Armstrong. Bud Greenspan, the celebrated creator of several documentaries on the Olympics said, "[Lance] is one of the top three athletes of all time, without a doubt, and maybe even higher." But Armstrong's contribution to the world extends well beyond athletics. Identifying athletic struggle as a metaphor for life, he sought to help people triumph over life-threatening illness, seeing it as an opportunity to tap into one's inner resources rather than as an excuse to abandon the struggle. To this end, he established the Lance Armstrong Foundation (LAF), a non-profit organization (URL: www.laf.org) dedicated to those who are living "with, through and beyond cancer." Within eight years since its inception in 1997, LAF has raised over $25 million for cancer survivorship programs and grants. The ubiquitous yellow wristbands, emblazoned with the logo "LiveSTRONG", are part of a sensational promotion (with 40 million in circulation by 2005) that raised revenue while spreading cancer awareness.

Undoubtedly, Armstrong will be known as a man who refused to be felled by cancer, an athlete who defied death and won. It is not just that he recovered, but that he used the experience to spur him to become greater than he had been before. He adamantly refused to lose the most arduous race, the race for survival. After that, he transformed the torturous heat and mountains of pain in the Tour de France from insurmountable obstacles to rich opportunities.

Coming from behind has been Armstrong's rallying call from childhood, underlying all he has achieved. He told the press during the 2003 Tour, "Watch me beat defeat, win over adversity and knock down all those barriers blocking my path to the top." Those forceful words emanated from the soul of a man who had the will to win against great odds. Breakdown had preceded his major breakthroughs. His struggle had begun with an uphill battle as an only child of a single mother living in the projects and grappling for survival–described two decades later in Linda's autobiography, *No Mountain High Enough*. Then testicular cancer threatened to destroy him. Next was the turn of the Alps and Pyrenees. Lance had always trained his body to be the best but until the cancer, his mind and heart were not as conditioned for eminence as they were afterward. That battle for life showed him how to attack with the heart and head as well as with the body. Speaking eloquently of this epic battle, he said, "I treated my illness like it was a sporting event, like the Tour de France." And when he crossed the finish line in Paris on Sunday July 28, 2002, he told the media, "There's never been a Tour de France victory by a cancer survivor before me. That's what I'd like to be remembered for."

Perhaps Lance Armstrong's greatest contributions were his books that shared his experiences and insights with those who are not touched by cancer. *It's Not About the Bike, My Journey Back to Life* and *Every Second Counts* describe his struggle for survival in a way that encourages us to dig deeper into ourselves to overcome obstacles. Capturing his message in a single succinct sentence, he explained (Armstrong, 2001, p. 267):

The one thing the illness has convinced me of beyond all doubt–more than any experience I've had as an athlete–is that we are much better than we know. We have unrealized capacities that sometimes only emerge in crisis.

Chapter 13

PRINCIPLE #13: PERFORM IN THE ZONE

I believe in every shot I hit that I can pull it off. It's just, I guess, my mind-set. I've always believed that.

–Tiger Woods

First-tee Jitters

If you're a golfer, the following scenario may be familiar. It's a beautiful Sunday morning. You are standing on the first tee, surrounded by a gallery of spectators awaiting their turn. You look down the fairway and see that the foursome ahead is now out of range. It's your turn to hit. Your hand shakes as you tee up your ball. The shot of adrenaline you felt when your name was called has set your heart racing. A thousand thoughts rush into your head at the same time. "Keep your head down, left arm straight, one-piece takeaway, and remember to follow through." You take a practice swing. A quick glance at the gallery reveals the expectant grins of a few friends and neighbors who will be judging your competence, based on this single shot. The butterflies in your stomach tell you that another shot of adrenaline has been sent to your muscles. Your position in the social hierarchy hangs precariously on the outcome of this ever-crucial tee shot, but your status as a weekend warrior warns that a successful outcome is unlikely.

As you move mechanically into your backswing, your attention is scattered and your focus is blurred. You just want the nervousness and anxiety to be over, preferably with a face-saving performance. Your downswing explodes into a violent lunge at the ball and, in an instant, your hands transmit the dreaded message–you've topped the ball! As the white sphere skitters to a stop 100 yards down the fairway, you observe the stifled laughs and smug smirks of your audience. You attempt to recover your dignity with a witticism like "tough course." You gather your wounded pride and walk down the fairway asking yourself, "After all the good shots I hit on the driving range, how could I duff my drive off the first tee?"

This familiar scenario is called "first-tee jitters." The bane of all high-handicap golfers and many low-handicappers, it has been experienced to some degree by all golfers. However, first-tee jitters provide a key insight into the emotional and physical harmony that is a prerequisite for optimal athletic performance. During the warm-up on the driving range, no drive is particularly important because it's a practice session and no one is watching. Consequently, there is not enough anxiety to cause the muscles to tighten or the focus to blur. It is reasonably easy to achieve a fluid, coordinated swing. However, under the spell of first-tee jitters, a successful swing is elusive. Performance falls victim to stress.

The Inverted-U Hypothesis

Without stress, an athlete never performs optimally. But too much stress is equally harmful. Optimum performance demands an emotional disposition somewhere between nonchalance and stress-out; being excited enough to outplay and out-hustle opponents, yet not so excited that the emotions override what the body knows how to do. Recall the "yips" from Chapter 5, "yips" that cause golfers to miss putts when suffering extreme stress. When the stakes are high, the muscles tighten, the "left brain" overrules instinct and the golfer is unable to execute what the "right brain" knows how to do.

In 1908, Yerkes and Dodson proposed a relationship between performance and psychological arousal (state of mental stimulation). They asserted that performance increases as the level of psychological arousal is increased, until it reaches an optimal level. Beyond that optimal arousal level, excitement gives way to anxiety and performance deteriorates. If performance is graphed as a function of arousal, the result is a curve shaped like an upside-down U, hence the relationship is described as the *inverted-U hypothesis*–a fancy name for a simple idea.

The graph shows that too little psychological arousal, corresponding to low motivation, yields a low performance. On the

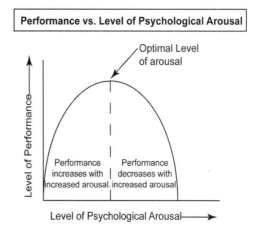

other hand too much arousal, corresponding to a paralyzing anxiety, interferes with focus and concentration and also yields low performance. A little nervousness before athletic competition activates the release of adrenaline, stimulating faster muscle contraction and enhancing performance. However, excessive amounts of adrenaline generate fatigue and decreasing performance, as predicted by the inverted-U hypothesis.

This relationship between arousal levels and performance has been validated by a century of empirical evidence and has undergone a series of successive refinements. For example, research shows that the optimal level of arousal depends upon the sport involved and the skill level of the athlete. The optimal level of arousal required for kicking a field goal is much less than that required to box fifteen rounds. Furthermore, highly successful athletes have a much higher optimal arousal level than neophytes or intermediate performers. In essence, the elite athletes have much greater stress tolerance and perform best when under substantial pressure. That is one reason why the lower-rated golfers might lead in the first-round of a major tournament on Thursday, yet are much less likely than the top-rated golfers to be in the lead in the final round on "pressure-cooker" Sunday.

Understanding the Link between the Mental and Physical

During the past 20 years, sports psychologists have discovered the powerful role of the mind in achieving peak performance in athletics. Famous baseball catcher Yogi Berra expressed this insight in his famous Yogism, "Ninety percent of this game is half mental." Athletic superstars understand that their success, relative to others, has more to do with focus and attitude than physical attributes. Arnold Palmer, who dazzled golfing fans by sinking long, formidable putts when his competitors were suffering from the yips, once observed, "You play [golf] from the shoulders up–it isn't all important, just 90%…and it may be over 90%." Palmer's insight is further elucidated by Deepak Chopra in his book *Golf for Enlightenment* (pp. 21–22).

Tournaments are won on Sunday because when players of equal skill attack the course, their emotions decide the outcome. Fear and anxiety are enormously amplified in this game; the tiniest tension in a major muscle group can throw the swing off drastically. Golf can't be mastered until you confront your emotions.

The way we think is the way we perform. On the surface this statement seems trite. So also does the familiar adage: *positive thinking yields positive results.* However, psychiatrist John Diamond validated these claims in his breakthrough book, *Life Energy* (1990), which became a seminal work in the science of kinesiology. In his research, he tested thousands of people from all walks of life, including many athletes, to investigate links between the mind and the muscles. Diamond found that a person's muscles become weaker when negative thoughts pervade the conscious mind. He found that football players who thought of nothing but catching the football tested with higher energy levels and stronger muscles than those who focused on the fear of the impact that would follow the catch. Positive thoughts stimulate the release of endorphins, while negative thoughts stimulate adrenaline. Each has an enormous impact on the way the body will function. Dr. David Hawkins (quoted in Chapter 6) asserted (p. 3), "Muscles strengthen and weaken from positive or negative emotional and intellectual stimuli. A smile will make you test strong, while the statement, 'I hate you,' will make you test weak."

Stress was found to be the physiological manifestation of negative thoughts. Conversely, those who thought positively suffered minimal stress. Diamond wrote (p. 232), "Your thoughts have the power to alter the physiological response of your muscles." This research reveals that negative thoughts are the culprits, causing athletes to press, to try too hard and to become stressed. It explains why players come back after a long layoff and perform much better. Excessive striving and stress lead to the staleness often associated with overtraining. However, during a layoff, athletes unknowingly enter an optimum mind-body place called "relaxed concentration." They have few negative expectations and intense focus, the panacea for performance in any sport.

Factors that Contribute to Competitive Anxiety

In their book *Competitive Anxiety in Sport*, sports psychologist Rainer Martens and his associates present a model that expresses the perceived threat experienced in athletic competition as a product of two variables: its perceived importance and the perceived uncertainty of the outcome (that is, Perceived Threat = Perceived Importance × Perceived Uncertainty). This means that a golfer who regards the outcome of a particular shot as important and highly uncertain will experience the shot as a significant threat and will suffer considerable anxiety. On the other hand, a golfer who is executing a shot that he perceives as unimportant and having a predictable outcome will suffer little or no anxiety. These situations and the two intermediate cases are summarized in the table.

Competitive Anxiety as a Function of Perceived Importance and Uncertainty

	Low Uncertainty	High Uncertainty
Low Importance	low perceived threat **low anxiety**	moderate perceived threat **moderate anxiety**
High Importance	moderate perceived threat **moderate anxiety**	high perceived threat **high anxiety**

This idea helps to explain why the athletic superstars are able to function in high-pressure situations without experiencing debilitating anxiety. During the thousands of hours of practice they invest in developing a skill, they become more proficient in its execution. More importantly, athletes begin to *believe* that they can execute the skill successfully. This belief becomes a self-fulfilling prophecy that further increases proficiency, resulting in high confidence in performing that skill. This high confidence minimizes the uncertainty of the outcome and hence the anxiety, *even when the perceived importance of the outcome is high*. Top professional golfers experience high arousal during an important tournament, but their confidence in their ability to execute a particular shot enables them to focus on executing the skill, thereby blocking out or substantially reducing the anxiety. As Tiger Woods, master of spectacular game-winning shots, once confided, "I believe in every shot I hit that I can pull it off. It's just, I guess, my mind-set. I've always believed that."

Transcending Anxiety and Achieving Relaxed Concentration

Most world-class athletes know from experience that it is impossible to focus while anxious. They develop techniques for avoiding the negative thoughts that generate anxiety. A technique that many use is to find a fantasy and escape into that world where doubts and "what-ifs?" can't exist. At crunch time, the mind must calm the emotions and allow the body to do what it has learned during the thousands of hours of practice. In *Breaking the Surface*, Greg Louganis spoke often about how he would enter a kind of metaphysical state prior to a critical Olympic dive. To focus with intensity, he would climb the high board and start envisioning perfection while reciting the words from *Wiz*, "You must believe." For him the state was euphoric and it drove out all negative energy inside him. He wrote, "If you have to think, it's over. It's reflex, so you must have it within, or you have already hit the water."

When Louganis says, "It's reflex," he is expressing what kinesiologists refer to as muscle memory, i.e., the sequences of neuron firings that are recorded in the right hemisphere of the brain. In Chapter 5, I explained that conquering the "yips" in golf is about quieting the left brain and allowing the right brain (the location of muscle memory) to prevail. Research by kinesiologist Debbie Crews at Arizona State University has provided recent evidence of a significant difference in brain activity between expert and novice golfers. As reported in the *Wall Street Journal* (April 18, 2005, R3):

Professor Crews fitted golfers with specially equipped helmets that record brain waves through an EEG, or electroencephalogram. She found that as experts get ready to swing, left-hemisphere activity–associated with analyzing the shots and planning their mechanics–quiets down. At that point, the right hemisphere, which is known for integrative and holistic thinking, takes over. But in less-skilled players, or those who choke, the brain does not hand off activity to the right hemisphere. Their left brain keeps frantically thinking, OK, head down, feet planted...It's trying to think the ball into the air or the hole. Sending information to the motor cortex right up until the moment of the swing can mean too much information to the muscles–and shots that go awry.

By quieting the left brain, the athletic superstar reduces anxiety and creates an optimum environment for concentration and focus. But quieting the left brain means trusting your instincts to execute the skill effectively. In golf, the adage is "Trust your swing." Even in a sport as intense as the 100-meter dash, optimal performance requires *relaxed* concentration. Florence Griffith-Joyner, reflecting on the new world record of 10.48 seconds that she set in the 1988 Olympic Trials, commented (Orlick, p. 126), "The 10.60 [time for the run in the first round of the competition] made me realize if I continued to concentrate on what I'm doing and stay relaxed, my times would continue to drop."

Reaching a Higher Level of Consciousness

Deepak Chopra described a higher level of consciousness that golfers experience when they enter a state of relaxed concentration (p. 51), "There are moments when the hole [seems to change size], or when a distant green suddenly jumps so near and you feel you could reach out and touch the flagstick. These are not optical illusions but a key to the game..." Referring to professional golfer Billy Mayfair, who achieved a record score of 27 for nine holes in the fourth round of the 2001 Buick Open, Chopra said, "When asked what happened during his 'near-perfect' round, Mayfair replied, 'Every hole looked as big as a bathtub. All I did was try to get out of my own way.'"

Michael Jordan was in a similar state during that memorable playoff game against Portland on June 14, 1998. He was amazed to see his shots, one after the other, ripping the basket. In his inimitable charismatic style he looked at the broadcast booth and just shook his head in bewilderment. In this state one feels invincible, as if lifted into a higher level of consciousness in which all things are achievable. He often played on a different plane, once stating, "Basketball is like meditation to me, it's all visionary." Jordan's trance-like focus even concerned the coaches of the Chicago Bulls: they worried that his teammates would be distracted by his surreal performance and become spectators.

Those who have visited this zone of relaxed concentration find the experience mystical and mesmerizing. When in this altered state of consciousness, every putt goes in, tennis aces are easy, and motoring down the ice or soccer pitch is pure ecstasy and is effortless. You may recall from Chapter 5 how Pelé described the "near mystical state" he entered while in the midst of action in the World Cup game against Sweden:

I felt a strange calmness...It was a type of euphoria; I felt I could run all day without tiring, that I could dribble through any of their team or all of them, that I could almost pass through them physically. I felt I could not be hurt. It was a very strange feeling and one I had never felt before. Perhaps it was merely confidence, but I have felt confident many times without that strange feeling of invincibility.

Describing a stage win in the 1999 Tour de France, Lance Armstrong recalled a similar state of seemingly boundless energy (Armstrong, 2001, p. 236):

On a small curve, I swung to the inside of the group, stood up, and accelerated. My bike seemed to jump ahead...Johan [in the follow car] checked my heart rate via the digital computer readout, so he knew how hard I was working and how stressed my body was. I was a 180 [heartbeats per minute], not in distress. I felt as though I was just cruising along a flat road, riding comfortably...It was strange, but I still didn't feel a thing. It was...effortless.

Many athletic superstars have been accused of leaving their consciousness in the locker room. Legendary coach Pop Warner said that Jim Thorpe ran the football like a man possessed. He told the press that Thorpe functioned in a kind of reverie, an ethereal state more supernatural than natural. Athletes who are able to achieve this altered state of consciousness are special. Sports commentators and other spectators witnessing their performances are often heard to utter in disbelief, "that shot was unconscious." It now appears that these phrases are more literal than figurative. Superstars are "unconscious" and that is why they are able to perform well beyond the norm. In *The Evolution of Consciousness*, medical researcher Robert Ornstein explained, "We cannot consciously control our actions and still function at peak. Quick actions are below consciousness." Renowned psychiatrist David Hawkins wrote (p. 172), "High states of consciousness are frequently experienced by athletes–sublime states of peace and joy."

The Zen Zone

In their quest to achieve the ultimate spiritual experience, Buddhists developed the Zen concept centuries ago. In its purest form, Zen is a state of the mind in which the mental and physical parts of one's being are brought together in a harmonious unity–a state in which man is at one with nature. This concept was applied to the martial arts where it was developed as a method of focusing mental power to execute physical actions with maximum effect. A visual exposition of Zen in this context was presented in the movie *The Last Samurai*, in the scenes in which actor Tom Cruise is taught the art of swordsmanship. In his book *Zen and Japanese Culture*, author Daisetz T. Suzuki further describes the concept of Zen in that context (pp. 94, 96):

If one really wishes to be master of an art, technical knowledge is not enough. One has to transcend technique so that the art grows out of the unconscious...In such cases, you cease to be your own conscious master but become an instrument in the hands of the unknown...it is for this reason that the sword moves where it ought to move and makes the contest end victoriously. This is the practical application of the Lao-tzuan doctrine of doing by not doing.

Sports psychologist Terry Orlick describes what is sometimes called the "Zen zone" (Orlick, p. 155–6):

Entering the Zen zone means becoming one with and inseparable from the essence of what you are doing during each moment you are actually doing it. It is being all here, totally present, absorbing yourself in, connecting yourself to, and becoming one with your body, your task, nature...There are times for thinking and reflection, but there are also times to connect totally with what you are doing and to leave your conscious thinking behind. Performance is a time for connection rather than reflection.

Orlick cites several examples of athletes from a variety of different sports who describe their mental states when achieving peak athletic performance. Among these is a vivid description from the great Spanish bullfighter Juan Belmonte whom Orlick quotes (p. 157):

All at once I forgot the public, the other bullfighters, myself, and even the bull...They say that my passes with the cape and my work with the muleta that afternoon were a revelation of the art of bullfighting. I don't know, and I'm not competent to judge. I simply fought as I believe one ought to fight, without a thought, outside of my own faith in what I was doing. With the last bull I succeeded for the first time in my life in delivering myself and my soul to the pure joy of fighting without being consciously aware of an audience.

Getting into the zone is about marrying the various elements of the self into one cohesive, directed and well-prepared automated machine. It isn't about trying hard or about transcendental meditation. It is about becoming so relaxed–removing the mind from the task at hand–while remaining totally focused. Action is then fluid and the conscious mind has deferred to instinct.

Jim Thorpe was the personification of "performance in the zone" long before sports psychologists coined the phrase. His ability to visualize, to be "at one with his environment" and to achieve relaxed concentration of the highest order enabled him to excel at every sport he attempted. This ability derived from the deep inner spiritual cadence that resonated with the naturally free culture of the Sac and Fox tribe. Dr. Joseph Alexander, who was a three-time All-American at Syracuse University, declared (Wheeler, p. 121):

> *[Thorpe's] movements were all easy, simple and flexible, and most important of all, he never played football with any anxiety or fear or anything to hinder his mind from acting on a split second's notice.*

It is not easy to enter the Zen zone. Like happiness, it cannot be pursued directly, but must ensue as a by-product of optimal functioning. Though we cannot prescribe a procedure for performing in the zone, we can identify some of the precursors for achieving this state. For example, we know that performance in the zone demands an inner confidence that borders on arrogance, coupled with total relaxation and the absence of anxiety. All of the athletes quoted above described the euphoric and strangely peaceful feeling that accompanied their performance in the zone. They were excited and psychologically aroused, but not anxious. Their confidence came from their belief in their ability to execute the skills they had learned in practice and their calm came from their ability to block out the negative and enjoy the intensity of their focus.

Recently, the concept of performing in the zone is personified by young phenomenon Tiger Woods. The man adorned in power crimson on Sunday afternoons is not there to lose. Prior to a crucial putt, he can be seen cupping his hands around his eyes to block out his peripheral vision and intensify his focus. Tiger is known for his remarkable ability to transcend the distractions of spectators and the media and then emerge from the intensity with a miraculous shot. He has become the model for performance in the zone.

Before we delve into what makes him tick, I invite you to use the following self-assessment to help you determine your own proclivity for performance in the zone.

ZONE PROPENSITY SELF-ASSESSMENT–Can You Get in the Zone?

Choose a number 1–5, with 1 the lowest and 5 the highest, to indicate the degree to which you believe the statement describes you or how you feel. Record for each statement the number you have chosen. The scoring key is at the bottom of the page.

	Strongly Disagree				Strongly Agree
1. I am able to relax even at crunch time.	1	2	3	4	5
2. I am able to psyche-up without psyching out, e.g. tossing clubs.	1	2	3	4	5
3. I can compete aggressively while having fun at competing.	1	2	3	4	5
4. I am able to become so absorbed in the moment that I block hecklers.	1	2	3	4	5
5. I often visualize my goals before I execute my skills.	1	2	3	4	5
6. Friends tell me I'm oblivious to what's going on around me.	1	2	3	4	5
7. I tend to lose track of time when I'm playing a game.	1	2	3	4	5
8. I have the ability to remain totally confident when things go wrong.	1	2	3	4	5
9. Even when upset, I am able to refocus on the task at hand.	1	2	3	4	5
10. I am able to suspend judgment to escape into a fantasy story.	1	2	3	4	5
11. I have an unquestioning belief in my ability to learn a new skill.	1	2	3	4	5
12. I don't believe that people can beat me on talent alone.	1	2	3	4	5
13. Friends say that I'm unrealistically optimistic.	1	2	3	4	5
14. When faced with a unique problem, I usually find options.	1	2	3	4	5
15. I trust my instincts, even when they contradict current wisdom.	1	2	3	4	5
16. I am willing to execute a skill without engaging the conscious mind.	1	2	3	4	5
17. I tend to be in control of my emotions in almost all situations.	1	2	3	4	5
18. I tend to rebound well from adversity and injury.	1	2	3	4	5
19. I find pleasure in focusing deeply during competition.	1	2	3	4	5
20. I sometimes sense that I will sink a long putt or hit a winning tennis shot, just before I execute the skill successfully.	1	2	3	4	5

Instructions	Scoring Key
Total the numbers you chose for all 20 items. Then use the scoring key to determine your propensity to perform in the zone.	**90–100:** You are well-suited to performing in the zone. **80–89:** With a little practice, you can perform in the zone. **70–79:** To perform in the zone, you need to learn to focus. **Below 70:** You need to learn to control your emotions.

TIGER WOODS

- In 2005, named by *Fortune Magazine* as second most influential celebrity in the U.S.

- U.S. Junior Amateur Champion in 1991, 1992 and 1993.

- U.S. Amateur Champion in 1994, 1995 and 1996.

- In 1997, won the Masters by 12 strokes–the largest margin in the history of that event.

- In 2001, won the U.S. Open by 15 strokes–the largest margin in the history of that event.

- In the four majors spanning 2000–2001, won the Grand Slam of Golf.

Tiger Woods: The Competitor Who Epitomizes Performance in the Zone

© Mitchell Gerber/CORBIS

**Tiger Woods
born Dec. 30, 1975**

When Tiger Woods walked to the first tee at Augusta National on Sunday, April 10, 2005, he was facing one of the greatest challenges of his life. Winless during the past ten major tournaments on the PGA Tour, he was experiencing the longest drought of his career–a drought spanning almost three years. There was already speculation that Tiger, at 29 years of age, was past his prime and that the era of his dominance of golf was now a chapter in its history. It was 8:00 a.m. Rain delays the previous day required that he now play the final nine holes of the third round of the Masters Tournament and then play the 18 holes of the final round. It would be a long day.

With a score of 74 on the first round of the Tournament, Tiger had been in danger of missing the cut, but a 66 in the second round put him back in the race. Gathering momentum like a racehorse coming down the home stretch, Tiger had served notice on the rest of the field by scoring birdies on his last four holes on Saturday. Chris DiMarco, who had been at the top of the leader board for the first three days of the Tournament, was now looking over his shoulder as Tiger approached the starting gate. Looking down the tenth fairway, Woods appeared to be gathering his focus. The world watched, wondering if the greatest force in modern golf could pull off a miracle in the home stretch and snatch the green jacket from DiMarco's grasp. He was trailing DiMarco by a formidable four strokes. If ever there was a time when "first-tee jitters" would rear its ugly head, this was it. But Tiger ripped his drive down the fairway and the race was on!

On that electrically charged Sunday morning, Tiger Woods launched his attack with birdies on the first three holes. He entertained the spectators with a masterful display of golfing skill, completing the third round of this revered tournament with a phenomenal 65. Before noon, Tiger had moved from four strokes behind DiMarco to a three-stroke lead.

Heading into the fourth and final round, Tiger and Chris were paired in what would become one of sports' most dramatic head-to-head battles of skill and focus. Tiger was on fire and had the advantage of momentum, but DiMarco, hungry for his first victory in a PGA major, was tenaciously trying to hold on to what had been in his grasp from day one. It seemed that the golf gods were determined to test the mettle of both combatants by hurling every possible adversity their way. Slick greens and tough pin placements that reward and punish risk-taking are typical challenges on Sundays, but this day they seemed ever more potent. Both DiMarco and Woods struggled through all the obstacles that Augusta National put between them and the Butler Cabin. By the time they reached the 16th hole of that final round, the drama was rising to an almost unbearable climax. DiMarco had moved to within a single stroke of Tiger and there were only three holes left to play.

The 16th hole at Augusta is a test of nerves disguised as an aesthetically pleasing, 170-yard, par-three hole. A menacing azure-blue pond runs along the left side of the lush fairway, threatening the intrepid golfer who dares hit to the left side of a giant green that slopes precipitously toward the water. When the pin is located on the back left portion of the green (where it usually resides on "pressure-cooker" Sunday), a cautious tee-shot is punished by a probable three-putt. Furthermore, a ball hit deep into the green often rolls off the back, making par particularly difficult to achieve. It was in this position that Tiger Woods found himself after his tee shot. DiMarco, launching an attack on Tiger's fragile lead, landed his tee shot on the green about 20 feet from the pin. It seemed highly likely that Tiger would bogey. If DiMarco sank his putt for a birdie, he would have the lead with only two holes to play–a huge psychological advantage. What happened in the minutes that followed has been recorded as one of the most spectacular moments in the history of golf.

The outcome of the first major tournament of the 2005 PGA Tour was hanging in the balance. All the practice throughout the winter months, culminating in three arduous rounds at Augusta, had come down to this single shot on the 70th hole of play! From the left backside of the green, Tiger studied the pin position and the steep left-to-right slope toward the pin. It was clear that a ball hit left and above the hole would roll down toward the cup, gathering momentum as it rolled past the hole and toward the water. A small error in the angle of approach or the force applied to the ball would inevitably result in a bogey. With all the world watching and the adrenaline pumping, the chances that Tiger would execute a flawless shot seemed miniscule. Who could possibly achieve the focus and emotional calm necessary to transcend this enormous pressure?

Tiger studied the position of his ball, visualized its curvilinear path, and rehearsed the execution of his stroke. Then, as the world hung in silence, he swept his club through the ball with the precision of a surgeon's knife, chipping it above the hole in the hope that it might roll toward the cup and stop within a foot or two of the hole. The ball landed on the green above the hole and checked up, seeming to pause momentarily as it changed direction and then began rolling toward the cup. As it rotated down the slope, gathering momentum, the Nike swoosh on the ball was intermittently blurred and visible until it came to rest on the lip of the cup. Suspended in limbo, hovering on the edge of the precipice, it wavered while the world gallery rose to its feet. And then, as if touched by a subterranean tremor, the Nike logo swooshed once more and the ball teetered into the cup.

The roar from aficionados throughout the golfing world acknowledged that the impossible can sometimes occur. When Chris DiMarco missed his birdie putt, Tiger took a daunting two-stroke lead. In one single swoosh, he had shifted the momentum, snatching a victory from the jaws of defeat. Though Chris DiMarco scrambled to tie the match by the end of the final round, there was an air of inevitability about the ultimate outcome of this epic battle. Tiger won with a birdie on the first playoff hole, capturing his fourth green jacket and winning his ninth major PGA tournament. He was now half-way to reaching his ultimate goal–the record 18 wins in PGA major championships held by Jack Nicklaus.

Though both golfers displayed remarkable shot-making abilities and showcased golf at its highest level, this contest was not really about golf. Rather, it was about superb athletic performance under enormous emotional pressure and stress. Both golfers exuded the ability to focus intensely and establish a harmony of mind and spirit needed to execute fine motor skills when the stakes were virtually infinite. In the end, it was Tiger Woods who, at the crucial moment of play, was able to perform in the zone and execute at a level that can only be described as surreal.

Tiger Woods' Trek to the Top

Early Imprints

Earl Woods was a man with a dream. Orphaned at age 13, he was mothered by his eldest sister Hattie who raised him and his four siblings. A talented baseball player, he won a scholarship to Kansas State University and became the only black player in what is now the Big Eight Conference. Racial taunts and hostile comments from baseball fans, and his prohibition from eating in the same restaurants as his white teammates, prompted Earl to say that there were two colors in America: white and non-white. These experiences forged his resolve to one day address the social inequities and enhance the status of blacks in the United States.

During the 1960s, he joined the U.S. Army, serving as a Green Beret in Vietnam and fighting alongside his closest friend Colonel Nguyen T. Phong, known as "Tiger." During their near-death experiences fighting the North Vietnamese, Earl and Tiger became as close as brothers. Earl credited his friend with saving his life on several occasions and resolved that if he survived to have children, he would name his first son Tiger in his friend's honor.

While on an information assignment to Bangkok, Thailand, Earl met a pretty Thai girl named Kultida Punsawad who was a secretary in the U.S. Army office there. Kultida, later known to the world as "Tida," came from a Buddhist background and exuded the disciplined, reflective nature of the Thai culture. Earl and Tida fell in love, and in 1969 they were married. When the war in Vietnam ended, they moved to Brooklyn, N.Y. where Earl served at Fort Hamilton. It was while stationed there that Earl Woods, at 42 years of age, was introduced to golf. A fellow officer, who happened to be a competent golfer, challenged Earl to a game at the Fort Dix golf course. Earl's natural athletic ability enabled him to score 91 in his first 17 holes of golf, but it was not enough to win the wager or the bragging rights from the hustler and Earl conceded without playing the last hole. The loss of his money and his pride drove Earl to practice his golfing skills with a vengeance in the months that followed. During a return match four months later, Earl scored an 81, recovering his money and his pride. He was now hooked on golf.

After retiring from the military, Earl and Tida moved to Orange County, California, where Earl found employment negotiating materials contracts for the McDonnell Douglas rocket program. A short time later, on December 30, 1975, Tida gave birth to their first and only child, Eldrick Tiger Woods.

Now obsessed with golf, Earl lamented that he had discovered the game too late in life to develop his skills to their full potential. He resolved that this would not happen to his son. Earl often placed tiny Tiger in a high chair in the garage where the young child could watch his father hitting golf balls into a net for hours at a time. Whether it was subliminal conditioning or a natural inclination is not clear, but when Tiger was ten months old he climbed down from the high chair and swung his dad's putter like an accomplished golfer. Charged with excitement, Earl summoned Tida to witness the birth of a champion.

Research scientists have recently uncovered what they call *mirror neurons* that may explain Tiger's precocity. Apparently, children learn to mimic the actions they see early in life. This so-called "muscle-memory of the mind" was reported by Christian Keysers of the University of Groningen, who explained (*Wall Street Journal*, 1A, Begley, March 4, 2005), "We start to feel actions and sensations (of others) in our own cortex as if we were doing these actions and having these sensations."

From that early episode, it was clear that Tiger was eager to play. Earl became Tiger's role model and the passion for golf passed from father to son as if by osmosis. Years later, in an interview with *Golf Digest*, Tiger reported, "I have been infatuated with the game of golf since my pop first put a club in my hands when I was a toddler. I was an only child and the club and ball became my playmates." By the time his son could walk, Earl took him to the golf course and showed him the nuances of this difficult game. With his father as coach and mentor, Tiger honed his strategies on the tees and greens, as well as in the sand and the rough. Before his third birthday, the young prodigy was featured on the *Mike Douglas Show* in a putting and driving contest against Bob Hope. At age three, he won a Pitch, Putt and Drive competition against 10- and 11-year-olds, and just before his fourth birthday, he shot a 48 from the red tees on the back nine of the Navy course in Cypress, California. On August 27, 1980, at the age of four, Tiger made his first birdie on the par-three 91-yard hole at Heartwell Park Golf Club.

At this time, Earl solicited the help of golf pro Rudy Duran to help coach Tiger and build on the foundation that Earl had established. By age six, Tiger was competing in tournaments throughout southern California. At eight, he won his first Junior World 10-and-under championship with a five-under-par 51 at Presidio Hills in California, and at ten years of age he added a second Junior World championship. On one occasion, Tiger complained to his coach, "I keep shooting for the pin and the ball keeps backing up. How can I stop it?" The amused golf pro advised him that achieving such backspin is the fantasy of almost every golfer in America and that he shouldn't change a thing.

During Tiger's evolution as a golfer, Earl subjected his protégé to what he called *psychological warfare*. Recognizing that golf is predominantly a mental game requiring total focus and emotional control, Earl would attempt to distract Tiger at critical moments. He would rip the Velcro on his glove when the lad was in his backswing or remind him not to hook when he was perilously close to the out-of-bounds markers on the left. Tida, who also played a role in helping Tiger develop mental toughness, took a different approach. She took him to the Buddhist temple where he learned meditation and mind-control skills. She explained that golf is a gentleman's game, and that the kind of spoiled-child behavior modeled by tennis stars like Conners and McEnroe was both reprehensible and unacceptable. However, not wishing to diminish his killer instinct, she cautioned (Rosaforte, p. 20), "When you are ahead, don't take it easy, kill them. After the finish, then be a sportsman." This mental conditioning from both parents helped Tiger learn how to achieve total focus and enter a state of relaxed concentration–a technique that would prove invaluable when he entered the realm of high-stakes competition.

When Tiger was ten, Earl retained golf pro John Anselmo of Meadowlark GC in Huntington Beach, CA to bring Tiger's game to the next level. Within a year, Eldrick Tiger Woods had eclipsed his father and mentor. In *Training a Tiger*, Earl admitted (p. 23), "Tiger first really beat me when he was eleven. I was trying my best, but he honestly whipped me. I haven't come close to beating him since, and I never will." Earl had nurtured and unleashed a Tiger that had now outgrown his trainer. In formulating his goals, the precocious pre-teen posted a chart on his bedroom wall showing the ages at which Jack Nicklaus had won each of the major tournaments. Years later, describing to Tim Crothers of *Sports Illustrated* the motivation behind the chart, he mused, "I wanted to be the youngest player ever to win the majors. Nicklaus was my hero, and I thought it would be great to accomplish all the things he did even earlier than he accomplished them."

The Relentless Climb to the Top

In 1988 at the age of 56, Earl Woods retired to help his son prepare for a future as a professional golfer. Tiger and his father became inseparable, traveling all over America, Canada and Mexico. Under the tutelage of John Anselmo, Tiger's game continued to improve and in August 1989 at the age of 13, Tiger entered his first national tournament, the 21st Insurance Golf Classic. After making the cut, he was paired in the third round with two-time Arkansas player of the year, John Daly. After nine holes, the 5' 6", 107-lb grade-eight student was three under par and the 23-year-old Daly was one over. Determined not to lose to this thirteen-year-old, Daly, who was already a PGA professional of some reputation, had to scramble to save face. He later opined, "That kid is great…I had heard a lot of good things about him, but he is better than I heard." At the conclusion of the tournament, Tiger had come second to seventeen-year-old Justin Leonard. While still in elementary school, Tiger had become almost unbeatable against amateurs of virtually any age and was already better than many professionals.

It was at this time that Dr. Jay Brunza, a sports psychologist and captain in the U.S. Navy, joined "Team Tiger." Brunza worked with the eager teenager to develop his powers of concentration and has been credited with teaching Tiger the secrets to "playing in the zone." In *Think Like Tiger*, author John Andrisani states (p. 63):

> *Tiger plays the game with such ease that it's obvious his subconscious mind allows him to execute impossible-looking shots due to a stress-free state of mind and a super-confident attitude that he learned through meditation and by working with Brunza.*

Observing Tiger's approach to golf as a teen, one teaching pro said (Strege, p. 78), "As a kid Tiger was composing shots in his head just as Mozart composed music in his head before writing it."

By the time Tiger was fourteen, he was a 2-handicap at the tough 6,820-yard Navy course. The course professional David Smith was effusive in his praise of his remarkable play (Rosaforte, p. 26):

> *What sets [Tiger] apart is his mental approach to the game. I have been a PGA professional for 13 years, almost as long as he's been alive, and he knows more about the game than I do. I have never known anyone who was so naturally adaptable mentally to the game as Tiger.*

The Contract in a Drawer

We live in a world of visual media, featuring corporate logos, celebrity endorsements, and images of superstars as prominent icons of billion-dollar marketing campaigns. Multi-national corporations and even institutes of higher learning seek to enhance their images by associating themselves or their products with celebrities. The quest to identify superstars early–long before they enter their supernova stage–drives these institutions to court potential celebrities in their infancy. Future NBA players are scouted in elementary school and often have what Pelé called a "contract in a drawer" before they are old enough to have a legally binding signature. Thus it is not surprising that Tiger was approached with an offer when he was only 13 years old and still in elementary school. What is surprising is that the first overture came not from a corporation, but from a most prestigious institute of higher learning–Stanford. Apparently, Wally Goodwin, the coach of Stanford's golf team, got wind of Tiger's remarkable achievements in junior amateur golf.

Urgently in need of golfing talent, he wrote to Tiger saying, "If you ever want to take a shot at Stanford, drop me a line." In a response dated April 23, 1989, Tiger wrote a letter, from which some excerpts are reprinted below:

Dear Coach Goodwin:

Thank you for your recent letter expressing Stanford's interest in me as a future student and golfer. At first it was hard for me to understand why a university like Stanford was interested in a thirteen-year-old seventh grader and after talking with my father I have come to understand and appreciate the honor you have given me.

...My goal is to obtain a quality business education...My GPA this year is 3.86 and I plan to keep it there or higher when I enter high school...Ultimately I would like to be a PGA professional.

Hope to hear from you again.
Sincerely,
Tiger Woods 5-5/100   (These numbers give his height and weight.)

The seeds that Goodwin sowed in 1989 would bear fruit four years later. On November 10, 1993, Tiger announced that he would be enrolling at Stanford after graduation from high school. In the fall of 1994, he enrolled in a customized program that combined business and economics courses.

Within a year after Goodwin's overtures on behalf of Stanford, Earl was approached by Hughes Norton, Vice-President of International Management Group (IMG), who had managed several top golfers including Arnold Palmer. Attempting to convince Mr. Norton of Tiger's potential as a commercial commodity, Earl said, "The first black superstar on the tour is going to make himself and somebody else a whole lot of money." Mr. Norton responded, "That's why we're here, Mr. Woods." Tiger was fourteen years old at the time.

During the ten years from age five to fifteen, Tiger was refining his game in amateur tournaments wherever they were played. In 1991, at the age of 15, he became the youngest golfer in history to win the U.S. Junior Amateur Championship. He repeated as U.S. Junior Amateur Champion in 1992 and 1993, becoming the only person ever to win this title more than once. The legend of the Tiger was growing, and stories of this wunderkind were circulating in ever-higher echelons of the golfing world. But many bright young stars have appeared on the horizon only to sputter, flare and then fizzle into oblivion. The ultimate test of Tiger's golfing prowess was yet to come.

Life's Best Teacher

In 1993, Tiger reached for the brass ring. Having just won his third consecutive U.S. Junior Amateur, he was poised to make history by winning in the same year the U.S. Amateur to be held at the Champions Golf Club in Houston, Texas. Next year he would be too old to play in the Junior Amateur, so this would be his only opportunity to capture this unprecedented double crown.

Tiger's press clippings preceded him into the U.S. Amateur Championship. From early in his career, a major part of the Tiger legend focused on his distance off the tee. At age 15, while playing in the Nissan Los Angeles Open, he drove the ball 344 yards and followed with a nine-iron to reach the 504-yard par-5 hole in two. In that same year he became the topic of post-competition conversation in the Bel Air clubhouse after reaching the 575-yard 14th green in two shots. Not only was this assumed to be impossible, but Tiger had reached the green with an iron! Then, the day after his 16th birthday, Tiger had a chance to play the Great White Shark, Greg Norman, on the Shark's home course in Florida. Norman was one of the superstars on the PGA Tour and the previous year was second longest off the tee with an average driving distance of 282.3 yards. Biographer Rosaforte captures the drama of that encounter after Greg Norman crushed his drive down the long fairway of the par-5 second hole (p. 49):

It was as if he was saying, "OK, kid, top that." Woods certainly tried. His drive came off the clubface like a tracer, and from the tee, it was hard to tell whose ball went farther, Norman's or Woods'. It was a macho thing, an immediate test of manhood, the 180-pound Shark and the 140-pound Tiger checking each other out for the first time. As they drove up to their balls making small talk, Norman was a little shocked to see that...damn! He had been outdriven by the U.S. Junior champion. It wasn't the last time that Norman hit first to the green. "He was 4–5 yards past me," Norman said. "That little shit was driving it by me all day."

Now, at 17 years of age, as he entered the U.S. Amateur, Tiger was no longer a 140-pound adolescent. His greater size and strength enabled him to drive the ball consistently over 300 yards and routinely reach the par-5 greens in two. Stories of his gargantuan tee shots were blowing through the golfing world like tumbleweed in a Texas windstorm. Tiger's presence in a tournament was beginning to intimidate his competitors.

The Champions Golf Club, site of the U.S. Amateur, is a long, punishing course well-suited to those who are long off the tee. Tiger's powerful drives would give him a significant advantage, particularly on the par fives. Furthermore, the Tournament was a match-play format (the winner being the player winning the most holes, not total score), so a long-ball hitter could let out the shaft, risking an errant drive without putting himself hopelessly behind. The odds were certainly stacked in Tiger's favor.

No one was surprised when Tiger Woods scored even par in the qualifying round of stroke play, nor when he breezed through his first round of match play, winning in 14 holes by scoring three birdies and an eagle. However, his head-to-head with English golfer Paul Page proved to be more of a challenge than anticipated. The Brit seemed to sink every putt in sight and after Tiger scored a double-bogey on the 16th hole, Page was two holes up on Tiger. When Tiger missed the fairway on the 17th hole and Page got up and down in par from a green-side bunker, Tiger lost the match and his only opportunity to capture the double-amateur crown.

As I've noted in previous chapters, failure is often the catalyst to breakthrough change. Tiger's defeat in the 1993 U.S. Amateur offers further validation. Realizing that his son's occasional hook was preventing him from reaching the next level, Earl Woods decided to enlist the help of Claude "Butch" Harmon. Harmon is the coach who was credited with the highly successful transformations in the swings of Greg Norman and Davis Love and has the reputation as the consummate guru in swing technique. Harmon instructed Tiger to widen his stance, reduce his hip turn, increase the length of his takeaway, and shorten his backswing. Modifying a swing that he had learned and grooved in his formative years would not be easy, but Tiger understood the importance of practice and tackled the transformation with passion and commitment. Harmon's coaching paid huge dividends. After almost a year of implementing the suggested swing changes, Tiger emerged with a more consistent swing and more confidence off the tee.

Tiger's loss in the U.S. Amateur Championship in 1993 cost him the opportunity traditionally granted the top amateur-to play the following year in the three great majors: The Masters, The U.S. Open and The British Open. To qualify for these tournaments in 1995, Tiger would have to win the U.S. Amateur Championship in 1994. What he needed now, more than anything else, was the opportunity to play against golfers at the highest level. They would challenge him to reach his full potential.

The 1994 U.S. Amateur Championship

It was at this time that Tiger's informal association with IMG began to pay dividends. As Tiger prepared for the 1994 U.S. Amateur, IMG used their powerful connections to arrange for him to play with top PGA professionals in overseas tournaments in Thailand, Indonesia and other locations in Southeast Asia. The wunderkind played with and against such golf superstars as Norman, Couples, Faldo and Langer. During early 1994, Tiger learned from the greatest and came to the U.S. Amateur ready to make his mark.

It is said that success is what happens when readiness meets opportunity. Indeed, Tiger was ready when he entered the U.S. Amateur at TPC-Sawgrass in Ponte Vedra, Florida. Harmon's coaching had stabilized his swing, giving him more consistency without loss of distance. Brunza had helped him learn how to achieve relaxed concentration in the midst of emotional chaos, and IMG had provided him with a rich opportunity to test his mettle against the best golfers in the world. As might be expected, Tiger breezed through the qualifying rounds with scores of 65 and 72 and won his first four matches–three without serious jeopardy. In the match against Buddy Alexander, Tiger was three down with five holes to play. Facing imminent elimination, Woods intensified his focus. Alexander self-destructed and Tiger managed to survive.

By the time he reached the final against the formidable Trip Kuehne, the drama was building. Kuehne birdied seven of the first 13 holes, putting him four holes up on Tiger at the end of the first 18. When Kuehne won the sixth hole of the final 18, Woods was trailing by five, with just 12 holes left to play. Tiger couldn't afford to tie; he had to win five holes outright just to force a playoff. It appeared he would have to wait another year for a crack at the U.S. Amateur Championship and an opportunity to play in the majors.

At a time when most golfers would mentally concede and fold their tents, Tiger dug in, winning five of the next 10 holes and splitting the others. Kuehne and Woods were dead even as they approached the formidable 17th hole at TPC-Sawgrass. This is the famous par-3 dragon with the island green, and the surrounding water that has literally (and figuratively) swallowed the balls of golf's greatest heroes. The PGA professionals have learned from harsh experience that hitting to the right edge usually ends in disaster as the slightest gust of wind or error in direction lands the ball in the water, resulting in a bogey or double-bogey. Of course, the pin was located on the right side of the green, perilously close to the water. Selecting a wedge, Tiger stared down the flag 139 yards away and slammed hard into the ball. It soared skyward, then plummeted like a rocket on re-entry into the atmosphere, bounced on the green between the pin and the water, then spun backward, coming to rest about three feet from a watery grave and about 14 feet from the cup.

By the time Tiger lined up his putt, he was already in the zone. As if guided by an unconscious force, he rolled the ball into the cup for a birdie that put him one hole up. Later, he was unable to recall any of the details of the putt. As biographer Rosaforte observed (p. 96), "Afterward Woods couldn't remember the distance, the break or the grain. He couldn't even remember hitting the putt or the celebration that followed. He was too zoned out."

As Tiger approached the 440-yard 18th hole, Jay Brunza encouraged him to stay in his state of relaxed concentration. Water on the left of the fairway intimidates right-handed golfers, reminding them of the dire consequences of a hook and fracturing their focus. But Tiger used the prudence he had learned from his earlier mistakes. He selected a two-iron and hammered the ball beyond the hazard. His tee shot was long enough for him to reach the green with a seven-iron, and he two-putted for a par to win the match by two holes. National coverage on ESPN enabled the world to watch what Rosaforte called "the greatest comeback in the 99-year history of the event."

Earl rushed to the 18th green and embraced his son, celebrating a watershed moment in their journey to the top of the world of amateur golf. Later Earl told his son, "You have done something that no black person in the United States has ever done, and you will forever be a part of history."

After winning the U.S. Amateur Championship in 1994, Tiger continued the winning streak that began after his loss in 1993. He won all his matches during the remainder of his amateur career, capturing the U.S. Amateur again in 1995 and 1996, achieving an unprecedented three consecutive U.S. Amateur titles.

Turning Professional

Superstars are always looking for higher mountains to climb. With his three-peat in the U.S. Amateur, it was clear that Tiger had outgrown amateur golf and it was time to turn professional. It was also time for the "contract in a drawer" to come out so that Tiger could begin receiving revenue from the pending endorsements that were swelling like a tsunami. Consequently, few were surprised at a press conference preceding the Greater Milwaukee Open on August 26, 1996, when Tiger, at age 20, announced that he was turning professional. Three days later, he dropped out of Stanford. On his son's behalf, Earl had negotiated the most lucrative school dropout deal in sports history. Tiger moved to Orlando to live in a condo provided by Nike and Titleist, comforted by a $60-million advance in the bank. When details of his contract leaked out, one professional golfer observed sardonically, "Here's a guy who hasn't even got his Tour card yet, and he's making $60 million."

The Greater Milwaukee Open was Tiger's first tournament as a professional. He tied for 60th and earned $2,544, placing him 344th in money winnings. However, to earn his Tour card enabling him to play on the PGA circuit in 1997, he would have to place in the top 125 in money winnings in 1996. Only ten weeks remained in the season. In a mind-boggling blitz, Tiger Woods played in six more tournaments. He finished in 11th place in the Canadian Open, fifth in the Quad City Classic, third in the B.C. Open, first in the Las Vegas Invitational, second in the LaCantera Texas Open, and first in the Disney Classic. This spectacular string of wins and high-placed finishes catapulted him into the 24th position in money winnings for the 1996 season–in a mere 10 weeks! Not only had Tiger earned his Tour card for 1997, but he had placed among the top 30 money winners. This qualified him for the PGA Tour Championship to be played at Southern Hills in Tulsa.

Following the win at Walt Disney World, Tiger Woods became an instant celebrity. He arrived at Southern Hills to a media frenzy–the beginning of a phenomenon that would become known as Tigermania. Television cameras could not sate the public's thirst for glimpses of Tiger lining up a putt, pounding a drive, chipping out of a trap, or frowning over an errant shot. Even when Tiger was not performing well, the television networks recognized that viewers found Tiger's travails more riveting than the performances of less dynamic (and more experienced) golfers, even if they were higher on the leader board.

The second round of the PGA Tour Championship was one such occasion. After scoring an even-par 70 in the first round, Tiger was just four strokes off the lead. However, on Friday his game disintegrated. He lost six strokes to par on the front nine, carding an astronomical 43. The golf world looked on incredulously, unaware that a few hours earlier Earl Woods had been rushed to the hospital with chest pains. His bypass surgery a decade earlier had revealed a tendency toward artery blockage, putting him at greater risk of heart problems. Tiger was suffering internal turmoil, agonizing over the possible loss of his closest friend, soulmate and father, yet he continued to grind through the back nine at par, finishing the second round with a 78. Then he announced, "There are more important things in life than golf. I love my dad to death, and I'm going to see him right now." Happily, Earl was declared to be "out of danger" and Tiger was able to return to the Tournament. He went on to finish the PGA Tour Championship tied for 21st, winning a total of $790,594 in 10 weeks!

Reaching into the Stratosphere of Golf

Every April, tens of millions of television viewers enjoy golf's rite of spring, feasting their eyes on the plethora of color from the budding dogwood trees, the brilliant azaleas, the majestic magnolias and the lush green fairways that define Augusta National. It is a beautiful spectacle that enhances the reputation of the Masters as the pinnacle of professional golf. No golfer is considered great until he has won a major and none can be considered the best until he has donned a green jacket, the symbol of a Masters champion. As the first major on the PGA Tour each year, a victory at the Masters yields exemptions from the grueling qualifying rounds of a multitude of tournaments. For professional golfers, and especially those from the U.S., the green jacket is considered the ultimate symbol of preeminence in golf.

Since its creation in 1933 by Bobby Jones and Clifford Roberts, Augusta National has become the symbol of the ultra-exclusive gentleman's country club. Throughout its history, it has striven for the highest standards of dress, deportment and gentlemanly conduct, commensurate with its exclusivity and old southern traditions. Characteristic of this tone is the following admonition to patrons, written by Bobby Jones in 1967 and distributed to spectators every year at the Masters.

In golf, customs of etiquette and decorum are just as important as rules governing play...Most distressing to those who love the game of golf is the applauding or cheering of misplays or misfortunes of a player. Such occurrences have been rare at the Masters, but we must eliminate them entirely if our patrons are to continue their reputation as the most knowledgeable and considerate in the world.

Membership at Augusta National is by invitation only and is closed to females. Reflecting the customs of the old south, membership was also closed to non-Caucasians until 1991 when African-American Ron Townsend became a member. In 1974, as an automatic invitee for his win in the Firestone

Classic, Lee Elder became the first black to play in the Masters. Similarly, Tiger Woods was an automatic invitee to the Masters in 1995 through 1997 for his wins at the U.S. Amateur in the preceding years. During his first Masters appearance in 1995, Tiger turned in a creditable set of scores (72–72–77–72), but in 1996, he missed the cut, having scored 75s in each of the first two rounds. Despite Tiger's poor performance that year, Jack Nicklaus was impressed by what he saw in the young man's game and made his oft-quoted prediction:

Both Arnold [Palmer] and I agree that you could take my Masters [wins] and his Masters [wins] and add them together, and this kid should win more than that. This kid is the most fundamentally sound golfer I've ever seen at almost any age.

Combined, Arnold and Jack had 10 Masters wins, so Nicklaus had set the bar high for Tiger when he came to the Masters in April 1997. No longer preoccupied with school, and with two professional tournament wins under his belt, he was ready to reach for a green jacket.

Tiger got off to a bad start in the first round, missing fairways and scrambling to recover. At the turn he was carding 40. Then he launched a charge, playing the back nine in 30 strokes–six under par–for a combined 70. Nick Faldo, the Masters Champion the previous year and Tiger's playing partner in that round, scored a 75. The next day, by capitalizing on his distance off the tee and hitting wedge shots to the pin on seven of the eighteen holes, Tiger burned up the course. He carded a 66 that put him at eight under for the tournament, giving him a three-stroke lead over Colin Montgomerie. Effusive in his praise of Tiger's spectacular performance, Jack Nicklaus said, "It's a shame Bob Jones isn't here. He could have saved the words he used for me in '63 for this young man, because he's certainly playing a game we're not familiar with."

When Tiger came to the first tee on Saturday, the field was missing several of the world's top golfers including Norman, Faldo and Mickelson who had missed the cut. Tiger had a three-stroke advantage and it was clear that he had the bit in his teeth. Though only 21 years of age, he prevailed over several seasoned professionals. He resolved to follow his mother's advice, "When you're ahead, don't take it easy, kill them." And kill them he did in the third round, scoring a brilliant 65 and tying the 54-hole record of 15 under, held by Ray Floyd. At the end of the day, Tiger led the field by nine strokes and it was clear he would be the next Masters Champion.

When Tiger Woods stepped to the first tee on Sunday, April 13, 1997, the only question in the minds of the fans was, "Will Tiger beat the record of 17 under par, held jointly by Jack Nicklaus and Ray Floyd?" As the drama unfolded, Tiger continued his pattern of long drives, followed by pitches to the green and mind-boggling putts, delivered in a calm, controlled demeanor that belied the intense pressure exerted by the elevated expectations of the golfing world. When he sank his final five-foot putt on the 18th hole, he registered a 69 for the day and a 72-hole score of 18 under par–a new Masters record and a win by a margin of 12 strokes over Tom Kite.

On what will always be considered one of the cardinal days in the history of golf, Tiger Woods transcended the field of the world's greatest golfers by a staggering margin that some believe will never be equaled. Before the 1997 Masters, winning a green jacket by 12 strokes with a record-breaking score of 18 under par was considered impossible for even the greatest seasoned golfer. After the 1997 Masters, NBC News reported, "People are talking about two types of golfers: Tiger Woods and everybody else." Achieving such stature at age 21 in one's first full season as a professional is unprecedented in any sport. It was clear to the golfing world on April 13, 1997, that Eldrick Tiger Woods had reached the stratosphere of golf.

The Grand Slam–The Holy Grail of Golf

After the 1997 Masters, few would doubt that Tiger Woods was the number one golfer in the world. However, when he failed to win a major during the next two-and-a-half years, there were rumblings among those who suggested that the '97 Masters was a flash-in-the-pan. Most of those skeptics were silenced in the fall of 1999 when Tiger won his second major, the PGA Tour Championship. He won this tournament in a dramatic showdown with the sanguine Spaniard, Sergio Garcia, who stalked him to the final hole. Later describing his thoughts in those final moments of the tournament, Tiger commented, "A bomb could be going off, [and I] probably wouldn't even know. That's the focus I had." Tiger proved once again that his ability to focus–to perform in the zone–made him the best player in the world. But the world hadn't seen anything yet.

Like all athletic superstars, Tiger's victories merely whet his appetite for even greater achievements that would destroy the record book and raise the bar beyond the reach of future generations. He had his eye on the holy grail of golf–the Grand Slam! You may recall that when Martina Navratilova was at the top of women's tennis, she etched her supremacy in the record books in perpetuity by winning the four majors–the Grand Slam of tennis. In each sport, the Grand Slam is the ultimate fist pump that tells the world, "I'm the best, and when I'm done, I'll take my place in the Pantheon atop Mount Olympus." Though Tiger continued to enter check marks on the chart of Nicklaus' majors, his eye was keenly fixed on winning the (modern) Grand Slam, something that no golfer had ever achieved.

In 1930, Bobby Jones won the U.S. and British Amateur Championships as well as the U.S. and British Open, four tournaments that constituted the *Impregnable Quadrilateral*–the forerunner of the modern Grand Slam of Golf. A year later, he and Cliff Roberts began building Augusta National, site of a new tournament (to be called the *Masters*) that would eventually become the first leg of the modern Grand Slam. Then in 1953, Ben Hogan won three legs of the Grand Slam with victories in the Masters, the U.S. Open and the British Open, but decided not to enter the PGA Tour Championship due to a scheduling conflict. Both Palmer in 1960 and Nicklaus in 1972 won the first two legs of the Grand Slam, but lost their bid for the holy grail in the British Open.

Tiger's hopes of winning the Grand Slam in the 2000 season were dashed when he failed to win at Augusta. Some suggested that the slate of first-rate golfers made it virtually impossible for an individual to prevail in four consecutive majors. However, the naysayers took pause in June of 2000 when Tiger demolished the competition, winning the U.S. Open at Pebble Beach by an unprecedented 15 strokes. It was the largest margin of victory in a men's major golf championship, bettering his margin in the 1997 Masters by three strokes! Anticipating the future, TV executive Dick Ebersol said, "We've had two athletes in my time–Muhammad Ali and Jordan–that draw fans from outside their sport. Every indicator we have says Tiger is the next one."

Indeed, Tiger drew fans from far and wide outside the world of golf when he followed his stunning U.S. Open conquest a month later with a dramatic victory in the British Open at St. Andrews. This win made Tiger only the fifth player in history, and the youngest, to have won all four of the majors (albeit not consecutively), achieving what is known as a *career Grand Slam.*

Coming into the PGA Tour Championship, Tiger was looking to win his third of the four majors on the 2000 PGA Tour. In a grueling battle requiring intense focus and concentration, Woods finally prevailed over Bob May in a three-hole playoff. In an interview with *USA Today* on February 11, 2004, May recalled that hard-fought contest four years earlier:

Tiger is the most mentally tough guy in sports, from race car drivers to football players to anyone…you can never get him down, and he will never let himself get down. That's where he really beats up on people.

Tiger finished the season having captured three of the four majors. This meant that if Tiger could win the Masters in April 2001, he would simultaneously be the reigning champion in all four majors. Though not all victories would fall in a single year of the Tour, they would be consecutive and span less than a full year.

When the 2001 Masters rolled around, the golf world was buzzing with anticipation. Would Tiger Woods, at 25 years of age win a Grand Slam? In April of that year, tens of millions of viewers world-wide tuned in to see if Tiger could do the impossible. Aficionados throughout the world were not disappointed. In a sensational showdown between David Duval and Tiger Woods, the top-rated golfer in the world won with a 72-hole total of 272–a remarkable 16 under par!

Refusing to concede that Tiger had won a Grand Slam, and insisting that the four majors had to fall in the same PGA Tour year, some purists referred to his achievement as "The Tiger Slam." (Recall that Navratilova had faced a similar situation, but was credited with winning the Grand Slam of Tennis by the International Tennis Federation who awarded her a bonus of $1 million.) Most of the golfing world credited Tiger with a Grand Slam, acknowledging him at the beginning of the 2001 season as the greatest golfer in the world.

As I noted in earlier chapters, reaching the pinnacle in any venture is often followed by a let down and so it was with Tiger. He was closed out of the three remaining majors in the 2001 season and appeared to be tired. In *Think Like Tiger*, Andrisani opines (pp. 126–7):

During the last three majors of the 2001 golf season, Tiger was distracted. And, by the look on his face, mentally exhausted, too…Tiger admitted to the golf press that his swing was out of sync…During the 2001 U.S. Open, British Open and PGA, Tiger simply swung too fast and thus lost control of his shots.

Tiger seemed to recover early in the 2002 season, winning the Masters and the U.S. Open, but he did not prevail in the other majors. At the end of 2002 he underwent a knee operation that accounted for his slow start in the 2003 season. Although he won five tournaments in that year–a third of the events he entered—and posted the second lowest scoring average ever, pundits insisted he was in a slump. Tiger ended the year with his engagement to Scandinavian model Elin Nordegren while on an African safari. In 2004 they were married. Vijay Singh took over during much of that time as the leading money winner and the top-rated golfer on the PGA Tour.

During this three-year hiatus from major wins, Tiger worked tirelessly with his coach Hank Haney to refine his swing for greater distance and control. When asked when he would be finished refining his swing, Tiger responded, "I don't think you're ever finished. As soon as you feel like you're finished, then I guess you are finished, because you've already put a limit on your ability and what you can attain." Tiger's reluctance to put a limit on his performance ultimately paid huge dividends in his Masters win in 2005, once again quieting speculation that he was past his prime. In the television interview following that victory, Tiger said that the long drought was due to significant changes he made to his swing. He explained, "I was willing to go backwards to go forward, and it's now beginning to pay off."

The payoff was evident again, two months later, when Tiger placed second in the U.S. Open and came within a putt or two of winning his second major in 2005. For those who would still doubt that Tiger Woods was the greatest golfer in the world, he launched an aggressive charge at the British Open that saw him break into the lead on Thursday, July 14 and move relentlessly away from the pack through Sunday afternoon. He never looked back as he conquered the hallowed links of St. Andrews for the second time in five years. His second victory in the British Open gave Tiger his second career Grand Slam, having won each of the majors at least twice. The only other golfer in history to have achieved this feat was Jack Nicklaus, and Tiger reached this pinnacle before his 30th birthday.

In the PGA Championship, the final major of the 2005 season, Tiger had a disastrous start. Carding a score of 75 on the first day of the tournament at the very difficult Baltusrol Golf Club, Tiger found himself near the bottom of the pack, trailing leader Phil Mickelson by eight strokes. As he approached the last hole on the second day, he was perilously close to missing the cut. A dramatic birdie on the tough par-5 eighteenth hole enabled him to survive. However, several television commentators, observing that he was trailing Michelson by twelve strokes with only two rounds remaining, had written off his chances of challenging for the lead. Then Tiger launched a charge. In the third round he carded a 66, reducing Michelson's lead from twelve to six strokes. Throughout the final round on Sunday, August 14, Tiger continued to climb the leader board as contender after contender succumbed to the unrelenting pressure. By the end of his round, Tiger had scored a 68, shaving another four strokes off Mickelson's lead. When Phil Mickelson came to the 18th hole, he was tied with Elkington and Bjorn and was one stroke ahead of Tiger. Playing in elegant style, Phil sank his final putt to score a birdie and win the PGA Championship (his second major) by a single stroke over Elkington and Bjorn and two strokes over Tiger and Davis Love. Though a multitude of contenders had chased Michelson throughout the tournament, none was more unrelenting and menacing than the Tiger that chased him in the final two rounds. It was clear that the Tiger was back, hungrier than ever for tournament victories.

Legacy

At the time of this writing, Tiger Woods is entering his fourth decade of life and his career is still in its ascent. He has won ten majors and is more than halfway to Jack Nicklaus' record eighteen. Most people, including Nicklaus himself, believe that Tiger will surpass that benchmark and realize his boyhood dream.

Sports Illustrated wrote, "If Tiger is on Sunday's leader board, that's worth an extra one and a half Nielsen points or more; that's huge." Tiger's colleagues on the PGA Tour speak of him with a respect bordering on adulation. His achievements led pro golfer Lee Jantzen to say, "He's on a level that nobody can catch." After playing a round with him, Gary Player said, "He's the most dominant golfer who ever lived." Tom Watson added to the lore saying, "Tiger will change the nature of the sport. He is something supernatural."

Indeed Tiger has changed the game itself in the way that Ruth, Ali and Jordan changed their sports. One of the first harbingers of this impending change came with his dramatic dominance in the '97 Masters. When Nicklaus played a few rounds with him in the early days he had gushed, "There are no longer any par fives on golf courses." Tiger's ability to reach par-fives in two would require that golf course design be modified, either in length or configuration.

Even more important than his gargantuan distance off the tee was his demonstration of the critical importance of golf's mental component. It is more than physical skill that enables Tiger to execute brilliant shots at the most crucial moments of a tournament and win important playoffs when the pressure is crushing. His ability to perform in the zone, focusing his instincts and his powers of concentration to summon the intangible inner self, is the hallmark of his success. This is what Jack Nicklaus was describing when he summed up Tiger's 2001 win in the Memorial Tournament, saying, "Tiger's the smartest player in golf."

Many members of visible minorities identify with Tiger as a role model and living proof that golf is a game that is accessible to all–no longer a preserve of the Caucasian. This has dramatically expanded the breadth of golf's appeal across all races and nationalities. Though Tiger is pleased that his presence has opened the golf world to all, he has said that reference to him as an African-American is an insult to his mother whose background is Thai. On that basis, he might equally claim to be an Asian-American. Since Earl's ethnic background is a mixture of African-American, Caucasian, American Indian and Chinese, while Tida's is Thai, Dutch and Chinese, Tiger asserts, somewhat facetiously, that he is *cablinasian* (ca-blin-asian)–a kind of acronymic amalgam of his roots. Whatever his race, Eldrick Tiger Woods has made an enormous contribution to golf–making it accessible to people of all ages and races. As Tiger once explained during an interview:

Now I'm starting to see more minority faces in the crowd. And it's cool to see these people taking a serious interest in golf. My goal from the outset was to make golf look like America. Hopefully, when I am finished with golf or six feet under, I can leave the game better than it was when I entered.

Earl Woods is convinced that Tiger was put on earth to serve a mission. Always passionate about Tiger's potential impact, Earl asserted (Rosaforte, p. 240), "He will transcend the game and bring to the world a humanitarianism which has never been known before. The world will be a better place to live in by virtue of his existence and his presence."

Though Tiger's legacy is still in the making, there is no doubt that he has fulfilled a significant part of his father's promise and that his contribution to the world will continue through the years ahead. He was the first player to win $2 million, $3 million, $4 million, $5 million and $9 million on the PGA Tour and is annihilating the record books in the way that Babe Ruth did in the 1920s and Wayne Gretzky in the 1990s. In June 2005, Tiger Woods was named in the *Forbes Magazine* Celebrity 100 list as second only to Oprah Winfrey as the most influential celebrity in America. As we enter the 2006

PGA season, it is clear that Tiger Woods is well on his way to becoming the most dominant golfer in history and one of the most important icons on the American landscape.

Chapter 14

KINESTHETIC KARMA

We found that flow activity, whether it involved competition, chance, or any other dimension of experience, transported the person into a new reality. It pushed the person to higher levels of performance and led to previously undreamed-of states of consciousness.

—Mihaly Csikszentmihalyi

Is Athletic Eminence Born or Bred?

Now that you've journeyed with me through 13 chapters of psycho-biographies and research, it's time to revisit the question I posed in the Introduction: Is athletic eminence born or bred? Though most people would agree that genetics and training are both factors in athletic achievement, many have tacitly assumed that genetics plays the major role. They assume that superathletes have genetically superior physical attributes. However, supported by the growing body of research in the fields of kinesiology, physiology and psychology, my research indicates that genetics plays a relatively minor role. Physical attributes are significantly less important than mental and emotional dispositions in determining athletic excellence. Early imprints, psychological dispositions and winning behaviors are really the deciding factors in determining those who reach the top. In fact, most of the athletic superstars themselves attribute their success to these factors, rather than to genetic gifts.

Pelé still preaches in soccer training manuals, "I don't think there is such a thing as a born soccer player." Wayne Gretzky conjectured that his preeminence in hockey came from his passion for the game rather than some genetic predisposition. James Jordan, Michael's father, agreed with Pelé and Gretzky, telling the media, "Michael made himself into a great basketball player." He told Al Thomy of *The Sporting News* in 1984, "His leaping just didn't happen. He worked at it." He even went so far as to claim that Michael had helped make himself taller than anyone in their family by hanging relentlessly on monkey bars and encouraging his body to lengthen during its period of growth. Such a claim may be a stretch, but it is worth noting that Michael at 6' 6" is the tallest in his family, while his tallest brother and his father are only 5' 7".

Early imprints are a major factor in igniting in a young person the dreams and motivations that later explode into megastar performance. Martina Navratilova's stepfather contributed greatly to her ascent to the top of the tennis world. During her formative years, he spent hours encouraging her to perfect her tennis skills, predicting that she would one day win at Wimbledon. Had Jeff Gordon's mother not raced her five-year-old around tracks in Northern California, it is highly unlikely he would have become a star in NASCAR. Without such imprints, Jeff might be selling fast cars instead of driving them. Had Earl Woods not been relentless in his molding of son Eldrick into a tiger on the links, it is unlikely that his son would today be the preeminent player in the world. Similarly, Wally's Coliseum was the arena in which the young Wayne Gretzky learned how to anticipate where the puck would be. Positive early imprints condition children to be great, just as negative imprints preordain many individuals of comparable potential to a life of lesser achievement or mediocrity. These early imprints are invisible to spectators who, observing mature athletes performing superhuman feats, attribute this surreal performance to genetic advantage.

As I explained in the Introduction, I had originally assumed that athletic eminence began with kinesthetic superiority (physical), was driven by passion (emotional), and supported by the intent (mental) to blend it all together. However, the evidence I have gathered has persuaded me that these factors rank in the reverse order of importance. That is, the mental component is the most important, followed by the emotional and then the physical. Greatness demands that the mind be in control, deriving its energy from the passion within, while keeping competitive anxiety at bay. The body merely executes the instructions that were encoded in the subconscious during the thousands of hours of practice and physical rehearsal. Once these three components are in synch, a warrior becomes a single synthesized unit, ready to go for the gold.

Talent vs. Achievement

In the preceding chapters, I have provided a plethora of anecdotal evidence to support the claim that high achievement in sports (and life) derives more from mental and emotional factors than from genetic gifts and talent. Recent research offers quantitative evidence supporting this claim. In 2004, Charles Murray, W. H. Brady Scholar at the American Enterprise Institute for Public Policy Research (Washington, D.C.), published the results of his comprehensive analysis of eminence (achievement) in *all* fields of human endeavor. In *Human Accomplishment*, Murray's data show that in every field of human enterprise, a handful of individuals stand head and shoulders above the rest in their contributions. He explains (p. 87):

The evidence for it is overwhelming: When you assemble the human résumé: only a few thousand people stand apart from the rest. Among them, the people who are indispensible to the story of human accomplishment number in the hundreds. Among those hundreds, a handful stand conspicuously above everyone else.

For example, among the authors of Western literature, Shakespeare, Goethe, Dante, Virgil and Homer are considered *hors de catégorie* (beyond category). And even among these giants, William Shakespeare is considered without peer. His contribution to literature is considered "off the scale." The eminent that Murray studied are not those who were merely excellent, outstanding or even legends in their own time. His subjects were those whose contributions redefined their field of enterprise, setting new standards against which all successors compared themselves. In Western Music, the three most eminent were Beethoven, Mozart and Bach. The top three in the pantheon of Physics were Einstein, Newton and Rutherford. In golf, it was Nicklaus and Palmer (but more about that later).

Murray's measures of eminence are based not only on the quantity and quality of the contributions, but also on the number of citations of their work in the works of others. In essence, Murray gathered data that measured the impact of the eminent in their fields as judged by their peers, their successors and the ubiquity of their ideas and techniques. When he graphed these data, he discovered something very surprising and profound about the difference between talent and achievement.

Before embarking on an explanation of his findings, I should warn the reader who finds mathematical explanations distasteful. The rest of this section involves a quantitative argument that you should skip if you already accept my assertion that talent is *not* the dominant factor in high achievement. Renowned physicist Stephen Hawking lamented in the introduction to *A Brief History of Time* that his publisher warned that every equation he included would halve the sales of his book. Heeding this advice, I have banished equations from the discussion. For the reader with a background in elementary statistics, I have included in the Appendix a brief review of the origins of the normal distribution as it was applied to the measurement of human characteristics and their distribution throughout the population. The explanation that follows uses only graphs to present an argument for the factors that play key roles in distinguishing the talented from the eminent. You will not need to understand the explanation in detail to gain a sense of Murray's findings.

To establish a quantitative measure of eminence, Charles Murray sought an area of human endeavor in which achievement is measurable in objective terms. This renders it less open to opinion and debate. Recognizing that team sports make individual contributions difficult to assess, Murray chose to investigate the sport of golf. Plotting frequency polygons from PGA statistics on the performance skills of the PGA players between 1991 and 2000, Murray obtained the graphs below. The graphs reveal what we might expect: the component skills in golf are essentially normally distributed, i.e., the frequency polygons have the shape of a bell curve.

The component skills of golf form bell curves, even among professionals.

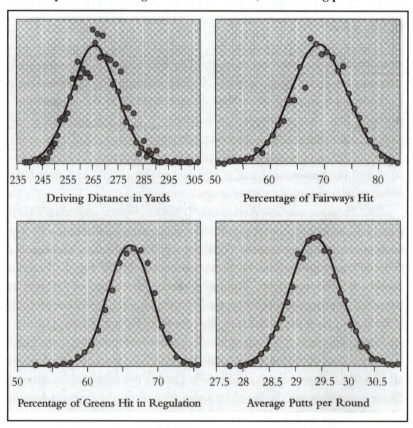

Murray considered using total money winnings as a measure of eminence but rejected this because money winnings over a span of decades favor recent golfers as the tournament prizes escalate. Ultimately, he adopted a standard that is more widely held in the golf community: the number of PGA tournaments won. Considering only those 170 golfers who had won at least one PGA tournament in their careers and had completed their careers by the end of the 2001 season, Murray graphed the frequency polygon for the number of PGA Tour victories. The graph that emerged from the data was not the tail of a normal distribution, but rather the graph shown below–a hyperbolic graph, known as a *Lotka curve*.

The leftmost dot on the graph shows that 26% of this elite group had only one tournament victory. About 12% had two victories and another 16% had three. Thus, more than half the golfers in this elite group won three or fewer tournaments. Furthermore, only four won more than 30 tournaments. At the extreme right end of the curve we have a single dot representing 61 tournament victories

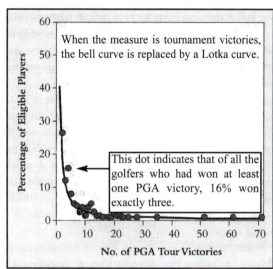

(Arnold Palmer) and another representing 71 tournament victories (Jack Nicklaus). The eminent in golf appear on the extreme right tail of a Lotka curve, rather than on the right tail of a normal distribution, indicating that while these golfers may be closer to the pack in component skills (or physical talent), when it comes to achievement, the truly eminent are way out in front of the pack. As Murray observed (p. 100):

Are we looking at fame or excellence? One of the satisfying simplicities of sports is that we can answer that question without agonizing. The men at the right-hand tail are not where they are because of social construction that artificially designate them as the best. No keepers of the golf canon awarded Jack Nicklaus his 71 PGA tour victories…The champions sit where they are because they were the best at what they did.

The truly eminent have physical skills that locate them on the right tail of the normal curve, but emotional and mental dispositions are the factors that combine to move the eminent to the extreme right tail of a Lotka curve, way ahead of the pack. Explaining this phenomenon in golf, Murray noted that all the top golfers who reach the fourth round of a major PGA Tournament (on a Sunday) have the requisite physical skills to win, but superior emotional and mental factors enable the eminent to prevail. He wrote (pp. 103–4):

> *...On Sunday, the opportunity to win the tournament is within reach [for those who have made the cut]. The individually simple tasks must be done under increased psychological pressure that makes the breath come shorter and the hands shake as you line up the putt. The number of people who are good enough to have survived the first three days to put themselves in that position is small; the number who can play well on Sunday under those conditions is smaller still...The number of people who can deal with that situation even a single time has dwindled to a few handfuls in every generation. To do such things repeatedly is given to a handful of golfers per century. Hence the Lotka curves.*

These emotional and mental dispositions embodied in the *13 Principles of Empowerment* account for the difference between talent and achievement.

WINNING EMOTIONAL DISPOSITIONS

The table below displays seven "winning" emotional dispositions or attitudes that facilitate the behaviors embodied in the *Principles of Empowerment.*

Winning Emotional Dispositions Linked to the Empowerment Principles

Winning Emotional Disposition	Empowerment Principle
Renegade Attitude	Principle #1: Value Your Difference.
High Risk Tolerance	Principle #2: To Win Big be Ready to Fail Big.
High Passion/Drive	Principle #3: Follow Your Passion.
Strong Self-Efficacy	Principle #6: Believe in Yourself.
Internal Locus of Control	Principle #7: Make 'em Play Your Game.
Strong Competitive Zeal	Principle #10: Ignite Your Competitive Zeal.
Type A Personality	Principle #11: Focus Your Type A Tendencies.

To what extent do the personalities of the thirteen athletic superstars reflect these emotional dispositions? In this table, I have graded each of the athletic superstars with respect to each of these winning personality traits. My assessments are based on the information gleaned from their autobiographies, biographies and interviews, and their performances on and off their fields of battle. Though specific assessments may be debatable, the general trends are clear. All of these athletic superstars possess most or all of the winning personality traits to a very high degree. (The bottom row gives the percentage of the total who possess a particular trait.)

EMOTIONAL DISPOSITIONS OF THE ATHLETIC SUPERSTARS

SUBJECTS	Renegade Attitude	Risk-Tolerance	Passion/ Drive	Self-Efficacy EGO	Locus of Control	Competitive Zeal	Type A/B
Jim Thorpe	R+++	H+	P+	E	I	C+	A
Babe Ruth	R+++	H+++	P+++	E++	I	C+++	A+++
Babe Zaharias	R+++	H+++	P+++	E++	I+	C+++	A+++
Wilma Rudolph	R	H	P+	E	I	C+	A
Pele	neutral	H++	P+	E	I	C+	A
Muhammad Ali	R++	H+	P++	E+++	I+	C+	A+
Martina Navratilova	R+++	H+++	P++	E	I++	C++	A+++
Greg Louganis	R++	H+	P+++	E	I	C	A+++
Wayne Gretzky	neutral	H	P+	E	I	C+	A+
Michael Jordan	R+	H+++	P++	E++	I+	C+++	A++
Jeff Gordon	R	H+++	P+	E	I	C+	A+++
Lance Armstrong	R+++	H+++	P+++	E+	I++	C++	A+++
Tiger Woods	R	H+	P++	E+	I+	C++	A+++
13 Subjects	R = 11 85%	H = 13 100%	P = 13 100%	E = 13 100%	I = 13 100%	C = 13 100%	A = 13 100%

To support the assessments in the table, I will review briefly some of the behaviors of the thirteen superstars that provide insights into their emotional dispositions. In some cases the evidence of a particular emotional disposition is overwhelming, while in other cases the evidence is suggestive rather than conclusive. Also, the presence of a particular emotional disposition may depend on the context, for example, Pelé may be a Type A in life and Type A+++ on the soccer pitch.

Renegade Attitude

The *renegade attitude* is a derivative of Principles #1 and #6: *Value your difference* and *Believe in yourself.* In essence, it is displayed as a psychological independence that rebels against conformity and asserts the uniqueness of self. It emanates from a strong self-efficacy combined with a reluctance to buy into conventional norms or traditions. Psychologist Rollo May offered a profound insight into the renegade attitude when he said, "In modern society the opposite of courage is not cowardice, it is conformity." In other words, to be great one must be different, and that takes courage. Most people conform even when it isn't in their best interest, because conformity is the path of least resistance. Institutions must maintain control to maintain power. That is the way to keep the masses in line. Only the renegade is willing to depart from convention, violate traditions and deal with threats and reprisals.

Carl Jung said, "Consciousness starts as an act of disobedience." Except for Pelé and Gretzky, all those profiled in this book personified irreverence toward authority. Jim Thorpe was a true iconoclast. One of his teachers said, "Jim was a reluctant and rebellious student and incorrigible youngster." Babe Ruth defied tradition by taking batting practice when he was pitching and going for the fences when singles were in vogue. Babe Zaharias was "shockingly deviant" according to biographer Susan Cayleff. Michael Jordan admitted, "I never listened to a coach, ever." Lance Armstrong wrote, "I am an anti-conformist in life and dress." Virtually all these athletic superstars had to fight prejudice of one kind or another. Ali had to fight the Government of the United States and Navratilova had to fight the Communist regime in the Czech Republic. Did they pay a high price for their defiance? You bet! Ali blatantly told the draft board "I don't have to be who you want me to be." They took his title and his passport but they didn't kill his defiant spirit. All of these superstars were renegades on and off the field of play. That is why they were able to revolutionize their sport. Departure from conventional wisdom and accepted practice is the origin of all paradigm shifts.

Risk-Taking Behavior

Big wins accrue only to those who take big risks. Risks are the price of rewards–no risk, no reward. Those unwilling to fail seldom make it in the big time. Why? Fear permeates everything they do. When excessive caution dictates the action, each step and every shot is tentative and the athlete suffers a kind of paralysis at crunch time. Reaping huge rewards in sports, as in any other endeavor, is about going where others fear to tread.

I used Babe Ruth as the model for Principle #2: *To win big be ready to fail big*, because he was the consummate risk-taker. He told reporters, "I swing big and I miss big." He scorned the cautious hit-and-run strategy, sacrifice bunts and other restrictive practices that dominated baseball in his era. Legendary sportswriter Grantland Rice wrote of Babe Ruth's mental power: "Can you imagine Babe Ruth ever considering the possibility of failure?" Ruth said to him, "Once my swing starts, I can't change it or pull up. It's all or nothing at all." A reporter stopped Babe outside Wrigley Field after his famous called-home run in the 1932 World Series and asked, "What if you had struck out?" Ruth responded in his unflappable style, "Never thought about that." That is the nature of Big T personality and what made him a superstar.

Lance Armstrong took the ultimate risk when he gambled his life on a high-risk aggressive chemotherapy treatment to kill his cancer. Greg Louganis risked death or serious injury in executing a dive that had killed Russian diver Sergei Shalibashvili just five years earlier. He said in his memoir, "You don't win gold medals playing it safe." Muhammad Ali risked public humiliation and injury when he entered the ring against reigning Heavyweight Champion Sonny Liston who was deemed unbeatable. Later, he risked a long prison term when he refused to be drafted. As a teenager, Jeff Gordon risked his life racing at speeds in excess of 200 miles per hour against professional drivers twice his age. The very nature of risk-taking personalities is that they live on the edge. They often feed on the adrenaline rush that comes from tempting fate and testing themselves at ever-escalating levels of danger.

Passion/Drive

Libidinal energy, the source of the sex drive, is what makes superstars tick. It pushes them beyond the norm both in practice and in the game. Frank Farley, the former President of the American Psychological Association, wrote, "The Big T (thrill-seekers) have high arousal thresholds and tend to have strong sex drives. Big Ts believe life is not worth living if they are not tested." These high testosterone, thrill-seeking athletes exude a libidinal energy that causes them to chase victory and sex with equal ardor.

Babe Ruth was an incorrigible example of a Big T athlete. When his roommate Ping Bodie was asked about the Babe, he responded, "I don't know him…I don't room with the Babe. I room with his suitcase." The testosterone raging through his body imbued the Sultan of Swat with both energy and drive. A similar sex energy led to Lance Armstrong's nickname "FedEx," because he just "had to have it absolutely, positively–overnight." Babe Zaharias, Martina Navratilova and Greg Louganis were all gay at a time when homosexuality was a serious impediment to an athlete's career and the prospect of lucrative endorsements. However, their strong libidinal energy drove them into the relationships they needed to satisfy their passions. All of the athletes profiled in this book exuded the passion to compete, to dominate and to win. It was exemplified in their relentless training, their fierce struggles through adversity and their refusal to accept less than first place.

Strong Self-Efficacy

When accused of arrogance, Muhammad Ali told the press, "It ain't braggin' if you do it." Although Muhammad Ali is our poster boy for Principle #6: *Believe in yourself*, every superstar profiled in this book came to their coliseum of contest with a positive sense of self and personal efficacy. Their success was not due to any special genetic predisposition, but had everything to do with their emotional and mental belief in their ability to prevail. Their self-efficacy was the fuel to a kinesthetic karma that made them great no matter the opposition, no matter the conditions and no matter their health.

Martina Navratilova wrote, "You have to have a positive attitude. You have to remember you have no control over anything but your attitude." She controlled her attitude and took Wimbledon by storm. Every tournament Tiger Woods enters he believes he will win. He has admitted, "The day I don't think that way is the day I quit." Like all superstars, he shows up with unbridled confidence and a strategy aimed at bringing home the gold. Wilma Rudolph, while settling into the blocks in the Rome Olympics told herself, "There's nobody alive who can beat me in the 200. Go get it!" Wayne Gretzky is always gracious and self-effacing, but inside his psyche rages a powerful and healthy sense of self. His gentle manner belies the inner volcano that erupted into the best game of his career when responding to the insult that he appeared to be skating with a piano on his back.

Also-rans allow failure to dominate their being and impede their performance. Instead of being convinced they can win, they wonder how not to lose. In *Competitive Anxiety in Sports*, R. Martens and his associates explained that although high energy is vital to athletic performance, an even more important factor is "a positive attitude." Tennis players who fear hitting a backhand down the line have a small chance of achieving this result because they lack the confidence in their ability to execute successfully. Those who can do it believe they can, while those who can't believe they can't. Psychologists have shown that until the *belief* in success is more than 50%, the chances of success are very low.

Both positive and negative attitudes yield self-fulfilling prophesies-one attitude makes you a success, the other a failure. This is true whether playing bridge, ping-pong, golf or tennis. According to Martens, until you can program your mind to believe that you have a better-than-50%-chance of success, you won't execute with conviction. Those who don't believe have programmed themselves for failure: those who believe have programmed themselves for success. Martens asserts (p. 222):

Uncertainty about winning or losing in competition can be determined by the person's perceived probability of success or probability of failure...uncertainty increases to a point at which there is an equal chance of the outcome being positive or negative.

Believing in advance of trying is fundamental to all things professional and personal. Those who question their ability to perform in sports or business are merely insuring they cannot. As I have often written, *success comes packaged in cans, failure in cannots!* The insecure merely function in response to their negative attitude; they sabotage their own talents. Michael Jordan did just the opposite. He was so confident he believed to the point of delusion. But it worked. Believing he could make every shot in the dying moments of a game enabled him to sink an alarmingly high percentage of them. He was unafraid of missing or losing. Wayne Gretzky commented, "You miss 100% of the shots you don't take." Gretzky utilized an "uncertainty index" to improve those hockey skills in which he felt inadequate. He practiced them relentlessly until he had built a high degree of confidence in executing them.

Locus of Control

Describing the ability of athletic superstars to take charge of a competition, Robert Lussier and David Kimball wrote in *Sport Management*,

"Internalizers obviously tend to perform better." By "internalizers" they were alluding to those having a strong *internal locus of control*. Such types believe they are in control of their destiny, while those oriented toward an external locus of control believe that fate plays a much greater role in the outcome of a competition. Externals capitulate to others; consequently, they rarely lead or attain greatness. Superstars, on the other hand, take full responsibility for the outcome of a contest and determine how the contest will play out. This behavior is captured in Principle #7: *Make 'em play your game*.

There is a substantial attitudinal difference between the athletic superstar and the average professional. Superstars come armed with a mystical, sometimes quasi-metaphysical sense of their destiny. They function as someone predestined to greatness and consequently execute their skills instinctively, as if serving as an agent through which an inevitable outcome is emerging. They amble through life in a kind of ethereal splendor, operating with a special sense of internal purpose resembling a Nietzschean will-to-power. Jim Thorpe was immersed in Indian lore and a mystical spiritualism that propelled him far beyond the norm. When he took control of the football, he taunted the opposition to attempt to tackle him. Then he dodged and evaded them, leaving a trail of powerless opponents strewn in his wake. Wayne Gretzky exercised a similar control from his office behind the net. Assessing the configuration of players on the rink, he orchestrated play, setting up goals and throwing the opposition into defensive mode. Pelé also controlled the soccer pitch by playing aggressively and forcing the other team into a reactive mode. "The object of the game" he liked to say, "is to score, not play defense." He insisted that the only way to play the game was to "Attack, Attack and Attack." He railed against coaches who recommended a more defensive style of play because he knew instinctively that the advantage belongs to the one who controls the game.

Competitive Zeal

Few athletes are as competitively driven as Michael Jordan. When he was playing out his last season with the Washington Wizards he told the media, "I just want to be remembered as a competitor that never gave up on anything." That will be his legacy. The competitive zeal that drove Michael Jordan also drove the other athletic superstars, manifesting often as a fierce tenacity. Refusing to yield to cancer, Lance Armstrong said, "I never back down." During his struggle against the disease, he tapped into his fierce competitive instincts to harness his energies and scream at the cancerous lesions (p. 131),

"You picked the wrong guy!" "I personalized the disease," he wrote, "I made it my enemy, my challenge." Babe Zaharias was similarly possessed by tenacity and a competitive zeal that manifested as controlled aggression. Her overt aggressiveness on her golf tour made most of her male competitors seem timid. Her female competitors bristled when Babe strolled arrogantly into the clubhouse of the U.S. Open and proclaimed, "They might as well give me the cup now, cause I'm goin' to take it."

Aggressive play was also the mantra of Martina Navratilova. Submissive females were in mortal fear of confronting this "competitive beast from the east." They were forced to play her game and paid a dear price for doing so. "I'm a serve-and-volleyer. Either I beat you or you beat me." She was not about to stand at the baseline and trade shots with a more capable opponent. She was an intimidator who went for the jugular on every shot. Wilma Rudolph learned to be competitive quite young, writing (p. 47), "I started acquiring a competitive spirit when I was unable to go to school; a spirit that would make me successful in sports later on." Following an interview with Tiger Woods, a writer from *Sports Illustrated* reported, "Tiger is the fiercest competitor I ever met."

As noted in Chapter 10, competitive zeal in sports derives from libidinal energy sublimated into athletic competition. The depletion of libidinal energy (hence competitive zeal) with age is probably the most important factor responsible for the gradual decline in an athlete's performance after the peak years. As the sex drive diminishes, the athlete loses some of the competitive zeal that fueled earlier successes. The aging athlete is less willing to suffer the pain and endure the hardship of staying in top physical shape and performing at the highest level of competence. Gordie Howe, one of the best-conditioned athletes of all time, explained that he decided to retire when getting in shape for the hockey season became too onerous. Boxer Mike Tyson announced his retirement in June, 2005 stating that at age 38, he had lost the discipline required to train hard and stay in shape.

Though the body undergoes a muscular depletion with age, the reduction in competitive zeal appears to be the more prominent factor in age-related decline. We observe, for example, that business tycoons generally come into their own later than athletes, yet when they step back from the helm of the corporation they created, it is usually a result of their reduced competitive zeal rather than any diminution of their business skills.

Type A Personality

Have you ever noticed how stars like Michael Jordan have limitless energy on and off the court? Coach Collins described his star saying, "Michael is always hyper." Jordan told the media, "I sleep sparingly and I almost always have energy." From day one Michael was the first to practice and the last to leave. This restless energy, often manifest as "hurry sickness," is a familiar defining characteristic of the Type A personality and is linked to competitive zeal. Jim Thorpe admitted to the press "I was always of a restless disposition." Throughout his life he would disappear for weeks, leaving his wife wondering about his whereabouts. Gene Sarazen said of Babe Zaharias, "She is very intense." Her fierce need to win and her burning passion to compete catapulted her to the top in every sport she tried. Race driver Jeff Gordon also exuded the restless energy described by his mother Carol, "He simply could not sit still, read books or watch television," she said in an interview. Lance Armstrong wrote, "I was a hyper kid and never able to do anything slow. I have an impossibly short attention span."

Type A behavior, described in some detail in Chapter 11, is sometimes seen as an obsessive quest for achievement and recognition. Martina Navratilova, Babe Ruth and Tiger Woods strove with inexorable fervor to break old records and create new ones. Martina competed in the professional tennis circuit beyond age 50, winning at Wimbledon an unprecedented nine times. Babe Ruth continued to swing for the fences in a quest for a home run record that would not be equaled in his generation. And Tiger Woods continues to chase relentlessly the 18 majors won by Jack Nicklaus to surpass the man who is his lifelong hero. After his 1997 Masters victory, Tiger told the media, "I can get into that totally obsessive state more easily than an older player."

WINNING MENTAL DISPOSITIONS

The *emotional* dispositions discussed above are personality traits that reflect attitudes and feelings about oneself and one's ability to prevail. Equally important in promoting winning behaviors are the *mental* dispositions. These are the rational or cognitive processes that reflect how we perceive and respond to events. The table on the facing page displays four winning mental dispositions and links them to the behaviors embodied in the *Principles of Empowerment*.

Winning Mental Dispositions Linked to the Empowerment Principles

Winning Mental Disposition	Empowerment Principle
Focus	Principle #5: Tap into Your Instincts.
Visualization	Principle #8: Visualize Your Goal
Holistic Thinking	Principle #9: Think Holistically
Self-Insight	Principles #4 & #12: See an Obstacle as an Opportunity

Focus

Though I used Pelé in Chapter 5 as the "focus" model, it is clear that all of the thirteen sports superstars profiled in this book were capable of achieving a laser-intensity focus. This mental disposition might be considered a prerequisite for success. Tiger's mental coach Jay Brunza said (*USA Weekend*, July 24–26, 1992):

Tiger is so advanced mentally, it's scary. I did some sports psychology with athletes at the [U.S.] Naval Academy where we worked on things like ways to focus attention, and Tiger is far ahead of anything I've ever seen.

Tiger himself reported his level of concentration in his win over Sergio Garcia at the 1999 PGA Championship: "A bomb could be going off, [I] probably wouldn't even know. That's the focus I had."

Michael Jordan was also renowned for his ability to focus. Tim Russet of *NBC News* reported (Smith, p. 32):

I've interviewed MJ a number of times, and the one word to describe him is focus*. He is singularly in that moment. Each question I asked him you could see him kick in to answer it. He wasn't on automatic pilot. He has a very compelling presence. He knows who he is.*

Similar comments have been made about the focus of Lance Armstrong and Jeff Gordon. Greg Louganis also reported how he recited the lyrics from *The Wiz* in order to focus his thoughts.

Visualization

In Chapter 8, we discussed visualization in considerable depth. The techniques of visualization involving mental rehearsal have recently become an integral part of training in all sports, though the great athletes have been practicing these methods for more than a century. Recall that Jim Thorpe was rehearsing his decathlon events in his head while sitting on board ship en route to the Olympic Games in Stockholm. Jack Nicklaus, in describing his "short, private, Hollywood spectacular" that preceded each shot, revealed the importance of the visualization technique in golf. Tiger Woods' coach John Anselmo used mental imagery to help Tiger enhance his swing and his shot-making. Andrisani explained (p. 25):

> To help Tiger take his mind off a water hazard fronting the green when playing short iron shots, [Anselmo] instructed him to imagine a colorful flag blowing at the top of the flagstick and aim for it.

Tiger described his own shot-making process, "I just *see* the shot and hit it." Greg Louganis envisioned himself performing a dive flawlessly, which gave him the confidence to function without stress. Though Greg Louganis was our model for the use of visualization, I could have chosen Michael Jordan who described visualization under pressure, "What happens to clutch guys in big moments is that everything slows down. You have time to evaluate the situation, and you can clearly see every move you have to make."

Holistic Thinking

Having internalized the specific skills of a particular sport, the superathlete is free to play unconsciously while he or she surveys the field of battle from a "zoomed-out" perspective. Pelé waxed eloquent about how he knew the positions of all the players on the field when he was playing "in the zone." Legendary coach Pop Warner said of Jim Thorpe, "I never knew a football player who could see holes through which to break as could the Big Indian." From his office behind the net, Wayne Gretzky orchestrated brilliant playmaking like a grand master in chess. A Russian hockey coach describing Wayne Gretzky's performance observed, "He sees the plays from 100 feet above the ice. He sees things before they happen." Lance Armstrong looked at *all* the stages of the Tour de France, analyzing those that he would attempt to win and those in which he would pace himself. Michael Jordan developed the ability to slash to the basket for a slam dunk as well as the ability to hit a field goal from outside. Thus, by surveying the positions of all the players on the court, he could exploit opportunities as they arose.

Self-Insight

Self-insight or tolerance for ambiguity is the mental disposition that enables an athlete to transform breakdown into breakthrough or see an obstacle as an opportunity (Principles #4 and #12). Like attaining a focus, interpreting obstacles as opportunities might be regarded as a prerequisite to performance at the highest level. Seeing an obstacle in a less positive light is self-defeating.

Lance Armstrong's mother Linda had frequently reminded her young son to see every negative as a positive and every obstacle as an opportunity. It is little wonder that he would eventually become the model for Principle #12. His conquest over cancer and then over the Tour de France were testimonials to his mental resolve to welcome adversity as a stimulus and a challenge.

Michael Jordan said in an interview:

I'm able to deal with failure and then try to turn that into a positive. I'm not going to let it get me down. If I have one bad day, that means I'm trying harder the next day to come back and make it a better day...failure always made me try harder next time.

Wilma Rudolph's ability to persevere relentlessly through agonizing therapy sessions month after month and year after year enabled her to recover from the crippling effects of polio to become the fastest woman in the world. Treating each obstacle as a challenge, she also triumphed over the crushing effects of poverty, racism and gender discrimination.

Banned from amateur golf, Babe Zaharias branched out into other sports, conducting exhibitions against the top professionals in billiards, basketball and baseball. After reinstatement as an amateur golfer, she began to win tournaments until banned for a second time. Picking herself up once more, she honed her golf game, returned to the links and became one of the greatest women golfers of all time and a co-founder of the LPGA.

The 13 psycho-biographies in this book revealed that all these sports superstars possessed a self-insight that enabled them to embrace obstacles as challenges. All of them recognized that obstacles were their allies in a conspiracy against their adversaries. They knew that their ability to meet and defeat these obstacles gave them the competitive edge over other contenders.

KINESTHETIC KARMA

Athletic eminence can only be achieved by reaching a state of "kinesthetic karma," in which the mind, emotions and body execute in harmony. Developing particular athletic skills often requires that these skills be broken down into their component parts (like a golf swing) during practice sessions and then synthesized or reconstituted into a single fluid motion. A similar analysis and reconstitution is involved in mental rehearsal and visualization activities. However, once the physical skills have been mastered and internalized, the athlete needs to let them reside in the subconscious and allow the mind to take a more holistic view. To perform in the zone the athlete must attain optimal emotional arousal, yet achieve a state of relaxed concentration. Freed from the encumbrance of "thinking" about the details of a particular skill, the athlete's mind is free to take a holistic view of the field, pitch or rink and execute the skills "unconsciously." It is in this semi-euphoric state that the athlete transcends the game and performs at a level that brings the spectators to their feet and turns the opponents into spectators. Research scientist Robert Ornstein explains, "Virtuoso performance is when another mind takes over and doesn't ask questions, doesn't require any conscious direction." In his recent book *In the Zone*, sports psychologist Michael Murphy asserts, "*Out-of-this-world* experiences are really *out-of-mind* experiences." The psycho-biographies I included in this book document many such episodes of superhuman achievement. On all of these occasions, the athletic superstars were performing in the zone, having achieved a kinesthetic karma.

The diagram on the opposite page shows the mental and emotional dispositions of an athlete that connect with the physical preparations to form an integrated whole. The four mental dispositions that contribute to performance in the zone were discussed in Chapters 4, 5, 8, 9 and 12 (Principles 4, 5, 8, 9 and 12) and are shown in one sector of the circle. The emotional dispositions, captured in Principles #1, 2, 3, 6, 7, 10 and 11, are shown as the seven sectors. Though the physical preparations involve the lion's share of the athlete's time, outstanding execution requires that the mental and emotional dispositions be integrated into both the practice sessions and the competition. (Recall, for example, how Michael Jordan practiced with the same intensity that he brought to the games.)

Kinesthetic Karma

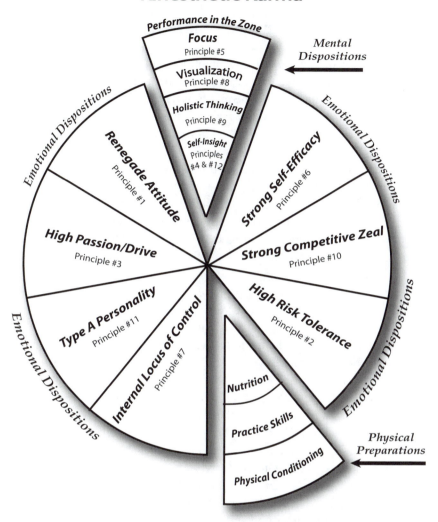

Performance in the Zone

Focus
Principle #5

Visualization
Principle #8

Holistic Thinking
Principle #9

Self-Insight
Principles #4 & #12

Mental Dispositions

Emotional Dispositions

Renegade Attitude
Principle #1

High Passion/Drive
Principle #3

Type A Personality
Principle #11

Internal Locus of Control
Principle #7

Strong Self-Efficacy
Principle #6

Strong Competitive Zeal
Principle #10

High Risk Tolerance
Principle #2

Nutrition

Practice Skills

Physical Conditioning

Emotional Dispositions

Physical Preparations

Landrum's 13 Principles of Empowerment

Principle #1: Value your difference. (Renegade attitude)
Principle #2: To win big be willing to fail big.
Principle #3: Follow your passion.
Principle #4: Transform breakdown into breakthrough.
Principle #5: Tap into your instincts
Principle #6: Believe in yourself.
Principle #7: Make 'em play your game.

Principle #8: Visualize your goal.
Principle #9: Think holistically to anticipate outcomes.
Principle #10: Ignite your competitive zeal.
Principle #11: Focus your type A tendencies.
Principle #12: See an obstacle as an opportunity.
Principle #13: Perform in the zone.

PERFORMING IN THE ZONE

Integration of the mental and emotional dispositions into the physical preparation is the balance that moves the superathlete into the zone (see the Kinesthetic Karma diagram on the previous page). Professional athletes would pay a king's ransom to have the key to what sportswriter George Plimpton called *The X Factor*–that magical land of optimum performance. Most athletes have their fifteen minutes in the sun, but fifteen minutes does not make a champion. During those brief interludes, some individuals have found the zone and used it to win. But only those who know how to access the zone frequently will reach eminence. The challenge is in getting there often. (Recall Murray's comments about golfers competing on the Sunday in a PGA major.) As shown in the Kinesthetic Karma diagram, entering the zone involves mental components such as visualization, holistic thinking, embracing obstacles as challenges and concentrating without stress. Chris Evert, the demure queen of American tennis, spoke of using positive visualization prior to every match. "I visualize playing. I feel like I've already played the match before I even walk onto the court." Michael Jordan said it in a slightly different way, "Basketball is like meditation to me." Pelé told the *New York Times Magazine* that his magnificent play often occurred when "I found myself in a kind of mystical state." Billie Jean King said when she was there [in the zone], "the ball looked huge." Tiger Woods' high school coach offered insight into his ability to go within. "As a kid Tiger was composing shots in his head just as Mozart composed music in his head before writing it."

The zone is a dichotomy. It lies on a continuum between being relaxed and being intense. Those who are there know it, yet is impossible to get there by trying. *The path is through optimal thinking in concert with optimal physicality.* Attaining a disposition of low stress but high focus creates the right environment for the mind and body to reach that ethereal state. With the head and emotions out of the way, the body's muscle memory functions optimally. The harmony between analytical left-brain activity and instinctive "unconscious" right-brain activity is optimal, each hemisphere yielding dominance to the other at appropriate times.

TIMELINE TO THE TOP–IS OVERNIGHT SUCCESS A MYTH?

My research has revealed that it takes about ten years to master any discipline and another ten to make it to the very top. This timeline is seldom violated. During the first phase, one learns the nuances of the domain, including strategies, weaknesses, and what works and what doesn't. Everyone would like to think that someone becomes an overnight phenomenon, but that just doesn't happen. Success is a by-product of those relentless hours in the gym or on the court working out the kinks.

Earl Woods, Tiger's father, provided him with constant tutelage in golf at an early age. From the night when Tiger at age 2 appeared on the Mike Douglas television show putting against Bob Hope, his destiny was set. He played his first tournament at age 6 and by age 15 he had won the U.S. Junior Amateur championship–roughly 10 years between his first tournament and his first flirtation with greatness.

By 21, Tiger was becoming a major threat. When he won the Masters by an unprecedented 12 strokes in 1997, he was on his way. Three years later, his legacy was intact when he became the #1 player in the game by winning the Grand Slam of golf. The time span from Tiger's first television appearance to his ranking as #1 in the World at age 21 was 19 years. Would he have been as good had he begun five years later? Probably! But it is very likely that he would not have won the U.S. Junior Amateur at 15 or become #1 in the world at 21. All learning curves are time related and that time is derived from the practice needed for skill building.

Michael Jordan was a stellar Little League baseball player at age 8 and an All-American basketball star at age 18. It took him 10 years to become a master athlete, and then another 10 years to grow from an All-American basketball player at the University of North Carolina to a member of the NBA World Championship winning Chicago Bulls in 1991. On his journey he won a number of NBA scoring championships and MVP honors. Jordan's timeline to the top was typical of most who reach eminence.

The table on the following page offers some insight into the timelines to the top across various venues. On average, these 13 superstars began playing competitively at age eight. They had refined their skills by the time they were 17 and by 25 many had struck gold. The median (middle value) total time elapsed from beginning to eminence was 20 years.

The two-decade timeline to the top is not only the norm in athletic ascendancy, it is also the norm in business, politics and the arts. In my previous book, *Entrepreneurial Genius: The Power of Passion* (Landrum, 2004), I profiled a dozen of the world's greatest entrepreneurs of the twentieth century and presented data to show that there are virtually no instant successes in business. Sam Walton didn't start Wal-Mart until he was 44, yet the pundits portrayed him as an instant success. They forgot to look at his twenty years of experimentation with small retail stores in Arkansas. For

Michael Dell the trek to eminence took exactly twenty years. He launched his first venture at 12 and became a billionaire at 32. No matter how generous your natural gifts, there are just no short cuts to success. We all pay a price for success and that price is time, effort and practice.

Given this approximate two-decade timeline, it is clear that the earlier you begin, the earlier you reach the pinnacle. Tiger Woods, Jeff Gordon and Wayne Gretzky started their journeys before they started school, which is why they got to the top in their early twenties. Henry Ford didn't start building cars until his late thirties, which is why his rise to prominence didn't take place until his fifties. That is just the nature of the game. For those who don't begin until age 20, eminence cannot be expected until somewhere around age 40. Those who began competing as children have the best chance of achieving early eminence. The romantic notion of instant stardom is almost always pure fiction. True eminence derives from years of toil during which one acquires mastery of a domain.

TIMELINE TO MASTERY & EMINENCE			
Superathlete	**Beginning Age**	**Age at Mastery**	**Age on Achieving Eminence**	**Total Timeline in Years**
Muhammad Ali	Boxing lessons 12	Olympic Champ 18	Heavyweight Champ 22	10
Lance Armstrong	Won first race 10	Champion cyclist 21	Tour de France 28	18
Jeff Gordon	Midget car racing 5	US Midget Champ 18	Winston Cup Champ 24	19
Wayne Gretzky	Competitve hockey 6	Junior Hockey Star 15	Best player in NHL 26	20
Michael Jordan	Little League Star 8	All-American BB 18	Best player in NBA 28	20
Greg Louganis	Acrobatic champ 4	US Olympic Team 16	Olympic gold medals 24	20
Martina Navratilova	Competitive play 6	Czech Champ 16	Best in the World 26	20
Pelé	Competitive play 5	World Cup Champ 17	World's Best 25	20
Wilma Rudolph	First race 12	All-state BB team 15	1960 Olympic Gold 20	8
Babe Ruth	St. Mary's BB team 7	Red Socks Pitching Ace 19	Home Run King 26	19
Jim Thorpe	First hunting trip 8	Carlisle football hero 20	Olympic gold medals 24	16
Tiger Woods	Competitive golf 5	US Amateur Champ 15	Best in the World 25	20
Babe Zaharias	School golf team 16	1932 Olympic Gold 21	Best in the World 36	20

Chapter 15

SELF EMPOWERMENT

Per ardua ad astra
[Through difficulties to the stars]

What Does this Research Tell Us about Gaining the Competitive Edge?

You have probably guessed by now that this book is not exclusively about sports or sports superstars. This context was merely the crucible for empirical research into the psychology of achievement and the winning behaviors of the super-achievers. Timothy Gallwey, renowned sports psychologist and author of best-selling books *The Inner Game of Tennis* and *The Inner Game of Golf*, notes that sports are really a microcosm in which we can observe and develop the character we need to achieve our goals (p. 213):

If the game [of golf] is played as Bobby Jones claimed to play it–as a conquest of oneself–it becomes truly recreational. It is a break from the routine and patterns of daily life that can truly enrich our existence. What players learn about themselves on the course can be transferred to every aspect of their lives and thus benefit the culture of which golf is only a small part.

Indeed, sports are a wonderful microcosm of life. They enable us to learn winning behaviors that we can apply to all facets of our careers, lifestyles and personal relationships. In athletics, winning and losing are more easily defined and the consequences of positive and negative behaviors are immediate. Thus we can experiment with different types of behaviors, discovering what works and what does not. From these observations we extract some fundamental principles that underlie winning behaviors in athletics and then extrapolate these to the worlds of business and life. Not surprisingly, we find that the very principles that I have described in this book underlie success in all domains.

Once we accept that eminence in sports, business or life has more to do with nurture than nature, we must conclude that the level of success or fulfillment we achieve in athletics and in our lives is a direct consequence of our early imprints and subsequent behaviors. Life is, indeed, a do-it-yourself kit. If most of our behaviors are winning behaviors, then we will tend to be successful. On the other hand, an operating style replete with self-defeating behaviors will inevitably bring a life of unresolved wants and needs.

Accepting that success is a direct result of our behaviors is the first step toward personal empowerment. We can no longer excuse our unresolved dreams by ascribing failure to bad luck, jealous adversaries or having "inferior genes." Those who feel unfulfilled in their careers often look at a more successful colleague and dismiss his success as a consequence of "sucking up" or attribute her success to "sleeping with the boss." Winners attack their weaknesses while losers deny or justify their ineptitudes. Those who feel unfulfilled in their quest for life's rewards observe superstars with mixed feelings of admiration and envy, ascribing the superstar's stellar success to some arbitrary stroke of genetic good fortune. However, those who understand the direct link between winning and losing take full responsibility for their setbacks and build on their strengths to attain their goals.

How Can this Research Benefit You?

These findings offer the ultimate empowerment to those who understand their implications. As we observed in Chapter 3, only a small fraction of the population ever achieve their dreams. The others, the vast majority of humanity, rationalize their unfulfilled aspirations by attributing them to inherited limitations or external factors beyond their control. This gives them some comfort, relieving them of the personal responsibility, but it imprisons them within their self-imposed limits. Recall Tiger Woods' admonition:

> *Knowing that you never arrive is a wonderful thing, because you never say, "This is my limit." You never put a limit on your own abilities. I think that's where a lot of players, a lot of athletes in general, put limitations: 'That's as good as I can play.' I hear that all the time...If you put a limitation on it, then you can't get any better."*

Tiger recognizes that he and he alone controls whether his skills improve, decline or remain static. If you are courageous enough to accept that your failures result from self-defeating behaviors or the absence of some winning behaviors, you are on the threshold of personal empowerment. By accepting full responsibility for your life's outcomes, you acknowledge that achieving your goals lies within your control. It's merely a matter of learning and acquiring the winning behaviors and divesting yourself of those behaviors that are self-defeating. Over 150 years ago, in his classic work *A Christmas Carol*, Charles Dickens captured the concept of self-empowerment through the character of Ebenezer Scrooge. Scrooge's miserly ways had made him friendless and miserable and his increasing cynicism had left him in a conundrum from which there seemed no escape. During visits from three spirits who coerced him into viewing his own behaviors from without, he recognized how he had been the architect of his own misery. Once he resolved to change his behaviors, Scrooge began to experience the joy that had eluded him for so many years. Dickens realized that our fulfillment in life is within our control through our ability to modify our behavior.

Through Adversity to Superstardom

Seeing possibilities in the impossible is the magic that makes people great. Relatively normal people with winning attitudes and behaviors display an uncanny ability to push through monumental adversity and win victories of the highest order. The inside stories of the athletic superstars and eminent entrepreneurs reveal over and over again lives fraught with misery, defeat and tragedy. Success arrived only after prolonged periods of trial and tribulation. Success did not occur *in spite of* adversity, but rather *because of* it. Ilya Prigogine, winner of the Nobel Prize in Chemistry for his work on dissipative structures, observed:

> *Breakdown is a harbinger of breakthrough. Psychological suffering, anxiety and collapse lead to new emotional, intellectual and spiritual strengths.*

Only by breaking down old barriers and beliefs can we free ourselves to explore creative new solutions to problems. In essence, adversity is an important catalyst in the problem-solving process. When apparently insurmountable obstacles arise, most people fold their tents and go home. For them the unknown is frightening. For those who see how adversity can lead to new opportunities, the pathway to the top is far easier. Those bound for greatness find adversity challenging and titillating. Also-rans capitulate.

In my *13 Principles of Empowerment* I have attempted to capture the winning behaviors that enable the eminent to push through adversity and reach the stars while the majority of humanity are defeated and settle for mediocrity. By learning and practicing these behaviors, you can push through adversity and achieve your dreams. However, before you proceed with a plan to implement these principles, you should develop a personal psychological profile by taking the self-assessments in the preceding chapters. To ensure an accurate assessment of your personality, it is essential that you try to answer each question as honestly as you can. Then in those areas where you discover a weakness, identify and practice the winning behaviors that you need to incorporate in your normal mode of operation. Identify your main goals and break them down into manageable sub-goals. Analyze the sacrifices you will need to make to achieve your goals and if you believe the goal is worth the price, go for it!

The Psychology of Winning

As noted in the previous chapter, athletic prowess has far more to do with the head and heart than the body. Performance at a high level in any venue is not about talent. Obviously, talent has some importance. You can't compete if you're not coordinated just as you probably can't play in the NBA if you are 4' 8" tall. When all else is equal, inherited characteristics matter. However, acquired skills usually override innate proclivities. K. Anders Ericsson, who has studied exceptional performance in athletics, academics and games such as chess and bridge, asserts that deliberate practice is the major factor and innate talent the minor factor in attaining excellence. Ericsson emphasizes that a training program involving continuous repetition and refinement of skills is the key to reaching the top in any field–sports, business or life!

Life in the fast lane demands a strong mental state and an indomitable will. Since the only limitations in life emanate from the heart and the head, you must look within to find the source of your energy. Introspection is the answer to most dilemmas. Ask what makes you tick and why. Many people are afraid to ask. They are deathly afraid of hearing an answer that will undermine their sense of self. But not so for the superstars. They are typically highly introspective–their own toughest critics.

Cognitive psychologist Douglas Hofsadter wrote of the necessity of introspection for the individual who faces chaos. Referring to the need to master oneself while in the midst of a frenetic environment, he observed (*USA Today*, Oct. 9, 1997), "An eerie type of chaos can lurk behind a façade of order–and yet, deep inside the chaos lurks an even eerier type of order."

The psychology of winning is about a strong sense of self fortified by the belief that you will ultimately achieve your goals. It is about a willingness to fail in the face of huge throngs screaming for your scalp. Winning is about setting a goal that you desperately wish to achieve and having the tenacity to chase it even when you are tired and hurt. Above all, being the best is about having a strong sense of self,

The first black Olympic gold medallist in the decathlon in 1956, Milt Campbell said, "If I don't wake up every day thinking I'm going to win the Olympic gold medal, I won't." Michael Jordan said, "This game is more mental than physical." Tiger Woods told *Golf Digest* (2003), "Every time I play, in my own mind, I'm the favorite." Such mental power is key to winning.

Where Does the Sense of Self Come From?

Superstars thrive on challenge and the unknown that intimidate and threaten the rest of us. Where does this difference originate? A study published in 2002 found that athletic prowess in adulthood could be traced back to early imprinting experiences. This research from the University of Otago in Dunedin, New Zealand, concluded "Children who show little fear of just about anything are three times more likely than their more anxious peers to achieve success as adults." This would indicate that grooming children early to tolerate risk pays long term dividends. D. McClelland, who spent much of his life testing the origins of achievement and power, concluded in his book *The Achieving Society* that greatness is programmed early:

> *Achievement can be developed. Achievement-motivated people are more likely to be developed in families in which parents hold different expectations from normal families. They expect their children to start showing some independence between ages six and eight, making choices and doing things without help, such as knowing the way around the neighborhood and taking care of themselves around the house.*

The 13 athletic superstars profiled in this book all thrived on challenge early in life. Their greatest fear was not of intimidation by adversaries, but rather of failure. As a young child, Tiger Woods told his first golf coach, "I'm never intimidated." He carried this disposition into adulthood. Thomas Edison and Walt Disney both displayed risk-taking behavior by riding the rails alone as adolescents. At age seven, Ross Perot had broken his nose several times while breaking horses. He credited his becoming a billionaire to this experience. The self-efficacy common to all athletic superstars is also evident in the great entrepreneurs.

Many great people were precocious, and the same is true of most of the super-athletes. Virtually all who are profiled in this book competed with much older children and even adults. They also tended to befriend and converse with adults long before reaching adulthood. A child who learns to compete with someone much older learns how to deal with bigger, stronger and more experienced adversaries. Picasso fraternized with older friends while living in the Pyrenees Mountains. To survive in Paris he lived with an older man and developed his skills as a wunderkind of the arts. Bill Gates skipped his senior year of high school to program computers for TRW. Michael Dell made more money in his senior year of high school than his economics teacher did. While their peers were chasing girls, they were chasing dreams.

How does precocity groom superstars for the climb to the top? Associating with older friends leads to greater maturity through a combined mental and social osmosis. Furthermore, it teaches the precocious child how to compete when at a physical and experiential disadvantage. They learn earlier than most that size doesn't matter, execution matters. Virtually all the superstars that we profile in this book were quite normal in size while growing up, but competed effectively with others who were older and much bigger. Consequently, they were forced to use skill and strategy to compete. They had nothing to lose and everything to gain, and that brought with it a winning attitude.

For those who did not get an early start, there is good news–it's never too late to develop winning behaviors. Shakespeare observed, "Some are born great, some achieve greatness and some have greatness thrust upon them." Those who are precocious are the ones who have learned the winning behaviors so young that they appear to have been born with these qualities. Those who achieve greatness are the ones who acquire the winning behaviors later and those who have greatness thrust upon them are the ones whose strong behaviors have been forged out of the fires of challenge and adversity.

The Main Impediment to Reaching Eminence

Most world-class athletes learn early that their greatest adversary lies within. In an interview with Larry King on June 10, 1998, Tiger Woods said, "There are two opponents in the game, yourself and the golf course. If you can somehow combat those two, you'll do all right." People who don't recognize this are in for a frustrating experience when they attempt to turn their hopes and dreams into reality. There is in all of us an inertial force that induces us to choose the path of least resistance. We would rather relax on the beach than endure a tough workout in the gym, the slopes, the links or the courts. Our innate desire for hedonistic pursuits beckons to us, "Stop working so hard," "Excessive practice is counterproductive," and "You deserve some R&R, some downtime. It's time to party." These inner battles are the biggest we fight on the road to achievement. External adversaries are easy by comparison. They are not present every minute of every day like those inner demons. Life's big wins all come from mastery of the self and control over that inner desire to take the easy path. This is particularly evident when things are toughest. When you hit the wall it is easy to quit, but that is when your inner strength must take over. When pain is unbearable, pleasure becomes more important than winning and only those with indomitable spirits can survive the powerful forces of inertia.

The quandary we face when we strive for physical achievement came into clear perspective one day when I observed a group of body builders working out. Their muscled physiques revealed their sacrifice and diligence. One of them was struggling in agony as he tried to complete one more chin-up to finish his set. His biceps and latissimus dorsi ("lats") were straining as he inched upward. On reaching the bar, he dropped to his feet and winced in pain. Then, catching his breath, he smiled with self-satisfaction and announced, "Ah, it's a great life if you don't weaken." There was a pause as his workout buddies contemplated his proud statement. Then the training partner whose turn had come, looked up at the chinning bar and observed, "Ya, but all the fun is in weakenin'." It was an insightful recognition of the dilemma we face when we wish to achieve. To enjoy life we must achieve something, but achievement requires that we sacrifice now for future rewards–"no pain, no gain." A corollary to this principle is that the degree of achievement we attain is roughly proportional to the amount of pain or sacrifice we can endure in our climb to the top.

Identifying problems and defining them is critical to the solution of all great dilemmas. Until we know our weaknesses on the field of play it is impossible to correct them. And until we also identify the weaknesses of our opponents, we are unable to attack them. Introspection and scrutiny are vitally important behaviors in winning any contest. We must look within and find those culprits that inhibit or limit our skills. If excess weight is holding us back, we must implement a healthy yet moderate diet. We must employ push-backs from the table rather than push-ups, and be brutally honest with ourselves about our eating habits. Some of us rationalize the consumption of a fourth slice of pizza or a third beer as a way of getting extra carbohydrates for energy, but our body merely stores as fat the carbohydrates that it does not burn. Martina Navratilova's rise to the top occurred only after she stopped living on Big Macs and chugging down milkshakes.

Among the most popular rationalizations for avoiding workouts is to yield to fatigue. We all get tired, but low achievers seem to get there more often than the winners. The eminent seldom tire until they reach the locker room. Then they collapse. They are in better condition because they run that extra mile. When tired of pushing weights, they push ten more. To make a difference they work harder, and when most are finished they do even more. During the practice for the 2003 cycling tour, the US team had completed two ascents of L'Alpe d'Huez in a grueling six-hour exercise. Team member George Hincapie reported (*USA Today*, February 17, 2004):

We were all trashed and eager to head back to the hotel, but Lance [Armstrong] just looked at us and said, "I think I'll go up one more time." We could barely stand, and he was ready to climb again...that was unbelievable.

It isn't the first 100 practice serves in tennis that make a difference. It is the last 50. Those are the ones that raise your game to a new level. It isn't the first 50 laps in the pool that make you grow. It is the last 5. Commitment to intense practice is a theme that is common to all the great sports superstars. You have met this theme again and again in the profiles of the previous chapters. There is no short cut to building skills in athletics, academics or business.

Watching Life from the Bench or Winning on the Field

Enlightenment and empowerment emanate from within. The body is but an agent of the mind. When the mind knows, the body has a tendency to respond to its intentions. Studies in kinesiology have revealed that the body weakens when the mind thinks negatively and strengthens when it thinks positively. Positive energy is transmitted from thoughts to the muscles. When Shakespeare wrote, "The eyes are the windows of the soul," he was acknowledging how powerfully the eyes convey the intentions of the brain. Michael Jordan often spoke of looking into the eyes of his adversary to determine whether they had what it took to compete.

In his book *Power vs. Force*, Psychiatrist David Hawkins implores us to acknowledge the need to reach "higher states of consciousness" in order to function optimally. For him, transcendence is going beyond the possible to consider the impossible; something that cannot happen in the presence of doubt or any form of pessimism. He asserts that to transcend normal achievement levels, competitors should remove the mind and allow the body to seek its limits. He estimated that 85% of society functions within the constraints of conventional thought, shown in the diagram below as a mediocrity box. The remaining 15% have so much positive energy that they escape mediocrity and attain a measure of peace and joy. Only a minuscule percentage of that 15% ever approaches the Shangri La known as *enlightenment*.

EMPOWERMENT

Only 15% of the world is energized positively. For them life is about joy, peace and optimism.

THE BOUNDED BOX OF MEDIOCRITY

"85% of the world is de-energized by fear, anger, grief and guilt–it is debilitating and antithetic to coping"
–David Hawkins

Winning behaviors set free the athletic superstars, the great entrepreneurs and the free thinkers in all fields

The Flow State

All athletes aspire to find that magical land known in sports as *The Zone*. Some speak of getting into the flow of the game. In *Flow*, eminent psychologist Mihaly Csikszentmihalyi describes the flow state that corresponds to performing in the zone in athletics, but also encompasses other creative pursuits (p. 4):

Flow is a highly focused state of relaxed concentration that obliterates all else out of consciousness. It is the state of self-actualization or transcendental behavior that is euphoric, the state in which people are so involved in an activity that nothing else seems to matter.

Csikszentmihalyi was describing a state of ecstasy that people involved in creative endeavors reach when in a highly charged state of inner bliss. It is a place that many cultists or religious mystics get to when they become so transfixed that they appear mesmerized to their disciples. Musicians go into what they call an aesthetic rapture. Picasso often spoke of a similar experience. "I never get tired," the founder of Cubism wrote, "That's why painters live so long. While I work, I leave my body outside the door, the way Moslems take off their shoes before entering the mosque." Functioning outside consciousness is the secret. People with this ability go into a trance-like state that is kind of supernatural. And it makes them perform supernaturally. Escaping reality makes them unreal, and their shots and moves are also unreal. It is a kind of surreal state where success is guaranteed. This is the land of ethereal brilliance.

In *The Psychology of Consciousness*, British psychiatrist Robert Ornstein described the brain's function during optimal performance. He observed, "The artist, dancer and mystic have learned to develop the non-verbal portion of their intelligence and therefore have become creative." Flow is a state of being in which instincts seem to guide us effortlessly to our goals. It is a state in which we know the right words to say in any given situation, where we start running to a position before the opposing player hits the ball to that spot, or where ideas flow onto our computer keyboard as if directed by a mysterious force. It is an epiphany or consummate rapture where centering takes place. Carl Jung called this place *syzygy*–the conjunction of the conscious and unconscious. In *Eight Keys to Greatness*, I described achieving this state as "synthesizing to success."

In his monumental work *The Farthest Reaches of Human Nature*, Abraham Maslow spoke of a transcendent personality destined to rule the world. He wrote, "The climax of self-actualizing is the peak experience." Being in the zone, describes that peak experience in which all things work–that magical place where the mental, physical, spiritual and emotional blend into one self-actualizing spirit. Csikszentmihalyi described perform-ance in the zone as an "eerie state of brilliance" or "Flow State." Russian coaches refer to it as "the white moment." In Japan it is known as *ki*. In China it is called *chi*. In India it is *prana*. It is known as *lung-gom* in Tibet. For Americans, it is merely getting into the zone.

Final Comments

My intention in writing this book has been to share with you the winning behaviors embodied in my *13 Principles of Empowerment*. By practicing these behaviors, you will begin to discover how to attain your goals. Follow the adage: Think big, start small. Create a sequence of attainable intermediate goals that build toward your ultimate goals. Then apply the winning behaviors relentlessly in your pursuit of these intermediate goals.

When you suffer a setback or meet an impasse in striving toward your goals, you must invoke Principle #12: *See an obstacle as an opportunity*, or in extreme cases, Principle #4: *Transform breakdown into breakthrough*. As discussed in Chapter 10, how you react to failure determines whether you become a winner or a loser. Recall the admonition of Confucius, "Our greatest glory is not in never falling, but in rising every time we fall." Eventually, you will develop the habit of dusting yourself off after a fall and renewing your resolve to achieve your goal. These periods that follow the minor setbacks and defeats offer the most valuable learning opportunities. When we succeed, we tacitly assume we are on the right track and we don't stop to analyze our actions. As Bill Gates observed in *The Road Ahead* (p. 35), "Success is a lousy teacher. It seduces smart people into thinking they can't lose." However, when we fail, we move into a problem-solving mode and begin to investigate alternative routes to our goals. By recognizing obstacles as challenges and then responding with the positive emotional dispositions shown in the Kinesthetic Karma diagram, you will move inexorably toward your goals and feel the exhilaration of personal empowerment. Like all worthwhile pursuits, your quest for self-actualization will exact a price, but that will make its attainment all the more precious. I wish you well in this endeavor, but I will not wish you luck–that's needed only by those with an external locus of control!

The Distribution of Human Talent

In the late 1800s, Sir Frances Galton measured the heights of 8585 men in Great Britain and recorded the number of men corresponding to each height. (Statisticians call this the *frequency* of each height because it's the number of times that height occurs in the list of measurements.) When the frequencies of all the heights were plotted, the resulting graph had the bell shape shown in the diagram below left. Observing that this shape is very close to the graph of the *normal distribution*, Galton conjectured that the heights of all males in a sufficiently large sample are normally distributed (below right).

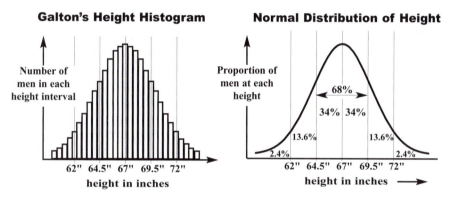

In fact, the normal distribution that fit his data has a mean of 67" and a standard deviation of 2.5". From the mathematical properties of the normal distribution, Galton was able to conclude the following:

- the average (mean) height was 67".

- heights were distributed symmetrically about 67", i.e., the number of men who deviated from 67" by a particular amount on the high side, equalled the number who deviated by that same amount on the low side.

- about 34% of all men had heights between 67" and 69.5" (i.e., 67" + 2.5") and about 34% of all men had heights between 64.5" and 67". That is, 34% of all men had heights within one standard deviation above the mean and 34% had heights within one standard deviation below the mean.

Subsequent research in the century that followed, has revealed that many physical, psychological and psychomotor attributes in the human population are normally distributed. Among the most widely studied examples is IQ. The popular Wechsler IQ test has been keyed to the normal distribution with mean 100 and standard deviation 15. This implies that when a large random sample of people take this IQ test, the average score will be 100. Furthermore, 34% will score between 100 and 115, (i.e., within one standard deviation above the mean) and 34% will score between 85 and 100 (i.e. within one standard deviation below the mean.) Only 2.4% will score more than two standard deviations above the mean, i.e., above 130 and only 2.4% below 70. SATs and other tests yield similar results. Since talents and skills are normally distributed within the human population, it might be expected that achievement, when measurable in quantitative terms, is also normally distributed.

GENERAL REFERENCES

Adler, Alfred. (1979) *Superiority and Social Interest*. 3rd rev. ed. New York: Norton & Co.

Adler, Jerry. (June 2, 2003) "Golf: Don't Think Twice–or at all, for that Matter." *Newsweek*, p. 14.

Baumeister, Roy, Laura Smart & J. Boden. (1996) "The Dark Side of High Self-Esteem." *Psychological Review*. v103, p. 68, 70-71.

Boorstin, Daniel. (1992) *The Creators*. New York: Random House.

Branden, Nathaniel. (1994) *Six Pillars of Self-Esteem*. New York: Bantam.

Buckingham, Marcus & Curt Coffman. (1999) *First, Break All the Rules*. New York: Simon & Schuster.

Conger, Jay. (1989) *The Charismatic Leader*. San Francisco, CA: Jossey-Bass.

Crothers, Tim & John Garrity. (1999) *Sports Illustrated Greatest Athletes of the 20th Century*. New York: Time Inc.

Csikszentmihalyi, Mihaly. (1996) *Creativity: Flow and the Psychology of Discovery & Invention*. New York: Harper Collins.

Farley, Frank. (May, 1986) "Type T Personality." *Psychology Today*, p. 46–52.

Frankl, Viktor. (1959) *In Search of Meaning*. New York: Pocket Books.

Franzini, Louis & John Grossberg. (1995) *Eccentric & Bizarre Behaviors*. New York: John Wiley & Sons.

Ferguson, Marilyn. (1980) *The Aquarian Conspiracy: Personal and Social Transformation in the 1980s*. Los Angeles, CA: J.P. Tarcher, Inc.

Gallo, Fred & Harry Vincenzi. (2000) *Energy Tapping*. Oakland, CA: New Harbinger.

Gallwey, W. Timothy. (1998) *The Inner Game of Golf*. New York: Random House.

Gardner, Howard. (1997) *Extraordinary Minds*. New York: Basic Books.

—— (1993) *Creating Minds*. New York: Basic Books.

—— (1983) *Frames of Mind: The Theory of Multiple Intelligences*. New York: Basic Books.

Garfield, Charles. (1986) *Peak Performance*. New York: Avon Books.

Gelb, Michael. (2002) *Discover Your Genius*. New York: Harper Collins.

—— (1998) *How to Think Like Leonardo da Vinci*. New York: Dell Trade.

Ghislin, Brewster. (1952) *The Creative Process*. Berkeley, CA: Berkeley Press.

Gilder, George. (1984) *The Spirit of Enterprise*. New York: Simon & Schuster.

Goleman, Daniel. (1995) *Emotional Intelligence*. New York: Bantam.

Gordon, Richard. (2002) *Quantum-Touch: The Power to Heal*. Berkeley, CA: North Atlantic Books.

Greene, Robert. (2001) *The Art of Seduction*. New York: Viking Press.

Gross, Ronald. (2002) *Socrates' Way: Seven Master Keys to Using Your Mind to the Utmost*. New York: Penguin Books.

Hawkins, David. (2001) *The Eye of The I*. Sedona, AZ: Veritas Publishing.

—— (1999) *Power & Force*. Sedona, AZ: Veritas Publishing.

Heatherton, Todd F. & Joel Weinberger. (1993) *Can Personality Change?* Washington, D.C.: American Psychological Association.

Herzog, Brad. (1995) *The Sports 100: The One Hundred Most Important People in American Sports History*. New York: Macmillan.

Hill, Napoleon. (1960) *Think & Grow Rich*. New York: Fawcett Crest.

Hirsh, Sandra & Jean Kummerow. (1989) *Life Types*. New York: Time Warner.

Homer-Dixon, Thomas. (2000) *The Ingenuity Gap*. New York: Knopf.

Hutchison, Michael. (1990) *The Anatomy of Sex & Power*. New York: William Morrow.

Jamison, Kay. (1994) *Touched with Fire*. New York: The Free Press.

Jung, Carl (1976) "The Stages of Life." *The Portable Jung*. New York: Penguin. Part 1, Chapter 1.

Jung, Carl & Joseph Campbell Ed. (1976) *The Portable Jung*. New York: Penguin.

Kanter, Rosabeth. (2004) *Confidence: How Winning Streaks and Losing Streaks Begin and End*. New York: Crown Publishing.

Keirsey, David. (1987) *Portraits of Temperament*. Del Mar, CA: Prometheus Books.

Keirsey, David & Marilyn Bates. (1984) *Please Understand Me: Character and Temperament Types*. Del Mar, CA: Prometheus Books.

Killy, Jean Claude. (1974) *Comeback*. New York: Macmillan.

Klein, Burton. (1977) *Dynamic Economics*. Boston, MA: Harvard University Press.

Kuhn, Thomas. (1962) *The Structure of Scientific Revolutions*. Chicago: University of Chicago Press.

Landrum, Gene. (2003) *Entrepreneurial Genius: The Power of Passion*. Burlington, ON, Canada: Brendan Kelly Publishing Inc.

—— (2001) *Sybaritic Genius*. Naples, FL: Genie-Vision Books.

—— (2000) *Literary Genius*. Naples, FL: Genie-Vision Books.

—— (1999) *Eight Keys to Greatness*. Buffalo, NY: Prometheus Books.

—— (1997) *Profiles of Black Success: Thirteen Creative Geniuses Who Changed the World*. Buffalo, NY: Prometheus Books.

—— (1996) *Profiles of Power & Success*. Buffalo, NY: Prometheus Books.

—— (1994) *Profiles of Female Genius*. Buffalo, NY: Prometheus Books.

—— (1993) *Profiles of Genius*. Buffalo, NY: Prometheus Books.

Leman, Kenneth. (1985) *The Birth Order Book*. New York: Dell Publishing.

Ludwig, Arnold. (1995) *The Price of Greatness*. New York: Guilford Press.

MacCambridge, Michael. Ed. (1999) *ESPN Sports Century*. New York: Hyperion.

Meadows, Dennis et al. (1972) *Limits to Growth*. New York: The New American Library Inc.

Martens, Rainer, Robin Vealey & Damon Burton. (1990) *Competitive Anxiety in Sport*. Champaign, IL: Human Kinetics Books.

McTaggart, Lynne. (2002) *The Field: The Quest for the Secret of the Universe*. New York: Quill.

Michener, James. (1976) *Sports in America*. Greenwich, CT: Fawcett Crest.

Moore, David. (2002) *The Dependent Gene: The Fallacy of Nature vs. Nurture*. New York: Henry Holt & Co.

Murphy, Michael & Rhea White. (1995) *In the Zone: Transcendent Experience in Sports*. Middlesex, U.K.: Penguin Books.

Murray, Charles. (2003) *Human Accomplishment: The Pursuit of Excellence in the Arts and Sciences, 800 B.C. to 1950*. New York: Harper Collins.

Nicklaus, Jack with Ken Bowden. (1974) *Golf My Way*. New York: Simon & Schuster.

Orlick, Terry. (2000) *In Pursuit of Excellence: How to Win in Sport and Life through Mental Training*. Champaign IL: Human Kinetics.

Ornstein, Robert. (1991) *Evolution of Consciousness: The Origins of the Way We Think*. New York: Touchstone.

——— (1972) *The Psychology of Consciousness*. New York: Penguin.

Orr, Frank & George Tracz. (2004) *The Dominators: The Remarkable Athletes Who Changed Their Sport Forever*. Toronto: Warwick Publishing.

O'Neil, William. Ed. (2004) *Sports Leaders & Success: 55 Top Sports Leaders & How They Achieved Greatness*. New York: McGraw-Hill.

O'Shea, Michael. (July 13, 2003) "How Important is Regular Exercise for My Sex Life?" *Parade*, p. 15.

Peterson, Karen S. (Sept 14, 1998) "Power, Sex, Risk." *USA Today*, p. 6D.

Pickover, Clifford. (1998) *Strange Brains and Genius*. New York: William Morrow.

Plimpton, George. (1990) *The X Factor: A Quest for Excellence*. New York: Whittle Books.

Prigogine, Ilya, and Isabelle Stengers. (1984) *Order Out of Chaos*. New York: Bantam Books.

Richman, Michael. (Feb 17, 2000) "Sportswriter Grantland Rice." *Investor's Business Daily*, p. A4.

Rosenzweig, Mark. (1971) *Biopsychology of Development*. New York: Academic Press.

Schwarzenegger, Arnold with Bill Dobbins. (1998) *The New Encyclopedia of Modern Bodybuilding*. New York: Simon & Schuster.

Sheldrake, Rupert. (2003) *The Sense of Being Stared At*. New York: Crown Publishing.

Siler, Todd. (1996) *Think Like a Genius*. New York: Bantam Books.

Simonton, Dean. (1994) *Greatness*. New York: The Guilford Press.

Storr, Anthony. (1996) *Feet of Clay: Saints, Sinners & Madmen–A Study of Gurus*. New York: Free Press.

——— (1993) *The Dynamics of Creation*. New York: Ballantine Books.

Sulloway, Frank. (1996) *Born to Rebel: Birth Order, Family Dynamics, & Creative Lives*. New York: Pantheon Books.

Vernacchia, Ralph. (2003) *Inner Strength: The Mental Dynamics of Athletic Performance*. Palo Alto, CA: Warde Publishers.

Walker, Harris. (2000) *The Physics of Consciousness*. New York: Perseus Books.

Weeks, David & Jamie James. (1995) *Eccentrics: A Study of Sanity & Strangeness*. New York: Villard.

Wilson, Robert Anton. (1990) *Quantum Psychology*. Phoenix, AR: Falcon Press.

Wolinsky, Stephen. (1994) *The Tao of Chaos*. Norfolk, CT: Bramble Books.

Woolum, J. (1992) *Outstanding Women Athletes: Who They Are and How They Influenced Sports in America*. Phoenix, AZ: The Oryx Press.

CHAPTER REFERENCES

JIM THORPE

Deagon, Brian. (Jan 16, 2002) "Jim Thorpe Earned the Gold." *Investor's Business Daily*, p. A3.

ESPN–Classics Special (Mar 9, 2003) "Jim Thorpe–All American."

Herzog, Brad. (1995) "Jim Thorpe." *The Sports 100: The One Hundred Most Important People in American Sports History*. New York: Macmillan. p. 105–109.

Richman, Michael. (Aug 16, 1999) "Olympic Track Champ Jim Thorpe." *Investor's Business Daily*, p. A8.

Wheeler, Robert. (1975) *Jim Thorpe*. Norman, OK: University of Oklahoma Press.

GEORGE HERMAN (BABE) RUTH

Barra, Allen. (Jul 7, 1999) "Baseball's Best Hitters." *Wall Street Journal*.

Blum, Ronald. (Dec 11, 1999) "It's Nearly Unanimous: The Babe is the Best." *Naples Daily News*, p. 2C.

Brady, Erik.(Feb 3, 1995) "Legend Keeps Going." *USA Today*, p. C–1.

Creamer, Robert. (1974) *BABE: The Legend Comes to Life*. New York: Penguin Books.

Costa, Gabe. (2002) "Babe Ruth Dethroned?" *The Baseball Research Journal*, p. 102–106.

Gallico, Paul. (1965) *The Golden People*. Garden City, NY: Doubleday & Co.

Gilbert, Brother, C.F.X. & Harry Rothgerber Ed. (1999) *Young Babe Ruth: His Early Life and Baseball Career, from the Memoirs of a Xaverian Brother*. Jefferson, NC: McFarland & Co.

Herzog, Brad. (1995) "Babe Ruth." *The Sports 100: The One Hundred Most Important People in American Sports History*. New York: Macmillan. p. 17–21.

MacCambridge, Michael. Ed. (1999) "Babe Ruth." *ESPN Sports Century*. New York: Hyperion. p. 80–91.

Miller, Ernestine. (2000) *The Babe Book*. Kansas City, MS: Andrews McMell Publishing.

Orr, Frank & George Tracz. (2004) "Babe Ruth." *The Dominators: The Remarkable Athletes Who Changed Their Sport Forever*. Toronto: Warwick Publishing. p. 112–115.

Thorn, John. (1975) *A Century of Baseball Lore*. New York: Hart Publishing.

Wagenheim, Kal. (2001) *Babe Ruth: His Life and Legend*. Milford, CT: Olmstead Press.

Wallace, Irving, Amy Wallace, David Wallechinsky & Sylvia Wallace. (1993) "Babe Ruth." *The Secret Sex Lives of Famous People*. New York: Dorset Press. p. 390.

Wood, Allan. (2000) 1918:Babe Ruth and the World Champion Boston Red Sox. New York: Writers Club Press.

MILDRED (BABE) DIDRIKSON ZAHARIAS

Cayleff, Susan. (1996) Babe: *The Life and Legend of Babe Didrikson Zaharias*. Chicago, IL: University of Illinois Press.

Herzog, Brad. (1995) "Babe Didrikson Zaharias." *The Sports 100: The One Hundred Most Important People in American Sports History*. New York: Macmillan. p. 110–114.

Orr, Frank & George Tracz. (2004) "Babe Didrikson." *The Dominators: The Remarkable Athletes Who Changed Their Sport Forever*. Toronto: Warwick Publishing. p. 28–31.

Zaharias, Mildred (Babe) Didrikson. (1935) *This Life I've Led: My Autobiography*. New York: Dell.

WILMA RUDOLPH

Biracree, T. (1987) *Wilma Rudolph*. New York: HP XT Publishing.

Chicago Tribune. (Jan 8, 1989) Interview with Wilma Rudolph.

Dixon, Oscar. (Nov 14, 1994) "Skeeter Took Fame in Stride. " *USA Today*, p. C1.

Gaines, Ann Graham. (1999) *Sports & Athletics–Female Firsts in their Fields*. New York: Chelsea House Publications.

Herzog, Brad. (1995) "Wilma Rudolph." *The Sports 100: The One Hundred Most Important People in American Sports History*. New York: Macmillan. p. 239–241.

Rudolph, Wilma with Martin Raibovsky. (1977) *Wilma*. New York: Signet Books.

Sherrow, Victoria. (1993) *Wilma Rudolph*. New York: Lert Publishing.

Wickham, Pete. (Nov 14, 1994) "Wilma Rudolph: Watching a Friend Die." *Naples Daily News*, p. C1.

Women in History. www.lkwdpl.org/wihohio/rudo-wil.htm

PELÉ (EDSON ARANTES DO NASCIMENTO)

Harris, Harry. (2000) *Pelé: His Life and Times*. London, UK: Robson Books.

Herzog, Brad. (1995) "Pelé." *The Sports 100: The One Hundred Most Important People in American Sports History*. New York: Macmillan. p. 366–369.

Orr, Frank & George Tracz. (2004) "Pelé." *The Dominators: The Remarkable Athletes Who Changed Their Sport Forever*. Toronto: Warwick Publishing. p. 84–87.

Pelé with Robert Fish. (1977) *My Life and the Beautiful Game*. New York: Doubleday.

MUHAMMAD ALI

Ali, Muhammad with Richard Durham. (1975) *The Greatest: My Own Story*. New York: Random House.

Brunt, Stephen. (2002) *Facing Ali: The Opposition Weighs In*. Toronto: Alfred A. Knopf Canada.

Early, Gerald. (1989) *The Muhammad Ali Reader*. New York: Rob Weisback Books.

Herzog, Brad. (1995) "Muhammad Ali." *The Sports 100: The One Hundred Most Important People in American Sports History*. New York: Macmillan. p. 9–16.

Howard, Allen. (2001) *Ali: The Movie & The Man*. New York: Newmarket Press.

McKenzie, Michael. (Jun, 1998) "Muhammad Ali Lessons from The Greatest." *Success*, p. 68.

Orr, Frank & George Tracz. (2004) "Muhammad Ali." *The Dominators: The Remarkable Athletes Who Changed Their Sport Forever*. Toronto: Warwick Publishing. p. 12–16.

Pacheco, Ferdie. (1992) *Muhammad Ali: A View from the Corner*. New York: Carol Publishing Group.

Remnick, David. (1998) *King of the World*. New York: Vintage Books.

Saracemp, Jon. (Dec. 10, 1999) "Athlete of the Century: Muhammad Ali." *USA Today*, p. 1A.

Strathmore, William. (2001) *Muhammad Ali: The Unseen Archives*. Bath, UK: Parragon Publishing.

MARTINA NAVRATILOVA

Blue, Adrianne. (1995) *Martina Unauthorized*. New York: Birch Lane Press.

Faulkner, Sandra. (1993) *Love Match: Nelson vs Navratilova*. New York: Birch Lane Press.

Herzog, Brad. (1995) "Martina Navratilova." *The Sports 100: The One Hundred Most Important People in American Sports History*. New York: Macmillan. p. 309–311.

Manning, Anita. (Feb 27, 1996) "Navratilova's New Life in the Crime-fiction Racket." *USA Today*, p. 4D.

Navratilova, Martina with George Vescey. (1985) *Martina*. New York: Alfred A. Knopf.

Orr, Frank & George Tracz. (2004) "Martina Navratilova." *The Dominators: The Remarkable Athletes Who Changed Their Sport Forever*. Toronto: Warwick Publishing. p. 72–75.

Shew, Donna. (July 2, 1999) "Tennis Champ Martina Narvatilova." *Investor's Business Daily*, p. A–5.

GREG LOUGANIS

Allen, Karen. (July 24, 1996) "Levity Eased Burden of Louganis' Secret" *USA Today*, p. 6E.

Louganis, Greg & Eric Marcus. (1995) *Breaking the Surface*. New York: Random House.

Marshall, John. (Apr 9, 1995) "Tell All Information In Bio Not Easy for Private Louganis." *Naples Daily News*, p. 7B.

Smith, Harry. (Apr 16, 2001) "Greg Louganis." *A & E Biography TV Special*.

WAYNE GRETZKY

Brady, Erik. (Jan 16, 1997) "Old Man of the Ice." *USA Today*, p. C1.

———— (Apr 19, 1999) "Hail Gretzky, Full of Grace." *USA Today*, p. C1.

Dryden, Steve & Hockey News. (1999) *Total Gretzky: The Magic, The Legend, The Numbers*. Toronto: McClelland & Stewart.

Herzog, Brad. (1995) "Wayne Gretzky." *The Sports 100: The One Hundred Most Important People in American Sports History*. New York: Macmillan. p. 174–178.

Orr, Frank & George Tracz. (2004) "Wayne Gretzky." *The Dominators: The Remarkable Athletes Who Changed Their Sport Forever*. Toronto: Warwick Publishing. p. 36–39.

Podnieks, Andrew. (1999) *The Great One: The Life & Times of Wayne Gretzky*. Chicago, IL: Triumph Books.

Taylor, Jim. (1994) *Wayne Gretzky*. Vancouver, BC: Opus Productions.

MICHAEL JORDAN

Halberstam, David. (2000) *Playing for Keeps: Michael Jordan & the World He Made*. New York: Broadway Books.

Herzog, Brad. (1995) "Michael Jordan." *The Sports 100: The One Hundred Most Important People in American Sports History*. New York: Macmillan. p. 76–79.

Krugel, Mitchell. (1998) *Jordan: The Man, His Works, His Life*. New York: St. Martin's Press.

Landrum, Gene. (1997) "Michael Jeffrey Jordan." *Profiles of Black Success: Thirteen Creative Geniuses Who Changed the World*. Prometheus Books, Buffalo, N.Y. p. 219–235.

Leahy, Michael. (2004) *When Nothing Else Matters: Michael Jordan's Last Comeback*. New York: Simon & Schuster.

Orr, Frank & George Tracz. (2004) "Michael Jordan." *The Dominators: The Remarkable Athletes Who Changed Their Sport Forever*. Toronto: Warwick Publishing. p. 44–47.

Smith, Sam. (1994) *The Jordan Rules*. New York: Simon & Schuster.

Speigel, Peter. (Dec. 15, 1997) "Jordan & Company." *Forbes*, p. 180–206.

Sports Illustrated. (1999) *Sports Illustrated Presents Michael Jordan a Tribute from the Pages of SI*. Special Collectors Edition 24203. New York: Time, Inc.

Sports Illustrated. (1995) Michael!: *The Story of Michael Jordan from his Childhood to his Comeback*. Collector's Edition for Kids. New York: Time, Inc.

Jordan, Michael with Mark Vanci. (1998) *For the Love of the Game: My Story*. Chicago, IL: Rare Air Media.

Williams, Pat. (2001) *How to be Like Mike*. Deerfield Beach, FL: Health Communications.

JEFF GORDON

Brinster, Dick. (2002) *Jeff Gordon*. New York: Chelsea House.

Graves, Gary. (Aug 13, 2001) "Gordon wins Global Crossing on a Dare: Holds on After a Bold Move." *USA Today*, p. 11C.

Jenkins, Chris. (June 21, 2002) "Gordon Stuck in a Rut." *USA Today*, p. C1.

Mair, George. (1999) *Natural Born Winner: Jeff Gordon*. New York: Ballantine Books.

Stewart. Mark. (2000) *Jeff Gordon*. Brookfield, CT: Millbrook Press.

Wood, Skip. (Feb 12, 1999) "Chasing Gordon." *USA Today*, p. 5C.

LANCE ARMSTRONG

Armstrong, Lance with Sally Jenkins. (2003) *Every Second Counts*. New York: Broadway Books.

Armstrong, Lance. (2001) *It's Not About the Bike: My Journey Back to Life*. New York: Berkley Publishing Group.

Armstrong, Kristin. (July 25, 2003) "Falling in Love with a Man and an Event." *USA Today*, p. 9C.

Lipsyte, Robert. (July 14, 2003) "What Makes a True Sports Hero?" *USA Today*, p. 11A.

O'Conner, Ian. (July 26, 2002) "Put Armstrong on US Pedestal." *USA Today*, p. 3C.

Orr, Frank & George Tracz. (2004) "Lance Armstrong." *The Dominators: The Remarkable Athletes Who Changed Their Sport Forever*. Toronto: Warwick Publishing. p. 16–19.

Ruibal, Sal. (July 30, 2001) "Armstrong Completes his Tour de Force Show." *USA Today*, p. 1D.

—— (May 22, 2002) "Cycling's Reluctant Saint." *USA Today*, p. 1A.

—— (Feb. 20, 2003) "A Tour de Force." *USA Today*, p. 3C.

—— (July 3, 2003) "Tour De France." *USA Today*, Section E

Tkacik, Maureen. (Jul 29, 2002) "Post Office Reject Spin on Cycling." *Wall Street Journal*, p. B1.

ELDRICK (TIGER) WOODS

Andrisani, John. (2002) *Think Like Tiger: An Analysis of Tiger Woods' Mental Game*. New York: G.P. Putnam's Sons.

Blauvelt, Harry. (Aug 17, 2000) "Playing in Tiger's Shadow." *USA Today*, C1–2.

Callahan, Tom. (2003) *In Search of Tiger: A Journey Through Golf with Tiger Woods*. New York: Crown Publishers.

Gordon, Devin. (June 18, 2001) "Tiger Rules: The Dominator." *Newsweek*, p. 42)

Johnson, Roy. (May 12, 1997) "Tiger: The Sports Business Will Never Be the Same." *Fortune*, p. 72–80.

Orr, Frank & George Tracz. (2004) "Tiger Woods." *The Dominators: The Remarkable Athletes Who Changed Their Sport Forever*. Toronto: Warwick Publishing. p. 140–143.

Richman, Michael. (Mar 8, 2000) "Tiger Woods." *Investor's Business Daily*. p. A4.

Rosaforte, Tim. (1997) *Tiger Woods: The Makings of a Champion*. New York: St. Martin's Press.

Triumph Books. (2000) *Tiger Woods: The Heart of a Champion*. Chicago, IL: Triumph Books.

Woods, Earl with Pete McDaniel. (1997) *Training a Tiger*. New York: Harper Collins.

Woods, Tiger with Editors of Golf Digest. (2001) *How I Play Golf*. New York: Warner Books.

Weir, Tom. (Apr 6, 2000) "On Course for Greatness?" *USA Today*, p. C1.

About the Author

Gene N. Landrum

7897 Cocobay Drive
Naples, Florida 34108
239-597-9545 -Fax 239-597-7347
E-Mail: genelandrum@earthlink.net
Web Site: genelandrum.com

Gene Landrum began his career in the Silicon Valley as an entrepreneur and hi-tech start-up executive where he interacted with many highly creative overachievers. He was fascinated by their difference from the rest of us in their mental and emotional dispositions, and intrigued by their similarities to each other in their winning behaviors. After earning his Ph.D. in psychology for his work on the innovator personality, he embarked on a more comprehensive program of study, investigating the personality dispositions and behaviors that lead to success in all walks of life. His research yielded some fascinating discoveries about overachievers that impelled him to reveal what makes them tick. ***Empowerment: The Competitive Edge in Sports, Business & Life***, his eleventh book, is the culmination of two decades of research, observation and investigation that reveals 13 overarching principles of behavior that underpin stellar success in any endeavor. Dr. Landrum has lectured extensively on various aspects of creative genius including the power of passion, visionary marketing, leadership, entrepreneurship and personal empowerment.

Some of Dr. Landrum's other books

The Superman Syndrome: The Magic of Myth in the Pursuit of Power (2005)

Entrepreneurial Genius: The Power of Passion (2004)

Sybaritic Genius: Sex Drive & Success (2001)

Literary Genius: A Cathartic Inspiration (2000)

Eight Keys to Greatness: Unlocking Your Hidden Potential (1999)

Prometheus 2000: Truth–Vision–Power (1997)

Profiles of Black Success: 13 Creative Geniuses (1997)

Profiles of Power & Success: 14 Geniuses Who Broke the Rules (1996)

Profiles of Female Genius: 13 Women Who Changed the World (1994)

Profiles of Male Genius: 13 Males Who Changed the World (1993)

"When it comes to geniuses, Gene Landrum wrote the book"
–Naples Daily News, **May 5, 1996**

Give the Gift of **EMPOWERMENT**
To your Loved Ones, Friends and Colleagues.

ORDER FROM YOUR FAVORITE BOOKSTORE OR ORDER HERE.

Please send me _____ copies of *Empowerment: The Competitive Edge in Sports, Business & Life* at $29.95 plus $5 for shipping/handling. My check is included with the completed form below.

To Pay By Check

1. Complete the following:

   Name _____

   Street Address _____

   City _____ **State (Province)** _____

   Zip (Postal) Code _____ **Country** _____

2. Write a check payable to *Brendan Kelly Publishing Inc.* for the number of books times $29.95 plus $5 for shipping/handling.

3. Send the check to: *Brendan Kelly Publishing Inc.*
   2122 Highview Drive
   Burlington, Ontario, Canada L7R 3X4

To Pay By Credit Card

1. Visit our web site at **www.brendankellypublishing.com**

2. Click on ORDER INFO, choose the $US or $CAD order form.

3. Add copy (or copies) of **EMPOWERMENT** to the shopping cart.

4. Press **SECURE CHECKOUT** and complete the form.